The Crisis and Renewal of American Capitalism

Despite the reversal of America's fortunes from the triumphalism of the Roaring Nineties to the gloom of the lost decade and the Great Depression, theoretical conceptions of US capitalism have remained surprisingly unchanged. This book departs from the American political economy literature to identify three common myths that have shaped our conceptualization of US capitalism: its reduction to a state market dyad disembedded from societal factors; the illusion of a weak state and the synchronic conception of the US variety of capitalism.

To remedy these pitfalls, the authors propose a civilizational approach to American political economy at the crossroads between cultural studies, history, sociology and political science. Drawing together contributions from a rich variety of fields (from geography to cultural studies, political science and sociology) this work sheds a new light on America's cultural political economy, combining theoretical reflection with empirical data and offering innovative perspectives on the crisis and renewal of American capitalism.

This book will be of interest to students and scholars interested in the dynamics of capitalism and its societal ramifications beyond economics. The multidisciplinary nature of this book also makes it a useful learning tool for students working in American politics, comparative political economy and urban sociology and capitalism and society.

Laurence Cossu-Beaumont is an Associate Professor in American Studies at the University Paris 3 – Sorbonne Nouvelle in Paris.

Jacques-Henri Coste is an Associate Professor in American Studies at the University Paris 3 – Sorbonne Nouvelle in Paris.

Jean-Baptiste Velut is an Associate Professor in American Studies at the University Paris 3 – Sorbonne Nouvelle in Paris.

Routledge Advances in International Political Economy

1 **The Future of the Nation-State**
Essays on cultural pluralism and political integration
Edited by Sverker Gustavsson and Leif Lewin
Co-publication with Nerenius and Santérus Publisher AB, Sweden

2 **Classical Liberalism and International Economic Order**
Studies in theory and intellectual history
Razeen Sally

3 **Coping with Globalization**
Jeffrey Hart and Aseem Prakash

4 **Responding to Globalization**
Jeffrey Hart and Aseem Prakash

5 **Japanese Capitalism in Crisis**
A regulationist interpretation
Edited by Robert Boyer and Toshio Yamada

6 **Globalization and Social Change**
Edited by Johannes Dragsbaek Schmidt and Jacques Hersh

7 **Multilateralism and the World Trade Organisation**
The architecture and extension of international trade recognition
Rorden Wilkinson

8 **Foreign Direct Investment, Democracy and Development**
Assessing contours, correlates and concomitants of globalization
Indra de Soysa

9 **Rethinking International Organization**
Deregulation and global goverance
Barbara Emadi-Coffin

10 **Technology, Governance and Political Conflict in International Industries**
Tony Porter

11 **America's Trade Policy towards Japan**
Demanding results
John Kunkel

12 **Chinese Capitalism in a Global Era**
Towards hybrid capitalism
Henry Wai-chung Yeung

13 **The World Bank and Africa**
The construction of governance states
Graham Harrison

14 **Welfare, Right and the State**
A framework for thinking
David P. Levine

15 **Regional Trade Integration and Conflict Resolution**
Shaheen Rafi Khan

16 **Contested Capitalism**
The political origins of financial institutions
Richard W. Carney

17 **Economic Growth, the Environment and International Relations**
The growth paradigm
Stephen James Purdey

18 **Variety of Capitalism, Types of Democracy and Globalization**
Edited by Masanobu Ido

19 **States, Nonstate Actors, and Global Governance**
Projecting polities
Edward A. Fogarty

20 **The Political Economy of Space in the Americas**
The new Pax Americana
Alejandra Roncallo

21 **Trade, Development and Globalization**
S. Javed Maswood

22 **Transatlantic Politics and the Transformation of the International Monetary System**
Michelle Frasher

23 **Global Criminal and Sovereign Free Economies and the Demise of the Western Democracies**
Dark renaissance
Edited by Robert J. Bunker and Pamela Ligouri Bunker

24 **Capitalist Alternatives**
Models, taxonomies, scenarios
Paul Dragos Aligica and Vlad Tarko

25 **International Mobility, Global Capitalism, and Changing Structures of Accumulation**
Transforming the Japan–India IT relationship
Anthony P. D'Costa

26 **The Crisis and Renewal of American Capitalism**
A civilizational approach to modern American political economy
Edited by Laurence Cossu-Beaumont, Jacques-Henri Coste and Jean-Baptiste Velut

The Crisis and Renewal of American Capitalism

A civilizational approach to modern American political economy

Edited by
Laurence Cossu-Beaumont, Jacques-Henri Coste and Jean-Baptiste Velut

Routledge
Taylor & Francis Group
LONDON AND NEW YORK

First published 2016
by Routledge
2 Park Square, Milton Park, Abingdon, Oxon OX14 4RN

and by Routledge
605 Third Avenue, New York, NY 10017

First issued in paperback 2021

Routledge is an imprint of the Taylor & Francis Group, an informa business

Publisher's Note
The publisher has gone to great lengths to ensure the quality of this reprint but points out that some imperfections in the original copies may be apparent.

British Library Cataloguing in Publication Data
A catalogue record for this book is available from the British Library

Library of Congress Cataloging in Publication Data
The crisis and renewal of American capitalism : a civilizational approach to modern American political economy / [edited by] Laurence Cossu-Beaumont, Jacques-Henri Coste, Jean-Baptiste Velut.
pages cm. – (Routledge advances in international political economy ; 26)
ISBN 978-1-138-90875-8 (hardback)
1. Financial crises–United States. 2. Capitalism–United States. 3. Finance–United States. 4. Monetary policy–United States. 5. United States–Economic conditions. 6. United States–Economic policy. I. Cossu-Beaumont, Laurence, editor. II. Coste, Jacques-Henri, editor. III. Velut, Jean-Baptiste, editor.
HB3743.C75 2016
330.973–dc23 2015028240

ISBN 13: 978-1-03-209814-2 (pbk)
ISBN 13: 978-1-138-90875-8 (hbk)

Typeset in Times New Roman
by Wearset Ltd, Boldon, Tyne and Wear

Contents

Figures

Maps

Tables

Contributors

Editors

Laurence Cossu-Beaumont is an Associate Professor in American Studies at the Sorbonne Nouvelle University of Paris. She joined the CERVEPAS research center on English-speaking economies in 2011, as a specialist on the United States' soft power through cultural industries such as the book industry. She wrote her PhD thesis on the editorial history of African-American writer Richard Wright. Her research focuses on book history in connection with African American Studies and transatlantic cultural history. Her recent publications include a contribution on editorial censorship in *Richard Wright in a Post-racial Imaginary* (Continuum Books, 2014) and a chapter on "Popular book clubs and the marketing of African American best sellers" in *Race, Ethnicity and Publishing in America* (Palgrave Macmillan, 2014). She recently prepared a new edition of Tocqueville's fellow traveler: *Marie ou l'Esclavage aux Etats-Unis – Portrait de mœurs américaines by Gustave de Beaumont* (Aux Forges de vulcain, 2014).

Jacques-Henri Coste is an Associate Professor in American Studies at the Sorbonne Nouvelle University of Paris and a member of the CERVEPAS research center on English-speaking economies. He has published scholarly articles on the development of business enterprise, innovation systems and the socioeconomic function of entrepreneurship. He edited and published a book entitled *Les sociétés entrepreneuriales & les mondes Anglophones* in 2013 at the Presses Sorbonne Nouvelle and a special journal issue on social entrepreneurship. His current research focuses on the evolutions of the US system of innovation and its embeddedness in the varieties of capitalism. He adopts a transdisciplinary perspective to analyze the joint development of economic models, paradigms, representations and fictions.

Jean-Baptiste Velut is an Associate Professor in American Studies at Sorbonne Nouvelle University of Paris and a member of the CERVEPAS research center on English-speaking economies. He wrote a dissertation entitled 'Free or fair trade? The battle for the rules of American trade policy from NAFTA to CAFTA' (2009). His research interests revolve around the role of the

United States in the process of economic globalization and the transformations of the American political economy in the contemporary period. He has published several articles on US international economic policies, the political economy of free trade agreements, antiglobalization debates and contemporary progressive movements in the United States. His latest research projects include a comparative analysis of US, EU and Chinese trade policies and a study of the governance of cross-regional free trade agreements.

Contributors

Pierre Arnaud teaches American Studies at the University of Paris Ouest Nanterre La Défense. He specializes in information technologies and the American economy from a sociological and cultural standpoint. Before joining the university, he taught for 13 years at ESCP Europe Business School. His most recent research at University Paris Ouest La Défense (CREA), CERVEPAS and Université Paris Dauphine deals with the US economy from a comparative perspective, including such topics as the social dynamics of consumption and debt, inequalities, cultural biases in the perception of the economy, etc.

Martine Azuelos is Emeritus Professor of Anglo-American studies at the Sorbonne Nouvelle – Paris 3 University. Her research deals with contemporary economic policies in Britain and the United States, the part these two countries have played in driving globalization and regional economic integration, and the dynamics of American capitalism. Her publications include *Mondialisation et domination économique: la dynamique anglo-saxonne* (Economica, 1998), *Intégration dans les Amériques: dix ans d'ALENA* (Presses de la Sorbonne nouvelle, 2004) and *Capitalisme anglo-saxon et monde(s) anglophones: des paradigmes en question* (a special issue of *LISA e-journal*, 13 (2), 2015).

Robert Boyer was Professor at Ecole des Hautes Etudes en Sciences Sociales and Senior Researcher at CNRS (National Center for Scientific Research) until 2008. He is now an economist at the Institute of the Americas in Paris. He has been active in the founding and diffusion of Régulation Theory, which investigates the long-run institutional transformations of capitalism and its various contemporary configurations. His major publications include *Regulation Theory: The State of the Art* (co-edited with Yves Saillard, Routledge, 2001) and *Diversity and Transformations of Asian Capitalisms* (with Hiroyasu Uemura and Akinori Isogai, Routledge, 2011). Other publications can be found at http://robertboyer.org.

Cécile Cormier is Associate Professor of American Studies at the University of Bordeaux, France. She researches topics in two very distinctive fields, namely public administration (especially policy analysis for the French Ministry of Foreign Affairs, and public budgeting and taxation in the United States at the federal, state and local government levels) and poetry (American poetry, French poetry and Chinese classical poetry).

Cynthia Ghorra-Gobin is a geographer and a CNRS senior researcher at the Research Center on the Americas (CREDA) at the Sorbonne Nouvelle University of Paris. She has published many books and articles on American cities (*Los Angeles, Le mythe américain inachevé, 1997, 2000*) and she edited the *Dictionnaire critique de la mondialisation* in 2012. Her research focuses on the social and economic impacts of globalization on cities and metropolitan areas.

James McBride, PhD, JD, is Clinical Assistant Professor of Liberal Studies at New York University. He practiced law as a securities attorney for nearly a decade at Schulte, Roth & Zabel, LLP in New York City, representing clients in Department of Justice, SEC and NYSE investigations. He is published widely in the areas of religion, law and culture, and is the author of *War, Battering and Other Sports: The Gulf Between American Men and Women on War and Domestic Violence* (Humanities Press).

Marie-Christine Pauwels is a former graduate of the French grande école "Ecole Normale Supérieure," with an "agrégation" in English and a PhD in American literature. She is currently working as an Associate Professor in American Studies in the department of foreign languages of the University of Paris Ouest Nanterre la Défense. Her current research focuses on collaborative consumption, peer-to-peer lending, prosumerism and the transformations of consumer culture.

Catherine Sauviat is a Senior Researcher at IRES, a research institute linked to major trade unions in France, and an Associate Professor at the University of Rennes 2. She has published on the US economy and social model, along with other research topics such as industrial and employment policies and corporate governance.

Bradley T. Smith is a PhD student and Graduate Teaching Assistant at Sorbonne Nouvelle University (Paris). His doctoral dissertation is entitled "The dialectics of neoliberalism in the United States: from the 'conservative revolution' to the crisis of 2008." His research interests include using a philosophical approach to studying American politics and the US economy. In 2009 he completed a master's thesis entitled "The roots of capitalist ideology in the United States: the American Revolution and the birth of the modern capitalist state."

Nicholas Sowels is a Senior Lecturer in English for economics at the University of Paris 1 Panthéon-Sorbonne. He also lectures on the economies of English-speaking countries and comparative capitalisms. His recent research and publications have focused on finance, macroeconomic policy, the financial crisis and the Great Recession.

Preface

Specificity, continuity and transformations of American capitalism

Robert Boyer

Since the early 1970s, the transformations of American capitalism have been a constant and major concern for researchers involved in the development of the French *régulation* approach (Aglietta, 1979; Boyer, 1990; Boyer & Saillard, 2001). It served as a reference point to test the predictions of conventional Marxist theory, the capacity of the mass production and mass consumption growth regime to spread to Europe and Japan, the long-term viability of *Pax Americana* after the collapse of the Bretton Woods international system and many other issues. Reading the present volume was an opportunity to reassess the respective merits and limits of various research questions in the light of the ambitious "civilizational approach" that brings together the various authors of the present volume. This brief preface deals with four questions around which the book gravitates. Can one assume that the United States of America is the typical liberal market capitalism or does it display specific features that most general theories do not capture? In retrospect, could the Golden Age of the post-Second World War era be sustained in the very long term or was it in direct opposition to the fundamental values that hold the New World together, and thus, would the new period, however turbulent and crisis-prone, mean a return to normal times? Do the representations of a weak and absentee state fit with the stylized facts observed, for instance, concerning innovation strategies and trade policy? Finally, will the financial collapse of September 2008 be a turning point in American history, or will capitalism use this structural crisis to bounce back and explore new alleys toward a new regime far faster-paced and adaptive than other brands of capitalism? Concerning these four issues, the book suggests convincing responses – with a high probability of "no" for all the first alternatives.

How distinctive is American capitalism?

Political economists and institutional researchers usually consider that North American capitalism is emblematic of a "liberal market economy," opposed to the German configuration supposed to define an institutionally "coordinated market economy" (Hall and Soskice, 2001). *Régulation* theory challenges this canonical opposition by pointing out the coexistence of at least five brands of capitalisms (Amable, 2003) among OECD countries, and capitalism extension to

Asia shows the novelty and specificity of the related brands of capitalisms (Harada & Tohyama, 2011). Nevertheless, all the taxonomies derived from comparative institutional analyses do cluster all English-speaking economies, including the United States, under the same heading of market-dominated capitalisms. This is simultaneously the merit and weakness of this kind of theorizing. This book warns us about the reductionism of such an approach: a civilizational-economic analysis points out both the exceptional features and the long-run transformations of North American capitalism. Let us mention its clear specificities and stress how important they are for understanding the long-term trajectory and the future of the country after 2008.

First of all, the United States represent a continental economy, organized according to the principles of market-preserving federalism (Weingast, 1995), quite a difference, for instance, with respect to the centralized government and limited size of the domestic economy in the UK. From a methodological point of view, the American states should be the relevant entities to be compared with European nation-states. Thus, many chapters of the book show the interest of such a regional/local disaggregation in terms of regulatory systems, economic specialization, real-estate bubbles, macroeconomic dynamics, unemployment, ecosystems, etc. This diversity might explain the versatility and dynamism of innovation – for instance from defense-related innovations to civilian applications – and the resilience of the American economy. An alternative would be to compare the United States with the European Union and China, i.e., equivalent continental economies, including a large diversity of regions/nation-states (Boyer, 2015a). From a macro point of view, the role of Wall Street in world financial intermediation is a second distinctive feature that explains why the post-2008 evolutions are so different in the United States and in the European Union. The real-estate bubble associated with the subprime crisis is closely related to the inflow of capital from abroad, especially Asia. Besides, the quantitative easing policy pursued by the Federal Reserve fully uses the asymmetry between the dollar and other currencies.

A second series of factors is embedded in typically American ideologies. Isn't a kind of Far West behavior governing financial innovations and practices boldly generating new risks in order to reap the benefits of exploring unchartered territories, whatever the cost for the population finally affected by foreclosures and unemployment? More important is the pervasiveness among the American population of a free-market vision of society: basically any allocation by the market is fair in the sense that relative income is believed to be a rough measure of the talent, ability and productivity – and not the outcome of power or chance, as most Europeans think. Furthermore, in a society propelled by the succession of migratory waves, generational upward mobility is a cornerstone of society. This deep-rooted belief can resist the counter-evidence provided by comparative international comparisons (Wilkinson & Kate, 2009) and the effective decline of this opportunity in contemporary North America: perceptions and representations matter! This gives the United States an extraordinary capacity to respond to major imbalances and structural crises. For instance, a poor or incomplete welfare state is partly overcome by the tradition of philanthropy, another American trait that turns out to have a significant ideological and practical impact in the contemporary period when the super-rich display a disproportionate fraction of national wealth (Piketty, 2014).

Last but not least, the Americans are the "consumers of last resort" given the symbolic role attributed to lifestyles, the typical mimicry and "mutual imitation" already noted by Tocqueville (1840), the demonstration effects of conspicuous consumption pointed to by Veblen (1899) and the wide acceptance of debt as an anticipation of future earnings or capital gains (as shown by real estate during the subprime bubble). Consumption is part of the American dream and the American way of life continues to seduce people all over the world. More generally, the United States is the matrix of fictional expectations (Beckert, 2016) that are exported to a large variety of societies, including the more traditional ones. This is largely a unique American competitive asset.

Thus, the civilizational approach unveils quite interesting features of the American trajectory that are downplayed by comparative institutional analyses in terms of variety or diversity of capitalisms. It is worthwhile to note that some *régulationist* authors have similarly evolved towards a "cultural political economy" (Jessop, 2012). Of course, this is not the only contribution of the present book.

Farewell to Fordism, updating core traditional values

Almost all chapters of the present volume provide deep historical roots for a series of contemporary characteristics of American capitalism. For instance, during the 1945–1963 period, consumption was fed by real income increases and a moderate and quasi-constant ratio of household debt to income, but since 1980 median real income has been nearly stagnant and thus consumption has been mainly driven by debt from one bubble to another. This is in full agreement with the periodization proposed by *régulation* theory: the crisis of the Fordist growth regime and then the progressive domination of a finance-led alternative model.

The regulation school also posited that the institutionalization of capital/labor relations would be largely irreversible and a new innovation-led industrial model was perceived as the American response to the rising performance of Japanese manufacturing. We were wrong and very early Michel Aglietta (1986) put the Golden Age in perspective and it appeared somehow as an oddity with respect to the specificity of American capitalism: a long tradition of market-led development, the domination of a few large enterprises, the difficult organization of labor, the checks and balances associated with the American Constitution had been long-lasting obstacles to the emergence of mass consumption in line with mass production. In a sense, the Reagan and Bush years rejuvenated and mobilized typical past American values (dynamism of entrepreneurship, Hooverian individualism, distrust for massive state intervention and belief in the intrinsic merits of markets) in order to eradicate most of the New Deal legacy. Only the Second World War had interrupted a former self-interest and laissez-faire tradition by promoting wide access to education, progressive and high taxation of income, recognition of the role of unions and finally the legitimacy of state interventions in the industry and the economy. The clear reduction of inequality is not the outcome of the victory of social-democratic ideas, but the unintended consequence of the World Wars in the reconfiguration of American and European societies (Piketty, 2014, 2015). As soon as product, labor and financial markets are deregulated, a new trend emerges with the recurrence of financial instability and economic crises. They appear as the new normality since most actors and analysts are under the illusion that "this time is different" (Reinhart & Rogoff, 2011) and seem to have forgotten that major economic downturns had almost disappeared until the early 1970s.

The second merit of this civilizational approach is then to insert the post-2008 American trajectory into the larger picture about the continuity and change within a society-wide approach that spans across all fields: representations and ideologies, household consumption, the state–market nexus, the relations between urbanization and financialization, the consequence of globalization upon the role of the state, the national innovation system and labor institutions transformations.

Beyond the myth: an evolving state–market nexus

Nearly all chapters develop a common and interesting finding: most analysts caricature the American regime as exclusively market-led and/or point out a weak federal state as a major obstacle to economic performance. This is a largely erroneous diagnosis, whereby the labeling and the ideology are hiding the reality of the synergy between state interventions and markets. Examples abound. Thus, industrial policy is largely absent from the official vocabulary, but many institutions do have the role of fostering the pre-competitive stage of innovation. The agency in charge of defense contracting is actually developing military technologies with an eye upon civilian spillovers, and they have been numerous since Reagan's "Star Wars" program. Similarly, the agency in charge of health has been quite instrumental in fostering biotechnological innovations in the private sector. The issue is not "how much public spending?" but "What kind of state intervention in order to upgrade and defend American competitiveness?" Similarly, trade negotiations focus on the sectors where American firms have a clear competitive advantage and specialization. The trump card of the United States is probably this organized but rather submerged synergy between the public and the private sectors.

Again, the competition among states is a powerful mechanism favoring innovation and thus the analysis has to take into account the regional and local entities involved in the innovation process: this explains the shift from one region to another according to the domestic and international contexts. The decentralization of the state–market nexus explains why hasty or distant observers conclude that the United States is an uncoordinated market economy. Similarly, the conflict between the prioritization of bondholders over the integrity of public services finds a solution at the regional level, and this is shifting the bargaining power against citizens' demands. This is a quite common issue of the present times, but this open conflict between citizenship and finance, democracy and capitalism (Streeck, 2014) finds a typical American solution. Even the subprime crisis is the consequence of a political program built upon the access to ownership by the less privileged via mortgage-refinancing public institutions.

Consequently, this civilizational approach delivers an important warning to the hasty and simplistic theorization economists are fond of. Clearly, the American brand of capitalism is different from the German model, not because of the primacy of markets over institutional coordination, but as contrasted configurations for the state–market nexus. The next question is, then: can the comparative international approach find adequate index in order to capture the stylized facts put forward by this alternative methodology? On one side, the experts in industrial policy have recognized the leading role of the federal government in the building of the American innovation system (Beffa, 2005, pp. 21–22). On the other side, institutional approaches now recognize that markets go along with authorities in charge of controlling them and thus coordination by markets and institutions are complementary (Boyer, 2015b).

Everything seems to change so that nothing changes?

The various chapters provide a kaleidoscopic vision of possible futures for the American society. The general impression is nevertheless that the legacy of the past will play a major role. One could have imagined a "return of the master" (Skidelsky, 2010), i.e., the defeat of free market fundamentalism and the restoration of the Keynesian form of interventionism as a durable inflexion of economic policy. Unfortunately, the vested interest of finance (Boyer, 2011) and the conception that markets are the least imperfect coordinating mechanism seems to have triumphed for economic and political elites (Greenspan, 2013), but also in public opinion as evidenced by the transitory and finally weak impact of the Occupy Wall Street movement. The embeddedness of American society-wide values is still operating.

Nevertheless, the economy is not converging at all to the pre-crisis configuration. The recovery is slow and creates fewer jobs than in the past and the participation rate is the lowest since 1978. The ideological polarization runs against a pragmatic approach of economic policy. The ownership society has shown its limit while some doubts emerge concerning the American model of urbanization, finally proved to be inefficient in terms of land use (*The Economist*, 2014). The collective rights of workers are eroded, but their individualization is not necessarily a good substitute; and a revival of philanthropy will not replace the implementation of a fully fledged social security system. Last challenge: we know why and how the United States adopted an unorthodox monetary policy, but no existing theory can guide the way out of this quantitative easing. The jury is still out, but again the United States is at the forefront of modernity, and its strategy will affect the rest of the world.

References

Aglietta, M. (1979). *A theory of capitalist regulation: The US experience*. London: Verso.

Aglietta, M. (1986). États-Unis: persévérance dans l'être ou renouveau de la croissance? In Boyer, R. (ed.) *Capitalismes fin de siècle*, Paris: PUF, 33–66.

Amable, B. (2003). *The diversity of capitalism*. New York: Oxford University Press.

Beckert, J. (2016). *Imagined futures: Fictional expectations and capitalist dynamics*. Cambridge, MA: Harvard University Press.

Beffa, J.L. (2005). *Renewing France's industrial policy*. Paris: La Documentation Française.

Boyer, R. (1990). *The regulation school: A critical introduction*. New York: Columbia University Press.

Boyer, R. (2011). *Les financiers détruiront-ils le capitalisme?* Paris: Economica.

Boyer, R. (2015a, July 2–4). 'Political organization matters: Comparing the reaction to the 2008 world crisis of the North American federal government, the fuzzy European governance and the Chinese party-state'. Presentation at the SASE Conference, London.

Boyer, R. (2015b). *Économie politique des capitalismes. Théorie de la régulation et des crises*. Paris: Grand Repères, La Découverte.

Boyer, R., & Saillard, Y. (eds.) (2001). *Régulation theory: The state of the art*. London: Routledge.

Economist, The, (2014). Roads of redemption, cities are bound to grow, but they need planning to be liveable, June 21. Retrieved from www.economist.com/news/international/21604576-cities-are-bound-grow-they-need-planning-be-liveable-roads-redemption/.

Greenspan, A. (2013). *The map and the territory: Risk, human nature, and the future of forecasting*. London: Penguin Books.

Hall, P., & Soskice, D. (eds.) (2001). *Varieties of capitalism: The institutional foundations of comparative advantage*. Oxford: Oxford University Press.

Harada, Y., & Tohyama, H. (2011). Asian capitalisms: Institutional configurations and firm heterogeneity. In R. Boyer, U. Hiroyasu & I. Akinori (eds.), *Diversity and transformations of Asian capitalisms*. London: Routledge, pp. 243–263.

Jessop, B. (2012). Crossing boundaries: Towards cultural political economy. An Interview with Bob Jessop. *Revue de la Régulation*, 12 (2). Retrieved from http://regulation.revues.org/9943.

Piketty, T. (2014). *Capital in the twenty-first century*. Cambridge, MA: Harvard University Press.

Piketty, T. (2015). Putting distribution back at the center of economics. *Journal of Economic Perspectives*, 29 (1): 67–88.

Reinhart, C., & Rogoff, K. (2011). *This time is different: Eight centuries of financial folly*. Princeton, NJ: Princeton University Press.

Skidelsky, R. (2010). *Keynes: The return of the master*. New York: Public Affairs.

Streeck, W. (2014). *Buying time: The delayed crisis of democratic capitalism*. London: Verso.

de Tocqueville, A. (1840). *Democracy in America*. Retrieved from www.gutenberg.org/files/816/816-h/816-h.htm#link2HCH0058/.

Veblen, T. (1899). *Theory of the leisure class: An economic study in the evolution of institutions*. New York: Macmillan.

Weingast, B. (1995), The economic role of political institutions: Market-preserving federalism and economic development, *Journal of Law, Economics, & Organization*, 11(1): 1–31.

Wilkinson, R., & Kate, P. (2009). *The spirit level: Why more equal societies almost always do better*. London: Allen Lane.

Acknowledgments

This book is dedicated to Martine Azuelos, who founded the CERVEPAS, a French research centre studying the drivers and agents of economic dynamism in the English-speaking world at the Sorbonne Nouvelle University of Paris, and to all the colleagues that have been part of this formidable intellectual experience. Martine Azuelos initiated and developed, for over 20 years, pioneering pluridisciplinary research on the idea that economic developments cannot be understood but in close correlation with social, political and cultural life. The series of research programs and publications that she launched and coordinated on the Anglo-Saxon model of capitalism were at the very origin of the book project and have inspired our research on 'economic civilization' and contemporary political economy. Our warmest thanks also go to her successor, Valerie Peyronel, for her unfailing support and contribution to this ambitious academic project and to all the colleagues of the CERVEPAS/CREW research centre with whom we entered in fruitful dialogues and conversations, including Juliette Bourdin, Nathalie Champroux, Catherine Coron, Louise Dalingwater, Taoufik Djebali, Olivier de Gromard, Anne Groutel, Ben Offerlé, Ruxandra Pavelchievici, Michel Péron, Marie-Claude Strigler and Christine Zumello.

We also extend our deepest gratitude to Professors Pierre Mélandri, Robert Boyer and Leo Panitch, who helped us contextualize and also conceptualize the US model of capitalism.

Like many edited volumes, this book started with a series of conferences that were held at the Institute of the Americas in Paris and, notably, the CERVEPAS/CREW international conference entitled 'The Health and Wealth of US Capitalism: A Critical Condition?' that gathered many academics from the United States, Canada and France on June, 14–15 2012. We would like to thank all those who took part in the scientific committee and the organization of this event: Martine Azuelos, Hélène Le Dantec-Lowry, Frances Fox Piven, Olivier Frayssé, Gerald Friedman, Régine Hollander, Pierre Mélandri, Vincent Michelot, François Vaillancourt, as well as Ondine Aza, Anna Kamalzadeh, Fanny Lauby, Cyrielle Pardanaud, Caixa Tan and Sébastien Wesser. We also want to acknowledge the kind support given to the event by Sorbonne Nouvelle Vice President of Research Carle Bonafous-Murat, the scientific committee and international relations department of Sorbonne Nouvelle University and the Directors of the CREW research centre.

We want to thank all the authors in this volume, several of whom did a lot more than contribute their own chapters, providing insightful comments and feedback, as well as corrections, at each stage of the work. Without their patience, support and encouragement, the book would not be what it is.

We also want to thank our colleagues Emmanuelle Avril and Christine Zumello for their valuable advice. We are grateful to all anonymous reviewers for their constructive feedback, and the editorial team at Routledge, including Nicola Parkin, Peter Harris, Lydia de Cruz, Hannah Riley and Gary Smith who supported the project from the start through to the final printing stage. All were extremely helpful and friendly and made this academic endeavor a very fruitful experience.

We hope that this volume will, through its readers, generate friendly and open debates on the state of the US political economy, the recent transformations and rejuvenation of the US model of capitalism and its embeddedness in an original form of 'economic civilization'.

Laurence Cossu-Beaumont, Jacques-Henri Coste, Jean-Baptiste Velut

Introduction

The crisis and renewal of American capitalism: a civilizational approach to modern American political economy

Laurence Cossu-Beaumont, Jacques-Henri Coste and Jean-Baptiste Velut

The unrivaled success of the US economy in the 1990s until the turn of the century long appeared as the uncontested victory of an unfettered free market-driven economy and the triumph of a vibrant neoliberal paradigm propagated worldwide. However, the Great Recession strongly affected perceptions of the US economy's performance and transformed the understanding and place of its economic model among the existing varieties of capitalism (Hall & Soskice, 2001; Amable, 2003; Baumol *et al.*, 2007). Domestically, the impact of this traumatic experience was devastating. Over seven million Americans were deprived of their homes by foreclosures; unemployment and poverty rates soared; and millions in the middle class saw the value of their homes and/or net worth of their retirement plans plummet. Internationally, the image of the United States was also tarnished. The contrast between its critical economic condition and the healthy growth of China and other emerging economies prompted both analysts and decision-makers to question the alleged superiority of the American variety of capitalism. More importantly, the American brand of capitalism was severely discredited for damaging the economic health of individual Americans, reducing national wealth, and even possibly leading the rest of the world down the wrong path. Thus, the Great Recession had immediate strong domestic and global impacts on business systems, institutional arrangements and political and cultural value systems (Streeck, 2011).

The persisting predicament of the American economic regime first brought about a renewed epistemological interest both in the diachronic and synchronic, the historical and the systemic dimensions of capitalism. It also brought to the fore the theoretical relevance of an all-encompassing concept (capitalism) able to embrace socioeconomic complexity and change. In the aftermath of the financial crisis, government interventionism signaled the visible return of the state in the economy and highlighted the intimate relationship between American capitalism and its political institutions. It also reflected the reassertion of the public sphere and an emerging order of regulatory capitalism (Levi-Faur, 2006; 2008). More recently, the failure of capitalism to "naturally" curb the rising concentration of wealth has sparked a vigorous debate on the persistent failure of the state to adequately address inequality (Piketty, 2014).

Yet, despite the reversal of America's fortune from the triumphalism of the "Roaring Nineties" to the gloom of the "lost decade," theoretical conceptions of US capitalism have remained surprisingly unchanged. In fact, if the crisis questioned the sustainability of the US capitalist paradigm, it did not fundamentally challenge academic theorization of American political economy. The laissez-faire brand of US capitalism was interpreted as a Faustian bargain whereby the United States traded social equity and economic stability for an artificial growth model inspired by supply-side economics.[1] In other words, many scholars concluded that the roots of America's demise lay in the intrinsic nature of its free market political economy. In such analyses, scholars tend to underplay the socio-political role of institutions in their interrelations with the market sphere and economic agents.

The idea of the American state as a cautious umpire of market actors has a long academic tradition. Early comparative political economy (CPE) studies described the United States as a "weak state" unable to implement coherent economic policy-making, as a result of its fragmented and decentralized political system vulnerable to the pressure of particularistic interests (Katzenstein, 1976; Krasner, 1978). In the 1980s, the rise of Japan as a major competitor to American firms contributed to sharpening the contrast between statist and liberal models of development. Many scholars deplored the conflicts, redundancies and lacunae of US economic policy in an increasingly competitive international economy and called for a more active and coherent trade and industrial policy (Reich & Magaziner, 1982; Zysman & Tyson, 1983; Hart, 1992).

This form of alarmism gradually faded in the 1990s, when America regained its economic leadership. Yet, this resurgence was rarely interpreted as a consequence of federal intervention. Amid scholarly debates on globalization and the decline of national sovereignty, America's success was too often seen as the payoff of its entrepreneurial model. Whether celebrated as engines of growth or denounced as harbingers of Americanization, US multinational corporations were often perceived as the central force behind America's economic resurgence, while the contribution of the American state was often downplayed or ignored, a phenomenon that Weiss defined as "state denial" (Weiss, 1998). Some proclaimed the "end of the nation state" in the event of rising regional, transnational and supranational actors (Ohmae, 1995; Mathews, 1997; see also Haass, 2008). Often convinced that the economic logic of globalization had supplanted the political and social spheres, they underscored government incapacity to regulate global supply chains, transnational trade and financial flows. In a much-hyped globalized economy, states were reduced to powerless entities dismantling welfare states and lowering their tax rates to win the favors of transnational capital in a so-called "race to the bottom" (Strange, 1996; Greider, 1997; Gray, 1998).

The next wave of political economy studies perpetuated traditional preconceptions about state–market relations. Placing firms at the center of their analysis, Hall and Soskice (2001) described the American "variety" of capitalism as a "liberal market economy" (LME), a capitalist system in which firm behavior was primarily driven by demand and supply conditions in competitive markets. This free market ideal type was distinguished from coordinated market economies (CMEs) where non-market modes of coordination prevail. Hall and Soskice's seminal contribution to institutional economics seemed to further entrench the well-established but largely mythic conception of the American state as a "weak" state (Novak, 2008).

The authors of the variety of capitalism school (VOC) shared a common focus on the concept of capitalism with the French regulation theory school (RT) pioneered by Michel Aglietta (1979) and Robert Boyer (1990). Both research programs converged in using international comparisons, questioning the primacy of liberal market economies and challenging the role of markets as the sole coordinating mechanism. VOC and RT stressed the search for an alternative form of capitalism after the crumbling of the "Fordist" regime (Boyer, 2000). They advanced the idea of "institutional complementarities" to explain the diversity, co-evolutions and pattern of interactions between subsystems within national models of capitalism. Internationalization and globalization deepened rather than diluted the competitive advantage associated with each institutional architecture.

RT first emerged as a major theorization of post-war Fordism, then developed into an analysis of the root causes of the transformations of capitalism. The dynamics of long-term cycles of socioeconomic stability and change resulted from unresolved contradictions within existing institutional arrangements and a lack of systemic and macroeconomic coherence. Regulation theory has generated multidisciplinary research for the past 40 years on how a wide range of economic, institutional, political and social factors interplay in the process of capital accumulation, produce singular growth regimes over time and legitimize various modes of institutional regulation. Laws, norms, forms of states, policies, paradigms, beliefs and representations were instrumental in the sustainability of what appeared as a predominantly endogenous model of capitalism (Orlean, 2004; 2014). While VOC highlighted private firm governance and external shocks, RT integrated its analysis of political economy with a study of civil society and the infrastructural power of the state. Modern capitalist economies differed internationally and produced several brands of capitalism (market-led, meso-corporatist, social democrat, state-led) that were the outcome of distinctive political economy compromises (Amable, 2004). Each capitalist type was characterized by specific institutional complementarities that first brought stability but nonetheless ended with a structural but largely endogenous crisis. Since it crossed economy and polity, agency and institutions, culture and values, the American model of capitalism had to be contextualized and examined from a multidimensional and multiscalar perspective including a more discursive stratum (Schmidt, 2008) and a "cultural turn" (Jessop *et al.*, 2012; Senett 2006).

As a consequence, it is the authors' contention that the interstructuration of the social, political and economic spheres has not been fully studied nor linked to framework conditions or to a wider "cultural political economy" (Jessop & Ngai-Ling Sum, 2012) specifically grounded, embedded in American civilization

(Granovetter, 1985). Hence, the need for a more integrated approach studying American capitalism with a "civilizational-economic analysis" (Swedberg, 2010) first re-embedding the economy in the American polity and society, then focusing on the centrality of the state–market nexus, and finally considering the dialectics and dynamics of US capitalism as an "economic civilization" marked off by more symbolic boundaries (Durkheim & Mauss, 1913; Eisenstadt, 2000) and shaped by sociocultural configurations and imaginaries (Taylor, 2007).

In short, for all the valuable insights of comparative case studies, many perspectives on American capitalism suffer from three major shortcomings: (1) their disregard for cultural and societal factors; (2) their reductive conception of state capacities; (3) their static interpretation of capitalism.

Re-embedding the economy

The first limitation of the comparative political economy literature has to do with its narrow focus on markets and political institutions, a "culture-blind" approach from which we strongly depart. Beyond the technicalities of flawed financial practices, how is American society to be appraised to enrich our understanding of the crisis and the transformations it may entail? Mainstream economists, central bankers and policy-makers have reconsidered both theory and practice to account for the Great Recession and search for policy prescriptions. Yet, they have often analyzed the economy as an object disembedded from its historical and cultural *milieu*. In doing so, they broke away from an older political economy tradition, best exemplified by the work of Polanyi and Braudel, which contended that the economy cannot be conceived of in a vacuum and needs to be reconnected with its territory, its historical and cultural background, as well as the constellation of stakeholders directly or indirectly engaged in the dynamics of capitalism. This is what Braudel describes as "civilization," a disfavored term that has the merits of encompassing the historical, cultural, institutional reality outside "which nothing can have full meaning" (Braudel, 1982, p. 23).

From institutional economics, we learnt that much was to be understood from considering the complex web of institutions when studying market mechanisms or the economy at large. But though institutions may have been a centerpiece for economic theory, they rather served as items to stage a static comparative framework (Hall & Soskice, 2001) or to discuss best practices and policies (North, 2005). And while comparative political economy did allow a useful focus on formal institutions, it often broke its promise to examine informal structures such as culture and beliefs.

At the Sorbonne Nouvelle University of Paris, the French research center on Anglo-Saxon economies (CERVEPAS) has been focusing on Anglo-Saxon varieties of capitalism since 1991 (Azuelos, 2012, 2015). Adopting an interdisciplinary approach, CERVEPAS scholars share the idea that economic reality cannot be understood but in close correlation with social, political and cultural life, and are committed to studying the *locus* of economic life (Azuelos, 2012; 2015). CERVEPAS has explored such themes as *entrepreneurship in Anglo-Saxon dynamics, innovation in Anglo-Saxon economies* and *the Anglo-Saxon model of capitalism*, with the postulate that capitalism is a relevant object of study, if not a model, whose appraisal can contribute to the study of US civilization. If the special brand of American capitalism lies at the heart of what makes US culture, politics and history, our intention as observers of contemporary America is to invite economists, historians and social scientists to offer a discussion on how the crisis may foster a shift in American civilization.

While CERVEPAS's interdisciplinary approach to economics clearly departed from the conventional disciplinary segmentation in French and Western academia, we are aware that other intellectual schools have also called for alternative approaches to the study of capitalism. To begin with, the study of capitalism as an institutionalized system – as opposed to a superposition of economic mechanisms – is at the heart of the work of many economists such as Marx, Keynes or Schumpeter, who have long recognized the interdependence between the economic, political and social spheres. Furthermore, the regulation school has long argued that capitalism cannot be reduced to an abstract, autonomous and functional market economy device resulting from fierce price competition and an asymmetric capital–labor nexus (Boyer, 2007). Instead, political economies should be understood as dynamic socioeconomic regimes that are constitutive of a complex web of political, cultural, social and institutional relations and the dynamics of these relations (Aglietta, 1979; Boyer, 2000, 2007; Aglietta & Bai, 2013). Finally, while Polanyi first argued that the market was to be re-embedded into the broader society, his claim has found new interest recently (Stiglitz, 2001; 2003). For instance, cultural political economists have defined their field as the confluence of culture, politics and clout (Best & Patterson, 2010).

In this book, we invited contributors to look at capitalism from the viewpoint not of standard monetary macroeconomics or classic business cycle literature, nor of the micro-economics of shareholders or corporate governance, but from the viewpoint of America's historical, cultural and social foundations. Indeed, the dynamics of capitalism cannot be distilled solely through the math of free capital flows and interest rates, but must be examined as a comprehensive and intricate system under the lens of social sciences.

Like CERVEPAS' series of publications on the dynamics of American capitalism and the emergence of an "entrepreneurial society" (Coste, 2013), the various schools aforementioned have shown that despite the useful insights that institutional economics may provide to the study of capitalism, the study of institutions needs to be supplemented with the analysis of ideologies, cultural values, power dynamics and the idiosyncratic politics of a given time. We depart from the initial notion that the economy rules supreme over society and that "economic capitalism" defines American civilization as its sole "driving force" (Braudel, 1995) to wonder about the political, societal and cultural forces at play in American capitalism (Neem, 2008; Eisner, 2011). Much in the same way as Aglietta and Bai (2013) accounted for China's particular experience of capitalism through its history, social fabric and collective memory, so we define our approach of America's recent experience of the crisis with an evolutionary perspective and a civilizational focus.

Subnational and shadow processes

The civilizational approach sheds light on one problem associated with CPE studies, namely their conventional focus on the national level of analysis, a prism ill-adapted to the multilevel power centers of decision-making under US federalism. Indeed, the crisis of American capitalism and the politics of austerity that emerged in its aftermath can only be fully captured by analyzing the dramatic economic losses undertaken by cities and states.[2] Similarly, while the federal government may seem at a loss to overcome institutional obstacles and pursue a coherent recovery policy, "entrepreneurial states" (Eisinger, 1988) "regional clusters" (Porter, 1990; Etzkowitz, 1998) and "global cities" or "metros" (Sassen, 2001; Katz & Bradley, 2013) serve as many examples that the subnational level is an important locus of decision-making power.

The analysis of subnational actors is all the more justified if one considers that the size of American states is comparable to that of other national economies in the world – one example being California's ranking as the eighth largest economy in the world. While the confinement of economic activism to regional or local government actors has often been interpreted as a weakness of the American state, the powers reserved to the states have in fact played a structuring force in the creative destruction of American capitalism. First, states serve as "laboratories" conducting experimentation in various policy spheres ranging from innovation policies to tax, social or regulatory reforms. Their behavior can have emulating effects on both state and federal actors – whether their policies are perceived as virtuous models (with best practices or "sunshine" effects) or negative examples (race-to-the-bottom scenario). This mimetic process is central to the political dynamics of American capitalism. Indeed, when federal decision-making is blocked by historical-institutional bottlenecks – as during the Gilded Age or in the contemporary era – cities and states become the *loci* of policy innovations and ventures in new issue areas.

Additionally, transnational processes have expanded the potentialities of local stakeholders by allowing them to confront, bypass or instrumentalize nation-states, thereby disrupting conventional hierarchies (Keck & Sikkink, 1998; Sassen, 2003, 2004; Wallerstein, 2000). Thus, while globalization has admittedly transformed the functions performed by national governments, global pressures have by no means made local avenues irrelevant. Following Sassen (2004), we call for a multiscalar analysis of American capitalism that takes stock of the impact of globalization on state capacities while acknowledging the importance of subnational actors.

The second lacuna of the variety of capitalism literature lies in its reductive conception of state capacities. At first sight, Hall and Soskice offer a sophisticated model to understand the intricacies of state–market relations in different national economies. But for all their meticulous efforts to avoid parsimony, the authors' focus on the contrast between LMEs and CMEs renews with a dichotomous vision of the state as interventionist or noninterventionist. Yet, as Evans shows, the question political economists should ask is not "how much" states intervene in the economy but "what kind" of involvement they undertake and what effects these measures have on the rest of society (Evans, 1995, p. 10).

By focusing on conventional modes of market intervention, political economists have often left aside hidden or submerged forms of economic activism that we describe here as shadow institutional processes. Scholars within and outside the American political development (APD) literature have long shed light on the economic guidance provided directly and indirectly by the US federal government.[3] Some scholars have documented the multiple functions operated by the military–industrial complex in the development of America's manufacturing and information technology sectors (Hooks, 1991; Fong, 2000; Block, 2008). Chang (2002) and Gindin and Panitch (2012) have analyzed the close relationship between state and market actors that led Washington to embrace protectionist policies before lecturing developing countries to open their markets to US exports in the interest of America's "informal empire." Scholars of financialization have also shed new light on the state–market nexus by revealing that state intervention was instrumental in the emergence of the modern financial capitalism – whether in relation to home mortgages (e.g., with the creation of government-sponsored enterprises Freddie Mac and Fannie Mae) or consumer credit (Aalbers, 2008; Trumbull, 2012).[4]

Weiss (2010) and Block (2008) delineated the contours of the American "hidden developmental state" by analyzing the recurrent pattern of economic activism through a wide array of technology, security and procurement policies. In a similar vein, Mettler (2011) unveiled the democratic dysfunctions of the "submerged state," defined as the intricate conglomeration of federal tax policies that benefit private organizations or households beneath the surface of US market institutions.

Our objective is to build upon this revisionist literature to show that the US federal government never took a backseat in the development of American capitalism. Instead, it resorted to subnational and shadow institutional processes that were mistaken as inaction. An avatar of the state–market nexus, this arsenal of policy tools is constantly reinvented by government actors at both national and subnational levels, which are neither systematically captured by business interests nor fully autonomous (Laffont & Tirole, 1991; Levine & Forrence 1990). They operate under the principles of "embedded autonomy." In Evans' words, they are "embedded in a concrete set of social ties that binds the state to society and provides institutionalized channels for the continual negotiation and renegotiation of goals and policies" (Evans, 1995, p. 12). In this sense, America has never really been a "weak state" nor a "liberal market economy." As Polanyi (2001) famously wrote, "*laissez faire* was planned" – an aphorism that remains as potent today as it was for the nineteenth century. Thus, while we recognize that business interests may dominate many policy spheres, we do not view power as a perpetual monopoly but rather as a historically contingent nexus that may be partly or radically altered by state, business and civil society actors.

The dynamics of agency, institutions and culture

The third shortcoming of conventional political economy models lies in their synchronic approach to capitalism and their tendency to minimize the transformative functions that crises perform to sustain or renew, destroy or create varieties of capitalism and their legitimate models.[5] This is partly due to the fact that institutionalist analyses of political economy have always been better equipped to explain continuity – e.g., through feedback loops, path dependency or policy legacies – than change. The old tradition of American institutionalism had first focused on the genesis and evolution of social institutions but soon envisaged political economy as incorporated in a broader societal and cultural process (Veblen, 1898). Institutions appeared as persistent social facts resulting from interaction and association. Maintaining socioeconomic equilibrium required striking political compromises that had to be enacted into law (Commons, 1924, 1934; Commons *et al.*, 1950). Mapping the formal institutions of the modern state and understanding system and power dynamics helped channel and control the disruptive forces of conflict into collective action. Politics regulated and stabilized social life by providing persistent rules and norms that had to be legitimized to become efficient. Shaping rules and norms constrained and modeled individual behaviors, warded off discontinuities in institutional architectures and fostered more linear trajectories. The focus was no longer on change but rather on social cohesion, collective consent and smooth institutional interdependencies between public and private institutions. Consequently, the new form of economic institutionalism that emerged with Coase (1937), developed with Williamson (1975, 2000) and North (1990, 2005), watered down the early political form of collective regulation and the public "turn" of the theories produced by the first generation of American institutionalists. The new approach was less concerned with social order, conflicts and hegemony, and more with transaction costs and the dialectic of markets and organizational hierarchies. It highlighted the relationship between externalization and internalization but also the impact on behaviors of socioeconomic constraints nested in institutional systems and societal values. "Rules of the games" and the notion of "adaptive efficiency" (North, 1990, 2005) became the prevailing characteristic and drivers of "productive," "maximizing" and resilient institutions. These powerful "governance structures" (Williamson, 2002) whose forms also extended to private and not-for profit organizations seemed to successfully regulate externalities and remedy market failures while compensating for weak state capacities. The dynamic role of other coordination mechanisms such as politics, actors' volition and agency was, however, ignored in such a framework, as also were the potential bifurcations of institutional trajectories resulting from endogenous contradictions and exogenous shocks.

The Great Recession has both highlighted the destructive power of finance when disequilibrium and instability become the rule and, paradoxically enough, evidenced the transformative power of crises and the hidden resistance force of existing models and implicit cultural patterns. The ensuing market and state failures have notably exposed the unresolved structural contradictions and tensions in the complex organization of a globalized capitalist economy (Hollingsworth, 1997, 2011) and the need to regulate and coordinate economic relations through norms and rules (North, 2005) that are also context- and culture-dependent. The constraining power of context and institutions and the central significance of politics and arenas that legitimize and implement sweeping institutional changes at critical junctures have become more salient, particularly when compromise must be reached to avoid, for example, congressional gridlock. The re-embedding of a partly deterritorialized US political economy has also become paramount since economic, social, political and cultural variables are jointly involved in the process of economic adjustment and institutional change (Hall & Thelen, 2009). These worlds are strongly intertwined and need to co-evolve into institutional complementarities so as to facilitate the emergence of a new compromise weaving the economic, political and societal spheres together both at the local and global levels. When faced with systemic risk, many US political and economic leaders have been forced to reconsider their guiding principles based on the self-instituted and self-regulated market dogma and the Lockean free will of the individual. The resistance force of existing economic models (free enterprise, proprietary rights, etc.) and imprinted cultural patterns that foster disruptive responses and conservative counter-reactions have been particularly strong in a newly polarized America. However, the destabilizing financial type of capitalism is no longer seen as the sole growth and value appropriation alternative, nor as the one best way toward a more "general welfare." In the face of strong opposition to state intervention, "re-forming" and "trans-forming" the existing economic model into a more sustainable and more mixed and coordinated socioeconomic system (Nelson, 2010) has become a much debated issue for liberals and post-Keynesians like Paul Krugman (2008), Robert Reich and other opinion leaders. This rejuvenated progressive stance jointly inscribes public policy, tolerable forms of state interventions, private forms of governance – in the business and non-profit sectors – but also acceptable value change at the core of a more domesticated economic dynamic and a less partisan polity.

Such paradigm shift, however, raises conceptual and normative questions on the intrinsic characteristics and dynamics of the US capitalist system, its boundaries, its destructive dimension but also its long-term institutional resilience and future adaptive capacity. We depart from conventional synchronic political economic models or dyadic approaches whereby American capitalism is only the logical product of structural forces or the fortuitous outcome of rational agents. Our objective is to demonstrate that the US political economy is rather a complex interaction and ever-changing dynamic system of agency, institutions and cultures. It is powered by contradictory forces, interacting actors, institutions, conflicting cultural values that drive its long-term development and produce a regime of growth and various modes and levels of regulation that are time- and space-specific (Aglietta, 1979). As a configuration of forces and institutions (Boyer & Hollingsworth, 1997) but also an interconnection between asymmetric spheres and spaces, American capitalism is intrinsically varied, multidimensional, changing and also transcultural. It is a locus, a focus and a transaction space whose boundaries extend to a wider globalized space of influence.

Admittedly, orthodox economists have never been fully blind to the power of agency or structure. However, for many American theoreticians of capitalism (public choice school), "free markets" remain the most rational and democratic economic system. The General Equilibrium model is said to coordinate actors via a competitive pricing mechanism that must be disconnected from society and polity since regulation is often appropriated by in-group elites that distort pure competition. Another dynamic pattern is also ascribed by agency theorists and particularly Schumpeter to the entrepreneur, a heroic figure of economic change that may develop his innovations into a firm and even an enduring institution (Schumpeter, 1934, 1942; Baumol *et al.*, 2007). In both cases, agency or actorhood predominates over hierarchical organizations and institutional structures in theoretical and ideological discourse, in the name of a long-standing American tradition of free enterprise and self-reliant initiative supposed to constantly rejuvenate civil society and democracy under the banner of a "Nation of Joiners" with highly valued entrepreneurship (Neem, 2008).

We posit that "the laws of motion" of capitalism (Boyer, 2010) are rather activated by a dynamic interplay between agency and structures, actors and institutions, a system of structured as well as structuring interactions that produces relevant socioeconomic forms able to tackle contradictions and produce change (Giddens, 1984; Nelson, 2010). Such a pluralistic form of regulation and constructivist function has always been a necessary condition for the dynamism and mutability of a multi-level governance structure. It is the way American capitalism acquired economic efficiency and discursive legitimacy (Schmidt, 2008) and produced a coherent narrative explaining crises and booms (Hodgson, 2009; Lipset, 1996) and also envisaged the possibility of the emergence of a new paradigm (Boltanski & Chiapello, 2005).

We define this rationalizing narrative process as "*focale*," a cultural prism that spotlights specific ideological representations while obscuring other ideational elements to make sense of the past, the present and the future of American capitalism (Beckert, 2013). This concept differs from the Gramscian notion of "cultural hegemony" to the extent that it is time- and space-specific and does not necessarily serve the interests of the ruling class. One of our objectives lies in identifying the processes under which this *focale* changes across history, i.e., how ideas, interests and institutions interact to catalyze paradigm shifts. To do so, we must take a second look at the developmental path of American capitalism that evidences far more intrinsic variety than is usually perceived. Shifting configurations are, indeed, correlated to economic and ideological cycles and highly dependent on social imaginaries (Taylor, 2007), actors' governing philosophies and institutional doctrines (Lichtenstein, 2006). This is, for example, the historical and cultural path Eisner (2011) has explored to describe the variegated process of change. He identifies three different regimes for the past century as the American political economy evolved: the Progressive regime and the regulatory state; the rise and consolidation of the New Deal and welfare state regimes; and a neoliberal market regime that is currently in turmoil.

To understand the development logic of American capitalism, it is necessary to first theorize capitalism as autonomization and prevalence of the economic sphere over the political and social spheres, but also as a flux of societal and cultural processes – counter-movements regulating the state–market nexus. The renewal dynamics of the US brand of capitalism may rely on this constant tug of war between a dual disembedding and re-embedding process, between an "agentic" and a more structural and institutional vision of the economic system. The dominant positivist economic framework explains the rise of capitalism as an open self-organizing process not guided by a central agent but reduced to rational economic relations and aggregated data. Another tradition emphasizes the role of political actors as originators of institutions, individual entrepreneurs, business firms or sovereign entity actors as the driving forces of societal change. A renewed regulatory tradition also underlines a shift of regulation in which the state is restructuring itself in cooperation with civil society and cultural values. We believe that a transdisciplinary approach that we term "civilizational approach" is needed to define US capitalism as a socioeconomic and cultural system in movement, a changing but resilient multi-level mode of coordination rather than a mere economic equilibrium.

To capture the complex societal dynamics of the American variety of capitalism, the present volume is divided into three main parts. Part I casts light on the transformation and resilience of the state–market nexus during the Great Recession. The purpose of this part is dual: (1) to go beyond dichotomous explanations of the crisis as market or regulatory failure to delineate its cultural, figurative and societal contours; (2) to de-construct the notion of crisis and understand its functions in the renewal and legitimation of the American political economy.

James McBride begins by examining the deep historical and cultural roots of the notion of "lawlessness" in the American psyche and its contemporary ramifications in the reconstructed "Wild West of Wall Street." At the crossroads between cultural studies and economics, the author demonstrates how symbolic factors can have very tangible – and destructive – effects on the social ecosystem of American capitalism. Nicholas Sowels' study reasserts the importance of ideational determinants by studying the long process of "ideological capture" undergone by successive Federal Reserve chairmen under the neoliberal political economic regime. Bradley T. Smith deconstructs the state–market dichotomy by arguing that government intervention has performed key functions to support the neoliberal regime over the past 30 years and is therefore unlikely to trigger a paradigm shift in American political economy. Finally, Pierre Arnaud seeks to re-embed the economy in its cultural and political milieu. The author demonstrates that household debts, rising inequality and financialization have long been constitutive elements of a coherent global equilibrium which the financial crisis has severely – though maybe not definitively – disrupted.

Part II interrogates the legitimacy of methodological nationalism by bringing into relief the imbroglio of subnational, national and global processes that drive, transform and constrain US capitalism. Martine Azuelos challenges monolithic representations of the American political economy in a sharp analysis of the heterogeneous impact of the financial crisis across cities, states and regions of the United States. Drawing upon economic geography, political economy and institutional economics, her study discusses the determinants of these regional disparities before calling for a cross-disciplinary approach to American capitalism that does full justice to its internal diversity. Cécile Cormier's chapter on state and local tax and budgetary policies corroborates the significance of subnational or "submerged" policies. Her quantitative analysis sheds light on the hidden role played by local governments in creating social inequality, a phenomenon often interpreted as the primary result of federal policies. In a multiscalar analysis of the housing market collapse, Cynthia Ghorra-Gobin connects the dots between local and global forces propelling US economic growth – and more specifically urbanization and financialization. The author goes beyond conventional interpretations of the subprime mortgage crisis as a financial bubble to discuss the societal and cultural underpinnings and implications of the housing collapse, i.e., its meaning for America's ownership society and the very essence of the American Dream. Finally, in his analysis of America's competitiveness policy, Jean-Baptiste Velut examines the extent to which globalization has reconfigured economic activism, giving birth to decentralized and hybrid forms of government intervention that conventional dichotomies between the public/private and local/global dichotomies can no longer capture.

Part III also focuses on the trajectory of American capitalism and more specifically on the role of agency and structure in its renewal. Jacques-Henri Coste studies the US "National System of Innovation" as a complex socioeconomic paradigm and a political economy construct at the core of the American variety of capitalism. He traces the development path and legacy of successive innovation regimes and considers the extension of an open governance and collaborative innovation model in the wake of previous transformations (closed/linear model, interactive triple helix, regional clusters, and entrepreneurial ecosystems). The new paradigm serves as a policy substitute and a pragmatic compromise underplaying the developmental and catalyzing role of federal and subnational instances within a decentralized and pluralist mode of innovation governance. His purpose is to depart from market perspectives that only interpret America's inventiveness as the product of the Invisible Hand, so as to unveil the broader political and cultural ecosystem that has nurtured innovation in the United States. Catherine Sauviat similarly examines the interplay between structure and conjuncture under the prism of the idiosyncratic US labor market, revealing that the American crisis has exacerbated long-term trends and undermined workers' rights under degrading employment conditions. The confluence of these short- and long-term factors is raising fundamental questions on the essence and the capacity of renewal of the US employment model. Marie-Christine Pauwels explores the difficulties inherent to challenging the current political economic regime through the experience of Occupy Wall Street. Not only do social movements contesting capitalism face an uphill ideological battle in the United States, but contentious power can also be co-opted for commercial purposes. By underlining the limits of mobilization outside democratic channels, the author reaffirms the crucial importance of the state in shaping the trajectory of US capitalism. If capitalism cannot be challenged from outside, it may be transformed from inside. Laurence Cossu-Beaumont draws a parallel between the origins of philanthropy and the latest forms of "philanthro-capitalism" in the form of *The Giving Pledge.* The civilizational focus on the current discourse of capitalists seeks to re-embed the American brand of capitalism in its essential historical and cultural *milieu*. It allows consideration of whether innovative partnerships between individuals, corporations and the state may redefine the contours of America's cultural political economy or simply act to reproduce and legitimize the US variety of capitalism.

Notes

1 For a discussion, see Pontusson (2005).
2 See the contributions of Azuelos and Cormier to this volume. See also Peck (2013).
3 For a discussion of the APD literature on the American state, see Orren and Skowronek (2002) and Novak (2008).
4 For an excellent review of the literature, see Van Der Zwan (2014).
5 A notable exception is Eisner (2011).

References

Aalbers, M. (2008). The Financialization of Home and Mortgage Market Crisis. *Competition & Change*, *12*, 148–166.

Aglietta, M. (1979). *A theory of capitalist regulation: The US experience*. London: Verso.

Aglietta, M. & Bai, G. (2013). *China's development: Capitalism and empire*. New York: Routledge.

Amable, B. (2003). *The diversity of capitalism.* New York: Oxford University Press.

Azuelos, M. (2012). Anglosphere. In Ghorra-Gobin, C. (ed.), *Dictionnaire critique de la mondialisation*. Paris: Armand Colin.

Azuelos, M. (ed.) (2015). Capitalisme anglo-saxon et mondes anglophones: des paradigmes en questions. *Revue LISA/e-journal*, *13*(2). Retrieved from https://lisa.revues.org/7184.

Baumol, W., Litan, R. & Schramm, C.E. (2007). *Good capitalism, bad capitalism and the economics of growth and prosperity.* New Haven, CT: Yale University Press.

Beckert, J. (2013). Capitalism as a System of Expectations: Toward a Sociological Microfoundation of Political Economy. *Theory and Society*, *42*, 219–240.

Bennet, J.C. (2001). An Anglosphere Primer. *The Anglosphere Institute*. Retrieved from http://explorersfoundation.org/archive/anglosphereinstitute.html

Best, J. & Paterson, M. (eds.) (2010). *Cultural political economy.* New York: Routledge.

Block, F. (2008). Swimming Against the Current: The Rise of a Hidden Developmental State in the United States. *Politics and Society*, *36*(2), 169–206.

Boltanski, L. & Chiapello, E. (2005). *The new spirit of capitalism.* London: Verso.

Boyer, R. (1990). *The regulation school: A critical introduction.* New York: Columbia University Press.

Boyer, R. (2000). Is a Finance-led Regime Growth a Viable Alternative to Fordism? A Preliminary Analysis. *Economy and Society*, *29*, 11–145.

Boyer, R. (2007). Capitalism Strikes Back: Why and What Consequences for Social Sciences? *Revue de la Régulation: Capitalisme, Institutions, Pouvoirs, 1*. Retrieved from http://regulation.revues.org/2142.

Boyer, R. (2010). Are there Laws of Motion of Capitalism? *Socio-Economic Review, 9*(11), 59–81.

Boyer, R. & Hollingsworth, J. Rogers (1997). From National Embeddedness to Spatial and Institutional Nestedness. In J. Rogers Hollingsworth & R. Boyer (eds.), *Contemporary capitalism. The embeddedness of institutions* (pp. 433–484) Cambridge: Cambridge University Press.

Boyer, R. & Saillard, Y. (1995). *Théorie de la régulation, Etat des savoirs*. Paris: La Découverte.

Boyer, R. & Saillard, Y. (eds.) (2002). *Régulation theory: The state of the art*. London and New York: Routledge.

Braudel, F. (1982). *Civilization and capitalism, 15th–18th century, vol. II: The wheels of commerce*. New York: Harper [Originally published as *Les Jeux de l'échange*, 1979].

Braudel, F. (1995). *A history of civilizations*. New York: Penguin Harper [Originally published as *Grammaire des civilisations*, Flammarion, 1987].

Chang, H.J. (2002). *Kicking away the ladder: Development strategy in historical perspective*. London: Anthem Press.

Coase, R.H. (1937). The Nature of the Firm. *Economica, 2*(1), 386–405.

Commons, J.R. (1924). *Legal foundations of capitalism*. New York: Macmillan.

Commons, J.R. (1934). *Institutional economics*. Madison, WI: University of Wisconsin Press.

Commons, J.R., Parsons, K.H. & Perlman, S. (1950). *The economics of collective action*. New York: Macmillan.

Coste J.H. (2013). *Les sociétés entrepreneuriales et les mondes anglophones, cultures, contextes, perspectives*. Paris: Presses Sorbonne Nouvelle.

Durkheim, E. & Mauss, M. (1913). Note sur la notion de civilisation. *L'Année Sociologique, 12*, 46–50.

Eisinger, P.K. (1988). *The rise of the entrepreneurial state*. Madison, WI: University of Wisconsin Press.

Eisenstadt, S.N. (2000). The Civilizational Dimension in Sociological Analysis. *Thesis Eleven, 62*, 1–21.

Eisner, M.C. (2011). *The American political economy, institutional evolution of market and state*. New York: Routledge.

Etzkowitz, H. (1998). The Triple Helix of Academia–Industry–Government: The US National Innovation System. In R. Anderson, T. Cohn, C. Day, M. Howlett & C. Murray (eds.), *Innovation systems in a global context* (pp. 127–147). Montreal: McGill-Queen's University Press.

Evans, P. (1995). *Embedded autonomy: States and industrial transformation*. Princeton, NJ: Princeton University Press.

Fong, G. (2000). Breaking New Ground or Breaking the Rules: Strategic Reorientation in US Industrial Policy. *International Security, 25*(2), 152–186.

Giddens, A. (1984). *The constitution of society: On the theory of structuration*. Cambridge: Polity.

Gindin, S. & Panitch, L. (2012). *The making of global capitalism: The political economy of American empire*. London and New York: Verso.

Granovetter, M. (1985). Economic Action and Social Structure: The Problem of Embeddedness. *American Journal of Sociology, 91*(3), 481–510.

Gray, J. (1998). *False dawn: The delusions of global capitalism.* New York: New Press.

Greider, W. (1997). *One world, ready or not: The manic logic of global capitalism.* New York: Simon & Schuster.

Haass, R.N. (2008). The Age of Nonpolarity: What Will Follow U.S. Dominance. *Foreign Affairs, 87*(3), 44–56.

Hall, P.A. & Soskice, D. (eds.) (2001). *Varieties of capitalism: The institutional foundations of comparative advantage.* Oxford: Oxford University Press.

Hall, P.A. & Thelen, K. (2009). Institutional Change in Varieties of Capitalism. *Socio-economic Review, 7*(1), 7–34.

Hart, J.A. (1992). *Rival capitalists: International competitiveness in the United States, Japan and Western Europe.* Ithaca, NY: Cornell University Press.

Hodgson, G. (2009). *The myth of American exceptionalism.* New Haven, CT: Yale University Press.

Hollingsworth, J. Rogers (1997). The Institutional Embeddedness of American Capitalism. In C. Crouch & W. Streeck (eds.), *Political economy of modern capitalism, mapping convergence and diversity* (pp. 133–147). London: Sage.

Hollingsworth, J. Rogers (2011). Comment on "The Complex Economic Organization of Capitalist Economies" (by Richard R. Nelson). *Capitalism and Society, 6*(1).

Hooks, G. (1991). *Forging the military–industrial complex: World War II's Battle of the Potomac.* Chicago, IL: Illinois University Press.

Jessop, B. & Sum, N.G. (2012). *Towards cultural political economy: Bringing culture back in the economy.* Cheltenham: Elgar.

Jessop, B. *et al.* (2012). Crossing Boundaries: Towards Cultural Political Economy, Interview with Bob Jessop. *Revue de la Régulation, 12.* Retrieved from http://regulation.revues.org/9943

Katz, B. & Bradley, J. (2013). *The metropolitan revolution.* Washington, DC: Brooking Institution Press.

Katzenstein, P. (1976). International Relations and Domestic Structures: Foreign Economic Policies of Advanced Industrial States. *International Organization, 30,* 1–45.

Keck, M.E. & Sikkink, K. (1998). *Activists beyond borders: Advocacy networks in international politics.* Ithaca, NY: Cornell University Press.

Krasner, S.D. (1978). United States Commercial and Monetary Policy: Unravelling the Paradox of External Strength and Internal Weakness. In P. Katzenstein (ed.), *Between power and plenty: Foreign economic policies of advanced industrial states* (pp. 51–87). Madison, WI: University of Wisconsin Press.

Krugman, P. (2008). *The return of depression economics and the crisis of 2008.* London: Penguin.

Laffont, J.J. & Tirole, J. (1991). The Politics of Government Decision Making: A Theory of Regulatory Capture. *Quarterly Journal of Economics, 106*(4): 1089–1127.

Levi-Faur, D. (2006). Varieties of Regulatory Capitalism: Sectors and Nations in the Making of a New Global Order. *Governance, 19*(3), 363–366.

Levi-Faur, D. (2008). Regulatory Capitalism and the Reassertion of the Public Interests. *Policy and Society, 27*(3), 181–191.

Levine, M.E. & Forrence, J.L. (1990). Regulatory Capture, Public Interest, and the Public Agenda: Toward a Synthesis. *Journal of Law Economics & Organization, 6,* 167–198.

Lichtenstein, N. (2006). *American capitalism, social thought and political economy in the twentieth century.* Philadelphia, PA: University of Pennsylvania Press.

Lipset, S.M. (1996). *American exceptionalism: A double edged sword.* New York: Norton.

Mathews, J.T. (1997). Power Shift. *Foreign Affairs*, *76*(1), 50–66.
Mettler, S. (2011). *The submerged state.* Chicago, IL and London: University of Chicago Press.
Neem, J.N. (2008). *Creating a nation of joiners: Democracy and civil society in early national Massachusetts.* Cambridge, MA: Harvard University Press.
Nelson, R.R. (2010). Capitalism as a Mixed Economy. Columbia University Center on Capitalism and Society, Working paper, 59. Retrieved from http://capitalism.columbia.edu/files/ccs/CCSWP59_Nelson.pdf.
North, D. (1990). *Institutions, institutional change, and economic performance.* Cambridge: Cambridge University Press.
North, D. (2005). *Understanding the process of economic change.* Princeton, NJ: Princeton University Press.
Novak, W.J. (2008). The Myth of the Weak State. *The American Historical Review*, *113*(3), 752–772.
Ohmae, K. (1995). *The end of the nation state.* New York: Free Press.
Orlean, A. (2004). What is a Collective Belief? In P. Bourgine & J.P. Nadal (eds.), *Cognitive economics* (pp. 199–212). Berlin, Heidelberg and New York: Springer-Verlag.
Orlean, A. (2014). *The empire of value: A new foundation for economics.* Cambridge, MA: MIT Press.
Orren, K. & Skowronek, S. (2002). The Study of American Political Development. In H. Milner & I. Katznelson (eds.), *Political science: State of the discipline III* (pp. 722–754). New York: W.W. Norton.
Panitch, L. & Gindin, S. (2012). *The making of global capital: The political economy of American empire*. New York: Verso Books.
Peck, J. (2013). Pushing Austerity: State Failure, Municipal Bankruptcy and the Crises of Fiscal Federalism in the USA. *Cambridge Journal of Regions, Economy and Society*, *7*(1): 17–44.
Piketty, T. (2014). *Capital in the twenty-first century.* Cambridge, MA: The Belknap Press of Harvard University Press.
Polanyi, K. (2001 [1944]). *The great transformation.* Boston, MA: Beacon Press.
Pontusson, H.R. (2005). Varieties and Commonalities of Capitalism. In D. Coates (ed.), *Varieties of capitalism, varieties of approaches* (pp. 163–188). London: Palgrave.
Porter, M. (1990). *The competitive advantage of nations.* New York: Free Press.
Reich, R.B. & Magaziner, I.C. (1982). *Minding America's business: The decline and rise of the American economy.* New York: Harcourt Brace Jovanovitch.
Sassen, S. (2001). *The global city: New York, London, Tokyo*. Princeton, NJ and Oxford: Princeton University Press.
Sassen, S. (2003). Globalization or Denationalization?, *Review of International Political Economy*, *10*(1), 1–22.
Sassen, S. (2004). Local Actors in Global Politics. *Current Sociology*, *52*(4): 649–670.
Schmidt, V. (2008). Discursive Institutionalism: The Explanatory Power of Ideas and Discourse. *Annual Review of Political Science*, *11*, 303–326.
Schumpeter, J.A. (1934). *The theory of economic development.* Cambridge, MA: Harvard University Press.
Schumpeter, J.A. (1942). *Capitalism, socialism and democracy.* New York: Routledge.
Senett, R. (2006). *The culture of the new capitalism.* New Haven, CT: Yale University Press.
Stiglitz, J. (2001). Foreword. In Polanyi, K., *The great transformation.* Boston, MA: Beacon Press [1944].

Stiglitz, J. (2003). *Globalization and its discontent*. New York: W.W. Norton.
Strange, S. (1996). *The retreat of the state: The diffusion of power in the world economy*. Cambridge: Cambridge University Press.
Streek, W. (2010). Taking Capitalism Seriously: Toward an Institutionalist Approach to Contemporary Political Economy. Max Planck Institute for the Study of Societies, Discussion paper 10/15. Retrieved from www.mpifg.de/pu/mpifg_dp/dp10-15.pdf.
Streek, W. (2011). The Crises of Democratic Capitalism. *New Left Review*, *71*. Retrieved from http://newleftreview.org/II/71/wolfgang-streeck-the-crises-of-democratic-capitalism.
Swedberg, R. (2010). A Note on Civilizations and Economics. *European Journal of Social Theory*, *13*(1), 15–30.
Taylor, C. (2007). *Modern social imaginaries*. Durham, NC and London: Duke University Press.
Trumbull, G. (2012). Credit Access and Social Welfare: The Rise of Consumer Lending in the United States and France. *Politics & Society*, *40*, 9–34.
Van Der Zwan, N. (2014). Making Sense of Financialization. *Socio-Economic Review*, *12*, 99–129.
Veblen, T. (1898). Why is Economics not an Evolutionary Science? *Quarterly Journal of Economics*, *12*(4), 373–397.
Wallerstein, I. (2000). Globalization or the Age of Transition? A Long-Term View of the Trajectory of the World System. *International Sociology*, *15*(2), 251–267.
Weiss, L. (1998). *The Myth of the Powerless State: Governing the Economy of a Global Era*. Oxford: Polity Press.
Weiss, L. (2010). The State in the Economy: Neoliberal or Neoactivist? In G. Morgan, J. Campbell, C. Crouch, O. Pedersen & R. Whitley (eds.), *The Oxford handbook of comparative institutional analysis* (pp. 183–209). Oxford: Oxford University Press.
Whitley, R. (2009). U.S. Capitalism: A Tarnished Model. *Academy of Management Perspectives*, *23*(2), 11–22.
Williamson, O. (1975). *Markets and hierarchies: Analysis and antitrust implications*. New York: The Free Press.
Williamson, O. (2000). The New Institutional Economics. *Journal of Economic Literature*, *38*(3), 595–613.
Williamson, O. (2002). The Theory of the Firm as Governance Structure: From Choice to Contract. *Journal of Economic Perspectives*, *16*(3), 171–195.
Zysman, J. & Tyson, L.D. (1983). *American industry in international competition: Government policies and corporate strategies*. Ithaca, NY: Cornell University Press.

Part I

Re-embedding the financial crisis in its cultural milieu

1 The "Wild West" on Wall Street

An analysis of and prognosis for the American model of postmodern finance capital in the global economy

James McBride

Introduction

In their introduction, the editors of this volume note the impoverishment of scholarly approaches to the study of American political economy that forego consideration of non-economic factors in their analyses of capitalism. Such research fails to reach the underlying dynamics that give birth to and shape the developments of American finance capital. Accordingly, they call for "re-embedding the economy" into the American historical and cultural milieu, which alone will yield an understanding of the forces that brought both the United States and, indeed, the world economy to the brink of collapse in 2008. This author takes their call seriously. The analysis that follows shall: (1) provide what the editors called an "economic civilization analysis" that will contextualize the developments of American investment banking, particularly the rise of the "New Breed" of American banker which produced the "Wild West" on Wall Street, in the American historical and cultural milieu; (2) describe the products and behaviors of the "lawless," i.e., unregulated, derivatives market, which led the world to the economic precipice; and (3) analyze the attempt by Congress and the Obama Administration to rein in Wall Street.

An economic civilization analysis

Although crime has markedly declined in the United States over the past two decades (Wood, 2012), there are more guns in America today than ever before, over three hundred million or almost one for every American (Lepore, 2012, p. 39). Why? In Baudrillard's postmodern hyperreality, Americans actually live their mythologies (Baudrillard, 1989, p. 28). Europeans are right. Americans are cowboys, or at least they believe themselves to be. Following the Jeffersonian dictum that "the government which governs best governs least," they are ideologically predisposed to distrust the state. The law appears to be weak, corrupt or intrusive. It therefore should come as no surprise that, in the postmodern American economy of the last decade, lawlessness, an attribute of the American psychic economy, marked the "Wild West of Wall Street."

Frequently, Europeans find the American penchant for violence and lawlessness bewildering and incomprehensible; yet there is something about the American predisposition that is also viscerally exciting. Americans are in love with the aura of freedom – not just freedom in the form of rights, but also freedom from constraint. It is a "siren call" that lures Americans frequently to their own destruction, for Americans do and will pay the price, sometimes with the sacrifice of their own children – e.g., the Newtown, Connecticut mass shooting – and sometimes with economic disaster. Where does this consciousness, this twist in the American psychic economy, originate?

To a dramatic extent, the source for lawlessness in the American psyche lies in the nation's experience of the frontier. In his classic 1894 paper, "The Significance of the Frontier in American History," the American historian Frederick Jackson Turner (1894) concluded that "the frontier is the outer edge of the wave—the meeting point between savagery and civilization." It was the boundary along which individuals and families had to wrest the means for their own survival without the aid of the state or law. Although government, as it followed behind the wave, extended its reach and at times provided the frontier with a modicum of security, it also infringed upon the freedom of settlers to reap the benefits of the natural order as they themselves deemed fit. Hence, "the frontier is productive of individualism. Complex society is precipitated by the wilderness into a kind of primitive organization based on the family. The tendency is anti-social" (Turner, 1894). Although Turner noted that a bulletin of the Superintendent for the Census in 1890 officially announced the "closing" of the American frontier, this liminality became indelibly etched in American consciousness – a place where "the bonds of custom are broken and unrestraint is triumphant" (Turner, 1894).

Structuralist analysis of the Wild West is helpful in understanding this consciousness. Will Wright, author of classic text *Sixguns and Society*, sees in the image of the West the superimposition of a symbolic order – a mythic structure – on American historical experience. In his words, "myth maps the present on the past in order to pose problems and propose solutions. Hence through myth the future is discovered in the past" (Wright, 1985, p. 210). Nowhere is this mythic structure more evident than in the cinematic depiction of the American West. Hollywood captured this conflict in its production of Western films and television shows during the 1950s–1970s that depicted a frontier marked by the skirmish between possessive individualism (the underlying ethos of an unrestrained free market)[1] and the institutional framework of social values.[2]

The heroes of these films, as well as the villains, were exponents of possessive individualism, beholden to no one, although most often the villain operated within the social order to subvert it for his own ends. The latter's unrestrained possessive individualism undermined the social values of a democratic society (freedom, equality, community, peace, love, mutual respect, satisfying work). Yet the hero was likewise a loner, who frequently lived outside social norms, in order to do battle with the villain on equal terms. Here lies what Wright called the "central dilemma" of the classic Western: "If the values of society are accepted [e.g., love, community, peace, harmony], they cannot be defended, and if they are defended, they cannot be practiced" (Wright, 1985, p. 162). In such instances, average citizens are supposed to turn to legal authority. Yet, in this cinematic world, on the frontier between possessive individualism and social values, Americans cannot rely on the law. The law here is fragile – too weak to even preserve itself. In other words, the paradox of classic Western films, indeed the paradox of the cinematic image of American society, which embraces both possessive individualism and social values, is this: to preserve society, you must break the law.[3]

The concept of vigilante justice remains one of the most powerful themes in American films and television. The "good guys" are those who operate outside social norms in order to subdue the villains. This theme appears *ad nauseam* in Hollywood films, the biggest export of the American post-industrial economy. The history of American film is replete with Western heroes (*Shane*, *Magnificent Seven*, *Unforgiven*), action heroes (the *Mission Impossible* and *Bourne* series) and superheroes (*Spiderman* and *Batman* series), to name just a few, all of whom operate outside the law to save society. Much in the American psychic economy, ranging from the gunslinger to the euphemistic "enhanced interrogation techniques" of American intelligence services, arises along this frontier of structuralist binaries: outside–inside, nature–culture, strong–weak, good–corrupt. A man, allegedly uncorrupted by and standing outside society, provides the natural strength and goodness to subdue those corrupted or weakened by the culture of the social order.

Although at first glance this anthropological analysis of the American psychic economy may seem to have little to do with American political economy, this approach tells us much about the mentality of Wall Street during the "Bull" years of the derivatives revolution. The Street has always had its suspicions about government regulation, which is commonly believed by players to strangle the free market. Talk to any broker on the Street and they will tell you their heartfelt belief that federal and state regulators (and even their very own compliance officers) stifle innovation with burdensome rules and paperwork. The Smithian dictum of "truck, barter and exchange" is deemed a natural attribute of free men, who have a right to the fruits of their labor through hard work and individual initiative (Smith, 1776, book 1, chapter 2). Government interference corrupts the natural process of bargaining, which is the hallmark of the Street. To free the natural forces of productivity, government should refrain from imposing regulations on the market – indeed, the fewer regulations, the better. Regulations not only shackle growth; they also invite corruption as individuals, be they hedge fund managers or investment bankers, try to circumvent them to maximize returns for their investors and their own proprietary interests. In short, players on the Street cannot help but see themselves as victims of governmental regulators who unfairly try to rein in the productive forces of capitalism. It would be far better without the regulation of the market, for it is only by establishing a legal lacuna – a law-free zone where financial professionals could go about their business unencumbered – that the "good guys" of Wall Street can bring prosperity to the American people. For them, the market is – or at least ought to be – the frontier. Hence, the notion that Wall Street had become the

"Wild West" is no cheap metaphor, but rather a reflection of the deep-seated belief of players in the justice of unregulated markets, emancipated from the unnatural impediment of law. The fin-de-siècle witnessed the opportunity for the Street to seize the moment and free itself from the ever-present watch of government and industry regulators by opening up just such a new frontier.

During the 1990s, groups of young insurgents (the "New Breed") in the banking industry orchestrated a "breakthrough" in the staid business of investment banking by creating two new financial products: credit default swaps (CDSs) and collateralized debt obligations (CDOs), brilliant fusions of securitization and credit derivatives. Derivatives are just what they sound like. Derivatives are contracts whose value is based on or derived from another set of assets. Because they were private contracts regarding the performance of assets, and not the buying or selling of the assets themselves, the parties and counterparties almost never conducted derivatives transactions on exchanges, preferring private deals arranged by their investment bankers and private clearing houses.[4] Since derivative transactions technically did not entail the purchase or sale of the underlying security or commodity, they were indicia of what we might call postmodern finance. Wall Street and its Republican allies prevailed upon the Clinton Administration, its economic advisors, e.g., Robert Rubin and Larry Summers, and the Congress to exempt derivatives from governmental regulation by the Commodity Futures Modernization Act of 2000.[5] In effect, the US government created a "law-free" zone in which the "good guys," i.e., the "New Breed" of investment bankers, could exploit the free market for the benefit of themselves, their employers, and, collaterally, the nation. The failure of the Congress to regulate derivatives unleashed a frenzy of securitization on Wall Street – a veritable "Wild West" in which anything goes – that ultimately ended in the near-total collapse of the world economy.

The structure of the credit derivative market and its 2008 collapse

Ironically, the origins of the 2008 economic crisis lie in the response of the Federal Reserve to the cycle of booms and busts in the 1990s and early 2000s. Investment banks handled the IPOs (initial public offerings) of small Silicon Valley operations, many of which had never turned a profit, and turned their founders into millionaires overnight. The investment banks made tens of millions of dollars in underwriting fees and stock sales. The boom, however, was short-lived and went bust in March 2000. The downturn from the dot-com bust was exacerbated by the 1998 collapse of Long Term Capital Management, an electronic trading hedge fund that lost $4.6 billion in 1998 in the Russian currency devaluation and almost pulled down America's leading financial institutions (Lowenstein, 2000). In 2001 Enron's collapse dealt another blow to a slowing economy, followed by the destruction of the World Trade Center in September. By October 2001 the DOW had fallen to 7,286, a 38 percent drop since January 14, 2000. During this period, Alan Greenspan, chairman of the

Federal Reserve, responded by cutting the Federal Reserve's discount rate – the rate at which banks borrow money from the Federal Reserve – from 7.5 percent in 2000 to 2 percent in October 2001.

The radical decline in the discount rate caused a crisis among institutional investors. Most institutional investors were largely limited to investing in bonds that were rated AAA by credit rating agencies (also called nationally recognized statistical rating organizations or NRSROs) like Standard & Poor's, Moody's and Fitch – in other words, they invested in US Treasury bonds, backed by the US government.[6] Many relied upon the steady return from safe investments in government bonds to fund their activities, including pensions, payrolls and operational expenses. However, because government bond interest rates mirrored the drop in the Fed's discount rate, the returns on Treasuries were no longer sufficient for institutional investors to meet their obligations. Now they faced a shortfall in income and either had to trim their expenses, lay-off employees or even reduce payouts to pensioners or other beneficiaries. Many scanned the horizon for other potentially AAA-rated financial products that would fill that void by providing a higher return than depressed US Treasury bond investments, even if it were only an extra 25–50 basis points (0.25–0.5 percent interest). Although most Americans feared the consequences of 9/11, investment banks saw the ensuing economic downturn as a golden opportunity.

The decline in the discount rate produced dramatic drops in mortgage rates, fueling a housing boom across the country. The "New Breed" reasoned that by marketing residential mortgages, which had been securitized as bonds (called residential mortgage-backed securities or RMBSs), to investors, investment banks could make billions of dollars in profits. Of course, the profitability of RMBSs depended on whether and how many investors would actually buy them, but most investors shied away from the idea. If you held a subprime mortgage, you would carry the risk of default by the borrower and a 100 percent loss. Compared to a US Treasury bond backed by the credit of the United States, a mortgage backed by the credit of a home owner was a risky proposition, to say the least.[7] However, if the bank bundled that mortgage in a package of 1,000 mortgages, "New Breed" risk managers (dubbed "Quants" because of their mathematical prowess (Patterson, 2010)) reasoned that the risk of default would be very low. Accordingly, the "New Breed" recommended packaging RMBSs into CDOs to be held by structured investment vehicles (SIVs), collateralized by the houses purchased by mortgagors. Quants discovered that risk could be cut further by splitting up the packages of mortgages into tranches, i.e., dividing the bond offering into different levels, based on the mortgagors' credit. No investor took the risk of the entire bond, but only assumed the risk of the tranche of the bonds they had purchased. Indeed, higher-level tranches received safer bond ratings if they paid bondholders first in case of default.

Part of the Quants' work also involved a form of prestidigitation. Investment bankers who structured these deals sought to maximize the size of this new financial product by rolling in the over $1 trillion US domestic market of credit card and auto loan debt (sold, e.g., by VISA, Mastercard or GMAC). By loading credit card and auto loans that traditionally have a higher rate of default into these mortgage loan tranches, Quants diluted their risk to investors (Patterson, 2010, pp. 180–181). However, this sleight-of-hand alone did not convince the credit rating agencies to give these CDOs the AAA rating that institutional investors needed. To answer that question requires an understanding of the structure of the CDO transaction developed by the "New Breed" of investment bankers. Figure 1.1 reflects that structure.

Figure 1.1 depicts what the Goldman trader, Fabrice Tourre, one of the key figures in the SEC fraud case, called the "monstrosity" (Gapper, 2010) and what Blythe Masters, a JP Morgan banker who helped build it, dubbed "the financial weapon of mass destruction" (Tett, 2009, p. 249). Of course, it wasn't seen as such when it was first built. It was, in fact, the most amazing money-making machine.

At the upper left is a box entitled institutional investors (such as pension funds, private equity funds, hedge funds, colleges, universities, non-profits, state

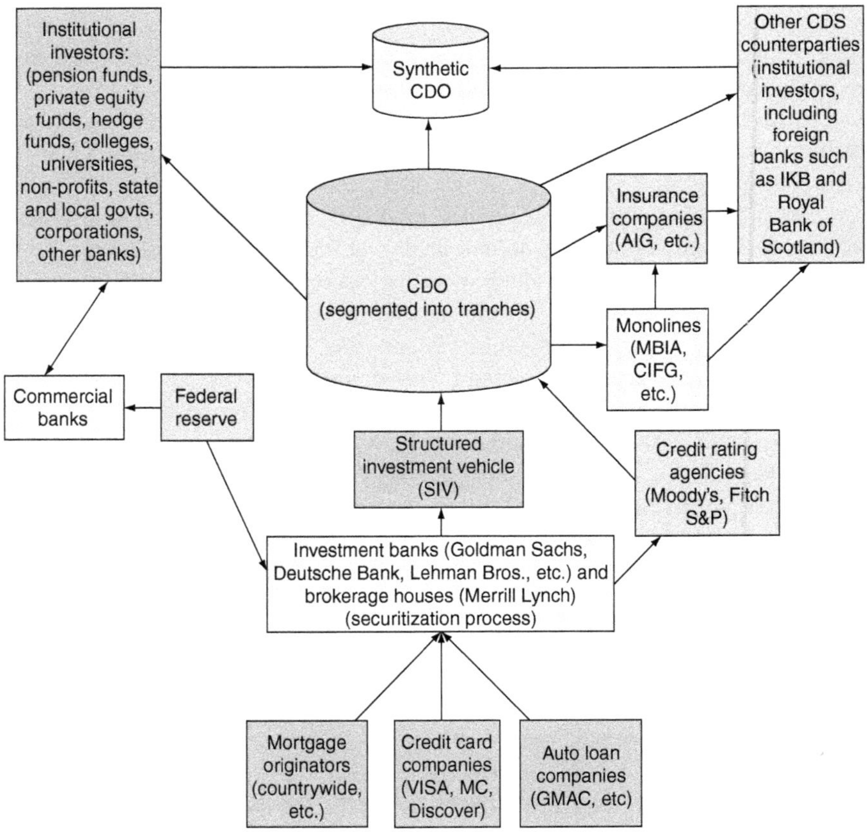

Figure 1.1 Collateralized debt obligations (CDO) deal structures (© James McBride 2013).

and local governments, corporations and banks.) The boxes at the bottom refer to mortgages, auto loans and credit cards. The historically low discount rate translated into historically low mortgage rates, which meant that many lower-middle- and lower-class Americans could afford to buy a home for the very first time, and home ownership meant increased credit lines for credit cards and auto loans. The "New Breed" at JP Morgan, Deutsche Bank, Goldman, Merrill Lynch, etc. (*see* center box) thought that if they could gather up these mortgages (*see* the left lower box), couple them with auto loans (the right lower box) and credit card loans (*see* the middle lower box), repackage them as new bonds called CDOs (*see* the barrel in the middle of the diagram) and sell them to institutional investors, their banks could make a fortune. So investment banks set up off-balance sheet entities, called structured investment vehicles or SIVs (*see* the center box below the CDO), which would hold these debt instruments, and issue the CDOs. But why would any institutional investor want to buy a bond based on a tranche of a CDO backed in part by subprime mortgages? The New Breed argued that because subprime mortgages were spread throughout all tranches of the CDO, the risks of default to the investor were substantially lessened. But to convince institutional investors to buy the CDO, the bankers concluded that they had to get a AAA rating from a credit rating agency (Fitch, Standard & Poor's, or Moody's) for at least the top tranche (*see* the credit ratings agencies box). How could they convince the credit rating agencies to give their CDOs an AAA rating, usually reserved for extremely safe investments like US Treasuries?

The "New Breed" came up with a novel idea – insurance. Smaller insurance companies, e.g., AMBAC, CIFG, MBIA, had offered insurance on municipal bonds for some two decades. Dubbed monolines because they specialized in this one line of business, these companies had issued over $150 billion worth of insurance on municipal bonds by 2007. The investment banks thought they could pay monolines, insurance companies with multiple types of business or even outside counterparties (see the boxes on the right of the barrel) to insure the investors in case any of the tranches of the CDO went belly-up. So the bank paid small premiums to insure the whole CDO. (AIG took only 12 basis points or one-tenth of 1 percent to insure the entire value of a CDO.) If the bond defaulted, the investors would be paid by the counterparties.

Assured by this insurance arrangement,[8] the credit rating agencies gave CDOs AAA ratings. Since there was virtually no record of default on small CDOs in the early 2000s, counterparties increasingly took the bait. It looked like a great deal with very little risk. These insurance deals were structured as "zero-sum" CDSs. If the CDO did not default, the counterparty received a steady flow of income. On the other hand, if the CDO defaulted, the counterparty assumed the entire cost of paying off investors. However, during the mid-2000s, most counterparties regarded default as remote, particularly since the housing boom continually enhanced the value of the borrowers' homes. Perhaps a tiny percentage might default due to personal circumstances, but virtually everyone else would pay their mortgages, even if they had to sell, because the value of houses continually rose. By 2005, AIG had insured $80 billion worth of CDOs, despite the fact that many CDOs were shot through with subprime mortgages.[9] And it wasn't just insurance companies. State and local governments, corporations, non-profit organizations, even small towns in Australia and Norway, got into what was called the Credit Default Swap game. Frequently fearing the remote possibility of default, cautious counterparties to the original CDSs, in turn, arranged to trade their CDSs on the secondary market or even swap part of their risk with even more counterparties to insure themselves if they could not afford to pay. As trading in the secondary market expanded rapidly, the web of CDSs binding countless institutions to each other spread around the world.

Once the credit ratings agencies rated CDOs AAA, institutional investors were all over them. CDOs paid more than government bonds and sold like hot-cakes. As a matter of fact, investment bankers couldn't produce the CDOs fast enough. They needed more and more mortgages, and they didn't care whether mortgages packaged into the CDOs were subprime or not. The CDOs still sold because they were "insured." So mortgage originators lowered the standards for mortgages. If you didn't qualify for a mortgage based on your documents, you could resubmit your application on a "non-document" basis. Mortgage originators didn't care if you paid back the loan because they sold your mortgage as soon as they issued it;[10] nor did the investment banks that bought your mortgage care because they covered it by selling CDOs to institutional investors. At the height of the boom, the notional value of derivatives totaled a jaw-dropping $636,431 billion (Van Duyn, 2010, p. 5).

The CDO/CDS structure proved to be so successful that investment banks could not keep up with the demand. There were simply not enough mortgages being issued. Some banks addressed the problem by buying separate CDOs, repackaging parts of separate tranches together and reissuing them as yet another CDO in a transaction called the "CDO squared" (Tett, 2009, p. 93). Yet, the CDO money-making machine required even more mortgages. So the "New Breed" came up with a new, brilliant idea. If they couldn't create more "real" CDOs, they decided to create "synthetic" ones. What's a "synthetic" CDO? It's a CDO whose value is based on the debt instruments of "real" CDOs which are used as referents. It's really a form of pari-mutual gambling, like betting on a horse race. A bank puts two parties together in a typical CDS arrangement. One party bets that the referent CDO will remain solvent and, in return, receives a stream of income from the counterparty. The counterparty believes that the CDO will default and will receive the entire notional value of the CDO if the instrument collapses. By 2006, half of all CDOs were synthetic (Lowenstein, 2010, p. 56).

John Paulson, the CEO of Paulson & Company, a multi-billion-dollar New York hedge fund, told Goldman Sachs that he wanted to "short" synthetic CDOs, i.e., bet that the referent CDOs would default. Goldman was more than willing to put together parties, of course, for a fee. Goldman made hard sells to its customers around the world that the synthetic CDO called Abacus would be a great investment, while privately Goldman traders disparaged it. Goldman sales managers looked for European banks, unsophisticated in the world of derivatives (what we might call financial "rubes"), that would be Paulson's counterparties in the Abacus deal. Goldman sales staff would attend banking conferences and trail European bankers like a pack of lions intent on the kill. They talked IKB Bank and Royal Bank of Scotland into the Abacus synthetic CDO deal (which later became the subject of Goldman's $550 million settlement with the SEC).

By the winter of 2005–2006, this structure became what appeared to be the very model of economic justice in a capitalist society. To be sure, there was no leveling here, but everyone seemed to benefit from its operation. With higher returns, pension funds could meet their obligations to pensioners, corporations increased their profits and raised dividends to shareholders, foundations could fund their grantees, and colleges and universities could pursue the expansion of their facilities and hire new faculty. Mortgage originators like Countrywide Financial took a cut off the top of the mortgages that they sold to commercial or investment banks and frequently contracted with the banks to service the mortgages they had sold, e.g., bill and collect the monthly mortgage payment for a fee. Investment bankers profited by taking 20 percent on the performance of a securitized package of mortgages and charging a 2 percent fee (dubbed in the industry the "2 and 20").[11] Credit rating agencies made enormous fees as deal advisers. Counterparties to CDSs received a stream of revenue from insuring the CDOs, and, best of all, Americans from even the poorest backgrounds gained admission to what George W. Bush called the "Ownership Society."[12] The surging American economy had not even reached the threshold of Pareto optimality (the notion that the economy is running at optimal efficiency if and only if no-one's utility can be raised without reducing the utility of someone else). Instead, the rich could get richer and so could the poor.

However, the housing prices in the United States ominously began to fall in the spring of 2006 (Tett, 2009, p. 143). Default rates began to spike, which in turn had an effect upon the value of CDOs, particularly because subprime mortgages were not located only in the lowest tranche but appeared in the higher tranches as well. CDO default rates rocketed to 36 percent by July 2008 (Scheeringa, 2011). The precariousness of CDOs meant that counterparties to CDSs which insured the CDOs became increasingly nervous. They needed to know how secure their investment was; however, counterparties had difficulty assessing the value of the CDOs with any certainty and the risk they carried by insuring them. In the mid-1990s, the SEC had barred the valuation of financial instruments based upon notional value. Instead, the equity and debt instruments were "marked to market," i.e., the price paid by buyers. Since CDOs and CDSs were traded in the private OTC ("over-the counter") market, they were priced by the last private, rather than exchange, sale of the CDO or CDS. Yet, those prices were not public. Without price transparency, the "Street" became rife with rumor. When certain tranches in CDOs became illiquid, i.e., could not be sold because of the rising default rate in the housing market, panic ensued. In June 2007, two Bear Stearns hedge funds that were heavily invested in CDOs collapsed (Tett, 2009, p. 169).

Confounded by the turn of events, the Street gave voice to their innermost fear, including the precipitous fall in their own fortunes. In the fall of 2007 on the brink of the massive implosion, a song made its way through the email boxes of Wall Street's best and brightest. Set to the tune of Don Maclean's "American Pie," the changed lyrics were perhaps better fitted to the title, "A Banker's Lament":

> A short, short time ago
> You can just remember
> How those CDOs used to make you smile
> You knew if you had the chance
> That you could make those returns dance
> And investors would be happy for awhile
> But subprime loans made them shiver
> With every default they would quiver
> Bad news on the home front
> You couldn't make a placement
> I do remember that you cried
> When you heard that AHM[13] had fried
> And something touched you deep inside
> The day the CDO died
> So bye-bye Mister CDO guy
> You piled the paper on when the market was high
> And the 2 and 20 made your living so fine
> Singing CDOs will keep me alive.

By the winter of 2007–2008, no one wanted to buy more CDOs and CDSs. When AIG, which had insured $80 billion of CDOs (Lowenstein, 2000, p. 55), wanted to trade away its CDS counterparty positions, PriceWaterhouseCoopers reported to AIG, "There's no there there" (Kelly, 2010, p. 48). CDO and CDS values plummeted. For institutional investors like corporations, pension funds, non-profit institutions, even banks like Lehman Brothers, that held CDOs and CDSs and borrowed against them, creditors demanded payment for the shortfall in the collateral's value against the amount the institutional investors owed. Moreover, since the values of CDOs and CDSs had dropped, no bank would loan more money to holders of these derivatives. Most corporations used short-term borrowing to cover their monthly expenses to pay for materials, capital goods and salaries/wages. They had to put up collateral. But now their collateral (CDOs and CDSs) was worth 80–90 percent less. So commercial banks (see the box on the left in Figure 1.1) stopped loaning money. Corporations, municipalities, state governments, etc. had to lay people off. Laid-off workers, even those who were holders of prime, rather than subprime, mortgages couldn't pay their mortgages or for that matter their auto loans and credit cards. They were either late or defaulted. In turn, the creditworthiness of more CDOs took a nosedive. The "insurers" of CDOs, the counterparties in CDSs transactions, did not have the money to cover the bondholders' losses because in an unregulated market counterparties had no capital requirements. And so the downward spiral continued. The value of CDOs plummeted in many cases to zero. Commercial banks reacted by shutting down their loan businesses. No more money would go out the door in the form of short- or long-term loans until the crisis passed. The actions of commercial banks produced the liquidity crisis. The circulation of money in the country declined. The US economy began to contract rapidly and threatened to grind to a halt. Unemployment rose and large financial institutions like Lehman Brothers, Wachovia and Washington Mutual, which had invested heavily in CDOs and CDSs, collapsed. Hank Paulson (no relation to John Paulson), the US Treasury secretary and former Goldman CEO, recalled that "banks were going down like flies" (Guha, 2010, p. 3).

Because the derivatives market linked financial institutions internationally, the failure of key financial institutions, most of whom had become players in the Credit Default Swap game, threatened to have a domino effect around the globe. The entire world stood at the brink of a precipice. We faced total international collapse. On September 18, 2008, Ben Bernanke stated, "It is a matter of days before there is a meltdown in the global financial system" (Paulson, 2010, p. 258). Forced by circumstances that promised a worldwide depression worse than 1929, the federal government intervened with the controversial bailout of Wall Street. It is said that Hank Paulson fell on his knees before House Speaker Nancy Pelosi to beg her help in passing the necessary legislation.[14]

The only victors who profited from the collapse of the CDO market were John Paulson and Goldman Sachs, which structured the most significant synthetic CDOs. Like John Paulson, Goldman shorted CDOs starting in February 2007, as indicated by Goldman internal emails published in the *Levin Report*. According to the Congressional investigation, Goldman turned a profit in 2007 of $3.8 billion on CDO "shorts" (Sen. Levin Calls Goldman Sachs Allegations "Deeply Troubling"). Paulson himself made over $1 billion on the Abacus deal in 2007 (Complaint, *SEC* v. *Goldman*, 2010, p. 3). Why did Paulson think that CDOs would implode? It doesn't take a genius to figure that out. CDOs only looked like AAA bonds. Actually the tranches were stuffed with questionable subprimes, credit card and auto loan debt. As soon as the bubble slowed down, it would all implode, especially since the tranches were correlated.

Although Goldman profited, most of us suffered – and many still suffer the consequences of the collapse. Most politicians placed the blame on Wall Street, while a few pundits placed the blame on the borrowers of subprime loans (similar to blaming the consumer for the lemon purchased from a slick used-car salesman). To be sure, the SEC fined Goldman Sachs some $550 million for the Abacus synthetic CDO deal which victimized RBC and IKB, among others (Khuzami & Reisner, 2010), and a recently resigned Goldman executive has claimed in the *New York Times* that Goldman over the years had lost its way, preferring to "screw its clients" for its own profit (Smith, 2012). Likewise, Countrywide Financial Corporation, the largest mortgage broker in the country, settled a class action suit in March 2011 for $624 million for failure to make full disclosure concerning its loan origination and underwriting practices and the creditworthiness of its borrowers and riskiness of its loans to investors in its stock options and corporate bonds (*Order Approving Plan of Allocation of Net Settlement Fund as Modified*, 2011). Countrywide's CEO Angelo Mozilo settled with the SEC for $22.5 million, plus an additional $45 million disgorgement of profits for failure to make full disclosure to investors and insider trading (SEC, 2010). More recently, in December 2011, the Civil Rights Division of the US Department of Justice announced a $335 million settlement approved by a federal district court in *United States* v. *Countrywide Financial Corporation* (C.D. Cal.) in which Countrywide admitted that it had discriminated against 10,000 African-American and Hispanic borrowers by giving them subprime loans while giving similarly situated white borrowers prime loans.

But even if every player in the derivatives market, including Countrywide and Goldman, acted legally, the financial structure still would have imploded. Although advocates for an unfettered free market argue that rational-maximization and self-interest are the engines that drive the economy and ensure the wellbeing of everyone, the economic crisis of 2008 proves them wrong. It is precisely because all the financial players acted in their own self-interest that the near collapse of the world economy happened. Greed is not good, neither for your soul nor the economy. The events in 2008 show that possessive individualism is not only insufficient to guarantee efficiency of capitalism; it actually is capitalism's own undoing.

Dodd–Frank: will it work?

In the wake of the financial meltdown of 2008, the Obama Administration pushed and the Congress passed the Dodd–Frank Wall Street Reform and Consumer Protection Act (Dodd–Frank Act, 2010). Signing the Act into law on July 21, 2010, the president stated that:

> [i]n the end, our financial system only works – our market is only free – when there are clear rules and basic safeguards that prevent abuse, that check excess, that ensure that it is more profitable to play by the rules than to game the system. And that's what these reforms are designed to achieve – no more, no less. Because that's how we will ensure that our economy works for consumers, that it works for investors, that it works for financial institutions – that it works for all of us.
>
> (White House, 2010)

Totaling some 2,200 pages in length, the Dodd–Frank Act was designed to address myriad problems governing the banking and insurance industries, particularly the credit derivative market, which played a central role in the near-collapse of 2008. Perhaps the most important element politically in the Dodd–Frank regime was the end of bailouts of major financial firms (Dodd–Frank Act, §716). Although the government would be permitted to intervene to help an economy when faced with an economic crisis, bailouts of the likes of Citibank and AIG would no longer be on the table. This provision places incredible pressure on the Dodd–Frank regime to ensure that Wall Street and the global economy never gets that close to collapse again.

Accordingly, Dodd–Frank creates an *über*-agency called the Financial Stability Oversight Council (FSOC), composed of representatives of the Federal Reserve, SEC, Commodities Futures Trading Commission (CFTC), Office of the Comptroller of the Currency (OCC), Federal Deposit Insurance Corporation (FDIC), Federal Housing Finance Agency (FHFA), National Credit Union Administration (NCUA), and the newly formed Consumer Financial Protection Bureau (CFPB), as well as state insurance, securities and banking regulators to coordinate the monitoring of the US economy's health (Dodd–Frank Act, §§111–123). The Act also establishes an Office of Financial Research that collects and analyzes economic data and reports on financial risk to the FSOC, the Congress and the public-at-large (Dodd–Frank Act, §§151–156). To eliminate the threat of financial institutions "too big to fail" (which the federal government could no longer bailout), FSOC will make recommendations to the Federal Reserve regarding capital and liquidity requirements, leverage and concentration limits, and "living wills" (plans to unwind) for financial institutions with consolidated assets equal to or greater than $50 billion (bank holding companies and supervised non-banks deemed large enough to require Federal Reserve oversight, e.g., AIG) (Dodd–Frank Act, §§116, 171, 172, 174, 201–217). Furthermore, Dodd–Frank limits these financial institutions to a debt-to-equity ratio of no more than 15 to 1. In addition to sharing information across federal government agencies and the Federal Reserve, the FSOC has the power to approve a recommendation by the Federal Reserve to order the divestment of holdings by these institutions if they pose a grave threat to the financial stability of the United States. In case of a financial institution's liquidation, costs will be borne by shareholders and creditors, rather than American taxpayers (Dodd–Frank Act, §214).

These FSOC provisions provide an "early warning system" for the US economy; however, they do not address the causes of the 2008 meltdown. Here the Dodd–Frank regime attempts to identify gaps in regulation (particularly in the credit derivatives market), modifies or prohibits certain activities that accelerated the rapid deterioration of that market and authorizes agencies like the SEC and CFTC to develop rules to enforce those modifications and prohibitions. However, will this new regulatory regime actually work as anticipated by President Obama? Or will both the self-interest of players in the credit derivatives market and their deep-seated resentment toward not only federal and state regulators, but even their own compliance personnel, subvert the hopes of Dodd–Frank? To establish a prognosis for the viability of the new regulatory regime, an analysis should begin with an assessment of the flaws in the CDO–CDS structures that led to the 2008 global economic retraction.

If you examine the CDO deal structures chart (Figure 1.1), you will recall that the implosion of CDOs were related to the existence of subprime mortgages that appeared in the tranches of CDOs sold to investors or served as referents for synthetic CDO/CDSs. Because of the enormous and incessant demand for home loans during the past decade to create RMBSs, mortgage originators engaged in mass mailings and cold-calls to interest potential borrowers. If these consumers did not meet the criteria to qualify for prime 30-year fixed mortgages, mortgage originators offered and frequently persuaded consumers to apply for ARMs, even though they might face balloon payments somewhere down the road. Moreover, mortgage originators frequently steered consumers into less desirable, more expensive mortgages that would generate higher fees. Dodd–Frank imposes a fiduciary duty of care upon mortgage originators to ensure that they do not engage in this sort of predatory lending (Dodd–Frank Act, §1402). To prevent such abuse, Dodd–Frank created the Consumer Financial Protection Bureau (CFPB), which was given broad discretionary authority to proscribe practices that are unfair or deceptive. Mortgage originators who fail to undertake their duty of care are subject to civil liability (Dodd–Frank Act, §1404). When a consumer did not qualify for the mortgage based on the documentation of their assets and income, mortgage originators commonly offered mortgages on a "no doc" basis, called NINJA loans (No Income No Job Assets). Mortgage originators did not really care whether the mortgagor could pay back the loan since they sold the mortgage as soon as it was issued. To address these problems, Dodd–Frank prohibits originators from offering residential mortgages without a good faith determination, based on the review of verified and documented information, that the mortgagor has the financial capacity to repay that loan (Dodd–Frank Act, §1411). Finally, to guarantee that mortgage originators comply with the good faith assessment of the borrower's capacity to repay, the Act requires them to hold 5 percent equity in the executed mortgages (Dodd–Frank Act, §15G).

Another key component in the CDO/CDS deal structure was the role of credit ratings agencies. These NSNROs used an "issuer-pays" business model during the housing boom (White, 2010). Why would Standard & Poor's, Fitch or Moody's give a triple AAA rating to a CDO when the CDS insurers of the bonds did not have any capital requirements and likely could not possibly cover the losses if the CDO defaulted? At the outset of the housing boom, small CDOs had good track records. The likelihood of default was miniscule; however, some critics suspected a darker reason. When investment banks structured CDO deals, NRSROs participated as a key party in the negotiations. Without their approval of the CDO as an AAA investment, the deal was a bust. Consequently, credit ratings agencies actually were paid on average $100,000 to help structure these deals. Accordingly, it was in their vested interest to approve them.[15] Moreover, the investment bank contracted with the ratings agency to provide ongoing rating evaluations of the CDO for which the NRSRO received a fee. Hence, the more deals, the more money made by the NRSROs. Investment banks soon learned that they possessed the leverage necessary to make credit ratings agencies compliant. NRSROs handed out AAA ratings for higher tranches of CDOs allegedly because it was in their financial interest to do so (Ford & Jones, 2010, p. 9). As Erik Sirri (2008), the director of the SEC's Division of Trading and Markets, later noted:

> In the case of structured finance products, we believe that the "issuer/underwriter pay" model creates a specific conflict because certain arrangers of structured finance products repeatedly bring ratings business to the NRSROs. As sources of constant revenue, active arrangers have the potential to exert great influence over an NRSRO relative to a corporate issuer that brings fewer ratings business to the NRSRO.

The government tried to correct this abuse through the Credit Rating Agency Reform Act of 2006 that allowed small credit ratings agencies to enter the market as "statistical ratings organizations." However, increasing the competition had the unintended effect of making credit ratings agencies more compliant with the wishes of investment banks. Indeed, investment banks could now effectively "shop" for the best rating.

The Dodd–Frank Act sought to address what, at the very least, had the appearance of impropriety. Henceforth NSNROs are required to erect a firewall between ratings and marketing/sales activities. Analysts will not be subject to coercive pressure to render a favorable crediting rating for a client in return for continued or further business. The Act requires NSNROs to submit information on analysts who receive employment by former clients. Ratings reports must include information on historical rating performance data and ratings methodologies, as well as the use of third-party due diligence efforts. By eliminating the exemption of NSNROs as a part of registration statements, the Act subjects credit rating agencies to civil liability under the 1933 Securities Act and the 1934 Securities Exchange Act. The Act places additional responsibility on the SEC to regulate NSNROs by authorizing the establishment of an Office of Credit Ratings (OCR) within the agency. Through the OCR, the SEC will create rules to separate ratings from marketing/sales activities, govern the training of ratings analysts, license the ratings analysts by examination and ensure that NSNROs establish an internal control system (Dodd–Frank Act, §939).

Although the activities of mortgage originators and NSNROs made the existence of CDOs possible, the panic on the derivatives market which followed the slowdown of the housing boom was caused to a large part by the lack of transparency in the CDO/CDS secondary market. CDO/CDS deals occurred largely as OTC transactions, leaving many other players in the credit derivatives market in the dark. Dodd–Frank seeks to cast sunshine on CDO/CDS deals by requiring that such transactions take place through clearinghouses which make information available to all players. (Notably, nonfinancial entities, dubbed "End-Users" by the Act, e.g., large corporations which use derivatives for hedging purposes, are not subject to the clearinghouse requirement.) Moreover, CDS dealers and market-makers will be subject to federal regulation. "Swap Dealers" will be regulated by the CFTC and "securities-related Swap Dealers" by the SEC, subject to their respective registration requirements and rules. In addition to dealers and market-makers, "Major Participants," i.e., those who maintain substantial positions in either securities- or non-securities based swaps or are highly leveraged financial entities or create substantial counterparty exposure, are also subject to regulation by the SEC or CFTC. Although it is assumed that clearinghouses will impose their own margin and capital requirements on CDS players, the SEC and CFTC are expected to generate minimum capital requirements and initial and variable margin requirements. The so-called "Lincoln Provision" of Dodd–Frank prohibits any Swaps Dealer, securities-related Swaps Dealer or Major Participant from leveraging federal monies borrowed from a Federal Reserve credit facility or the Fed's discount window for engaging in swaps transactions (Dodd–Frank Act, §§711–774).

The implosion of the CDO/CDS derivatives market in 2008 produced a financial crisis for individual investment banks and therefore the banking system as a whole. Many investment banks, large and small, borrowed money from the repo market at low interest rates to invest in higher return CDOs and CDSs. Because the returns were so thin, these banks had to borrow massive amounts of money to make these transactions worthwhile. Accordingly, banks hazarded tremendous risk exposure which compromised their viability with the implosion of the credit derivatives market. The consequences seriously threatened the world financial system. Named after the former chairman of the Federal Reserve, Paul Volcker, the so-called "Volcker Rule," which took effect on July 21, 2012, is designed to prevent any repetition of 2008 by barring banks from engaging in proprietary trading (Dodd–Frank Act, §619). Certain exemptions to the Volcker Rule exist. A banking entity may retain a 3 percent interest in a fund offered by the bank to unaffiliated investors and may invest in US Treasuries and Agencies (GSE bonds). Moreover, a banking entity may still function as an underwriter of CDOs or other market-making activities. Finally, under the "Merkley Provisions" designed to curb any transactions akin to the Abacus synthetic CDO deal, a bank may not engage in any transaction that would cause a material conflict of interest with investors.

These elements of the Dodd–Frank Act suggest that government intervention may well eliminate the abuses that led to the events of 2008; however, it appears that the American psychic economy may play a significant role in preventing the cure of what ails Wall Street. The effectiveness of Dodd–Frank is contingent upon the development and implementation of rules by federal regulators, such as the SEC, CFTC and the quasi-independent Federal Reserve. In May 2012, the chairman of the CFTC, Gary Gensler, and the chairwoman of the SEC, Mary Shapiro, testified before Congress that their agencies are grossly underfunded (*Derivatives Market Regulation and Oversight*, 2012). They simply do not have the monies available to hire the staff to do all that they are required by the Dodd–Frank Act. Gensler (2012) noted that the CFTC Enforcement Division is understaffed by 70 attorneys. He explained to the Senate Banking Committee:

> Confidence in the futures and swaps markets is dependent upon a well-funded regulator. The CFTC is a good investment of taxpayer dollars. This hardworking staff of 710 is just 10 percent more than what we had in the 1990s though the futures market has grown fivefold. The CFTC also will soon be responsible for the swaps market – eight times bigger than the

> futures market. Picture the NFL expanding eightfold to play more than 100 football games in a weekend, leaving just one referee per game, and, in some cases, no referee. Imagine the mayhem on the field, the resulting injuries to players, and the loss of confidence fans would have in the integrity of the game.

The annual budget of the CFTC is a mere $202 million, less than one half of the fine paid by Goldman for the Abacus deal. Although funding for the SEC has marginally increased by under 7 percent to $1.18 billion, Shapiro testified that "[w]e're still way outgunned by the firms we regulate in terms of technology" (Levine, 2012). The SEC had no money to even fund the creation of the OCR, mandated by Dodd–Frank. Federal regulators have been put in the position of riding buses to New York City from Washington, covering depositions with one attorney, and even paying for their own rooms on agency business (Protess, 2011). The underfunding of federal regulators is no accident. As Senator Dick Durbin (D-IL) stated in 2011, "There are many Republicans who did not support Wall Street reform who believe that they can starve the SEC into submission by refusing to put enough people, personnel – lawyers and accountants and others – monitoring the activities of the exchanges" (Mattingly, 2011).

Under the Administrative Procedures Act of 1946, federal agencies are required to publish proposed rules that they have created to give the public an opportunity for comment and to conduct cost–benefit analyses. According to the *Davis Polk Dodd–Frank Progress Report*, as of January 2, 2013, rule-making requirement deadlines have been missed in 237 cases, although of these, 95 rules (40.1 percent) have now been finalized. Of the total 398 required rule-makings, regardless of whether the deadline has been passed, only 136 (34.2 percent) are finalized. The remainder have yet to be approved, and 129 (32.4 percent) have not even been proposed (Harvard Law School Forum on Corporate Governance and Financial Responsibility, 2013). The reasons for the delay are two-fold. As Jacqueline McCabe, executive director for research at the Committee on Capital Markets Regulation, has stated, "We are deeply concerned that the inadequate cost–benefit analysis in the vast majority of rulemakings under Dodd–Frank could expose these rules to judicial challenge, prevent important rules from taking effect, and contribute to uncertainty in our markets over their fate" (*Written Testimony of Jacqueline C. McCabe*, 2012). Although McCabe praised the SEC for recent changes to its cost–benefit analysis procedure, she was highly critical of the CFTC's lack of in-depth treatment of proposed rules. While the CFTC could improve its procedures as well, clearly the agency's limited staff is completely overwhelmed in light of underfunding. Opponents of Dodd–Frank have already successfully challenged a proposed Dodd–Frank rule on the basis of inadequate agency cost–benefit analysis.[16] In addition, the players in the derivatives market have hired the best law firms on Wall Street to submit extensive documents analyzing the effect of the proposed rules. Because the SEC and CFTC are obligated to respond to these public comments, the process for the approval of final rules has been slowed to a crawl.

Ironically, the investment banking community has been helped by what some might consider an "unholy alliance" with the radical right. Viewing government itself as their enemy, "Tea Party" advocates, who vociferously condemned the federal bailout of financial firms and automakers, are actively working to dismantle the Dodd–Frank regulatory regime. Two years ago, Michelle Bachmann, former Republican presidential candidate and founder of the Tea Party caucus in the US House, introduced H.R. 87, which would repeal the Dodd–Frank Act. As one Tea Party pundit, Walter Coffey (2011) argued:

> The ultimate losers under this new legislation are (once again) the taxpayers and small business owners. Taxpayers will continue to be responsible for funding bailouts of privileged institutions. This hurts small business, which cannot compete with the big firms when the big firms have the luxury of getting bailouts. Those bailouts can be used by big firms as leverage to drive smaller competitors out of the market. Less competition means less choice; less choice means less consumer spending; less spending means less production; and less production means less jobs. So the law not only hurts taxpayers and small businesses, but it is a potential job killer as well. *This is nothing more than government siding with business against the people*, which is what got us into this mess in the first place. We can only hope that the new Congress will push to repeal this potentially destructive legislation. (Emphasis added).

The Tea Party therefore opposes Dodd–Frank because it allegedly continues bailouts, an action specifically forbidden by the text of the Act. However, hedge funds and investment banks will take support anywhere they can get it, and, as a consequence, Wall Street has been involved in financially supporting the reelection of Republican Tea Party candidates with substantial campaign donations (Przybyla & Mattingly, 2012).[17]

The Mitt Romney campaign, which blamed the Obama Administration for the continuing effects of the 2008 meltdown, likewise wanted to gut Dodd–Frank. As Romney's campaign position paper stated, the Act "delegated an extraordinarily wide scope of rulemaking to the same agencies that had failed to prevent the financial crisis" (*Believe in America: Mitt Romney's Plan for Jobs and Economic Growth* [Believe], 2011, p. 2). Defying logic, Romney argued that the SEC and CFTC, which were barred by law from regulating derivatives, ought to be blamed for their collapse. Although Romney admitted that "some of the concepts in Dodd–Frank [like "greater transparency" and "enhanced capital requirements"] have a place … [t]he government's response was to layer on new regulations and invent new bureaucracies that do not address the underlying causes of a crisis driven by the over-leveraging of our financial institutions and our homeowners" (Believe, 2011, p. 4). Although Romney failed to win the 2012 presidential election, the mix of political conservatives, Tea Party activists, and Wall Street lobbies will carry on the campaign to undo the regulation of the derivatives market.

Conclusion

The confluence of lawlessness in the American psychic economy and the contemporary crisis in American finance capital comes at a very dangerous juncture. The proposed repeal of the Dodd–Frank Act threatens to unleash not the power of capital, but the free-for-all that so characterized Wall Street during the first decade of the twenty-first century. By appealing to a deep-seated attribute of possessive individualism, those on the Street and in the halls of Congress, who wish to restore this legal lacuna, thereby threaten to destabilize the world economy again in the next decade.

Notes

1 Resulting from the individual's assimilation of the values of the free market, possessive individualism is marked by an overriding self-interest. Wright's analysis draws upon the work of MacPherson (1962) (Wright, 1985, p. 136).
2 Wright appropriates the term "institutional framework" from the work of Jürgen Habermas (1970). Habermas contrasted the values and norms of social communication and interaction with a society's "underlying purposive-rational subsystems," e.g., the capitalist mode of production. Whereas in traditional societies the institutional framework limited the underlying purposive-rational subsystem, entrepreneurial capitalism in modern societies contrasted sharply with traditional norms and values. As the manifestation of free market consciousness in interpersonal relations, possessive individualism represents the challenge of the "underlying purposive-rational subsystem" to the dominance of traditional norms and values (Wright, 1985, pp. 130–138).
3 Wright's analysis responds to Dave Grossman's unanswered query in *On Killing: The Psychological Cost of Learning to Kill in War and Society*: "Somewhere along the line we began to accept role models who 'had' to go outside the law to kill criminals who we know 'deserved to die.'" (Grossman, 1996, p. 321).
4 At the height of the CDO boom, 96 percent of derivatives traded "over-the-counter" through interdealers like ICAP and Tullet Prebon (van Duyn, 2010, p. 5).
5 Alan Greenspan, chairman of the powerful Federal Reserve Board, backed the position of the Republican Party and the Clinton advisers. "The Board continues to believe," concluded Greenspan in his testimony to the House Committee on Banking and Financial Services, "that, aside from safety and soundness regulation of derivatives dealers under the banking or securities laws, regulation of derivatives transactions that are privately negotiated by professionals is unnecessary" (Greenspan, 1998) (*Commodity Futures Modernization Act*, 2000, Title 1). As Senator Phil Gramm (R-TX) stated to the chairman of the SEC, Arthur Levitt, "Unless the waters are crimson with the blood of investors, I don't want you embarking on any regulatory flights of fancy" (Seligman, 2003, p. 744). President Clinton regrets not regulating derivatives. "Now I think if I had tried to regulate them – because the Republicans were in a majority in the Congress – they would have stopped it. But I wish – I should have been caught trying" (Braithwaite, 2010, p. 3).
6 Of the three major credit ratings agencies (Standard and Poor's, or S&P, Moody's and Fitch), S&P and Fitch use the same scale (AAA, AA, A, BBB) to designate the levels of risk in investment grade bonds. Moody's uses a scale of Aaa, Aa, A, and Baa. In the financial industry, AAA or Aaa represents a 1 in 10,000 chance of default; AA or Aa represents a 1 in 1,000 chance of default; A represents a 1 in 750 chance of default; and BBB or Baa represents a 1 in 500 chance of default (Lewis, 2010, pp. 50–51).

7 Although many homeowners had excellent credit, a significant proportion had poor credit ratings. Bankers called these mortgages subprime. Other mortgagors had marginal credit, and their mortgages were dubbed Alt-A.

8 Although CDSs act very much like insurance policies, there is some question about whether these arrangements can be legitimately called insurance. In the insurance industry, a defining characteristic of insurance is an "insurable interest." In other words, the insurer must have a cognizable claim on whatever is insured in case of default. *See* "Insurable Interest" (Rubin, 2000, p. 243). While counterparties in CDS arrangement on CDOs do have such a claim on the underlying bond if the insured defaults, CDS counterparties offering protection for "synthetic CDOs," *infra*, have no such claim. Hence, CDS arrangements for synthetic CDOs, which dominated the derivative market by 2006, arguably should not be considered insurance.

9 By 2004 $2 trillion subprime and Alt-A loans were outstanding (Lowenstein, 2010, p. 37).

10 Along with the Federal Reserve, eight institutional investors later sued Countrywide, the largest mortgage originator, which was bought by Bank of America, for $47 billion in losses related to mortgage-backed CDOs (Baer & Guerrera, 2010, p. 17).

11 By 2006, the banking fees for CDO deals totaled some $2.3 billion. The average transaction in 2006 returned $1.8 million in fees. The average bonus in the investment banking industry totaled $190,000 and grew at the rate of 11 percent per year (McGee, 2010, pp. 159, 191).

12 *See* Bush (2005) ("To give every American a stake in the promise and future of our country, we will bring the highest standards to our schools, and build an ownership society. We will widen the ownership of homes and businesses, retirement savings and health insurance preparing our people for the challenges of life in a free society").

13 American Home Mortgage.

14 Taken aback, Pelosi reportedly replied, "I didn't know you were Catholic" (McGee, 2010, p. 21).

15 For example, by 2005 Moody's received half of its revenue from structured finance (Tett, 2009, p. 101).

16 *See*, e.g., the successful challenge by the US Chamber of Commerce and Business Roundtable regarding the shareholder proxy access rule established by the SEC in 2011 (Madigan, 2011).

17 Tea Party Republicans on the House Financial Services Committee have set up a Dodd–Frank "Burden" Tracker to illustrate the slow pace of rule adoption, which they and their Wall Street allies have intentionally caused (Dodd–Frank Tracker, 2012).

References

ABC News. (2010, April 27). Sen. Levin calls Goldman Sachs allegations "deeply troubling." Retrieved from http://abcnews.go.com/GMA/Business/goldmans-blankfein-fabulous-fab-testify-today/story?id=10479173&page=4.

Baer, J. & Guerrera, F. (2010, October 20). Institutional investors join forces in bond losses fight. *Financial Times*. p. 17.

Baudrillard, J. (1989). *America*. (Trans. Chris Turner). New York: Verso.

Believe in America: Mitt Romney's plan for jobs and economic growth. Retrieved from www.mittromney.com/sites/default/files/shared/Regulatory.pdf.

Braithwaite, T. (2010, April 19). Treasury chief hardens stance on derivatives. *Financial Times*, p. 3.

Bush, G.W. (2005, January 20). Second inaugural address. Retrieved from www.gutenberg.org/files/925/925-h/925-h.htm#link2H_4_0056.

Coffey W. (2011, January 11). Why financial reform must be repealed. *Tea Party Tribune*. Retrieved from www.teapartytribune.com/2011/01/30/why-financial-reform-must-be-repealed/.

The Commodity Futures Modernization Act. (2000, December 21). Public Law 106-554. Retrieved from www.gpo.gov/fdsys/pkg/PLAW-106publ554/html/PLAW-106publ554.htm.

Complaint, *SEC* v. *Goldman* (S.D.N.Y.). (2010, April 16). Retrieved from www.sec.gov/litigation/complaints/2010/comp-pr2010-59.pdf.

Derivatives Market Regulation and Oversight. Testimony of Gary Gensler (CFTC Chairman) and Mary Shapiro (SEC Chairwoman) before the Senate Banking, Housing and Urban Affairs Committee. (2012, May 22). Retrieved from www.c-spanvideo.org/program/306162-1.

Dodd–Frank "Burden" Tracker. (2012) Retrieved from http://financialservices.house.gov/uploadedfiles/dodd-frank_pra_spreadsheet_7-9-2012.pdf

Dodd–Frank Wall Street Reform and Consumer Protection Act. An act to promote the financial stability of the United States by improving accountability and transparency in the financial system, to end "too big to fail," to protect the American taxpayer by ending bailouts, to protect consumers from abusive financial services practices, and for other purposes. (2010, July 21). Public Law 111-203. Retrieved from www.gpo.gov/fdsys/pkg/PLAW-111publ203/content-detail.html.

Ford, J. & Jones, S. (2010, June 10). A tricky pick. *Financial Times*, p. 9.

Gapper, J. (2010, April 19). SEC has its work cut out in Goldman case. *Financial Times*. Retrieved from www.ft.com/cms/s/0/e3ad8ab4-4b49-11df-a7ff-00144feab49a. html#axzz1PSFOeUMY.

Gensler, G. (2012, May 22). *Testimony Before the US Senate Committee on Banking, Housing and Urban Affairs*. Retrieved from www.cftc.gov/PressRoom/SpeechesTestimony/opagensler-114.

Greenspan, A. (1998, July 24). *Testimony on the Regulation of OTC Derivatives, Before the Committee on Banking and Financial Services, U.S. House of Representatives*. Retrieved from www.federalreserve.gov/boarddocs/testimony/1998/19980724.htm.

Grossman, D. (1996). *On killing: The psychological cost of learning to kill in war and society*. Boston, MA: Little, Brown & Co.

Guha, K. (2010, February 1). When the markets froze there was going to be a painful impact. [Interview with Hank Paulson]. *Financial Times*. p. 3.

Habermas, J. (1970). *Toward a rational society*. Boston, MA: Beacon Press.

Harvard Law School Forum on Corporate Governance and Financial Responsibility. (2012, May 16). *January 2013 Davis Polk Dodd–Frank Progress Report*. Retrieved from http://blogs.law.harvard.edu/corpgov/?s=tracker&submit=Go.

Kelly, A. (2010, March 1). Inside the Crisis at AIG. *Fortune*. p. 48.

Khuzami, R. & Reisner, L. (2010, July 15). Speech by SEC staff: remarks at news conference announcing landmark $550 million Goldman Sachs settlement. Retrieved from www.sec.gov/news/speech/2010/spch071510rsk.htm.

Lepore, J. (2012, April 23). Battleground America: one nation, under the gun. *The New Yorker*. Retrieved from www.newyorker.com/magazine/2012/04/23/battleground-america.

Levine, D. (2012, May 22). JPMorgan Hearing: Market Regulators Warn They're Broke, Outgunned by Wall Street. *Huffington Post*, Retrieved from www.huffingtonpost.com/2012/05/22/jpmorgan-hearing_n_1536596.html.

Lewis, M. (2010). *The big short: Inside the doomsday machine*. New York: W.W. Norton.

Lowenstein, R. (2000). *When genius failed: The rise and fall of long term capital management.* New York: Random House.

Lowenstein, R. (2010). *The end of Wall Street.* New York: Penguin.

McGee, S. (2010). *Chasing Goldman Sachs.* New York: Crown Business.

MacPherson, C.B. (1962). *The political theory of possessive individualism.* Oxford: Oxford University Press.

Madigan, P. (2011, October 3). CFTC and SEC facing legal anxiety over cost–benefit analyses. Retrieved from www.risk.net/risk-magazine/feature/2111501/cftc-sec-facing-legal-anxiety-cost-benefit-analyses.

Mattingly, P. (2011, January 6). Tea Party caucus founder pushes to repeal Dodd–Frank. Retrieved from www.bloomberg.com/news/2011-01-06/tea-party-caucus-founder-bachmann-pushes-measure-to-repeal-dodd-frank-law.html.

Order Approving Plan of Allocation of Net Settlement Fund as Modified (C.D. Ca., Western Division). (2011, March 4). Retrieved from www.countrywidesecuritiesclassaction.com/CourtDocuments.htm.

Patterson, S. (2010). *The quants.* New York: Crown Business.

Paulson, Jr., H.M. (2010). *On the brink.* New York: Business Plus.

Protess, B. (2011, May 3). U.S. regulators face budget pinch as mandates widen. *New York Times.* Retrieved from http://dealbook.nytimes.com/2011/05/03/u-s-regulators-face-budget-pinch-as-mandates-widen.

Przybyla, H. & Mattingly, P. (2012, April 30). Tea Party congressmen accept cash from bailed-out bankers. Retrieved from www.bloomberg.com/news/2012-04-30/tea-party-congressmen-accept-cash-from-bailed-out-bankers.html.

Rubin, H.W. (2000). Insurable interest. In *Dictionary of insurance terms*, 4th ed. (p. 243). Hauppauge, NY: Barron's.

Scheeringa, D. (2011). Dodd–Frank credit rating agency reform in the crosshairs. *Illinois Business Law Journal.* Retrieved from www.law.illinois.edu/bljournal/post/2011/03/29/Dodd-Frank-Credit-Rating-Agency-Reform-in-the-Crosshairs.aspx.

SEC (2010, October 15). *Former Countrywide CEO Angelo Mozilo to pay SEC's largest-ever financial penalty against a public company's senior executive.* Securities and Exchange Commission. Retrieved from www.sec.gov/news/press/2010/2010-197.htm.

Seligman, J. (2003). *The transformation of Wall Street: A history of the securities and exchange commission and modern corporate finance.* New York: Aspen.

Sirri, E. (2008, June 11). Opening remarks before the Commission open meeting. Retrieved from www.sec.gov/news/speech/2008/spch061108ers.htm.

Smith, A. (1776). *An Inquiry into the Nature and Causes of the Wealth of Nations.* Retrieved from http://geolib.com/smith.adam/won1-02.html.

Smith, G. (2012, March 14). Why I am leaving Goldman Sachs. *New York Times.* Retrieved from www.nytimes.com/2012/03/14/opinion/why-i-am-leaving-goldman-sachs.html?pagewanted=all.

Tett, G. (2009). *Fool's gold.* New York: Free Press.

Turner, F.J. (1894). The significance of the frontier in American history. *Annual Report for 1893.* Washington, DC: American Historical Association. Retrieved from www.learner.org/workshops/primarysources/corporations/docs/turner.html.

Van Duyn, A. (2010, August 12). Derivative dilemmas. *Financial Times*, p. 5.

White, L.J. (2010) Markets: the credit rating agencies. *Journal of Economic Perspectives*, 24, 211–226.

White House (2010, July 21). *Remarks by the President at Signing of Dodd–Frank Wall Street Reform and Consumer Protection Act.* Office of the Press Secretary, the White

House. Retrieved from www.whitehouse.gov/the-press-office/remarks-president-signing-dodd-frank-wall-street-reform-and-consumer-protection-act.

Wood, D.B. (2012, January 9). US crime rate at lowest point in decades: why America is safer now. *Christian Science Monitor.* Retrieved from www.csmonitor.com/USA/Justice/2012/0109/US-crime-rate-at-lowest-point-in-decades.-Why-America-is-safer-now.

Wright, W. (1985). *Sixguns and society: A structural study of the western.* Berkeley, CA: University of California Press.

Written Testimony of Jacqueline C. McCabe, Executive Director for Research at the Committee on Capital Markets Regulation. (2012, April 17). Retrieved from http://oversight.house.gov/wp-content/uploads/2012/04/4-17-12-McCabe-Testimony.pdf.

2 Why and how the Fed contributed to massive failure in asset markets

Nicholas Sowels

This contribution argues that the "Great Recession" was no accident. The precise collapse of the housing bubble via the subprime crisis let alone the way it spread internationally may not have been forecast by many, yet there were clear straws in the wind as of the early 2000s that the US economy was suffering from financial imbalances, manifest in its huge and expanding current account deficit and a housing market that was overheating. These were not accidental phenomena. Instead they were almost an inevitable result of the neoliberal paradigm and economic structure which had been created progressively since the 1970s, and which had already led to several financial crises and severe stock market collapses in 2000–2001.

In the introduction of this book, it is argued that the US economy experienced a turning-point at the end of the 1990s and early 2000s. The evolution of monetary policy, finance and household debt supports this view, as the stock market crashes at that time and the subsequent mild recession (in 2001) were dealt with by substantial monetary easing. The pick-up of growth in 2003 then did restore the illusion of economic success. But it was much financed by cheap, borrowed money: as Kenneth Rogoff (2003) noted at the time, the US upturn was "the best economic recovery money can buy."[1] But such growth based on borrowing paved the way for a new, far more dangerous cycle in asset-price speculation in the housing market.

I argue here that these developments in the real economy – and in particular the growth of the house-price bubble – were almost inevitable and fairly clear outcomes of monetary policy and events in the financial sphere. In the final analysis, these can be traced right back to the collapse of the Bretton Woods system in 1971 and its fixed exchange rate system between countries. When this broke down, it inaugurated an era of (global) financial liberalization, innovation and market interconnection, helped by information and communication technology (ICT). These factors taken together amounted to – and still constitute – a reflection of the paradigm shift to neoliberalism both in the United States and internationally. Neoliberalism replaced the more "mixed-economy," New Deal paradigm that was created during the 1930s. This was then massively consolidated during World War II, and functioned so successfully as a macroeconomic and macro-social manifestation of "Fordism."[2]

In response to the crisis of the New Deal Fordist economy in the late 1960s and 1970s, neoliberal policies were implemented in the United States and internationally. These included, significantly, financial liberalization. Retrospectively, it can be seen that these policies helped pave the way for bouts of financial instability reminiscent of the nineteenth and early twentieth centuries when free finance in the United States led to repeated "panics," culminating in the Great Crash of 1929 (Burgin, 2012). Thus, as the globalization of financial markets expanded rapidly from the 1970s onwards, the US and world economies began experiencing repeated financial crises, including notably: the Third World Debt Crisis of the 1980s; a major stock market collapse in October 1987; the US savings and loans crisis in the late 1980s; the Mexican peso crisis in 1994; the Asian crisis in 1997; the LTCM crisis on the New York market in 1998; and the collapse of the Internet/TMT (technology, media and telecommunications) bubble in 2000, followed by the strong fall of traditional stocks thereafter, which was aggravated by the 9/11 terrorist attacks.

Despite these repeated financial crises, the US authorities – the government and the Federal Reserve – did not change their policy orientations in the years preceding the Great Recession (Greenspan, 2007). On the contrary, broad policies of non-intervention and market deregulation, as well as providing cheap capital when necessary to compensate financial instability, were pursued throughout. And, in some ways they were effective, as the period from the mid-1980s to the eve of the financial crisis in 2007/2008 is frequently referred to as the "Great Moderation" (Bernanke, 2004), when inflation was low and growth on the whole steady.

Indeed, the mid-2000s were often presented as the heyday of "Anglo-Saxon" capitalism, typically defined as the transactions-based capitalism of the "liberal market economies" (as identified, for example, in the *Varieties of Capitalism* approach by Hall and Soskice). But, actually, as we can see now, the stock market collapses in 2000–2001 were tackled using cheap money, while the underlying performance of the US economy deteriorated.

The first section of this chapter outlines key aspects of the progressive development of open, unregulated, international financial markets, within the context of the spread of neoliberalism. The next section examines how neoliberal ideology came to dominate the policy of the Federal Reserve, in particular through the influence of Alan Greenspan. The third section reviews the pursuit of monetary policy and the Fed's doctrine of not intervening in asset markets. The fourth section analyzes how fears of deflation led the Fed to implement very low interest rates in the early 2000s, leading to massive moral hazard in mortgage finance and the US housing boom. The last section concludes and seeks to place Fed policy in a broader historical context.

The rise of neoliberalism and the emergence of international capital markets

To a large extent, neoliberalism emerged as a reaction to the economic crisis of the 1970s. To be sure, neoclassical economics as a means for promoting economic liberalism had existed as a current in economic thought, going back until the end of World War II (Jones, 2012; Mirowski & Plehwe, 2009). Early, founding moments of what critics today call "neoliberalism" include the publication of Hayek's *The Road to Serfdom* in 1944 and the creation of the Mount Pelerin Society in 1947 "to discuss the state and the possible fate of liberalism (in its classical sense) in thinking and practice."[3]

In the subsequent decades, prominent neoliberal thinkers, Hayek and, of course, Milton Friedman (1962) in particular, developed economic theory critical of the broadly Keynesian/New Deal consensus of the post-war world, accompanied by the belief that government was an ineffective actor in managing the economy and society. While actual state ownership in the United States was always very limited, what was later derided as "Big government" did appear to be successful in leading major public policies, until the late 1960s.

Apart from conducting wars (relatively successfully in Korea and disastrously in Vietnam), the US government played a pro-active role during the long, post-war boom: expanding education, for example, with the GI Bill at the end of the war; building the interstate highway system from the 1950s onwards; supporting the military–industrial complex; and leading the "war against poverty" in the 1960s. Such policies are generally viewed as extensions of the New Deal paradigm on the one hand. They can also be viewed as macroeconomic components of the Fordist economy. Equally spectacular, if arguably less useful, government action did succeed in fulfilling Kennedy's space-race pledge of "landing a man on the moon and returning him safely to Earth" by the end of the 1960s.

As so often in history, however, this symbolic, crowning moment of what government was capable of doing occurred when the very economic foundations of the post-war boom were manifesting serious weaknesses: the international monetary system – built around the dollar and its link to gold at $35 an ounce – was crumbling under inflationary pressures and the emergence of international capital markets. The Bretton Woods system then finally collapsed when the Nixon Administration took the dollar off the gold standard officially, in August 1971. This sent massive shock waves through the world economy, and was a key factor in stoking the surge in inflation that gripped the industrialized countries at the time. The hike in inflation was, of course, compounded by the first oil-shock in 1973/1974, although it was also partly a consequence of the devaluing dollar.

Significantly, as the dollar and other currencies started floating, financial markets quickly developed to deal and hedge in currencies, as they were already doing in commodities. Not surprisingly, this occurred first in Chicago. The Windy City was and is home to some of the world's largest commodity markets. It is also the home of the "Chicago School of Economics," based on neoclassical economics, and where Milton Friedman was a leading figure in the 1970s along with George Stigler, Robert E. Lucas and Eugene Fama. Specifically in late 1971, Leo Melamed, as chairman of the Chicago Mercantile Exchange (CME), commissioned a report from Friedman on the possibility of creating financial futures to hedge and speculate on exchange rate movements. Friedman endorsed the creation of such markets – in the United States – wholeheartedly (Friedman, 2011). And on May 16, 1972, the international monetary market was created at the CME (Melamed, 1972). Derivative trading in money had started.

From a macroeconomic perspective, the rise in inflation and the slowdown in growth of the 1970s – stagflation as *The Economist* magazine had termed it – led to a profound reappraisal of economic policy. This favored a clear shift toward controlling inflation by the end of the decade: in 1979, Paul Volcker was appointed as chairman of the Federal Reserve by President Jimmy Carter (a Democrat and president from January 1977 to January 1981). P. Volcker was given the explicit task of bringing down inflation using monetary policy, as suggested by monetarist economists, again led by Milton Friedman and the Chicago School. The hiking of the short-term interest rate by the Fed – peaking at 20 percent in June 1981 – did the job. The economy entered a double-dip recession (contracting in 1980 and 1982), unemployment at one point topped 10 percent, and the Third World – having massively borrowed in dollars at floating interest rates and exchange rates in the 1970s, and encouraged to do so by US banks – suddenly found itself unable to honor its debts. This led to a decade-long crisis for Latin America and much of the developing world. But US inflation came tumbling down.

The Third World Debt Crisis, which left many leading banks in the industrialized countries holding non-performing debts, was one factor that contributed to the subsequent "securitization" of debt, as debts were partly converted into tradable bonds at the end of the 1980s. Such securitization has been a key feature of neoliberal finance. Instead of debts being contracted between two parties – the borrower and a bank – international bond markets were developed as a means for non-state entities to borrow money directly in the wholesale capital markets. Historically, this had been very much the privilege of governments which for long had sold bonds to cover deficits, especially in times of war. During the 1960s, however, bonds became increasingly used by private companies and financial institutions, which could turn to the markets directly to raise capital more cheaply, rather than borrow from banks: so-called Eurobonds thus emerged as an investment instrument, capable of harnessing Eurodollars (i.e., dollars held outside the United States) circulating in international capital markets.

Securitization was further encouraged by the growth of government borrowing, as of the 1970s, and the expansion of company shares traded both nationally and internationally. With the slowdown in growth in the 1970s, governments faced public pressure to maintain spending, just at a time when middle class and wealthier voters began rebelling against paying high rates of tax. The US tax revolt – which began with Proposition 13 voted by referendum in California, to cut property taxes – became prominent nationally with the election of Ronald Reagan in 1980 (as had already happened when Margaret Thatcher's Conservative Party was elected to office in May 1979).

To pay their bills, governments, and especially the US government, massively sold bonds into the markets. Significantly, too, securitization also received a boost in 1970 when Ginnie Mae (the Government National Mortgage Association, which is a wholly owned government corporation within the US Department of Housing and Urban Development, or HUD) began to guarantee mortgage-backed securities (Cowan, 2003) in order to facilitate household borrowing and greater homeownership. In the decades to come, this new type of mortgage finance made it possible to access wholesale (and international) capital markets, opening up the way to expanded homeownership. But this also encouraged the speculative nature of the housing market and the rise of private debt.

Similar phenomena occurred concerning shares. Stock markets exploded as of the 1980s, and traded shares proliferated everywhere, partly in response to company restructurings (the 1980s witnessed a merger and acquisitions boom, and a profound reorganization of large firms which shifted away from conglomerate structures to concentrating on core businesses). Also, the number of shares available for trading increased dramatically as privatization swept the industrialized world. This followed the successful privatization of British Telecom in 1984, which at the time was the world's largest stock market flotation ever.

In parallel to the development of new instruments and the expansion of securitization, finance also burgeoned thanks to deregulation. Again, the process of deregulation was something which took hold during the Carter presidency. In reaction to stagnation, government policy under Jimmy Carter changed, not only at the macroeconomic level (see above), but also at the microeconomic level. In line with neoliberal thinking, this change was based on deregulating markets. In particular, the Carter Administration deregulated transport (road haulage and air travel) and telecommunications, and in 1980 (its last year in office) legislation was passed to end interest rate ceilings on deposit accounts.

President Ronald Reagan (January 1981 to January 1989) subsequently extended such deregulation, including into the area of finance. The Garn–St. Germain Depository Institutions Act of 1982, in particular, deregulated America's savings and loans industry. Significantly, the Act also allowed banks to provide adjustable-rate mortgages, later a major characteristic of subprime mortgages.

Neoliberal ideology at the heart of the Fed

The return to laissez-faire economics may not have been exactly "planned," to draw on Polanyi's expression presented in the Introduction. But, the consolidation of neoliberal ideology at the Federal Reserve was actively encouraged by Alan Greenspan, who was appointed chairman of the Fed in 1987, to succeed Paul Volcker. Dr. Greenspan was (and still largely is) a true believer in free markets, and in the virtue of market self-regulation. He was a long-time friend of Ayn Rand, and much influenced by her Objectivist, individualistic ideas. For example, in 1963, writing in *The Objectivist Newsletter* edited by Rand, he asserted that:

> Capitalism is based on self-interest and self-esteem; it holds integrity and trustworthiness as cardinal virtues and makes them payoff in the marketplace, thus demanding that men survive by means of virtues, not of vices. It

> is this superlatively moral system that the welfare statists propose to improve upon by means of preventive law, snooping bureaucrats, and the chronic goad of fear.
>
> (Greenspan, 1963)

More than 30 years later, as chairman of the Federal Reserve, Alan Greenspan continued to defend the powers of markets to self-regulate, while criticizing government action in principle. In 1997, for example, in a speech made at the Financial Markets Conference of the Federal Reserve Bank of Atlanta, he clearly states that:

> But if private market regulation is effective, then government regulation is at best unnecessary. At worst, the introduction of government regulation may actually weaken the effectiveness of regulation if government regulation is itself ineffective or undermines incentives for private market regulation. We must be aware that government regulation unavoidably involves some element of moral hazard – if private market participants believe that government is protecting their interests, their own efforts to protect their interests will diminish to some degree.
>
> (Greenspan, 1997)

This ideological orientation held by Greenspan was very much in tune with the times. And it had fundamental consequences in the years ahead. In particular, he supported the Clinton Administration's policy of deregulating banking, as well as the self-regulation of expanding derivative markets (Bill Clinton was president from January 1993 to January 2001). A further significant policy approach to emerge during the Greenspan years, and which was also broadly supported by his successor at the Fed, Ben Bernanke, is the view that the monetary authorities should not intervene in asset markets to limit the development of price bubbles.

Concerning banking, Alan Greenspan at the Fed contributed to the repeal of the Glass–Steagall Act. This act was passed in 1933, and was a legacy of Wall Street's Great Crash in 1929. The main impact of the Act had been to prevent commercial/retail banks from trading in financial markets or engaging in insurance activities. As part of the wave of deregulation in the 1980s and 1990s, the Fed had progressively allowed commercial banks to develop business in securities trading: notably in December 1996 the Fed announced that the proportion of revenue which commercial banks could earn through their securities trading subsidiaries would rise from 10 percent to 25 percent (Federal Reserve, December 20, 1996). This effectively gutted the Glass–Steagall Act of much of its powers. But, it was not repealed until 1999, following the *preceding* merger between the Citicorp bank and the Travelers insurance company. Both Citicorp's CEO John Reed and especially Travelers' CEO Sandy Weill lobbied Congress, the Administration and the Fed to ensure the repeal of Glass–Steagall and hence the future of the merger (PBS/Frontline, 2003). The repeal was duly signed into law by President Clinton as the

Gramm–Leach–Bliley Act in September 1999, only a few weeks after Robert Rubin, President Clinton's Treasury secretary, had left government to become chairman of Citigroup (the name of the merged company)!

This, of course, was a historic moment. The separation of financial activities – and especially the separation of investment banking and commercial banking – had been one of the two key legacies of financial markets and banking reform in the 1930s: the other restriction was on interstate banking, which had already been freed up in 1994 (under the Riegle-Neal Interstate Banking and Branching Efficiency Act). By undermining and finally repealing the Glass–Steagall Act, the US authorities took a big step in helping with the securitization of finance and the financialization business in general (defined here as the transformation of any kind of asset, including physical assets like real estate, to be converted into some form of security that can be traded in the financial markets).[4] This was a deliberate policy move by the Clinton Administration which had always been relatively close to Wall Street, and it was a very clear expression of the way finance has managed to capture the political process.

Significantly, Alan Greenspan was also opposed to any form of regulation for derivative markets. As trading in derivatives grew, especially with financial innovation, ICT and the proliferation of instruments, it could have been brought under the supervision of public markets, like stock exchanges for shares and bonds. And indeed, derivative trading (of swaps) was later brought into regulated, formal markets by the Dodd–Frank Act of 2010. However, at the time, Greenspan was clearly unfavorable toward this, noting in 1997 that:

> The application of the Commodity Exchange Act to off-exchange transactions between institutions seems wholly unnecessary – private market regulation appears to be achieving public policy objectives quite effectively and efficiently.
>
> (Greenspan, 1997)

As a result, so-called over-the-counter trading, which occurs directly between buyers and sellers outside a formal exchange, was allowed to develop unhindered. But Alan Greenspan was not alone, and his views were shared by key players in the Clinton Administration. These included the aforementioned Robert Rubin (2003), who was a former co-chairman of Goldman Sachs. He first became an economic adviser to President Clinton, before being appointed Treasury secretary in 1995, a post he held until leaving for Citigroup (see above). Similarly, Mr. Rubin's successor at the Treasury, Lawrence Summers, was also an advocate of the non-regulation of derivative markets.[5]

In short, the deregulated and liberalized trading environment in which financial institutions were operating at the start of the twenty-first century was a deliberate, conscious historical construction (Stiglitz, 2003). There may not have been an overall plan, but the drive to deregulation was consistent and went on unabatedly. It was, of course, fundamentally facilitated by computer technology and the internet.

Monetary policy and the Fed's position of not intervening in asset markets

Along with its general stance favoring deregulation, the Fed also narrowed its policy-making on the whole to maintaining price stability by using interest rates. This means that it had (and arguably still has) few means to intervene in asset markets, and indeed it formulated a clear policy over time of not intervening. There are two sides to this story. On the one hand, the Fed broadly followed what became known as the so-called "Jackson Hole consensus." This takes its name from the mountain resort of Jackson Hole in Wyoming, where central bankers, finance specialists and monetary policy economists meet every August to discuss policy. The consensus refers to the orthodoxy that emerged during the 1980s and 1990s about how monetary policy should function and what it should aim to do. On the other hand, the Fed developed a policy over time of deliberately avoiding any actions which intervened in asset markets, preferring instead to deal with the consequences of bubbles once they had burst.

Looking at monetary policy first, the policy shift which Paul Volcker had undertaken while Chairman of the Fed became the new economic orthodoxy in the years that followed. Throughout the industrialized world (and indeed even in many developing nations), macroeconomic policy moved very much to the control of inflation through the use of short-term interest rates. Moreover, as part of the Jackson Hole consensus, central banks should be independent from politics, so that policy can be set by committees of experts. Such arrangements reflect, broadly speaking, the success of monetarist economic theory in supplanting Keynesianism. Instead of seeking to pursue growth (and full employment) via demand management, governments throughout the world switched to pursuing price stability, a task delegated to central banks. Price stability may be defined in slightly different ways from country to country; for example, following the original example of New Zealand, many central banks had adopted clear inflation targets for monetary policy (in the UK, the New Labour government set a target for the Retail Price Index less mortgage rates (PRIX) of 2.5 percent ±1 percent in 1997; the European Central Bank moved to an inflation target of 2 percent or less in 2001). Although Alan Greenspan himself did not favor a specific target (a 2 percent target was finally adopted under the Chairmanship of Ben Bernanke in January 2012) the Fed did indeed pursue its primary mission of holding down price increases. The instrument to do this is the short-term interest rate, or more precisely the federal funds rate: i.e., the rate at which banks lend reserves held in the Federal Reserve System to each other overnight, once their books are closed at the end of each trading day. If necessary, the Fed intervenes in this market by buying and selling bonds to hit the target rate. This rate is set collegiately by the Federal Open Market Committee, which also fixes other short-term interest rates that are less important in monetary policy.

There was a certain simplicity and elegance in these arrangements. Using one instrument to aim at one target conforms to the so-called Tinbergen Rule, named after Jan Tinbergen, the Dutch Nobel laureate in 1969. The rule states that the number of goals of policy should not exceed the number of instruments. As financial deregulation had essentially stripped monetary authorities (in the United States and elsewhere) of other instruments – such as credit controls – the logic of using the only remaining powerful instrument to obtain low inflation was implacable. It was also a policy that was fairly easy to communicate to markets, politicians and the public. This fits in with what has become one of the defining values of running monetary policy, namely that the authorities needed to be explicit, transparent and credible. Only by stating clearly to markets what their overall objectives and policies are can central banks properly ensure transparency and only then can they have any hope of being credible. Credibility, in turn, is deemed as vital in shaping agents' expectations about future inflation, and expectations of low inflation are in themselves a key component of actually achieving low inflation without needing to use excessively high interest rates (as Paul Volcker had been forced to do in the early 1980s, when inflation was high and expectations of future inflation were high too: see above).

It should be noted, however, that unlike other central banks (notably the ECB), the Federal Reserve also has a mandatory objective of supporting maximum employment. This may conflict with its goal of ensuring price stability, but it does make the Fed's statutory remit more flexible than is the case for other central banks. Significantly also, Raghuram Rajan has argued that the more limited welfare support for unemployed persons in the United States puts greater pressure on the central bank to stimulate growth in times of recession than is found in countries where public safety nets are more developed (Rajan, 2010, pp. 83–100). Moreover, the Fed sets the federal funds rate for a national, albeit continental, economy (compared to the ECB, which faces a much more complex task of setting a single rate for the whole euro area, comprising 17 countries with differing economic performances). As a result of these factors, the Fed has tended to be more reactive and flexible in varying rates than the ECB, and such reactivity did indeed play an important role in policy during the early 2000s, which partly explains why the housing credit bubble occurred.

Up until the 2007–2008 crisis, it was generally argued that the Jackson Hole policy framework was successful. Once inflation and inflationary expectations had been broken throughout the industrialized world – usually with recourse to considerable unemployment to break the power of labor and force down wage demands – it was relatively easy for the authorities to hold down consumer price rises. The overall policy was also helped by expanding international trade and investment, both of which acted (and still act) to strengthen price competition and weaken wages. What the Jackson Hole consensus on policy did not do, however, was to provide any means for managing asset price bubbles and/or financial crises.

These came and went with quite some regularity. Indeed, scarcely after taking office, Alan Greenspan had to handle the biggest stock market crash since 1929, when the Dow Jones Industrial Average plummeted by 23 percent on 19 October 1987. The crash shook global confidence – at least for a short time. However, the Fed led central banks worldwide in a policy of aggressively cutting interest rates and injecting liquidity into financial markets (by buying up bonds and hence pumping money into markets). This worked. Instead of the collapse of share prices leading to a global recession or worse, growth by the real economy was only marginally affected by the crash (Ferguson, 2008, pp. 165–169).

Similar interventions occurred in the wake of later crises, most notably following the Asian crisis in 1997 and the collapse of the New York hedge fund LTCM in the autumn of 1998, and especially in the wake of the collapse in internet/TMT stocks in 2000 as well as the large, subsequent falls in conventional stocks. The latter occurred due to knock-on effects of the internet/TMT crash, the mild US recession in 2001 and the impact of the 9/11 terrorist attacks. In each of these cases, Alan Greenspan led the Fed in cutting interest rates strongly and providing markets with liquidity. It was a policy response which the markets came to call the "Greenspan put" because it guaranteed investors that they could sell their investments at a high price in the future, as with a put option. The Fed's apparent success in dealing with all these crises did much to boost Mr. Greenspan's reputation. He became the "maestro," the deft central banker capable of ensuring low inflation and preventing financial crises from spilling over into the real economy ... too much. Indeed, a whole personality cult emerged around him. Analyzing his often cryptic statements became a kind of latter-day Kremlinology, while his every utterance as an "oracle" could sway markets (Zumello, 2011).

The maestro, of course, was not alone, and a policy consensus developed within the Fed about the difficulties of trying to intervene in asset markets to prevent bubbles. This was very cogently laid out, for example, in a speech made by Ben Bernanke in October 2002, during his first spell as a governor at the Fed. In this speech, B. Bernanke begins by noting that the central bank should use the "right tool for the job," and specifically that "the Fed should use monetary policy to target the economy, not the asset markets." He also states that the Fed does have regulatory tools to address issues of financial market stability, and notes:

> the Fed [should] use its regulatory, supervisory, and lender-of-last-resort powers to protect and defend the financial system. In particular, alone and in concert with other agencies, the Fed should ensure that financial institutions and markets are well prepared for the contingency of a large shock to asset prices.
>
> (Bernanke, 2002)

Dr. Bernanke goes on to state quite explicitly that he does not believe that the Fed should "lean against bubbles," let alone "pop" bubbles aggressively. He puts forward several reasons for this, including that it is not actually easy to identify bubbles and that monetary policy is too blunt an instrument to prick bubbles. More specifically, he asserts that,

> [t]hough the price of (say) a share of stock is readily observable, the corresponding fundamentals – such as the dividends that investors expect to

receive and the risk premium that they require to hold the stock – are generally not observable, even after the fact.

Significantly, he very clearly supports the prevailing point of view that competitive markets are more efficient than government agencies:

> there is the additional difficulty that the prices of equities and other assets are set in competitive financial markets, which for all their undeniable foibles are generally highly sophisticated and efficient. Thus, to declare that a bubble exists, the Fed must not only be able to accurately estimate the unobservable fundamentals underlying equity valuations, it must have confidence that it can do so better than the financial professionals whose collective information is reflected in asset-market prices.
>
> (www.federalreserve.gov/boarddocs/speeches/2002/20021015/default.htm – fn7)

> I do not think this expectation is realistic, even for the Federal Reserve. Moreover, I worry about the effects on the long-run stability and efficiency of our financial system if the Fed attempts to substitute its judgments for those of the market. Such a regime would only increase the unhealthy tendency of investors to pay more attention to rumours about policymakers' attitudes than to the economic fundamentals that by rights should determine the allocation of capital.
>
> (Ibid.)

As for monetary policy as an instrument, Ben Bernanke asserts that:

> Although neither I nor anyone else knows for sure, my suspicion is that bubbles can normally be arrested only by an increase in interest rates sharp enough to materially slow the whole economy. In short, we cannot practice "safe popping," at least not with the blunt tool of monetary policy.
>
> (Ibid.)

In fact, the general view to emerge at the Fed was that intervention should occur after an asset price collapse, to limit the consequences to the real economy. This was a position which Alan Greenspan had already stated in the late 1990s, when stock market prices already appeared very high – especially for internet/TMT stocks. Specifically, in 1999, before the House Committee on Banking and Financial Services, Alan Greenspan had made the case that stock market values were perhaps over-valued, but that pre-emptive intervention to affect prices was not really possible. However, he clearly said that "[i]t is the job of economic policymakers to mitigate the fallout when it occurs and, hopefully, ease the transition to the next expansion" (Greenspan, 1999).

Significantly, he restated this position at the Jackson Hole meeting of 2002, after the massive stock market crashes of 2000 and 2001! In fact, Greenspan makes quite a sophisticated analysis acknowledging how risk-taking – especially by financial investors – may spread in the wake of prolonged economic growth, and may even be boosted by minor increases in interest rates, as had occurred in the 1990s:

> Prolonged periods of expansion promote a greater *rational* willingness to take risks, a pattern very difficult to avert by a modest tightening of monetary policy. In fact, our experience over the past fifteen years suggests that monetary tightening that deflates stock prices without depressing economic activity has often been associated with subsequent *increases* in the level of stock prices.
>
> (Greenspan, August 2002)

Thus, once again, he refutes the arguments in favor of pre-emptive policy to limit bubbles developing, and reiterates the Fed's role to "mitigate the fallout" of crashes, and "ease the transition to the next expansion" (ibid).

Fears of deflation, low interest rates, moral hazard and the housing market

The "Greenspan put" reached it apotheosis in the following two years, notably as the central bank brought down the federal funds rate to 1 percent in June 2003, and kept it there for a whole year. At the time, this was a record low, unparalleled in modern history (though it pales into insignificance compared to the way the Fed has kept interest rates at 0–0.25 percent since December 2008!). It was justified by the fact that the Fed was actually worried about deflation. Haunted by the specter of the Great Crash in 1929, when the collapse of Wall Street led to the Great Depression, or what Milton Friedman later called the "Great Contraction" of the money supply, Alan Greenspan and others like Ben Bernanke (who's PhD research had been on the collapse of banking during the Great Depression) worried that there were risks of consumer price falls. In December 2002, Greenspan stated specifically that:

> Although the US economy has largely escaped any deflation since World War II, there are some well-founded reasons to presume that deflation is more of a threat to economic growth than is inflation. For one, the lower bound on nominal interest rates at zero threatens ever-rising real rates if deflation intensifies. A related consequence is that even if debtors are able to refinance loans at zero nominal interest rates, they may still face high and rising real rates that cause their balance sheets to deteriorate.
>
> Another concern about deflation resides in labour markets. Some studies have suggested that nominal wages do not easily adjust downward. If lower price inflation is accompanied by lower average wage inflation, then the prevalence of nominal wages being constrained from falling could increase as price inflation moves toward or below zero. In these circumstances, the effective clearing of labor markets would be inhibited, with the consequence being higher rates of unemployment.

> Taken together, these considerations suggest that deflation could well be more damaging than inflation to economic growth.
>
> (Greenspan, December 2002)

These concerns had a direct impact on encouraging the Fed to bring interest rates down to historically low levels. But at such low levels, interest rates contributed to providing capital for the next asset price boom, namely in housing. While the US economy only grew slowly out of its mild recession of 2001 – the recovery at the time was qualified as "jobless" – house prices in the United States began to rise, at first in coastal markets (the Eastern seaboard, Florida and California), and then as the decade wore on throughout the national market.

This is not the place to review the emerging house price boom, which culminated in widespread subprime mortgage lending. Nor can we deal here with the crucial issue of how rising house prices and rising household indebtedness (especially via the substantial recourse to negative equity borrowing) helped sustain the US consumer boom, and offset stagnating median incomes.[6] Suffice it to say, loose monetary policy at the Fed, combined with massive international capital flows into the United States that were financing the current account deficit, all contributed to a generalized climate of careless borrowing and lending, and generalized moral hazard on a gigantic scale. The mammoth *Financial Crisis Inquiry Report*, published in January 2011, unequivocally points to the systematic breakdown of prudent financial practices:

> The prime example is the Federal Reserve's pivotal failure to stem the flow of toxic mortgages, which it could have done by setting prudent mortgage-lending standards. The Federal Reserve was the one entity empowered to do so and it did not. The record of our examination is replete with evidence of other failures: financial institutions made, bought, and sold mortgage securities they never examined, did not care to examine, or knew to be defective; firms depended on tens of billions of dollars of borrowing that had to be renewed each and every night, secured by subprime mortgage securities; and major firms and investors blindly relied on credit rating agencies as their arbiters of risk. What else could one expect on a highway where there were neither speed limits nor neatly painted lines?
>
> (*Financial Crisis Inquiry Report*, 2011, Conclusions, p. xvii)

The Report clearly quantifies households' reactions when the Federal Reserve cut interest rates early in the new century:

> [as mortgage] rates fell, home refinancing surged, climbing from $460 billion in 2000 to $2.8 trillion in 2003, allowing people to withdraw equity built up over previous decades and to consume more, despite stagnant wages. Home sales volume started to increase, and average home prices

> nationwide climbed, rising 67% in eight years by one measure and hitting a national high of $227,100 in early 2006.
>
> (p. 5)

Nor can the Fed say it did not know what was happening. In the very speech Alan Greenspan made in December 2002 [*sic*] warning about deflation, he also clearly stated that:

> To be sure, the mortgage debt of homeowners relative to their income is high by historical norms. But, as a consequence of low interest rates, the servicing requirement for that debt relative to homeowners' income is roughly in line with the historical average. Moreover, owing to continued large gains in residential real estate values, equity in homes has continued to rise despite very large debt-financed extractions. Adding in the fixed costs associated with other financial obligations, such as rental payments of tenants, consumer instalment credit, and auto leases, the total servicing costs faced by households relative to their income appears somewhat elevated compared with longer-run averages. But arguably they are not a significant cause for concern.
>
> (Greenspan, 2002)

These contradictory views of developments in the housing market were reaffirmed later on several occasions by Alan Greenspan and leading members of the Fed. On the one hand, they were fully aware of the exceptional nature of the housing bubble. On the other hand, they repeatedly downplayed its dangers, arguing that markets would self-adjust, without necessarily leading to a major economic downturn:

> Borrowing against home equity has been a staple of household finance for decades, but as I noted earlier, it has been only in the past decade or so that such practices have been encouraged by lenders. We need to far better understand the economics of this major addition to household finance and its impact on the economy. One hopes, new data will form the basis of better insights.
>
> (Greenspan, 2003)

Or again in October 2004:

> In summary, although some broader macroeconomic measures of household debt quality do not paint as favorable a picture as do the data on loan delinquencies at commercial banks and thrifts, household finances appear to be in reasonably good shape. There are, however, pockets of severe stress within the household sector that remain a concern and we need to be mindful of the difficulties these households face.
>
> In addition, a significant decline in consumer incomes or house prices could quickly alter the outlook; nonetheless, both scenarios appear unlikely

> in the quarters immediately ahead. If lenders, including community bankers, continue their prudent lending practices, household financial conditions should be all the more likely to weather future challenges.
>
> (Greenspan, 2004)

Even when the warning lights began to flash red, little immediate action was taken to offset a market crash. In early 2007, worries about subprime loans led to a crash in the Shanghai stock exchange, which plunged by nearly 9 percent on February 27, 2007. This in turn led to a sharp fall in stocks on Wall Street, with the Dow Jones dropping by 416 points (Peters & Barboza, 2007). Still, the Federal Reserve remained relatively unperturbed by events. By this stage Alan Greenspan had retired, being replaced in January 2006 by Ben Bernanke. But, in line with efforts to reassure markets, the transition of chairmen at the head of the Fed was very much marked by continuity.

As 2007 wore on, the stormclouds were manifestly gathering, even if not all troubles were local. It was in Britain that the bank Northern Rock had to be rescued by the authorities in September 2007, following the first British bank run in more than 100 years. Northern Rock may not have been a US bank, and ironically its exposure to US subprime mortgages was limited. But its immediate difficulties in the autumn of 2007 did result from it being cut out of the US inter-bank market, so that Northern Rock was unable to rollover its borrowing and hence continue to finance its operations. This was a clear indicator of extreme market nervousness, and the Fed did ease rates in the last months of the year.

By early 2008, the US authorities, including the Fed, had indeed woken up to the immanent dangers facing the US banking system and the economy. In January the Fed reduced the federal funds rate from 4.25 percent to 3.5 percent, the largest cut in more than two decades (La Monica, 2008), while in March 2008 it participated in a deal which was brokered between the authorities and JP Morgan Chase for the buyout of Bear Stearns, a Wall Street investment bank that was on the brink of bankruptcy.

When the crisis finally exploded worldwide in September 2008 (following the collapse of Lehman Brothers), the Federal Reserve and the US government did pull out all stops to prevent domestic and international capital markets from freezing up entirely and bringing the world's real economy to a sudden stop. Whatever the final assessments of policy during the crisis will be, the package of measures put together by the out-going Bush Administration, the Federal Reserve and the international community did prevent a complete freezing up of markets, and hence did allow the world economy to carry on operating.

Criticism is far more legitimate, however, concerning both the run-up to the crisis and subsequent policy. Significantly, despite the fact that the writing had been on the wall for a number of years, the Federal Reserve (and authorities worldwide) had refused to act to calm the US housing boom and to rein in the excess of international financial speculation which had grown up in the preceding years. Little or nothing was done to stem the unfettered development of finance, in accordance with the neoliberal policies pursued by Alan Greenspan, the Federal Reserve System as a whole and financial authorities across the globe. When the crisis broke, their plea was one of not knowing, of not being able to predict the unpredictable. This response and the previous "group-think" which it patently reflected have been well described by Joseph Stiglitz, a specialist in the information imperfections of markets, and economics Nobel laureate in 2001:

> When the bubble breaks, everyone says, "Who could have predicted it?" I was at a meeting in Davos in January 2008: the bubble had broken the preceding August, though the optimists were still of the view that it would have little consequence. As I and a couple of other colleagues explained how the bubble had developed and what its breaking meant, a chorus of central bankers in the front row chimed in: "No one predicted it," they claimed. That claim was immediately challenged by the same small band that had been talking about the bubble for several years. But the central bankers were, in a sense, right: no one with credibility in their circle had challenged the prevailing view, but there was a tautology: no one challenging the prevailing view would be treated as credible. Sharing views was part of being socially and intellectually acceptable.
>
> (Stiglitz, 2009, p. 253)

Yet even such willful ignorance is quite a hard claim to explain. It is particularly notable that the world's leading central bankers and monetary experts received a clear warning concerning weakness in the global banking system at the Jackson Hole conference in August 2005. This was Alan Greenspan's last conference as chairman of the Fed, and in many ways his swan song. But the meeting also contained a very forthright and unambiguous warning by Raghuram Rajan, chief economist at the IMF at the time, about massive exposure in the banking sector to systemic risks (Rajan, 2005). Having also previously worked at the Booth School of Business at the University of Chicago, and becoming Governor of the Reserve Bank of India in September 2013, Mr. Rajan was (and is) an insider's insider. Nevertheless, his warning was roundly derided at the time, and he noted later that "I exaggerate only a bit when I say I felt like an early Christian who had wandered into a convention of half-starved lions." Yet he also noted that "[a]s I walked away from the podium [...] I felt some unease [...] because the critics seemed to be ignoring what was going on before their eyes" (Rajan, 2010, p. 3).

As for the US housing bubble, which culminated in the widespread use of subprime mortgages that were then "sliced-and-diced" and sold off as securities throughout the international financial system, it was in fact very much a classical asset price bubble. Like other asset prices bubbles, it was fueled by cheap capital and the hope of ever-rising asset prices, leading to ever-greater risk taking. Or significantly, as the French, heterodox financial economist André Orléan (2011) has noted with great simplicity, the price mechanism in asset markets broke down. Instead of rising prices inducing a fall in demand – as usually occurs in goods markets – higher prices, and the prospect of higher future prices, stimulated the demand for housing assets. This demand was in turn financed with cheap credit.

This of course raises important questions about the functioning of the price mechanism. While Hayek's view is that prices provide sufficient information to allow producers to make output decisions, the observation here by A. Orléan strongly challenges the role of prices in asset markets. It fundamentally raises the question of how efficient asset prices, and therefore asset markets, are in allocating resources. The Fed's policy of just looking at price inflation for goods and services, in line with this use of the short-term interest rate instrument, would appear to be gravely flawed.

Conclusion and the broader historical context

This chapter has tried to show that the Federal Reserve under the chairmanship of Alan Greenspan in particular played an instrumental role in supporting the deregulation of finance in the United States. In its application of monetary policy, the Fed has also had a direct hand in encouraging asset market bubbles and in particular the US housing boom of the 2000s. This of course ended in the subprime crisis, the ensuing international financial crisis and the subsequent Great Recession, whose impact is still shaping the world economy. Both of these policy approaches – financial market deregulation and the way monetary policy has been implemented – are key elements in the shift away from the New Deal Fordist public policy paradigm, toward neoliberalism. Together, they also contributed to the repeated financial crises that have characterized neoliberalism, in a way that is reminiscent of financial "panics" that marked US capitalism during the nineteenth century, and through to the Great Crash of 1929. From a "civilizational" point of view, neoliberalism does therefore appear to reconnect, to some extent, with classical liberalism in the field of finance.

On the whole, the policy orientations of Alan Greenspan were shared by his successor Ben Bernanke. Differences in their approaches to monetary policy – the explicit setting of an inflation target, more collegiate decision-making by the FOMC and a clearer communication of Fed policy to markets – are hardly fundamental, or at least they were not important prior to the onset of the financial crisis.

Since 2008, when the financial crisis really took hold, the Federal Reserve has gone to great lengths to support the US economy. During the most acute phase of the financial crisis in late 2008, the Federal Reserve to a large extent acted as a substitute for failing international financial markets, including the interbank market, the commercial paper market, etc. The Federal funds rate was also cut to a range of 0 percent to 0.25 percent in December 2008, where it has remained since. As the imminent dangers of the collapse of the US (and indeed international) financial system receded, the Fed nevertheless continued to pursue unconventional monetary policies, with the aim of meeting its mandated objectives of maximum employment and price stability. Thus, in a semi-annual statement on monetary policy to Congress in February 2013, Chairman Bernanke listed these as including:

> "forward guidance" regarding the FOMC's anticipated path for the federal funds rate, in order to influence longer term interest rate in the markets and hence "support a stronger recovery." Specifically, the interest rate will be kept low as long as unemployment is above 6½ percent, provided that expected inflation remains within half a percentage point of its 2 percent target and expectations of inflation remain low.
>
> The large-scale purchase of longer-term securities, including agency (i.e., Fannie Mae, Freddie Mac and Ginnie Mae) mortgage-backed securities in addition to government bonds. Since end 2012, these purchases have been running at $85 billion a month (respectively $45 billion for mortgage-backed securities and $40 billion in Treasury securities), and are set to continue until the FOMC observes a substantial improvement in the outlook of the labour market.
>
> (Bernanke, 2013)

Bernanke went on to assert that such policies were providing important support to the US economy, and were in particular helping the recovery of the housing market. However, he also noted that they carried risks. These include:

> concerns that public confidence in the Fed to maintain price stability could weaken and may lead to problems exiting its policy of purchasing securities;
>
> the possibility that very low interest rates, if maintained for a considerable time, could impair financial stability. For example, portfolio managers dissatisfied with low returns may "reach for yield" by taking on more credit risk, duration risk, or leverage.
>
> implications for the US federal budget, as the Fed's present portfolio of securities means that it is making large interest payments to the government, which could fall substantially in the future.
>
> (Ibid.)

Needless to say, Ben Bernanke was reassuring about these risks. But there are indeed dangers inherent in the extremely permissive and unconventional monetary policy pursued by the Federal Reserve. To be sure, the program of quantitative easing was brought to an end in October 2014, without causing significant financial market disruptions. Ben Bernanke's successor as chair of the Fed, Janet Yellen, who took over in February 2014, appears to have carried forward the collective policy of the Fed board seamlessly.

Doubts, however, remain about the future of the Fed's interest rate policy, and the possible consequences which a rise in interest rates may have on financial markets and the global economy. At the time of writing (late December 2014), there appear to be two major worries concerning the return to higher, more normal levels of interest rate. One concerns the bond markets, the other concerns the value of shares. It is widely believed that a rise in short-term interest rates set by the Fed could lead bond prices to fall. This in turn would automatically lead to a rise in long-term interest rates which are set in markets: such a rise follows automatically as lower bond prices mean that the absolute annual (coupon) payment bonds carry then actually become higher percentage yields. Similarly, at the end of 2014, the Dow Jones Industrials stood at record highs, breaching 18,000 points in the run-up to Christmas. Even though it was also announced on December 23, 2014 that the US economy had recorded annualized growth of 5 percent in the third quarter of 2014 – the fastest rate since 2003 – it may legitimately be asked whether such high stock values are justified by underlying economic activity.

It is far beyond my capacity to judge these risks, let alone predict the timing of a turnaround in market sentiment. Indeed, predicting the timing of crashes is virtually impossible by definition. Nevertheless, numerous analysts and commentators have already issued clear warnings of a future financial crisis. Thus, in March 2013, for example, David Stockman – President Reagan's budget director from 1981 to 1985 – caused quite a stir with a stinging article in the *New York Times*. For him, twentieth-century Keynesianism, government policy to expand welfare and crony capitalism have fundamentally weakened the US economy, while monetary policy pursued by the Fed since the end of the gold standard has completely debauched the US currency. Over this period, public and private debt has been piled up massively, while production has only expanded at a moderate pace. As a result, the ratio of America's total debt to economic output has risen from about 1.6 to about 3.6. David Stockman concluded that the "United States is broke – fiscally, morally, intellectually – and [that] the Fed has incited a global currency war … that will soon overwhelm it. When the latest bubble pops, there will be nothing to stop the collapse" (Stockman, 2013).

More recently, in August 2014, Raghuram Rajan (2014) warned that the world economy could face another Great Depression, such as in the 1930s. He has pinpointed "competitive easing" between central banks, and hence their failure to coordinate policy, as a major risk. The resulting cheap money has led investors to chase high yields, which in turn has driven up asset prices that risk subsequent, unpredictable price movements. Similarly, the *Financial Times*' chief economics editor, Martin Wolf, also clearly stated in September 2014 that: "The pre-crisis orthodoxy proved defective. The new orthodoxy is an improvement. But it is open to question in important respects. The financial system remains fragile. The risks of further crises are not small" (Wolf, 2014).

The danger is that for all the re-regulation which banking in the United States (and elsewhere) has undergone since the crisis, the basic structural mechanisms of neoliberalism in finance remain in place. The Dodd–Frank Act of 2010 is indeed a massive piece of regulatory legislation and has addressed many of the problems that led to the crisis. But other major causes for concern remain. The wall of money the Fed has thrown into the banking and financial system since the crisis dwarfs the enormity of the "Greenspan put" in the early 2000s. The US banking system too is today also much more concentrated than previously, and is again reasserting direct influence in Washington. In a truly hair-raising article penned by Edward Luce, the *Financial Times*' chief US commentator, on

December 14, 2014, the latter noted that: (1) Jamie Dimon, the chief executive of JP Morgan, had directly "arm-twisted" Congress to pass a $1.1 trillion spending package, thus ending the threat of a government shut-down, and in exchange got a measure in the bill which allows banks to resume derivatives trading from their taxpayer-insured arms; and (2) that the big four US bank groups today – JP Morgan, Citi, Bank of America and Wells Fargo – "account for 68 per cent of US deposits and an even higher share of US derivatives trading." Not surprisingly, Mr. Luce's article carries the subtitle: "There will be another crisis. No law can stop it, no regulator can foresee it." This may be overly deterministic, and historical processes are not easily described by laws of motion like physics. However, the fundamental structural characteristics of the US economy and the functioning of finance have not changed substantially since the 2007–2008 crisis, and there are good reasons to be worried about future, significant crises.

Notes

1 Kenneth Rogoff was chief economist at the IMF from 2000 to 2003.

2 Fordism is the term the French "Regulationist school" of economics developed in the 1970s to describe an economic regime based on a compromise between capital and labor. As its name suggests, capital has the managerial prerogative to organize production, and in exchange labor receives high wages. This compromise leads to high levels of employment and growth due to the resulting favorable interaction between production and demand, and the fact that very long production runs allow large economies of scale to be achieved. See, for example, the seminal work on Regulation Theory by Michel Aglietta (1997).

3 See "About MPS," retrieved May 19, 2013, from www.montpelerin.org/montpelerin/mpsAbout.html.

4 For an overview of financial deregulation see: Sherman (2009).

5 In 1998, Lawrence Summers, acting as deputy secretary of the Treasury, testified to Congress on the issue of derivative market regulation, noting that "To date there has been no clear evidence of a need for additional regulation of the institutional OTC derivatives market, and we would submit that proponents of such regulation must bear the burden of demonstrating that need" (Summers, 1998).

6 These issues are extensively analyzed in the seminal work by Mian and Sufi (2014).

References

Aglietta, M. (1997). *Régulation et crises du capitalisme* (3rd edn.). Paris: Editions Odile Jacob.

Bernanke, B. (2002). Asset-price "bubbles" and monetary policy. *Remarks before the New York Chapter of the National Association for Business Economics*, New York. Retrieved from www.federalreserve.gov/Boarddocs/Speeches/2002/20021015/default.htm.

Bernanke, B. (February 20, 2004). The great moderation. *Remarks by Governor Ben S. Bernanke at the meetings of the Eastern Economic Association, Washington, DC.* Retrieved www.federalreserve.gov/boarddocs/speeches/2004/20040220/.

Bernanke, B. (February 26, 2013). *Semiannual monetary policy report. Statement by Ben S. Bernanke, Chairman Board of Governors of the Federal Reserve System, before the*

Committee on Banking, Housing, and Urban Affairs, US Senate. Retrieved from www.federalreserve.gov/newsevents/testimony/bernanke20130717a.htm.

Boyer, R. & Saillard, J.P. (1997), *After Fordism*. London: Palgrave MacMillan.

Burgin, A. (2012). *The great persuasion: Reinventing free markets since the Depression*. Cambridge, MA: Harvard University Press.

Cowen, C.L. (November 5, 2003). *Statement on behalf of the American securitization forum, before the Subcommittee on Housing and Community Opportunity and the Subcommittee on Financial Institutions and Consumer Credit, United States House of Representatives*. Retrieved from http://financialservices.house.gov/media/pdf/110503cc.pdf.

Federal Reserve. (December 20, 1996). Press release.

Ferguson, N. (2008). *Ascent of money: A financial history of the world*. London: Penguin Books.

Financial Crisis Inquiry Report (2011). Final Report by the National Commission on the Causes of the Financial and Economic Crisis in the United States, submitted by the Financial Crisis Inquiry Commission. Official government edition. Retrieved from www.gpo.gov/fdsys/pkg/GPO-FCIC/pdf/GPO-FCIC.pdf.

Friedman, M. (1962). *Capitalism and freedom*. Chicago, IL: University of Chicago Press.

Friedman, M. (2011). The need for futures markets in currencies. Reprinted in *Cato Journal*, *31*(3). Retrieved from http://object.cato.org/sites/cato.org/files/serials/files/cato-journal/2011/9/cj31n3-15.pdf.

Greenspan, A. (1963). The assault on integrity, *The Objectivist Newsletter*, August 1963; reprinted in Ayn Rand (ed.), *Capitalism: The unknown ideal*. New York: Signet, 1967, pp. 118–121. Retrieved from https://docs.google.com/document/d/1UamlhxrEe_tW6zms1_gTT1czVweHkkLfa-PGXu6GvJM/edit?pli=1.

Greenspan, A. (1997). Government regulation and derivative contracts. *Remarks at the Financial Markets Conference of the Federal Reserve Bank of Atlanta*, Coral Gables, Florida. Retrieved from www.federalreserve.gov/boarddocs/speeches/1997/19970221.htm.

Greenspan, A. (July 22, 1999). The Federal Reserve's semiannual report on monetary policy. *Testimony before the Committee on Banking and Financial Services*, U.S. House of Representatives. Retrieved www.federalreserve.gov/boarddocs/hh/1999/july/testimony.htm.

Greenspan, A. (August 30, 2002). Economic volatility. *Opening remarks at a Symposium Sponsored by the Federal Reserve Bank of Kansas City*, Jackson Hole, Wyoming.

Greenspan, A. (December 19, 2002). Issues for monetary policy. *Remarks before the Economic Club of New York*, New York City.

Greenspan, A. (March 4, 2003). Home mortgage market. *Remarks at the Annual Convention of the Independent Community Bankers of America*, Orlando, Florida (via satellite), Retrieved from www.federalreserve.gov/BOARDDOCS/SPEECHES/2003/20030304/default.htm.

Greenspan, A. (October 19, 2004). The mortgage market and consumer debt. *Remarks at America's Community Bankers Annual Convention*, Washington, DC.

Greenspan, A. (2007). *The age of turbulence*. New York: Penguin.

Hall, P. & Soskice, D. (eds.) (2001). *Varieties of capitalism: The institutional foundations of comparative advantage*. Oxford: Oxford University Press.

von Hayek, F. (1944). *The road to serfdom*. Chicago, IL: University of Chicago Press.

Jones, D.S. (2012). *Masters of the universe: Hayek, Friedman and the birth of neoliberal politics*. Princeton, NJ: Princeton University Press.

La Monica, R.R. (January 22, 2008). Fed slashes key rate to 3.5%. *CNNMoney*. Retrieved from http://money.cnn.com/2008/01/22/news/economy/fed_rates.

Luce, E. (December 14, 2014). Too big to resist: Wall Street's comeback. *The Financial Times*. Retrieved from www.ft.com/intl/cms/s/0/b048dbde-8383-11e4-8a84-00144feabdc0.html#axzz3Xyos4TKS.

Melamed, L. (1972). A futures market in currency, presented to the New York Society of Security Analysts, Inc., New York. Retrieved from www.leomelamed.com/essays/72-fut.htm.

Mian, A. & Sufi, A. (2014). *House of debt: How they (and you) caused the Great Recession, and how we can prevent it from happening again*. Chicago, IL and London: University of Chicago Press.

Mirowski, P. & Plehwe, D. (eds.) (2009). *The road from Mont Pelerin: The making of the neoliberal thought collective*. Cambridge, MA: Harvard University Press.

Orléan, A. (2011). De l'euphorie à la panique. In P. Askenazy & D. Cohen (eds.), *16 nouvelles questions d'économie contemporaine*. Paris: Arthème Fayard/Pluriel, pp. 37–116.

PBS/Frontline. (May 8, 2003). *The long demise of Glass–Steagall: In the Wall Street fix*. Retrieved from www.pbs.org/wgbh/pages/frontline/shows/wallstreet/weill/demise.html.

Peters, J.W. & Barboza, D. (February 28, 2007). Dow average falls 416 points after China sell-off. *New York Times*. Retrieved from www.nytimes.com/2007/02/28/business/28stox.web.html.

Rajan, R. (2005). Has financial development made the world riskier? *NBER Working Paper* No. 11728. Retrieved www.nber.org/papers/w11728.

Rajan, R. (2010). *Fault lines: How hidden fractures still threaten the world economy*. Princeton, NJ and Oxford: Princeton University Press.

Rajan, R. (August 6, 2014). RBI's Rajan warns of possible asset price collapse; euro "too strong." *Central Banking*. Retrieved from www.centralbanking.com/central-banking/news/2358938/rbi-s-rajan-warns-of-possible-asset-price-collapse-euro-too-strong.

Rogoff, K. (September 18, 2003). *Transcript of the September 2003 World Economic Outlook Press Conference*, Dubai, International Monetary Fund. Retrieved from www.imf.org/external/np/tr/2003/tr030918.htm.

Rubin, R. (2003). *In an uncertain world*. New York: Random House.

Sherman, M. (2009). *A short history of financial deregulation in the United States*, Washington, DC: CEPR. Retrieved from www.cepr.net/documents/publications/dereg-timeline-2009-07.pdf.

Stiglitz, J. (2003). *Roaring nineties*. New York: W.W. Norton.

Stiglitz, J. (2009). *Freefall: Free market and the sinking of the global economy*. London: Penguin Books.

Stockman, D.A. (March 30, 2013). State-wrecked: the corruption of capitalism in America. *New York Times*. Retrieved from www.nytimes.com/2013/03/31/opinion/sunday/sundown-in-america.html?pagewanted=all.

Summers, L. (July 30, 1998). *Treasury Deputy Secretary Lawrence H. Summers Testimony before the Senate Committee on Agriculture, Nutrition and Forestry on the CFTC concept release*. Retrieved from www.treasury.gov/press-center/press-releases/Pages/rr2616.aspx.

Wolf, M. (September 3, 2014). Financial reform: Call to arms. *Financial Times*, Retrieved from www.ft.com/intl/cms/s/0/152ccd58-3294-11e4-93c6-00144feabdc0.html#axzz3Xyos4TKS.

Zumello, C. (2011). *L'intermédiation en question: finance et politique aux Etats-Unis de Clinton à Obama*. Paris: Presses Sorbonne Nouvelle.

3 The resilience of American neoliberalism

Bradley T. Smith

Introduction

The intervention of the US federal government to contain the 2008 financial crisis was commonly interpreted as a departure from the free market neoliberal paradigm that had dominated federal economic policy since the Reagan era of the 1980s. Reagan (1981) had set the tone for the following three decades in his first inaugural speech, by claiming in relation to the "stagflation"[1] of the 1970s: "In this present crisis, government is not the solution to our problem; government is the problem." In the crisis of 2008, however, Republicans and Democrats alike seemed to agree – perhaps grudgingly – that government intervention was the only workable solution to prevent a complete collapse of the international financial system.

The idea that the United States was entering a new era characterized by "the return of the state" (Grewel, 2010) was echoed in the mainstream media of the time. In November 2008, *Time* magazine ran a cover entitled "The New New Deal," with an image of freshly elected president Barack Obama dressed like Franklin D. Roosevelt, as to suggest a return to the interventionist policies promoted by FDR in the 1930s to fight the Great Depression (Beinart, 2008). In February 2009, *Newsweek* magazine went so far as to claim "We are all socialists now," hereby suggesting a new consensus in favor of a more European-style activist state (Meacham, 2009). Though with hindsight these headlines now seem far-fetched, they nevertheless reflected a dichotomous conception of the American state equally present in academia: that of a state that is either interventionist or non-interventionist, without taking sufficiently into account, as Evans (1995, p. 10) suggests, the actual nature of the intervention taking place.

The same dichotomy can be found in Hall and Soskice's (2001) distinction between "liberal market economies" (LMEs), of which the American neoliberal model would be one variety, and "coordinated market economies" (CME), to which the United States was perhaps transitioning in the aftermath of the 2008 crisis. Several influential economists, such as Joseph Stiglitz (2008), Paul Krugman (2009a), Robert Skidelsky (2008) and J. Bradford Delong (2008), also interpreted the federal intervention of 2008 as a potential shift away from a

30-year neoliberal cycle of "market fundamentalism" (Stiglitz, 2008, ¶ 1) and toward a new era they hoped to be characterized by Keynesian interventionism.

Yet, seven years on from the crisis, what is striking is not how much the United States has shifted away from neoliberalism, but rather how *little.* Indeed, as Colin Crouch (2011) puts it, instead of the dawn of a new era, what we have witnessed since the 2008 crisis is rather *The Strange Non-death of Neoliberalism.* This "non-death" may seem "strange" within a dichotomous vision of the state. However, if we take a closer look at neoliberalism from not only a political, but also an economic and ideological point of view, this dichotomy becomes quite problematic – and the reasons for the resilience of American neoliberalism, more apparent.

Three factors in particular can shed light on this resilience and the complexity of neoliberal dynamics in the United States:

1. From an ideological point of view, federal intervention does not necessarily signal a departure from neoliberal ideology.
2. From an economic point of view, the financial crisis does not seem to have diminished the power of financial capital, a centerpiece of the neoliberal economy.
3. From a political point of view, no mass movement seems powerful or organized enough to seriously challenge the established order, and neither Republicans nor Democrats seem to propose a radical break with neoliberalism.

It goes without saying that this list is not exhaustive and that other factors play into the equation. Nevertheless, by focusing on these three interrelated dimensions, this "civilizational" approach allows for a more in-depth comprehension of the nature of American neoliberalism.

Neoliberal interventionism

To begin, let us suppose just for an instant that the American state is indeed either interventionist or non-interventionist, and that neoliberalism is synonymous with non-interventionism. In this case, the expression "neoliberal interventionism" would appear to be an oxymoron. However, if we now push the dichotomy to the extreme and place anarchy on one end and totalitarianism on the other, it would be difficult to seriously argue, for example, that Milton Friedman, one of the most outspoken proponents of free-market capitalism, was an anarchist, and Keynes, a totalitarian. As Friedman (2002) puts it himself, "The consistent liberal is not an anarchist" (p. 34); and as both he and Keynes (Friedman, 2002, p. 5; Keynes, 1978) identify themselves as belonging to the liberal tradition of limited government, this places their theories somewhere in between a complete absence of government intervention and a government that intervenes in every aspect of life. Likewise, Reagan's oft-quoted axiom "government is the problem" is widely known, but the nuance he adds later in the same speech seems to have gone under the radar:

> Now, so there will be no misunderstanding, it's not my intention to do away with government. It is rather to make it work with us, not over us; to stand by our side, not ride on our back. Government can and must provide opportunity, not smother it; foster productivity, not stifle it.
>
> (Reagan, 1981, ¶ 12)

In short, the debate within liberalism is not about whether the government should intervene everywhere or nowhere, always or never; it's about which forms of intervention are legitimate and which are not. As all schools of liberal thought support state intervention to some extent, what distinguishes them from one another is exactly what forms of intervention their theories can justify and where they place the limits. As such, "neoliberal interventionism" is not an oxymoron, but rather an expression we can use to refer to the specific forms of intervention that are legitimate within a neoliberal framework.

If we now take a brief look at the history of neoliberal thought, it becomes even more apparent just how problematic it is to equate neoliberalism with non-interventionism or radical laissez-faire. As Dardot and Laval (2010, p. 8) put it, neoliberal thought, contrary to what one might expect, "appeared historically as an attempt to reestablish liberalism *against the naturalist ideology of* laissez-faire." By this they refer to the classical liberal notion of natural economic laws that are universal and ahistorical, which man can discover through science, but which he should not interfere with because they spontaneously produce maximum economic harmony and prosperity. In this sense, the positive laws of government are only legitimate when they are based on and uphold these natural laws. Neoliberal thought, on the other hand, appeared in the 1930s at a time when faith in this hands-off approach, which relies on the "invisible hand" (Smith, 1776) of "natural" market forces to correct economic imbalances, was utterly discredited. Direct government control of the economy was an alternative approach that was being adopted to various degrees in communist, social-democratic and fascist regimes alike.

Within this context, liberal intellectuals from several countries convened in Paris in 1938 at the Walter Lippmann Colloquium to reflect on ways to redefine liberalism in a way that would surpass "old" laissez-faire liberalism without falling into state-planned economies (Audier, 2012, p. 413).[2] The defining features of this "neo"-liberalism, as expressed in the "Agenda of Liberalism" at the end of the colloquium (Audier, 2012, pp. 485–486), were its rejection of "administrative interventionism" (Dardot & Laval, 2010, p. 166), that is, government management of part or all of the economy, and its support of "juridical interventionism" (ibid.; Audier, 2012, p. 415), that is, the creation of a strong legal framework, or "order," which serves to establish and maintain a free market economy. Liberal capitalism, in this sense, was no longer considered to be a "natural" order; it was henceforth to be understood as a political construction requiring the intervention of the state (Audier, 2012, p. 485).

Friedman (2002), leader of the Chicago School of economics, would later echo this position in *Capitalism and Freedom*. On the one hand, he states, "The role of government … is to do something that the market cannot do for itself, namely, to determine, arbitrate, and enforce the rules of the game" (p. 27); he hereby affirms the legitimacy of juridical interventionism due to the absence of a "natural" market order. On the other hand, he lists a series of "activities … undertaken by government in the U.S. that cannot … validly be justified" (p. 36) according to his liberal principles, most of which fall within the realm of administrative interventionism.[3] Even once the market order is juridically established, however, Friedman does admit that certain "market imperfections," such as monopoly and "neighboring effects" (i.e., negative externalities), are impossible to resolve through "strictly voluntary exchange" (p. 28). When this is the case, state intervention may be unavoidable, though prudence is necessary: "In any particular case of proposed intervention," Friedman writes, "we must make up a balance sheet, listing separately the advantages and disadvantages" (p. 32). As such, he affirms, "We do not wish to conserve the state interventions that have interfered so greatly with our freedom, though, of course, we do want to conserve those that have promoted it" (p. 6).

Thus, between the "Agenda of Liberalism" expressed at the Walter Lippmann Colloquium and Friedman's notion of a "balance sheet," it is a misconception to conceive of neoliberal theory as a radically anti-interventionist ideology. Indeed, it is much more subtle than that; and due to the very ambiguity of whether or not state interventions may be seen as having more advantages than disadvantages, differing or contradictory analyses can be made within the same ideological framework. Libertarians, for example, have argued that the 2008 crisis was not due to a lack of financial regulation, but to *excessive* intervention in financial markets (Allison, 2010, 2012; Randazzo, 2009). On the other hand, it is equally possible to consider an imminent meltdown of the entire international financial system as falling under the category of "market imperfections" having "neighboring effects" that are "practically impossible" to resolve through "strictly voluntary exchange." In this case, the need for state intervention can arguably be justified within a neoliberal framework – especially if the intervention is mostly juridical and if any administrative intervention is designed to be temporary.

This indeed seems to be the case for the federal intervention to contain the 2008 crisis. If some or all of the large American banks or car companies in trouble had been permanently nationalized, this would have amounted to significantly increasing administrative interventionism, which neoliberal ideology firmly opposes. Instead, the Dodd–Frank Wall Street Reform and Consumer Protection Act of 2010, which we will come back to later, modifies the "rules of the game" rather than imposing direct government administration of Wall Street financial institutions; it is therefore a form of juridical interventionism. Likewise, through the Troubled Assets Relief Program (TARP), signed into law by George W. Bush on October 3, 2008, the federal government has avoided permanent nationalization by preferring the conservatorship model, which involves temporarily taking control of troubled corporations and/or buying more than 50 percent of their assets, with the intention of selling them back to the private sector and ending federal control as soon as the companies get back on their feet. According to a Congressional Budget Office report (2014), of the $313 billion provided to financial institutions through the TARP, only $2 billion remained outstanding in March 2014, and 99 percent of the stock purchased by the Treasury had been repurchased by the issuing institutions (pp. 3–4). Likewise, of the $80 billion lent to the automotive industry, namely to GM and Chrysler, only $6 billion remained outstanding, and the Treasury had "sold all of its securities in the two companies" (p. 6). Thus, by avoiding permanent administrative intervention and preferring juridical interventionism, the federal government's interventionist response to the crisis does not seem to signal a departure from neoliberal ideology.

Understanding how specific forms of state intervention fit into neoliberal ideology not only undermines the relevance of an interventionist/non-interventionist dichotomy, but it can also partly account for the "non-death" of neoliberalism in the wake of the crisis. However, ideological consistencies, or inconsistencies for that matter, only capture part of the picture. Neoliberalism is not a mere ideology; it is also a set of real economic developments that have taken place over the course of three decades, and to which the crisis may or may not have put an end. Let us now take a look at the resilience of neoliberalism in the US from an economic perspective.

The rise and persistence of financial power

Many phenomena characterize American economic development since the late 1970s. These include *globalization*, or the increasing internationalization of American business activities made possible through technological progress and political agreements lifting barriers to the international flow of capital; *post-industrialism*, or the relative decline of the industrial sector and the rise of the service sector; and *economic inequality*, or the rising gap in the distribution of wealth between the richest and the poorest segments of American society. One development that deserves particular attention for our purposes, however, is *financialization*, or the increasing preponderance of financial capital in the US economy, thanks in large part to financial deregulation (Sherman, 2009; Krippner, 2005; Duménil & Lévy, 2011, part IV). Indeed, financialization was not only one of the prerequisites for these other phenomena, but it was also at the heart of the crisis that was initially interpreted as a turning point away from neoliberalism and toward a new New Deal. The power of financial capital had been significantly diminished during the Great Depression and through New Deal policies, and neoliberal policies contributed to restoring that power starting in the late 1970s. Has financial power been diminished since 2008 in the same way that it had been in the 1930s?

Just before the crash of 2008, the distribution of income and savings was about as unequal as it had been before the crash of 1929. In 1928, as in 2007, the richest 10 percent of Americans received nearly 50 percent of all revenues (including capital gains), with the top 1 percent receiving about 21 percent (Piketty & Saez, 2012). Samuel Rosenberg (2003) explains that in the 1920s, only the small wealthy minority "had any connection with the stock market"

(p. 6). The crash itself, therefore, primarily affected what Marx (2003) called the "finance aristocracy" (p. 36).[4] The financial system took another serious blow as more and more people defaulted on their loans, which in turn led to numerous bank failures and the infamous bank runs between 1930 and 1933. During this time,

> The Federal Reserve stood by passively as banks began failing in large numbers. Rather than supply monetary reserves to the banking system so as to lessen the number of banks likely to close, the Federal Reserve allowed the liquidation of the banking system to run its course.
>
> (Rosenberg, 2003, pp. 8–9)

On top of that, much of federal policy at the time was based on "the notion that the federal budget should always be balanced" (ibid., p. 8). For Rosenberg, this led to rather "perverse policies being implemented," namely Herbert Hoover's decision to eliminate the deficit through a large tax increase that

> went into effect in June 1932, near the trough of the Great Depression. As taxes are increased, individuals have less disposable income and with less disposable income, consumption is reduced thereby lowering the demand for goods and services. Such a policy was contrary to what was needed at the time.
>
> (Ibid.)

The tax increase concerned all income levels and thus decreased all sources of demand, making the Great Depression even harder for low-income earners. However, high incomes were also subject to significantly higher marginal rates, with the top rate passing from 25 percent to 63 percent. This was yet more bad news for large money holders: between the stock market crash, the bank failures, and now the tax increase, not only had they taken a swift blow to their wealth, but as Keynes (1964) would say, there were few "psychological and business incentives" (p. 194) for them to invest, for lack of aggregate demand and a predictable business climate. By the time Roosevelt came to power in 1933, the "finance aristocracy" had lost much of its economic and political clout.

The New Deal changed financial regulation in a way that significantly limited the power of finance for the subsequent decades. New federal regulatory and insurance agencies were created, such as the Federal Deposit Insurance Corporation (FDIC) and the Securities and Exchange Commission (SEC), and banks were henceforth subject to strict regulations through the Banking Act of 1933, also known as the Glass–Steagall Act. In order to reduce systemic risk induced by market speculation and competition, the act separated commercial and investment banking, and Regulation Q placed ceilings on the interest rates that banks were allowed to pay on various types of accounts.[5] The resulting system was relatively stable, for the US economy was free of financial crises all the way until the 1970s. It was also a period of decreasing inequalities in revenue, with the richest 10 percent of Americans no longer receiving nearly 50 percent of all revenues, but just over 30 percent, and the richest 1 percent receiving 9 percent instead of 21 percent (Piketty & Saez, 2012). In many ways, this can be attributed to the very progressive tax system that reigned throughout this period; indeed, top rates set between 70 percent and 92 percent limited the incentive for corporate executives to pay themselves lavish salaries.

The shift to neoliberal policies starting around the late 1970s/early 1980s put an end to these tendencies and ushered in a new era of increased financial power and economic inequalities. High inflation rates offered long-time critics of New Deal-era financial regulation a golden opportunity to successfully push for deregulation. As Sherman (2009) explains:

> In the late 1970s, inflation caused market interest rates to rise above the limits mandated by Regulation Q. The restrictions may have been prudent when inflation was around 3 or 4 percent, but with inflation as high as 10 or 11 percent, investors began to seek out and find alternatives to traditional deposit accounts.
>
> (p. 6)

The search for alternatives led to several financial innovations, notably the creation of money market mutual funds, which were not subject to Regulation Q and could therefore offer higher returns. However, regulated institutions struggled to compete with these new types of funds. As a solution, President Carter signed the Depository Institutions Deregulation and Monetary Control Act of 1980, which completely eliminated interest rate ceilings within six years. Two years later, President Reagan signed the Garn–St. Germain Act of 1982, which this time was aimed at making savings and loans institutions (thrifts) more competitive by allowing them to "enter into new financial territory with new risks" (Sherman, 2009, p. 7). New Deal regulations were on the way out, through both Republican and Democrat initiatives.

In addition to financial deregulation, the Reagan Administration pushed for supply-side economic policies ("trickle-down economics") that were based on the idea that lowering taxes on wealthy individuals and corporations and eliminating regulatory barriers would spur investment, create jobs, stimulate growth and increase federal revenues all at the same time. Through the Economic Recovery Tax Act of 1981 (ERTA) and the Tax Reform Act of 1986, top marginal rates were lowered from 70 percent to 50 percent and then all the way down to 28 percent, the lowest top rate since the 1920s. In subsequent years, the top rate averaged around 35 percent. This set the stage for increased inequalities in revenue after 1981.[6] Lower marginal rates meant there was more incentive for CEOs, for example, to pay themselves higher salaries. "The CEO-to-worker compensation ratio was 20-to-1 in 1965 and 29.9-to-1 in 1978, grew to 122.6-to-1 in 1995, peaked at 383.4-to-1 in 2000, and was 295.9-to-1 in 2013" (Mishel & Davis, 2014). Through supply-side policies, wealth was not trickling down, but up: "Overall, the rich were getting richer and the poor were becoming even more destitute" (Rosenberg, 2003, p. 235).

Reagan's supply-side economics did not balance the federal budget either. On the contrary, because of a combination of tax cuts and increased military spending, the deficit exploded during the Reagan era, with the total amount of federal debt tripling from $1 trillion to $3 trillion over the course of the decade (Office of Management and Budget [OMB], 2014). After the massive 1981 ERTA tax cuts, subsequent tax bills in 1982, 1984 and 1986 attempted to increase tax revenues, not by increasing marginal rates, but rather by closing loopholes while still pursuing low marginal rates (Fullerton, 1994). The elimination of tax shelters for real estate through the Tax Reform Act of 1986 was a major contributing factor to the savings and loan crisis of 1987. The industry's deregulation in 1980–1982 led to increased investment in higher-risk real-estate loans. As the 1986 reform eliminated incentives to invest in real estate, deposits fled the industry, and hundreds then thousands of institutions began to fail (Sherman, 2009, p. 8). In the midst of this, on October 19, 1987, there was a stock market crash even worse than that of 1929, as the Dow Jones Industrial Average decreased by a staggering 22.4 percent. Deregulation and "Reaganomics" had indeed made the financial system more volatile as a whole.

Considering the magnitude of these crises, one might imagine that the neoliberal experiment of the 1980s would have ended right there. However, the Fed and the Reagan and Bush Administrations' responses to these crises illustrate a defining feature of American neoliberalism and a central factor of its resilience: swift government bailouts in the wake of financial crises (Harvey, 2005, p. 73). Indeed, the day after the stock market crash, the newly appointed chairman of the Federal Reserve, Alan Greenspan, declared, "The Federal Reserve, consistent with its responsibilities as the Nation's central bank, affirmed today its readiness to serve as a source of liquidity to support the economic and financial system" (Zaretsky, 1996). By doing so, confidence was preserved and a 1930s-style panic was avoided. Likewise, the US Treasury used about $210 billion of taxpayer money to bail out the savings and loans industry, and the Financial Institutions Recovery and Enforcement Act of 1989 (FIRREA) expanded the government's ability to oversee the industry and provide a greater safety net if needed (Sherman, 2009, p. 8). In other words, as the government proved its commitment to corporate welfare, and as Greenspan affirmed the role of the Fed as a lender of last resort, the financial sector could rest assured that any risks involved with deregulation would be counterbalanced by the guarantee of state intervention designed to preserve the integrity of the free market system.

Thus, neoliberalism and financial power continued to develop throughout the 1990s and 2000s. Under Greenspan's chairmanship (1987–2006), the Fed progressively loosened Glass–Steagall restrictions by allowing commercial banks to derive a higher and higher percentage of their revenues from activities traditionally reserved for investment banks (Sherman, 2009, pp. 10). Glass–Steagall was eventually repealed in 1999, when President Clinton signed the Financial Modernization Act – a "modernization" that consisted of reverting back to the pre-New Deal era, when banking, investment and insurance activities could be combined without restriction. This encouraged a wave of mergers and the creation of financial mega-firms, such as Citigroup. More "modernization" was brought about by the Commodity Futures Modernization Act of 2000, which completely exempted financial derivatives from federal regulation. The bill was quietly adopted "without debate or review" as a "rider to an 11,000-page spending bill," "the day after the Supreme Court effectively decided the fate of the 2000 Presidential election" (ibid., p. 11). The rest is history: a housing boom inflated the bubble between 2000 and 2007, much like in the 1980s; extremely profitable mortgage-backed securities were pooled together into AAA-rated collateralized debt obligations (CDOs), which were then traded among investment banks; since the original mortgage lender no longer owned the loan, this created an illusion of security, since risk was constantly transferred to someone else; risky sub-prime mortgages thus proliferated and standards for attributing loans were lowered in order to respond to the phenomenal demand for mortgage-backed securities; the bubble burst when housing prices stopped rising, interest rates shot up, thousands of families began defaulting on their loans, the value of mortgage-backed securities collapsed, and the large banks that owned them began to fail (Demyanyk & Van Hemert, 2008; Schwarcz, 2009; Sherman, 2009, pp. 12–15; Duménil & Lévy, 2011, parts 6–7).

As seen earlier, the Bush Administration's response to the crisis was to create the TARP – in other words, to inject billions of dollars into the financial system to prevent it from collapsing like it had done in the early 1930s. This makes the situation more similar to the savings and loan crisis than to the Great Depression. Moreover, though the bailout probably prevented the economic downturn from worsening, it also prevented the "finance aristocracy" from losing its hegemonic power, as it had in the 1930s. Initially, the top 1 percent of Americans did suffer bigger losses than the bottom 99 percent during the 2007–2009 recession; their real income dropped by 36.3 percent, while that of the bottom 99 percent dropped by 11.6 percent (Piketty & Saez, 2012). However, during the recovery of 2009–2012, their real income grew by 31.4 percent, while that of the bottom 99 percent grew by only 0.4 percent (ibid.). That means that the top 1 percent captured 95 percent of total income growth during this period, which is more unequal than both the Clinton expansion of 1993–2000 and the Bush expansion of 2002–2007, when the top 1 percent captured, respectively, 45 percent and 65 percent of total income growth. In other words, with inequalities in revenue that are even greater today than they were before the crisis, the neoliberal trend of increasing inequalities has not at all been reversed. Financial profits and Wall Street bonuses have also increased continuously since the crisis, eventually surpassing their pre-crisis levels to reach some of their highest levels on record in 2013 (Federal Deposit Insurance Corporation [FDIC], 2014; Office of the New York State Comptroller, 2014). Meanwhile, the banking industry has continued its long-term drift toward increased consolidation, with the ten largest commercial banks holding nearly 50 percent of all US deposits in 2010 (Wheelock, 2011).

Thus, unlike the Great Depression, which severely weakened the power of finance, so far the 2008 crisis seems to have *consolidated* financial power, thanks in large part to federal intervention. Trends associated with the development of neoliberal economic policies in the United States, namely starker inequalities, financial hegemony and federal bailouts, have continued. Other policy responses of Congress and the Obama Administration have also contributed to the resilience of these trends. As we will now see, in addition to neoliberal interventionism and the persistence of financial power, the policy orientations of both the Obama Administration and the Republican opposition in Congress bear little resemblance to the dramatic shift that New Deal policies had brought about.

The absence of organized opposition and political alternatives

Has the crisis pushed either of the two major political parties to propose a fundamental break with the neoliberal economic model that has dominated for the past three decades? It was tempting to think so during the presidential campaign of 2008, which opposed Democratic candidate Barack Obama and Republican candidate John McCain. Early in his campaign, Obama denounced deregulation as a major source of the economic downturn and called for a new, "21st century regulatory framework" (Obama, 2008, ¶ 13). Though McCain had consistently supported financial deregulation from his seat in the Senate, he suddenly switched gears at the height of the crisis in September 2008 and began to embrace regulation (Shear, 2008). With three decades of financial deregulation on trial and both candidates calling for change, such a debate would have been unthinkable a couple of years earlier. High hopes were placed on Obama when he won the election in November – hence the speculation about a "New New Deal" (Beinart, 2008).

However, a fundamental catalyst for progressive change, which had been present in 1932, was strikingly absent in 2008: radical, organized, sizable opposition to the established order. Indeed, the social backdrop to FDR's New Deal was a strong and radicalized labor movement, backed by socialist and communist parties, along with increasing civil disobedience and rebellion (Zinn, 2003, p. 393). These movements were daunting enough to worry the powers that be. Who doesn't see the fear of revolution in FDR's "New Deal Speech" (1932) when he warns against the potential spread of "wild radicalism" (¶ 10)? Though this "danger" may have been limited, it was apparently significant enough for wealthy men like Roosevelt to consider outright "reaction" and stubborn conservatism to be potentially disastrous (ibid., ¶ 11), for it could have led to further radicalization and perhaps the downfall of the capitalist system. "Workable reforms" aimed at improving the material conditions of the working class, making concessions to labor unions, and helping the economy to recover seemed like a better way to head off revolution at the time (ibid., ¶ 11).

The situation was completely different in 2008. Since the 1930s, American capitalists have been incredibly successful in reducing the labor movement to near impotence and the American Left to near oblivion (Debouzy, 2009; Rosenberg, 2003; Sexton, 1992; Van Elteren, 2011). Prevailing anti-communism and the branding of anything outside of liberal capitalism as "un-American" has severely weakened the political Left since the Cold War period. Union power has been curbed in a variety of ways: by moving plants first to the less unionized South and Southwest throughout the postwar era, and eventually abroad; by outsourcing many activities to precarious non-union workers; by replacing workers with machines; by reorienting the economy toward new, hard-to-unionize service sectors, especially since the 1980s; through management's "hard line"; etc. While total union membership was already down to 20.1 percent in 1983, it had dropped to 11.3 percent by 2013 – continuing its decline despite the crisis – with union membership of private-sector workers at only 6.7 percent (Bureau of Labor Statistics, 2014). With a weak labor movement and an absence of influential parties to the left of the Democratic Party, political outlets are scarce for people committed to overhauling the system, not to speak of overthrowing it.

The Occupy Wall Street movement that peaked in 2011 was the largest left-wing attempt to push for radical change outside of mainstream politics. It was certainly a change to see large numbers of Americans out on the street voicing their critiques of capitalism in terms of class conflict ("We are the 99%!"), for this hadn't really been seen since the 1960s and 1970s. However, without national coordination, permanent structures and a clearly defined political program, the movement was unable to move from the initial stage of angry outburst to the development of an organized, long-term strategy. As was the case for the New Left of the 1960s, the movement was mostly anarchist in nature, which undermined its ability to organize; many refused to support the Democrats against the Republicans; and a small minority considered terrorist-style violence to be the only way to get attention (Hampsen, 2011; Unger, 1974, pp. 170–183). As such, terrorism would have been a last resort to make up for the lack of a mass movement and positive results. This is the route that one New Left group, the Weatherman, followed in the early 1970s, and it resulted in the complete dismantling of the movement and the radicalization of the neoliberal New Right that eventually brought Reagan to power (Unger, 1974).

Thus, with union influence at an all-time low and a lack of organized radical opposition, Obama has not at all had the same left-wing pressure that FDR was under during the Great Depression. As Obama's first term began, it quickly became apparent that the change he had promised would in fact be quite limited. In his first inaugural speech, he announced his pragmatic approach to government: "The question we ask today is not whether our Government is too big or too small, but whether it works.... Where the answer is yes, we intend to move forward. Where the answer is no, programs will end" (Obama, 2009a, ¶ 14). Does this not sound strangely familiar to Milton Friedman's balance sheet? "Nor is the question before us whether the market is a force for good or ill," Obama continues. "Its power to generate wealth and expand freedom is unmatched. But this crisis has reminded us that without a watchful eye, the market can spin out of control" (ibid., ¶ 15). In other words, for Obama, the market remains the central reference for growth and progress, but it also requires a legal framework in order to function correctly. Though Friedman and Hayek would not speak in terms of "keeping the market under control," we saw earlier how the whole premise of neoliberalism is the need for a certain amount of juridical interventionism to set up and maintain the market system. Thus, so far, we are still within the sphere of neoliberalism, though perhaps in a hemisphere that allows for more juridical interventionism.

Whom now did Obama appoint to keep a "watchful eye" on the market? Many of the same men who had helped to close that eye during the Clinton years and who have personal ties to Wall Street – Timothy Geithner, who replaced former Goldman Sachs CEO Henry Paulson as secretary of the Treasury, had been the president of the Federal Reserve Bank of New York from 2003 to 2009 and undersecretary of the Treasury from 1998 to 2001, under Robert Rubin and Lawrence Summers. These are the men alongside Alan Greenspan and Wall Street who successfully pushed for the repeal of Glass–Steagall and the deregulation of the derivatives market. Obama appointed Lawrence Summers as the director of the National Economics Council – the same Summers who had been a member of Reagan's Council of Economic Advisors, had pushed for financial deregulation in the Clinton Administration, had made millions of dollars in the financial sector thereafter, and had published a grand tribute to Milton Friedman in 2006, claiming that "any honest Democrat will admit that we are all Friedmanites now" (Summers, 2006, ¶ 2). Rubin, who had been chairman of Goldman Sachs before championing financial deregulation in the Clinton Administration, and who became chairman of Citigroup in 2007, continued to exercise his influence on the Democrats by founding the Hamilton Project in 2006, an influential think tank within the circles of White House counselors (Planel, 2012, chapter 3). The person whom Obama appointed to the head of the Commodity Futures Trading Commission (CFTC) was Gary Gensler, a long-time employee of Goldman Sachs who as undersecretary for domestic finance in 1999–2001 had fought for the Commodity Futures Modernization Act that prevented the CFTC from regulating the derivatives market. This all poses quite an obstacle to any significant change. As all of these men are notorious for making full use of the "revolving door" between the financial sector and the federal government, we can safely assume that the financial sector is especially keeping a "watchful eye" to be sure that Wall Street reform, even if it involves adding new regulations, will not seriously threaten the power of financial capital.

This is quite apparent with the Dodd–Frank Wall Street Reform and Consumer Protection Act of 2010. Often presented as the most sweeping financial reform since the New Deal, the bill does reverse some of the previous deregulatory trends by re-regulating the derivatives market; limiting the amount of capital that banks can invest in hedge funds (the "Volcker Rule"); promoting transparency; protecting consumers against predatory lending techniques; restructuring the regulatory apparatus through the creation of new agencies; and transferring additional powers to the FDIC, the SEC, the CFTC and the Fed. What the bill does not do, however, is restore the Glass–Steagall Act, put bankers on trial to hold them accountable for the crisis they caused, and provide compensation to those who lost their homes or jobs (Rivlin, 2013). Moreover, one of the aims of restructuring the regulatory agencies is to allow them to more efficiently liquidate failed banks in an orderly manner; in other words, the bill presupposes that its preventative regulatory measures may be insufficient to prevent future financial crises and therefore increases the federal government's capacity to reestablish order.

This makes the reform more similar to the one adopted in 1989 (FERRIA) in the wake of the savings and loan crisis. Indeed, unlike New Deal legislation, which used federal intervention to significantly restructure financial markets, FERRIA and Dodd–Frank are more about adapting federal regulations and agencies to existing markets. Not only that, but while Wall Street had already spent more than $1 billion on lobbying to water down Dodd–Frank and to prevent it from passing, since its adoption Wall Street has been spending even more money on lobbying to make sure its implementation is as slow, ineffective and filled with loopholes as possible. "Dodd–Frank's Achilles' heel is that it leaves the tough work of writing the actual regulations to existing federal agencies" (Rivlin, 2013, ¶ 7); and with swarms of lobbyists putting pressure on authorities, who themselves often have close personal ties with Wall Street, progress has indeed been extremely slow. Three years after the bill's adoption, only about 40 percent of its 398 rules had been finalized (McCoy, 2013). As former FDIC chairman Sheila Blair puts it:

> This stuff doesn't get any better with time. The longer you wait to finalize the rules, the more they get watered down, the more exceptions that get built in, people's memories about the crisis begin to fade and the pressure isn't there.
>
> (Kaufman, 2013, ¶ 7)

"Stuff" has not gotten any better either since the Republicans regained the House majority in 2010, many of the newly elected Republicans being affiliated with the ultraconservative Tea Party movement. Indeed, since then, not only have Republicans supported all efforts to delay, weaken or repeal Dodd–Frank, but they have also concentrated their efforts on obstructing two other major policy orientations of the Obama Administration: federal economic stimulus through the American Recovery and Reinvestment Act of 2009 (ARRA), and healthcare reform through the Patient Protection Affordable Care Act of 2010. While pressure from the Left was already weak and unorganized, the Right managed to effectively impose itself after 2010. Yet, like Dodd–Frank, before these reforms even became subject to gridlock, they were already quite underwhelming to those who hoped for a more drastic break with neoliberalism.

The recovery bill was based on the Keynesian notion that in times of crisis, an increase in public spending can be used to offset the negative effects of a decrease in private spending. This is at odds with the neoliberal notion that the federal budget should always be balanced and that market forces will eventually lead to recovery. However, Paul Krugman (2009b, 2009c, 2014), for example, repeatedly warned that the stimulus was not even one-third of what was needed, and that "by falling short, the act would end up discrediting the very idea of stimulus" (2014, ¶ 11). This indeed seems to be what has happened. Republicans have seized upon the shortfall to present the federal deficits as the main roadblock to recovery, which led to fierce congressional battles over the debt ceiling. Subsequent legislation has enacted fiscal austerity, with much more emphasis on spending cuts than on tax increases for the wealthy. The Budget Control Act of 2011, passed with bipartisan support, required spending to be reduced by $2.4 trillion over the next ten years, and sequestration would be used if deadlines were not met. Sequestration indeed went into effect in 2013. Meanwhile, the Bush tax cuts of 2001 and 2003 were temporarily extended in 2010, and though many tax cuts on the wealthy were allowed to expire in 2012, this merely set them back to pre-2003 levels, with a top rate of 39.6 percent instead of 35 percent. This was nothing compared to the extremely progressive tax system that reigned throughout the mid-twentieth century. Thus, stimulus through federal spending was short-lived, tax policy remains relatively generous to the wealthy and social welfare programs have been put under tremendous pressure to be reduced – hardly a radical change from past decades.

Congressional gridlock over the budget reached a peak in 2013, when House Republicans provoked a 16-day government shutdown by refusing to adopt the 2014 budget unless the Affordable Care Act (ACA) was defunded. After more than 40 failed attempts to repeal the ACA and the failure to have the Supreme Court rule it unconstitutional, this was the Republicans' most desperate attempt to eliminate a healthcare reform that many of them considered to be "socialist" and "un-American" (Volsky, 2013). Given the extreme rhetoric and the clear partisan divide on the issue (the bill passed without a single Republican vote), one might expect to find two fundamentally different visions confronting each other, one in favor of a socialized public health system and another in favor of a private health insurance market. However, if we look at the actual substance of the ACA, the possibility for consensus between the two parties is much stronger than the rhetoric would suggest. To be sure, the aim of the ACA is progressive: to gradually provide all Americans with healthcare insurance. The means by which the ACA achieves this, on the other hand, are in fact neoliberal ones that conservatives had supported in the past, and that reflect Obama's pragmatism. Early on, he discarded the option of creating a single-payer national health system as being unworkable in the American context: "The problem … is that we have an employer-based system that has grown up for decades. For us to completely change our system, root and branch, would be hugely disruptive" (Obama, 2009b). Instead, he voiced support, at least initially, for a "public option," meaning a government insurance program that would compete alongside private ones.

This was already an unchallenging stance toward the role of the market and of private insurance companies. In the end, even the public option was dropped in order to reach enough votes in the Senate. The resulting law is a market-based solution that creates "a new open, competitive insurance market" designed to "give Americans new affordable choices of private insurance plans that have to compete for their business based on cost and quality" (White House, Title I, ¶ 2). This fits quite perfectly within the neoliberal assumption that the private sector and competitive markets are the most efficient ways to produce and distribute goods and services at low costs, and that the government's role is to create markets where they don't already exist. We can perhaps call it "progressive neoliberalism" in that the juridical interventionism of the ACA does entail new rules that, for example, protect patients against abusive insurance company practices, extend coverage to a majority of Americans through individual and employer mandates, and expand Medicaid coverage. New government requirements are nevertheless different from a new national health system; yet, it is through these interventionist measures that Republican opponents try to depict the ACA as state socialism. The irony of it all is that this market- and individual-mandate-based solution to providing all Americans with health coverage was a Republican idea in the first place. The Heritage Foundation defended it in 1989 (Butler, 1989), and it was a template for Republican Mitt Romney's reform of Massachusetts' healthcare system in 2006. If these ideas are now considered to be "Big Government" solutions, this just goes to show how far to the right the debates have shifted.

In essence, while federal stimulus, financial reform and healthcare reform have all entailed some degree of government intervention, the fact that these measures have been either insufficient or filled with loopholes has reinforced Republican claims about government inefficiency. In a black-and-white world where "neoliberal interventionism" is an oxymoron, if people see that the *government* has used taxpayer money to bail out the *rich elite* and that Obama's supposedly "Big Government" approach has been unable to pull the economy out of the crisis, that's all the Republicans need to direct popular anger against the government and present further neoliberalization as the solution. Since the types of state interventions that the Obama Administration has supported are essentially neoliberal ones that presuppose market superiority, this means that neither political party is offering a radical break with neoliberalism and that debates are trapped within the narrow perimeter of conservative neoliberalism vs. progressive neoliberalism.

Conclusion

Thus, neoliberal interventionism, continued financial hegemony, disorganized and powerless resistance and a lack of politically viable alternatives are some of the reasons for the resilience of American neoliberalism. As a final remark, let us come back to the man who is generally credited for having set neoliberalism in motion in the United States – Ronald Reagan. When confronted with the deficits that his administration was piling up, despite his promise to do the opposite, his reaction is quite revealing. Historian Bruce Schulman (2001) writes:

> In discussing the deficit, many of Reagan's economic advisers recalled, he frequently repeated his favorite anecdote about the boy who looked at a pile of manure and assumed he must have received a new pony. One aide recalled the president's views on the deficit "going through three stages: one, they won't occur; two, they'll be temporary; three, when they stick they

> serve a good purpose—they keep the liberals from new spending programs. Oh, sure, that was Reagan." On that last point, Reagan was right. The unpaid bills choked off future spending and prevented even the most committed liberal activists from proposing new programs. Reagan's budgets ensured that Reaganomics would continue long after the president had departed the White House.
>
> (p. 238)

Therein perhaps lies the secret of the Reagan legacy, which lives on, as we have seen, even in the midst of today's crisis. For how much longer is yet to be known. One thing is sure, however: there's a vital limit to just how much wealth can be transferred from the bottom up before this becomes socially and economically unsustainable. Once this limit has been passed, future crises are to be expected – unless bolder change is undertaken.

Notes

1 This term was coined to designate a combination of economic stagnation and high levels of inflation.

2 Notable participants were Walter Lippmann, Louis Rougier, Friedrich von Hayek, Ludwig von Mises, Raymond Aron, Michael Polanyi, Wilhelm Röpke and Alexander Rustow.

3 Examples include "government control of output," "detailed regulation of industries," "present social security programs," "public housing," "national parks," "the legal prohibition on the carrying of mail for profit," and "publicly owned and operated toll roads." (Friedman, 2002, pp. 32–33).

4 In *The Class Struggles in France*, Marx uses the term "finance aristocracy" to refer to the fraction of the French bourgeoisie that ruled under Louis-Philippe, namely "bankers, stock-exchange kings, railway kings, owners of coal and iron mines and forests, a part of the landed proprietors associated with them" (p. 36). A similar category of capitalists existed in the United States at the same time and still exists today, though the concrete nature of their property has obviously evolved since the nineteenth century (the railway industry, for example, lost its importance in the twentieth century). In any case, the term "finance aristocracy" does not refer to small shareholders or individuals who simply have pension funds invested in the stock market, but to a relatively small group of individuals who, through their ownership or management (or both) of large amounts of financial assets, are able to exert an enormous amount of power on political and economic decision-making, often in a way that is disconnected from the so-called "real" economy (traditional industry and agriculture). In America, this group is often simply referred to as "Wall Street," since this is the center of financial activity in the United States. In recent decades, financial power has become so concentrated that many large banks and insurance companies have been deemed "too big to fail," since their failure could very well lead to the collapse of the entire international financial system.

5 "Under Regulation Q of the Banking Act of 1933, savings accounts were capped at 5.25 percent, and time deposits were limited to between 5.75 and 7.75 percent, depending on maturity. Checking accounts were restricted to an interest rate of zero" (Sherman, 2009, p. 6).

6 Other important factors include the proliferation of minimum wage jobs in the service sector, the decline in the real minimum wage itself, and the decline in union membership (Gordon & Dew-Becker, 2008).

References

Allison, J.A. (2010). The financial crisis and the deregulation myth. Cato Institute, December 10, 2010. Retrieved from www.cato.org/publications/commentary/financial-crisis-bank-deregulation-myth.

Allison, J.A. (2012). *The financial crisis and the free market cure: Why pure capitalism is the world's only hope*. New York: McGraw-Hill.

Audier, S. (ed.). (2012). *Le colloque Lippmann: aux origines du néo-libéralisme.* Lormont, France: Le Bord de l'Eau.

Beinart, P. (2008). The new liberal order. *Time*, November 13, 2008. Retrieved from www.time.com/time/magazine/article/0,9171,1858873,00.html.

Bureau of Labor Statistics (2014, January 14). News release: union members – 2013. Retrieved from www.bls.gov/news.release/pdf/union2.pdf.

Butler, S.M. (1989). Assuring affordable health care for all Americans. *The Heritage Lectures*, Vol. 218. Washington, DC: The Heritage Foundation.

Congressional Budget Office (2014). Report on the Troubled Assets Relief Program – April 2014. Congressional Budget Office. Retrieved from www.cbo.gov/sites/default/files/cbofiles/attachments/45260-TARP.pdf.

Crouch, C. (2011). *The strange non-death of neo-liberalism.* Cambridge: Polity Press.

Dardot, P. & Laval, C. (2010). *La Nouvelle raison du monde.* Paris, France: La Découverte.

Debouzy, M. (2009). *Le Monde du travail aux États-Unis: Les temps difficiles (1980–2005).* Paris, FR: L'Harmattan.

Delong, J.B. (2008, February 28). The end of the age of Friedman. *Project Syndicate.* 2008. Retrieved from www.project-syndicate.org/commentary/the-end-of-the-age-of-friedman.

Demyanyk, Y. & Van Hemert, O. (2008). Understanding the subprime mortgage crisis. Federal Reserve Bank of St. Louis Supervisory Policy Analysis Working Paper. Retrieved from http://ssrn.com/abstract=1020396.

Duménil, G. & Lévy, D. (2011). *The crisis of neoliberalism.* Cambridge, MA: Harvard University Press.

Evans, P. (1995). *Embedded autonomy: States and industrial transformation.* Princeton, NJ: Princeton University Press.

Friedman, M. (2002). *Capitalism and freedom* (40th anniversary edn). Chicago, IL: University of Chicago Press.

Fullerton, D. (1994). Inputs to tax policy-making: the supply-side, the deficit, and the level playing field. In M. Feldstein (ed.), *American economic policy in the 1980s* (pp. 165–208). Chicago, IL: University of Chicago Press.

Gordon, R.J. & Dew-Becker, I. (2008). Controversies about the rise of American inequality: A survey. Retrieved from http://faculty-web.at.northwestern.edu/economics/Gordon/NBER_Final_080421.pdf.

Grewel, D. (2010, February 1). The return of the state. *Harvard International Review.* Retrieved from http://hir.harvard.edu/big-ideas/the-return-of-the-state.

Hall, P.A. & Soskice, D. (eds.) (2001). *Varieties of capitalism: The institutional foundations of comparative advantage.* Oxford: Oxford University Press.

Hampsen, R. (2011, November 14). "Occupy" movement faces challenge from violent fringe. *USA Today.* Retrieved from www.usatoday.com/news/nation/story/2011-11-13/occupy-movement-violent-fringe/51188258/1.

Harvey, D. (2005). *A brief history of neoliberalism.* Oxford: Oxford University Press.

Kaufman, T. (2013). Set up to fail: Dodd–Frank leaves bank regulators overwhelmed, underfunded. *Forbes*. Retrieved from www.forbes.com/sites/tedkaufman/2013/07/19/set-up-to-fail-dodd-frank-leaves-bank-regulators-overwhelmed-underfunded/.

Keynes, J.M. (1964 [1936]). *The general theory of employment, interest, and money*. New York: Harcourt, Inc.

Keynes, J.M. (1978 [1925]). Am I a liberal? In E. Johnson & D. Moggridge (eds.), *The collected works of John Maynard Keynes* (Vol. 9, pp. 295–306). Saint Andrews: Royal Economic Society.

Krippner, G.R. (2005). The financialization of the American economy. *Socio-Economic Review*, 3, 173–208.

Krugman, P. (2009a). *The conscience of a liberal*. New York: W.W. Norton.

Krugman, P. (2009b, February 12). Failure to rise. *New York Times*. Retrieved from www.nytimes.com/2009/02/13/opinion/13krugman.html?ref=paulkrugman.

Krugman, P. (2009c, January 6). Stimulus arithmetic (wonkish but important). *New York Times*. Retrieved from http://krugman.blogs.nytimes.com/2009/01/06/stimulus-arithmetic-wonkish-but-important/?_php=true&_type=blogs&_r=0.

Krugman, P. (2014, February 20). The stimulus tragedy. *New York Times*. Retrieved from www.nytimes.com/2014/02/21/opinion/krugman-the-stimulus-tragedy.html?_r=0.

Marx, K. (2003). *The class struggles in France* (1850). Chippendale, Australia: Resistance Books.

Mccoy, K. (2013, 12 September). Dodd–Frank Act: after 3 years, a long to-do list. *USA Today*. Retrieved from www.usatoday.com/story/money/business/2013/06/03/dodd-frank-financial-reform-progress/2377603/.

Meacham, J. (2009, February 6). We are all socialists now. *Newsweek*. Retrieved from www.thedailybeast.com/newsweek/2009/02/06/we-are-all-socialists-now.html.

Mishel, L. & Davis, A. (2014, June 12). CEO pay continues to rise as typical workers are paid less. *Economic Policy Institute*. Retrieved from www.epi.org/publication/ceo-pay-continues-to-rise.

Obama, B. (2008, March 27). Renewing the American economy. Campaign speech at Cooper Union. Retrieved from http://usatoday30.usatoday.com/news/mmemmottpdf/obama-econ-speech-3-27-2008.pdf.

Obama, B. (2009a, January 20). Inaugural address. *The American Presidency Project*. Retrieved from www.presidency.ucsb.edu/ws/?pid=44.

Obama, B. (2009b, June 24). Remarks at ABC's "Prescription for America" Town Hall meeting and a question-and-answer session. *The American Presidency Project*. Retrieved from www.presidency.ucsb.edu/ws/?pid=86336.

Office of Management and Budget (2014). Table 7.1 – Federal debt at the end of the year: 1940–2019. Retrieved from www.whitehouse.gov/omb/budget/Historicals.

Office of the New York State Comptroller (2014, March 14). Wall Street bonuses went up in 2013. Press release. Retrieved from www.osc.state.ny.us/press/releases/mar14/031214.htm.

Piketty, T. & Saez, E. (2012). Income inequality in the United States, 1913–1998. *Quarterly Journal of Economics*, *118*(1), 2003. Updated to 2008 at http://emlab.berkeley.edu/users/saez.

Planel, N. (2012). *Obamanomics: Comment Barack Obama a réformé l'Amérique*. Lormont, France: Le Bord de l'Eau.

Randazzo, A. (2009, June 19). The myth of financial deregulation. *Reason Foundation*. Retrieved from http://reason.com/archives/2009/06/19/the-myth-of-financial-deregula.

Reagan, R. (1981). Inaugural address – January 20, 1981. *The American Presidency Project.* Retrieved from www.presidency.ucsb.edu/ws/?pid=43130.

Rivlin, A.M. (2013). Thoughts about monetary and fiscal policy in a post-inflation world. Brookings. Retrieved from www.brookings.edu/research/speeches/2015/03/10-monetary-fiscal-policy-post-inflation-rivlin.

Roosevelt, F.D. (1932, July 2). Address accepting the presidential nomination at the Democratic National Convention in Chicago. *The American Presidency Project.* Retrieved from www.presidency.ucsb.edu/ws/?pid=75174.

Rosenberg, S. (2003). *American economic development since 1945.* New York: Palgrave MacMillan.

Schulman, B.J. (2001). *The seventies: The great shift in American culture, society, and politics.* Cambridge, MA: Da Capo Press.

Schwarcz, S.L. (2009). Understanding the subprime financial crisis. *South Carolina Law Review, 60*, 549–572.

Sexton, P.C. (1992). *The war on labor and the left: Understanding America's unique conservatism.* Boulder, CO: Westview Press.

Shear, M.D. (2008, September 17). McCain embraces regulation after many years of opposition. *Washington Post.* Retrieved from www.washingtonpost.com/wp-dyn/content/article/2008/09/16/AR2008091603732.html.

Sherman, M. (2009). *A short history of financial deregulation in the United States.* Washington, DC: Center for Economic Policy and Research. Retrieved from www.cepr.net/documents/publications/dereg-timeline-2009-07.pdf.

Skidelsky, R. (2008, September 15). Farewell to the neo-classical revolution. *Project Syndicate.* Retrieved from www.project-syndicate.org/commentary/farewell-to-the-neo-classical-revolution.

Smith, A. (1776). *The wealth of nations.* London: Everyman's Library.

Stiglitz, J. (2008, July 7). The end of neo-liberalism? *Project Syndicate.* Retrieved from www.project-syndicate.org/commentary/the-end-of-neo-liberalism-.

Summers, L.H. (2006, November 19). The great liberator. *New York Times.* Retrieved from www.nytimes.com/2006/11/19/opinion/19summers.html.

Unger, I. (1974). *The movement: A history of the American new left, 1959–1972.* Lanham, MD: University Press of America.

Van Elteren, M. (2011). *Labor and the American left: An analytical history.* Jefferson, NC: McFarland.

Volsky, I. (2013, August 30). Jim DeMint: Providing health care for seniors and veterans is "un-American" and grounded in "socialism." *Thinkprogress.* Retrieved from http://thinkprogress.org/health/2013/08/30/2555561/jim-demint-programs-like-medicare-veterans-health-care-American-grounded-socialism.

Wheelock, D.C. (2011). Banking industry consolidation and market structure: Impact of the financial crisis and recession. *Federal Reserve Bank of St. Louis Review, 93*(6), 419–438.

White House (2015), Title I. Quality, Affordable Health Care for All Americans. Retrieved from www.whitehouse.gov/health-care-meeting/proposal/titlei.

Zaretsky, A.M. (1996). Learning the lessons of history: the Federal Reserve and the payments system. *The Regional Economist*, July. Retrieved from www.stlouisfed.org/publications/re/articles/?id=1805.

Zinn, H. (2003). *A people's history of the United States: 1492–present* [1980]. New York: HarperCollins.

4 Consumption, money flows and the crisis of American capitalism

Pierre Arnaud

Much of the discussion about the decline of the United States is based both on the rising clout of China, as observed through its fast-paced growth and growing commercial surplus, as well as on the imbalances of the American economy, best revealed by its deficits: federal deficit, commercial deficit and stockpile of private – household and corporate – debt. The aim of this chapter is to suggest an alternative view, grounded in the editors' and CERVEPAS's multi-factorial and civilizational approach. More specifically, the current situation of the US economy can be interpreted as the result of dynamic interactions between the international role of the dollar and the cultural factors that have shaped America's consumer markets and contemporary revenue distribution. This postulate, which is at the heart of CERVEPAS's work, is grounded in the fundamental perspective that the economy should be re-embedded within its historical, cultural, political and institutional dimensions to be fruitfully analyzed. A similar approach has irrigated the current work of heterodox economists such as Veblen (1899), Polanyi (1944) and Galbraith (1967), but also authors like Boyer (1990) and Orléan (2014). In this perspective, the 2008 crisis and the current imbalances of the US economy can be seen as expressions of an original form of world leadership, rather than the symptoms of its decline.

The first section of this chapter examines how the dual flow of the dollar,[1] international and domestic, revolving around the American consumer, impacts both global imbalances and domestic inequalities, while fueling America's geopolitical leadership. The second section looks at the cultural factors that have historically driven the American brand of debt-driven consumerism. The third section studies how specific consumer and debt dynamics have stimulated the US economy since the end of World War II and how they have interacted with the evolution of inequalities. More precisely, debt is part of the "complex interactions and ever-changing dynamic system of agency, institutions and cultures" which characterize the US political economy in the perspective of the present publication (see Introduction, p. 1). This leads to the conclusion that the US economy has long derived its strength from underlying imbalances. However, these social and economic imbalances have now reached such a level that their effects are no longer positive. But curbing them cannot be done without revising the international function of the dollar, a driving force behind these imbalances.

Much has been written about the international role of the dollar. Our first step here is to look at the general picture of how the US dollar flows out of, and back into, the United States, before moving to the domestic implications of these flows. Figure 4.1 shows that, over time, there is an overall balance: dollars flowing out of the United States through the purchase of goods, services or payment of capital revenues significantly outnumber those flowing in from equivalent US sales to the rest of the world, resulting in a large deficit of the balance of payments (C). However, this deficit is approximately compensated for by the net financial investment (D).

Dollars flowing out through the trade deficit loop back in the form of financial investment, a large chunk of it being treasury bonds (as shown by the gray bars in Figure 4.1).

Not surprisingly, countries running large commercial surpluses are also the main buyers of US federal debt: Japan and China together account for almost half of foreign-held federal debt.

This connects the participants in the flow into an intricate web of shared risks. The United States has become increasingly dependent on foreign savings. At the other end, surplus countries, notably China, are exposed to solvency and exchange risks. As the subprime crisis has clearly showed, capital invested in US debt is not immune to the risk of default or devaluation.

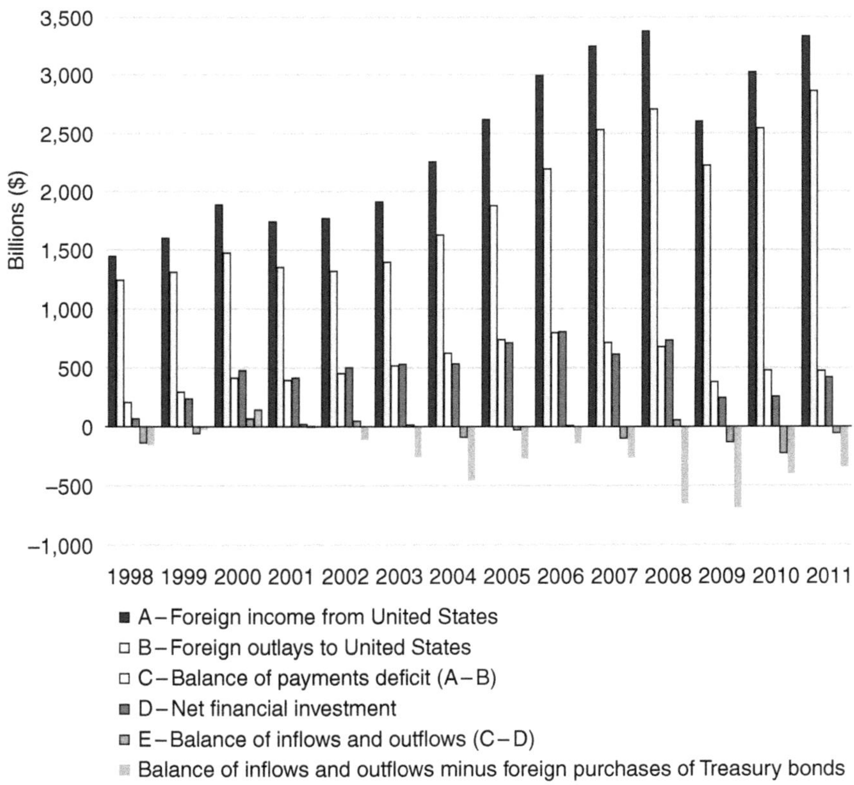

Figure 4.1 US international accounts, $ billion.

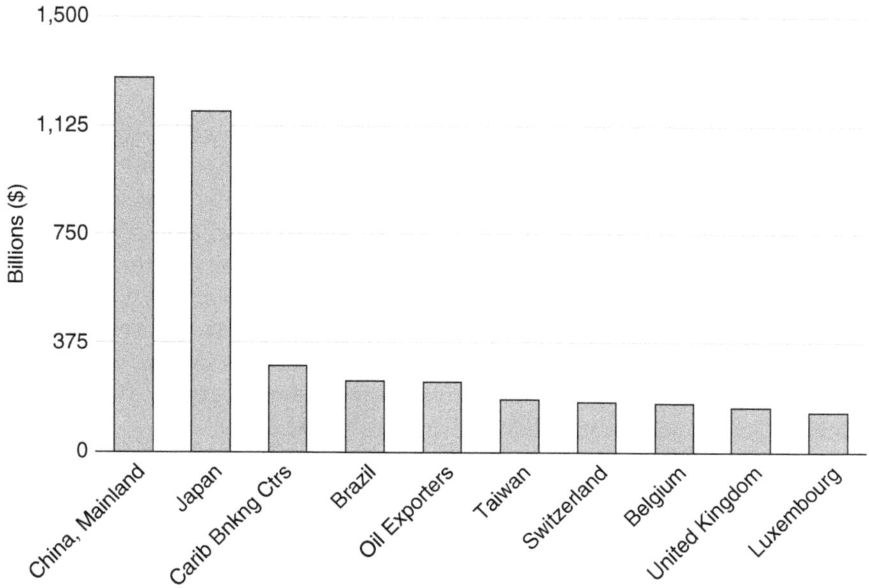

Figure 4.2 Major foreign holders of treasury securities, September 2013, $ billion (source: Department of the Treasury/Federal Reserve Board).

The sustainability of these growing imbalances has been questioned, especially after 2000, in the wake of the internet bubble and the ballooning of the federal deficit, after the surplus years of the Clinton Administration (Obstfeld & Rogoff, 2000; Mann, 2002; Bourguignat, 2003). Yet, in 2009, one year after the onslaught of the subprime crisis, Pierre-Olivier Gourinchas of the University of California, Berkeley, observed that "the dollar crisis that was predicted by the central view is the only one that hasn't happened" (*The Economist*, 2009). If anything, it was the currencies of emerging countries that were under fire as speculation about the end of the Fed's lax policy spread in 2013.

There is no doubt that America's "exorbitant privilege" rests on the willingness of foreign investors to buy US assets in spite of the growing deficit of the US balance of payments. Many reasons have been given for such willingness. In 2005, Ben Bernanke argued that America's low savings rate was a response to the global "savings glut" (*The Economist*, 2009), caused by a variety of factors, including ballooning revenues in oil-producing countries, aggressive export-driven economic policies in Southeast Asia in the wake of the 1997–1998 crisis (Sapir, 2009), undersized financial markets in developing and emerging countries (Forbes, 2008) and the low Yuan policy forcing China to keep its surplus in dollar-denominated securities.

These tensions were reinforced by geopolitical factors. According to Varoufakis (2013), allowing the deficits to grow was a calculated decision by the US administration, insofar as reining them in would have resulted in a reduction of the US geostrategic reach. In a broader historical perspective, Arrighi (2007) argues that in its financialization phase, the United States became a net importer of capital because, contrary to Great Britain that was in a similar situation at the end of the nineteenth century, it could not impose inequitable trade terms upon countries dominated under colonial rule.

Financialization must be understood, in the perspective given by Greta Krippner (2005), as a phase where increasingly accumulation takes place through financial processes rather than other economic activity. In that view, financialization is not characterized by the growth of the financial sector alone. Industrial corporations, for instance, also turn to financial activities and derive an increasing share of the profits from them. During the Reagan Administration restoring US leadership could only be effected at the expense of the balance of payment. The contradiction between a deficit-financed military budget and Volker's anti-inflationary policy led to high interest rates, triggering the initial inflow of foreign capital which would establish the long-term sustainability of America's deficits.

In this perspective, growing imbalances were not a sign of fading dominance, but the price to pay for continued leadership. The trade and public deficits of the 1980s did not just provide for Reagan's military build-up; it also established the country as the consumer of last resort and international provider of attractive financial investments, thus contributing to its soft power.

Domestic implications of the international flow of the dollar

Financialization and inequalities

If the international flow of the dollar can be interpreted as one of the cornerstones of the economic processes through which the United States maintained its geopolitical leadership, it also has profound domestic implications. The outflow of dollars through trade implies that the aggregate value of what is consumed has to be superior to the aggregate value of what is produced. This has to translate into a relative lack of productive investment.

The trend can be evidenced in at least three ways:

1 Net investment has significantly declined since 1980, from a trend average of 5 percent of GDP down to roughly 2.5 percent of GDP in 2010.[2]
2 Corporations have increasingly invested in financial assets rather than in tangible assets. In 1946, non-financial corporations held 22 percent of financial assets against 78 percent of tangible assets. In 2009, financial assets represented slightly more than half of all their assets.[3]
3 In the same period, the ratio of portfolio income to cash flow has dramatically increased for non-financial corporations.

All three observations point to accumulation strategies that are less entrepreneurial and more patrimonial, a tendency that is consistent with Arrighi's financialization thesis. This takes us to the heart of America's growing inequalities.

On the one hand, if net investment decreases, it stands to reason that revenues entirely dependent on such investments are likely to suffer. As corporations invest less in their productive activity and more in financial assets, the amount of money paid in salaries should decline in relative terms. On the other hand, more money allocated to financial assets will increase their value, hence favoring those in a position to hold large amounts of financial assets.

As Picketty and Saez (2003) and Saez (2012) clearly show, there has been a staggering growth of revenue inequalities in the United States since the beginning of the 1980s (see Figure 4.3).

Between 1980 and 2007, the share of total income accruing to the top 10 percent increased from less than 35 percent to nearly 50 percent. In a detailed analysis of Figure 4.3, Picketty (2014) warns that the figures fail to fully reflect the real share collected by the 10 percent richest, as they are based on IRS statements. Capital gains are probably underestimated given the numerous legal and extralegal ways to underreport them. In a context of moderate growth, this means that the 1 percent richest collected 60 percent of the growth, while for the lower 90 percent, growth was in fact limited to a meager 0.5 percent per year. The result is a massive transfer of the US national revenue – about 15 percent – from the bottom 90 percent to the top 10 percent. This is reflected in wealth inequalities.

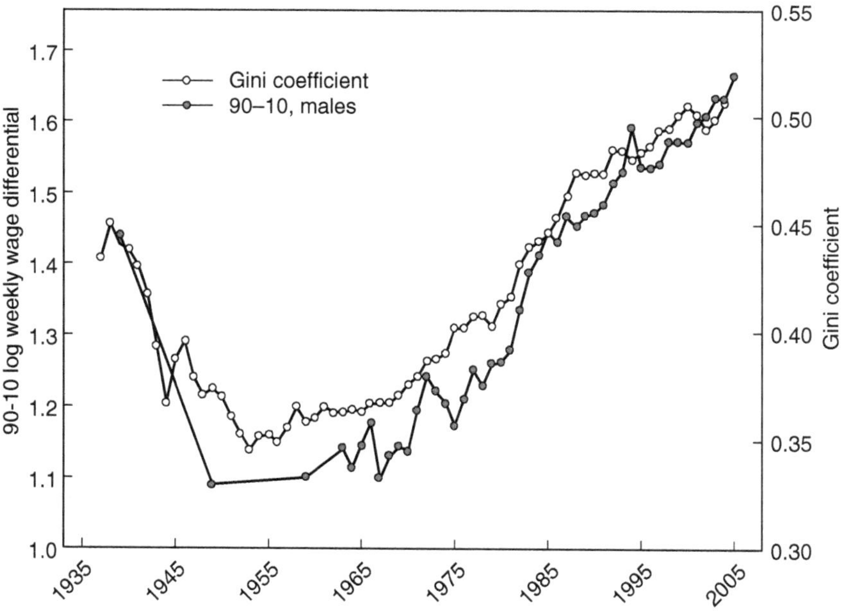

Figure 4.3 Revenue inequalities in the United States (1935–2005) (source: graph reproduced from Goldin & Katz, 2007).

Note

Source of data: annual earnings of male commerce and industry workers for 1937 to 2004 from the Social Security Administration earnings history data constructed and documented by Kopczuk *et al.* (2009), posted at www.columbia.edu/~wk2110/uncovering.

While according to Picketty (2014) the increase of top revenues is mostly due to the advent of "super-salaries" granted to top corporate executives, and only to a lesser extent to capital gains, wealth inequality exceeds revenue inequality. In 2007, the top 10 percent held 72 percent of all wealth (Wolff, 2010). The top 20 percent held 85 percent. Restricting the comparison to non-home wealth (that is, financial wealth in a broad sense) delivered even more staggering inequalities, with the top 10 percent holding 83 percent of all non-home wealth, and the top 20 percent, 93 percent.

Credit: the missing link between consumption and inequalities

To perpetuate its role as both a provider of international liquidities and a consumer of last resort, the United States has to maintain a high level of consumption. But as international liquidities are partially provided through the trade deficit, entailing a relative lack of production and, as a consequence, a relative lack of salaried revenues, both roles in effect conflict, since consumption is underfunded. Assuming an actual decrease of consumption is of course inconsistent with a range of statistical data as showed in Figure 4.4.

It is also hard to argue that the increased consumption of the top 10 percent might compensate for lost consumption in the bottom 90 percent. In fact, Kumhof and Rancière (2010) show that consumption inequality grows much slower than income inequality.

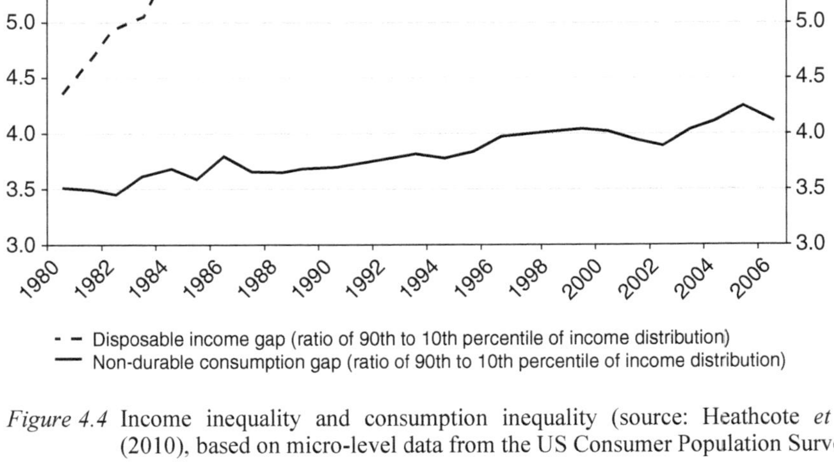

Figure 4.4 Income inequality and consumption inequality (source: Heathcote *et al.* (2010), based on micro-level data from the US Consumer Population Survey).

Of course, it was credit which allowed for a high level of consumption while revenues stagnated for a majority of households. As Figure 4.5 shows, US household debt has dramatically increased since World War II.

There are two phases to that increase, one between 1945 and the mid-1960s, another starting at the beginning of the 1980s. Phase 2 coincides with the deepening of the trade deficit (Figure 4.6).

The link between inequalities and debt is demonstrated by Kumhof and Rancière (2010). As revenues of the poor and middle classes stagnate or decrease, while revenues of the richest increase rapidly, the bottom majority compensates for the relative lack of revenues by borrowing. The rich enjoy not only the gratification of increased consumption, they are also in a position to save significant amounts of money. These savings are partially reinvested in the form of loans to the lower and middle class. In the real world, it is possible to correlate the growth of household debt with the growth of the share of income accruing to the top 5 percent.

Also, growing inequalities generate a political response. In general, the measures taken do not tackle the root causes of inequalities; rather, they aim at reducing borrowing costs for households and financial institutions. These measures, such as further liberalizing the free flow of capital, put downward pressure on the balance of payments. Also, as borrowing rates decrease, the upper class tends to allocate more resources to financial assets than real assets. Initially, this allows the lower and middle classes to consume much more than they would have otherwise, but it also results in long-term underinvestment in real assets (plants, machinery, etc.). That, in turn, further depresses the revenues of the lower and

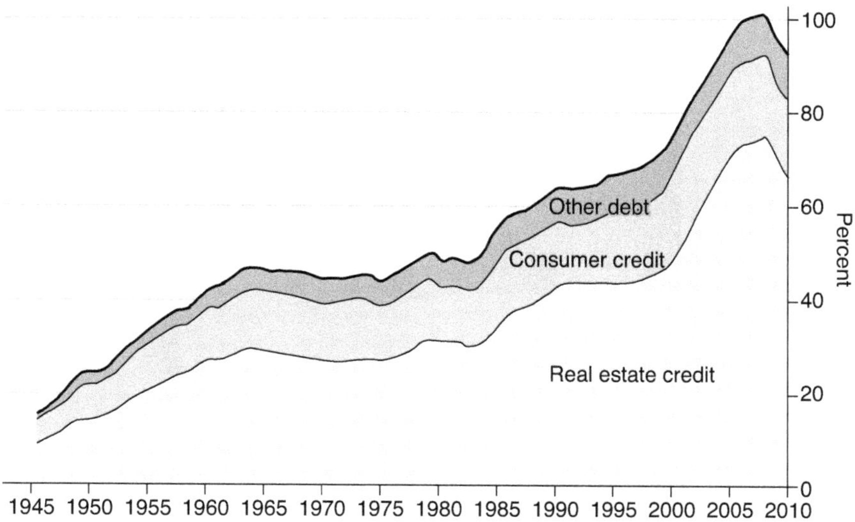

Figure 4.5 Evolution of total US household debt (1945–2010) (percent of GDP) (© Olivier Berruyer, www.les-crises.fr, 2011).

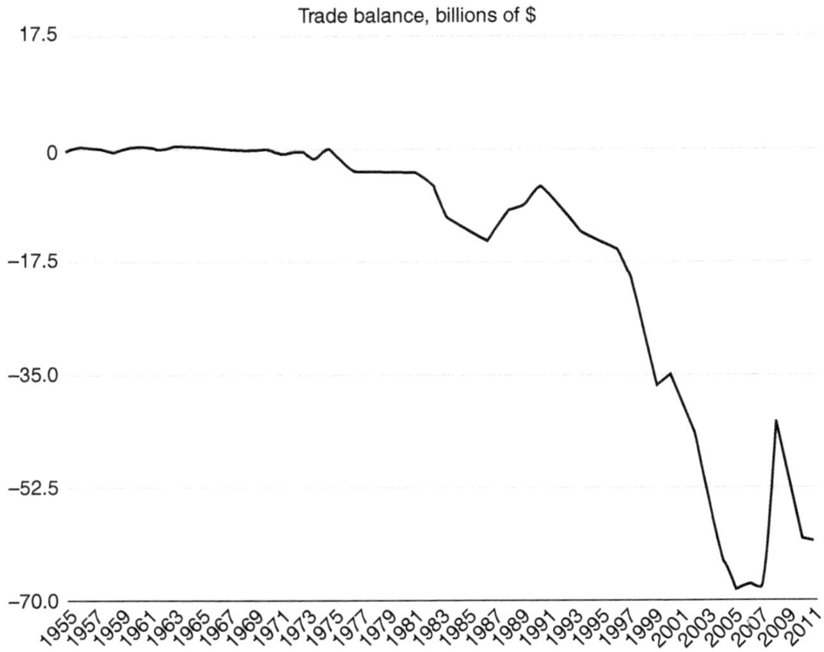

Figure 4.6 US trade deficit (data source: OECD).

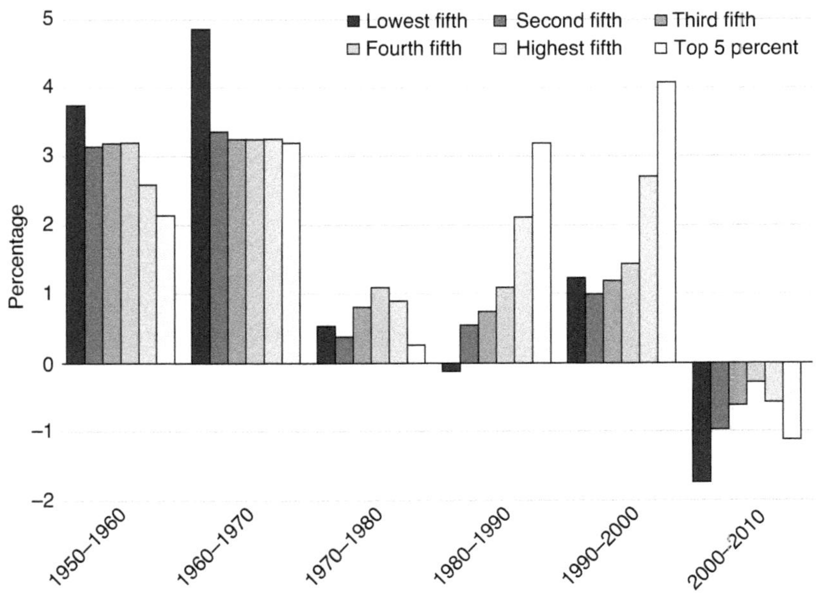

Figure 4.7 Average annual change in mean family income, by quintile and for the top 5 percent (1950–2010).

middle classes. Particularly noteworthy is that this theoretical demonstration is consistent with some of the observations made at the beginning of this chapter, regarding the downward trend of investment.

The dual flow of the dollar and the US consumer

In other words, the general circulation of the dollar can be described as a dual flow, domestic and international, each flow feeding on the other, and both generating worsening imbalances at their respective scales – domestic and international. The pivot of these two flows seems to be the American consumer. This, of course, leads to two obvious questions: why did American consumers maintain a level of consumption higher than that of most other consumers in developed countries? Why did they accept to carry such a high level of debt?

One answer is: because they could. Kumhof and Rancière observe that growing inequalities in China, for instance, did not result in higher household debt and deficit. On the contrary, the surplus increased. This is because financial markets are less developed than in the United States. As the sophisticated financial processes which channeled domestic and international savings to household debt in the United States did not exist in China, growing inequalities resulted in a lack of demand and the need to resort to export-driven growth strategies. This takes us back to the beginning of this analysis: how the geopolitical objectives of the United States translated into political decisions that reshaped the foundations of capital accumulation in the United States – the end of the gold standard, financialization, globalization, free flow of capital and structural deficits, leading to the end of the equalitarian era of the Golden Age.[4]

There is no doubt that the existence of sophisticated intermediation is a defining factor linking inequalities, household debt and the deficit-driven international flow of the dollar. However, we wish to argue that other factors are also at play, notably cultural factors. After all, the American households *could* borrow; they did not *have* to.

The culture of debt

Comparative patterns of debt in the United States and elsewhere

At first glance, it seems that US consumption and household debt patterns no longer differ strongly from that of other developed economies (Figure 4.8).

In fact, in some countries, debt ratios were higher than in the United States in the early 2000s. However, the first difference is that the increase of household debt in these countries is a relatively recent phenomenon (see Figure 4.9), starting at the end of the 1970s, whereas the first phase of US household debt increase begins right after World War II.

In fact, household indebtedness in the United States is a historical trend (Calder, 1999; Durkheim *et al.*, 2014). Twenty-first-century Americans seem thrifty in comparison with their forebears of 1890, when household debt was 186

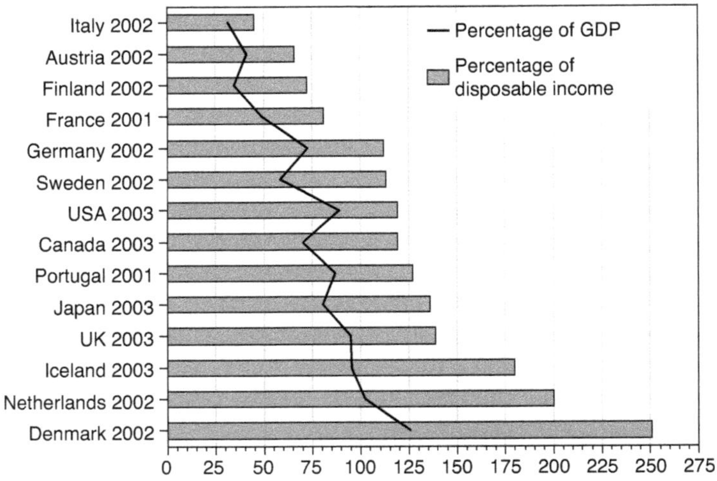

Figure 4.8 Household debt in selected countries (sources: Eurostat, OECD, Central Bank of Iceland).

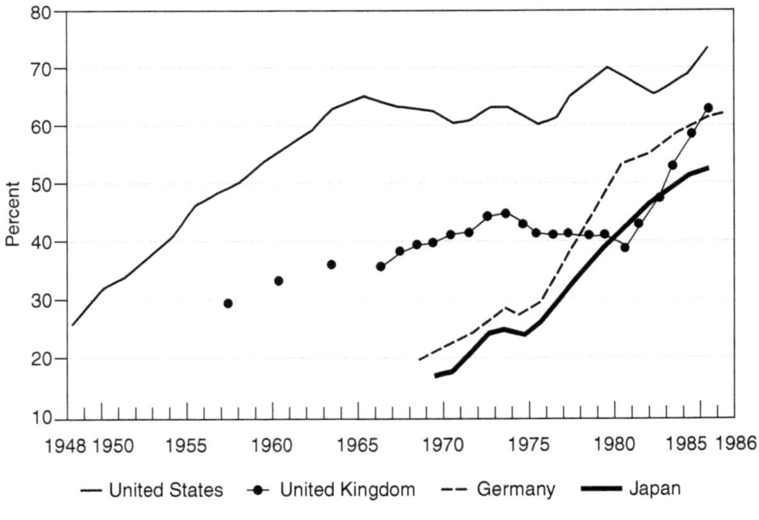

Note: United Kingdom data for three-year intervals for 1957–1966

Sources: United States – United States Department of Commerce (National Income and Product Accounts Tables), Survey of Current Business, Board of Governors of the Federal Reserve System, Flow of Funds Accounts.
United Kingdom – Central Statistical Office, Economic Trends, Financial Statistics, and author's estimates.
Japan – Economic Planning Agency, Annual Report on National Accounts.
Germany – Monthly Report of the Deutsche Bundesbank, Statistisches Bundesamt, Wirtschaft und Statistik, and author's estimates.

Figure 4.9 Household debt as share of disposable income.

percent of GDP (Jorion, 2006, p. 324). As early as 1925, 75 percent of all car purchases were financed with installment plans, as well as 70 percent of furniture, 75 percent of radios, 80 percent of phonographs and 80 percent of appliances (Cross, 2000, p. 29).

Although household debt has generally increased since the 1980s among OECD countries, there are significant differences. In the period leading to the 2008 crisis, debt levels stabilized in Japan, France and Germany, while increasing sharply in the United Kingdom and the United States (Figure 4.10).

However, the similarity between the United Kingdom and United States is superficial, as the increased household debt in the UK did not finance consumption. According to Spencer Dale (2009), some households, reaching retirement age, sold their houses that had become too big for their needs, making handsome profits as real-estate prices were breaking records. They used the extra cash to purchase financial assets in order to secure a steady revenue for their old age. The younger families, purchasing these houses at the top of the market, had to go into heavy debt. In other words, real-estate loans indirectly financed the purchase of financial assets. At the same time, consumption remained in line with the trends of the past 40 years.

On the contrary, in the United States, consumption growth accelerated after 2000 (Figure 4.11), in fact exceeding GDP growth in 2003.

This is particularly remarkable insofar as 2000–2003 was a period of quasi-stagnating GDP and decreasing corporate investment (−4.5 percent in 2000, −7 percent in 2001). Since the 1950s, in all downturn periods, consumption either stagnated or decreased, picking up only after investment and job creation recovered. In other words, in the sluggish context of 2000–2003, consumption ran counter to historical trends. If US consumers had reacted then as they had reacted before, some $125 billion would have been missing from the GDP, amounting to some 2.5 percent of the GDP in nominal terms.

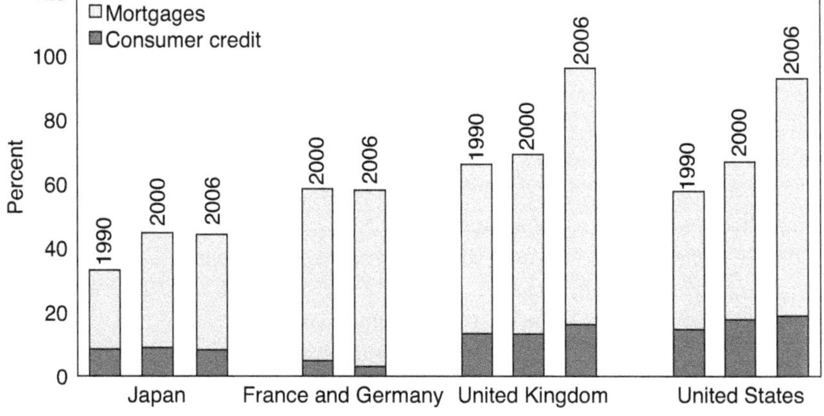

Figure 4.10 Household debt of a percent of GDP (source: BIS Papers n°46, Houshold debt: implications for monetary policy and financial stability, May 2009).

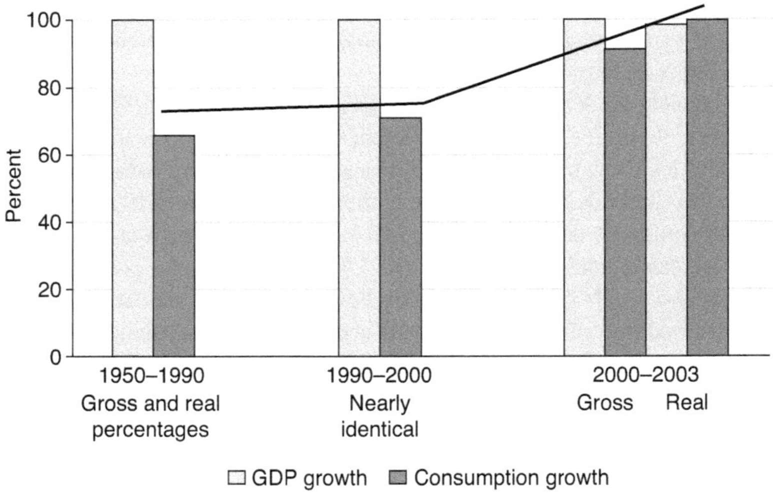

Figure 4.11 Consumption growth and GDP growth (source: US Bureau of Economic Analysis (BEA) National Economic Accounts (3/2004)).

Note
Graph by Marubeni Research Institute (www.marubeni.com/dbps_data/_material_/maruco_en/data/research/pdf/0407.pdf).

One reason for the resilience of US consumption in the years before the crisis is that, in contrast to what happened in Britain, the share of debt going to finance consumption increased. Not only did credit card debt increase by 315 percent between 1989 and 2006 (Ruben, 2009, p. 8), but a significant portion of mortgage loans were diverted to consumption through home equity extraction. As Table 4.1 shows, in a context where consumption was practically the only contributor to growth, home equity extraction had a decisive impact on economic activity. For instance, in 2007, subtracting the contribution of home equity extraction to the economy results in a revised figure for growth of 0 percent instead of the 2.2 percent actually recorded.

Another way to measure the resilience of the US consumption is to look at the evolution of GDP per capita and retail sales after 2000 (Figure 4.12).

Strikingly, retail sales diverge upwards from GDP per capita growth in the years before the subprime crisis. It then decreases faster than GDP per capita, but the pattern of upward divergence is back as early as 2010, at a time when the effects of the crisis were far from having been absorbed.

Finally, in a comparative study including the United States, the Netherlands, Spain and Italy, Crook and Hochguertel (2007, p. 34) show that a much greater proportion of US households apply for credit than in other countries of comparable level of development. This is in spite of the fact that US households' disposable income is on average 50 percent higher than that of European

Table 4.1 Home equity extraction and GDP growth (%)

	Real GDP growth rate	*Home equity extraction percentage of real consumer spending*	*Contribution of home equity extraction to growth in GDP percentage points*	*GDP growth rate recalculated without home equity extraction*	*Growth rate recalculated based on average home equity extraction 1990–1999*	*Growth gains attributable to home equity extraction increase*
2002	1.6	1.6	1.1	0.5	0.80	**0.80**
2003	2.5	1.9	1.3	1.2	1.51	**1.00**
2004	3.6	1.8	1.2	2.4	2.71	**0.93**
2005	3.1	2.4	1.6	1.5	1.74	**1.33**
2006	2.9	3.3	2.2	0.7	0.94	**1.93**
2007	2.2	3.3	2.2	0.0	0.27	**1.93**

Source: US Bureau of Economic Analysis and Fanny Mae data.

Note
From Jacques Sapir, L'économie politique internationale de la crise et la question du "nouveau Bretton Woods": Leçons pour des temps de crise, https://france.attac.org/archives/IMG/pdf/Crise___Bretton_Woods.pdf

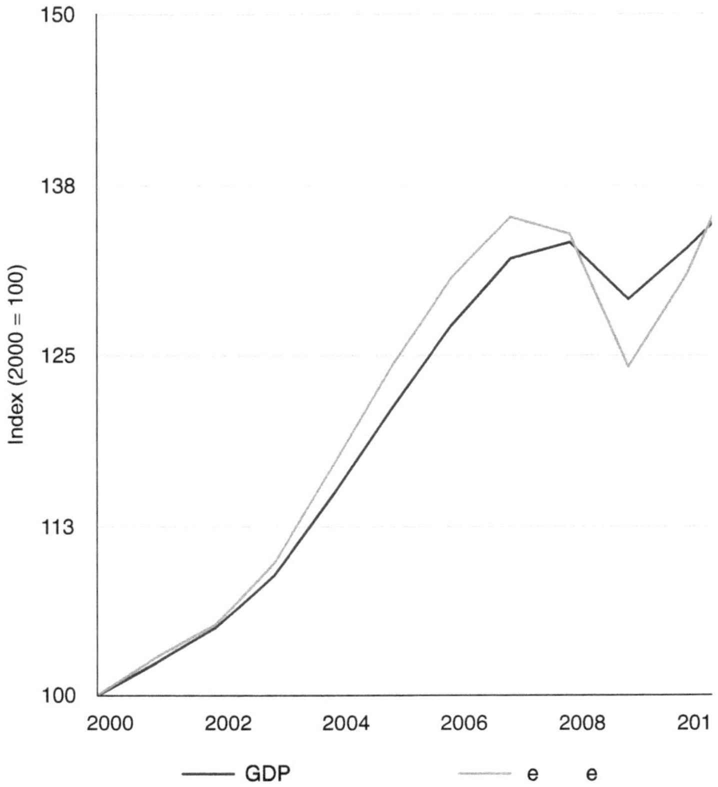

Figure 4.12 GDP per capita and retail sales (source: Census Bureau Annual Retail Trade Survey and World Bank (GDP per capita)).

households. Consequently, final consumption per household in the United States is about twice the average of the European Union.

From the self-made man to the self-made consumer

Without this particular dynamic of debt-driven consumption, there is reason to believe that it would have been much more difficult for the United States to follow the path it took at the end of the 1970s, with both domestic and external debt acting as engines of growth and global leadership.

The extensive tolerance of debt might find roots in history. The large waves of immigration, especially between the mid-nineteenth and early twentieth centuries, brought to the shores of America mostly underprivileged people who were used to living "on the brink of financial catastrophe" (Jorion, 2006, p. 32). Also, in a country populated by a steady inflow of newcomers, the proportion of individuals starting in life with no wealth previously accumulated was high, making debt more of an accepted norm than elsewhere. Paradoxically, the Calvinist foundation of the United States might have reinforced this. An early success, rested on debt, interpreted as evidence of predestination, could push the successful to take on even more risk. Financial risk was taken for business purposes, but also as an act of faith in the American Dream (Jorion, 2006; Calder, 1999). This perception of risk is clearly at work in the myths of the Frontier and of the self-made man. Both the pioneer and the businessman derive their success – and their contribution to the building of the nation – from their bold ability to face risk.

The question, of course, is how such a vision of risk, rooted in an entrepreneurial culture, could spill over to consumer credit, that is, the exposure to financial risk for the sake of personal gratification, something that contradicted founding Calvinist values. This evolution has to do with a shift in the definition of economic virtue. Thrift as a strategy through which to acquire the means to invest now in activities that may produce wealth later implies a fundamental measure of optimism. As the US economy matured, turning the United States into a nation of salaried employees with very little entrepreneurial prospect, the discipline of investment lost ground, and economic virtue was redefined simply as a belief in the good fortune that awaits the righteous, persistent and audacious citizen.

> When twentieth-century American consumers took to indebtedness as a way of life, they followed in the tracks of seventeenth-century colonists, eighteenth-century planters, and nineteenth century farmers and small businessmen. It is often forgotten, but from Plymouth Rock to the present, American dreams have usually required a lien on the future.
>
> (Calder, 1999, p. 27)

What this means is that consumer credit inherited the positive bias of entrepreneurial credit. The same kind of continuity may explain how consumerism could flourish within a cultural context where personal material gratification was essentially seen as sinful. In the nineteenth century, industrialization and the development of railroads produced the emergence of large-scale, nationwide, production. Industrial investment and economies of scale made it much more difficult for would-be entrepreneurs to establish and develop their own small-scale activity. At the same time, the new industrial behemoth developed huge needs for a salaried workforce (Beatty, 2001, pp. 129–140; Rifkin, 1995).

The same evolution was also at work in Europe. But in the United States it produced a profound cultural contradiction. In the nineteenth century, being successful was not limited to achieving a degree of material wellbeing. What mattered more was *how* one became rich: through the development of one's own independent activity. The mythical figure of the businessman did not just define success, it was also a cornerstone of the American identity, as the businessman was revered for his role in the building of the nation and the conquest of the west (Boorstin, 2000).

In the second half of the nineteenth century, a salaried employee could make a decent living. Nevertheless, he experienced a sense of "respectable mediocrity," as explained by Jocelyn Wills (2003) in her analysis of the diaries of an average American between 1876 and 1890. In 1887, Michael J. Boyle was employed by a prestigious store in Saint Paul, Minnesota. He lamented over the meagerness of his $1,500 annual salary, at a time when the average salary, excluding agriculture, was $475. But what he really regretted was "that he had never acquired the arts of economy, industry, and willpower, and the investment acuity necessary for economic independence."

While still floating in the collective consciousness as ideals of social achievement, these arts had essentially become superfluous for the great majority of Americans at the beginning of the twentieth century. Statistically, their chances of moving outside of the realm of salaried employment were minimal. Even worse, some of the qualities celebrated in the myth of the self-made man – initiative, independence – were repudiated under the new Taylorist organization which required that workers strictly applied procedures defined at the higher echelons of the corporate command structure. Even though revenues and purchasing power increased, there was a significant degree of dissatisfaction, causing a noticeable loss of work ethic. According to Rifkin (1995), at the turn of the century, economists remarked that working people were prone to trading work and extra revenue for additional leisure time.

> The fact that people preferred to trade additional hours of work for additional hours of leisure time became a critical concern and a bane to businessmen whose inventories of goods were quickly piling up on factory floors and in warehouses across the nation.
>
> (Rifkin, 1995, p. 19)

To solve this inventory crisis, the industrialists did their best to entice "those still working to buy more and save less. (…) Their crusade to turn American workers into 'mass' consumers became known as the gospel of consumption" (Rifkin, 1995, p. 18).

By itself, such a propaganda effort could not produce a fundamental social change. It did so because it resonated with what Calder (1999) calls a redefinition of the American Dream, from aspiring to the status of the small independent businessman to pursuing a degree of material wealth. In other words, if the real life of the businessman was out of reach, at least the average American could acquire some of the symbols of the happy few. According to Cross (2000, pp. 25–27), the nascent automobile industry exemplifies the emergence of the concept of democratic luxury. In 1900, cars were a rich man's toy, with a price tag some 15 times the mean annual income. In 1908, Ford introduced the Ford T at a price of $950, about two years of mean annual income. In his own words, his goal was to "build a car for the great multitude." In the next 19 years, he sold 15.5 million units of what had previously been the very symbol of the high life.

Consumer and debt dynamics in the United States

The two phases of debt in the post-war era

The reinterpretation of the American dream, from its entrepreneurial premises to debt-based consumerism, is the main cultural factor which contributes to the specific dynamics of America's consumerist economy. Maintaining a sufficient level of consumption, and going into debt for that purpose, is profoundly rooted in the American Dream.

> The puzzle begins with attempts to define [the American Dream]. The term seems to have originated with historian James Truslow Adams, who wrote in 1931 of "that dream of a land of which life should be better and richer and fuller for every man, according to his ability or achievement."
>
> (Calder, 1999, p. 4)

Calder defines the American Dream as being double-natured in essence, combining noble ends such as "freedom, self-fulfillment" and a "better life" with "a particular means to these ends – a house, a yard, a couple of cars – the things sociologist David Riesman termed the 'standard package' of consumer goods and leisure opportunities" (Calder, 1999, p. 4).

What this means is that reducing consumption and debt in order to face changes in the economic circumstances is a more complex process in the United States than elsewhere, as it affects how individuals relate to their sense of citizenship: how they define themselves as Americans. This, in turn, implies that consumption and household debt patterns are more rigid in the United States than elsewhere. This takes us back to Figure 4.5, showing the evolution of debt in the United States since the end of World War II. As already noted, there are two phases in the growth of household debt, an earlier phase of expansion from 1945 to the mid-1960s, then another one starting in the 1980s and culminating before the onset of the subprime crisis. In between, there are some 15 years of relative stability.

The easiest way to account for these two phases is to look at the contextual factors. Phase 1 (1945–1965) takes place during decades of diminishing inequalities and growing revenues for a majority of households. Phase 2 (1980–) is characterized by stagnating revenues, growing inequalities and, more generally speaking, the dual cycle of domestic and international accumulation of imbalances.

Different levels and dynamics of inequalities should affect the social role of consumption. The best conceptual tool to analyze this is the model of mimetic consumption established by Orléan (2014) in his criticism of neoclassical economics and, more precisely, of Walras' model and methodological individualism. Orléan challenges the independence of economic agents that is at the center of Walras' model, suggesting rather that consumption is a social dynamic operating along the following lines: not knowing what they really want, consumers turn to others in order to determine what is desirable. Their desire for specific goods is mediated by the example of other consumers' choices.

There are, thus, two sorts of mediation: internal and external. In the case of external mediation, individuals imitate an exogenous model. This is the pattern envisaged by Veblen (1899): each social class tends to imitate the behavior of the social class positioned one step higher in the social hierarchy. There is a degree of stability in this system, as the consuming patterns and desires are regulated by a unanimously accepted model.

But what happens if no clear exogenous model emerges to channel the preferences of the group? Each agent is left with no explicit consumption model to imitate. Individuals face their own lack of certainty regarding what should be considered as desirable. They turn to the other members of the group and scrutinize their consumption habits in an attempt to determine the "correct" consumption model. In that case, the mimetic model is endogenous, mediation is internal. This unleashes a chain of positive feedback. The behavior of individual A influences the behavior of B, which in turn influences the behavior of A. Such a system is unstable, prone to self-reinforcing excesses.

External mediation and national identity in the United States

According to Veblen, because the consumer looks up to the higher class for a model, a general agreement emerges about what should be considered as the proper signs of prestige, success and wealth. This agreement stabilizes the patterns of consumer behavior within the social group.

Of course, such external mediation works because there is a prior consensus over the identity of the higher class which should be emulated. In other words, there is a clear understanding of the social hierarchy and of the relative positions within it. The question is therefore how such external mediation can operate in the United States, a society which pictures itself as classless.[5] The historical origin of consumerism in the United States, as described above, suggests that the exogenous model of consumption is based on the mythical figure of the businessman. As consumerism became a substitute for a model of social achievement that is no longer within reach of the vast majority, American consumers bought what they believed were the symbols of a successful businessman's lifestyle. As Rifkin (1995, p. 20) puts it: "The common man and woman were invited to emulate the rich, to take on the trappings of wealth and prosperity previously reserved for the business aristocracy and social elite."

There are two important implications for this particular mimetic model. First, contrary to Veblen's description, the model has no objective reality. Consumers do not relate to an existing class of individuals; they imitate what they believe are the consuming habits of the mythical businessman. This belief is shaped by a range of factors including social interaction, advertising and marketing, media content, etc. In other words, the model does not emerge from a concrete, observable example. It emerges as a social norm or an archetype. This means that this mimetic, exogenous model is more fragile than elsewhere. It may be subjected to swift changes as collective representations change. It may become so elusive that external mediation will be replaced by internal mediation, if for some reason there is a lack of consensus over what the social norm of consumption should be, leading to the positive feedback pattern which Orléan (2014) calls "the model of mimetic competition."

The second implication is that the stakes of social recognition through consumption are particularly high in the United States. Consuming is not just the acquisition of additional material comfort or status, it is also, to some extent, participating in the American Dream. In other words, maintaining the appropriate consumption pattern also expresses the willingness of the consumer to be part of the nation. Reflecting on the negative consequences of debt-driven consumerism, Sullivan *et al.* (2000, p. 19) say that "to hint at economic vulnerability seems at best naive, perhaps unpatriotic."

Consumption, equality and public interest

These specificities of the mimetic model of consumption in the United States help us understand why the evolution of household debt has been correlated with changes in inequalities since World War II. Phase 1 of household debt growth (from 20 percent to 50 percent of GDP) expands from the end of the war to the mid-1960s, in a context of rapidly decreasing inequalities and expanding revenues. Growing household debt in such conditions may seem paradoxical. In fact, it actually contributed to the prosperity of the Golden Age.

In the two decades following the war, suburbanization was encouraged both as a response to the housing crunch and as a strategy of economic stimulation. Measures taken for that purpose included the development of the infrastructures connecting suburban neighborhoods with the inner cities, as well as the implementation of public policies facilitating and guaranteeing mortgage loans (Cohen, 2004). The ensuing housing boom did not stimulate the economy only through the profits and through the jobs generated by the housing industry. Newly acquired homes also meant new consumption needs, as these dwellings, generally larger than those that families had left behind in the inner cities, had to be furnished and equipped. Furthermore, longer distances between home and the workplace stimulated the car industry. It is not surprising, then, that consumer credit grew in parallel with the growth of mortgage credit.

In addition to the concrete effects of suburbanization, consumption was encouraged as a means to facilitate the conversion of the US industry from wartime to peacetime production. Fear that with the end of the war effort the economy would fall back into the depression of the 1930s justified the recourse to a new measure of national mobilization. In a country still marked by the trauma of the Great Depression, combining the materialistic appeal of consumption with patriotism could only succeed. What was in effect promoted was the virtuous circle of consumption, production, jobs and salaries, leading to more affluence, more consumption and more jobs, elevated to the dignity of a patriotic duty. According to Cohen (2004, p. 236), this propaganda was upheld not only by business circles, marketers and advertisers, insofar as union leaders, government agencies, etc., also participated in the spreading of the good word, that "mass consumption was not self-indulgence. Rather, it was a civic responsibility designed to improve the living standards of all Americans."

Hence consumption was not just a matter of personal gratification. It was also a question of public good. Consumption stimulated the economy and made the country and its citizens richer. But as the Cold War unfolded, consumption was also promoted as a process that brought the social benefits of improved equality: "politicians never tired of tying America's political and economic superiority over the Soviet Union to its more democratic distribution of goods" (Cohen, 2004, p. 237).

Consumption was thus at the core of a societal project promoting equality and affluence. Mass consumption, especially in an era of highly standardized production, equalized the lifestyles across the social pyramid, and reinforced the effects of homogeneous suburban housing. Also, economic growth was deemed to foster a form of equality which was all the more desirable as it did not have to rely on redistribution.

> It promised a socially progressive end of social equality without requiring politically progressive means of redistributing existing wealth (...) an ever-growing economy built around the twin dynamics of increased productivity and mass purchasing power would expand the overall pie without reducing the size of any of the portions.
>
> (Cohen, 2004, p. 237).

The idea that economic growth could put an end to the tortuous question of sharing was not a novelty. It was at the core of Taylor's utopian view of how the scientific management of work could foster an ideal society, where:

> Under scientific management (...) both sides take their eyes off the division of the surplus as the all-important matter, and together turn their attention toward increasing the size of the surplus until this surplus becomes so large that it is unnecessary to quarrel over how it shall be divided.
>
> (Boorstin, 2000, p. 364)

Just before the 1929 crisis, the Committee on Recent Economic Changes for the Hoover Administration based its optimistic conclusion on the principle of a boundless economy:

> The survey has proved conclusively what has long been held theoretically to be true, that wants are insatiable; that one want satisfied makes way for another. The conclusion is that economically we have a boundless field before us.
>
> (Rifkin, 1995, p. 23)

The idea that the economy can grow without limit is rooted in the historical conditions of early economic development in the United States: a phase that combined the revolutionary productive dynamics of industrialization with the opportunities given by a territory the size of a continent. That shaped an original vision of the economy as an open, limitless field, as opposed to the zero-sum game vision more prevalent in Europe (Arnaud, 2015).

Calling on this vision in the post-war era resonated with the core beliefs of American culture. It also reactivated the stimulative effect of this belief about indebtedness. In a limitless, ever-growing economy, the chances are high that most individuals will see their economic fate improve, thus mitigating, in the future, the debt burden taken in the present. In this context it is rational to accept a level of debt that might challenge one's current reimbursement capacity, since such risk-taking is merely an anticipation of higher future revenue.

All of these dynamic factors were at play in the cycle of growth and debt-driven consumerism of the Golden Age. But there is also a fundamental moderating factor: the relative equalitarianism, which materializes in at least three forms: diminishing revenue disparities, policies aimed at lifting the underprivileged out of poverty and the institutionalization of consumption as a matter of public interest. In this context, unsurprisingly, a consensus has emerged over what the exogenous model of consumption should be. In other words, there is, by and large, an agreement on the embodiment of the American Dream, in the form of a relatively well-defined model of suburban life, moderate affluence and personal homeownership. This model channels consumption behavior and reins in the risk of mimetic competition. It is also a model that is relatively close to a majority of households – that is, within their financial reach, all the more so as diminishing inequalities tend to reduce economic disparities. From a population with converging revenues, a social norm emerges, defining what the "correct" ideal lifestyle and model of consumption should be.

This may help us understand why household debt growth stabilized after 1963. There are several concrete factors which may explain this phenomenon, all linked to the crisis of the 1970s: inflation, increasing interest rates, the oil shock of 1973 and the end of Bretton Woods. A climate of growing uncertainty is not conducive to risk-taking. However, the flattening of the debt curve starting in 1963 predates all of these events. Strictly from a chronological point of view, it seems that the weakening of household debt dynamics should be regarded as a contributing factor of the crisis rather than a consequence of it.

One assumption here is that the flattening of the debt curve signals the maturing of the exogenous consumption model of the post-war era. This process may take place in several ways. (1) As more and more people achieve the American Dream in its post-war embodiment, the number of new entrants diminishes. (2) Those homeowners now experiencing the material comfort of the suburban lifestyle have little incentive to go much beyond that model. Ostentatious consumption is moderated by a common representation of wealth. This is precisely the stabilizing effect of the exogenous mimetic model.

Consumption and inequalities: the pivot of the 1980s

In this perspective, the leveling off of debt growth can be seen as both a cause and a symptom of the loss of dynamics of the post-war regulation system. And in the same way, its renewed ascent in the 1980s signals a new dynamic resulting from a new regulation system, or rather it shows the effect of the sociocultural changes that combine with the neoliberal regulation system. The defining social difference between the Fordist era and the neoliberal era is the evolution of inequalities: diminishing during the Fordist era, growing in the neoliberal era (Figure 4.3).

It would take too much space to examine in detail the multiple causes of this change, the result of complex interactions between economic, political and sociocultural factors, including deregulation, globalization, new tax policies, changes in employee compensation schemes within companies, etc. Rosanvallon (2013) describes one profound sociocultural shift in the perception of individualism, which loses its universalist roots of the nineteenth century and is replaced by a more radical, dichotomous form, which Rosanvallon calls "singularity individualism."

In this new form of individualism, society is no longer seen as a structure that, through appropriate rules and institutions, guarantees individual rights. Rather, there is a claim for a fully personal life possibly breaking away from common norms. The perception of a community of destiny is weakened, as individuals define themselves less as members of a given social group than in terms of their own personal history and prospects. The effects of this change are far-reaching. They include the retreat of many from collective political activism, thus facilitating the shift in the labor–capital power balance of the 1980s, or the acceptance of strictly individualized systems of human resource management, as opposed to the collective arrangements typical of the Golden Age.

In the consumer market, this change is both reflected and amplified by new production techniques and marketing strategies that allow for a far more segmented approach than that of the Fordist production model. It is not hard to understand how all these factors combine to adversely impact a consensual definition of the American Dream in its consumerist, materialistic form. In other words, its function as a stabilizer of consumption patterns is weakened. This gives more amplitude to endogenous mimetic dynamics, as the exogenous mimetic model weighs less in the overall consumer behavior patterns. The runaway household debt increase starting in the 1980s can be correlated with this shift.

Obviously, the primary reason for the debt increase is the stagnation of revenues and the loose monetary policies since the 1990s, along with the redefinition of housing as a financial asset rather than an expense (Théret, 2011). But the question remains as to why American households did not choose the alternative to debt that is to reduce their spending. Warren and Tyagi (2005) criticize the over-consumption thesis, arguing rather that households' main increases in expenses were in mortgage costs, health insurance and tax burden, while what they spent in clothing, food and appliances decreased relative to the generation of the 1970s.

However, their explanation of why mortgage costs increased, especially for families with kids – more competition for neighborhoods providing good school opportunities – is a good example of how price increases produce increased demand with positive feedback acceleration, a phenomenon Orléan links with mimetic competition. Similarly, Warren and Tyagi (2005) justify higher car budgets as a consequence of the purchase of larger, safer vehicles.

> After all, a family doesn't need a new SUV with a CD player, at least not in the same way that it needs decent day care or a home in a safe neighborhood. But we pause here to offer a bit of sympathy for the much-maligned buyer of the family car. The car industry's song has changed pitch over the past generation. Glance at an advertisement from any maker of family cars, and there you'll see the new message: safety for sale.
>
> (Warren & Tyagi, 2005)

But shouldn't we look at the safety argument as an after-the-fact justification for what seems to be a typical example of mimetic competition, especially considering that the commendable drive for increased safety has not caused the same kind of vehicle-size inflation in other countries? As Warren and Tyagi themselves recognize,

> A generation ago, the typical family owed about five percent of its annual income in consumer debt – non-mortgage debt such as car loans and credit cards. Today such debt adds up to more than a third of total annual income.

This should be correlated with the fact that, as noted above, a significant portion of mortgage loans was diverted to consumption through home equity extraction; a clear indication that mortgage costs are not the only issue. Finally, another indicator that somewhat weakens Warren and Tyagi's argument is that retail sales increased faster than GDP (Table 4.2).

In the end, between Warren and Tyagi's thesis that American households were strained by the increase of basic expenses and the argument of overspending, the

Table 4.2 Comparison of GDP per capita, retail sales and final consumption (1992–2007)

$ current	*GDP/capita*	*Retail sales*	*Final consumption ($ millions)*
1992	24,527	1,815,716	4,236,900
2007	46,627	4,005,798	9,806,300
coeff.	1.9	2.21	2.31

Source: US Census Bureau and Annual Retail Trade Survey.

contradiction is superficial and essentially caused by a moralist approach that fails to take into account the social dynamics of consumption. The explanation suggested here is that spending more to enter better neighborhoods and spending more to achieve a level of consumption in line with what one believes is the "correct" material status, is equally important in maintaining a given social standing. In other words, starting in the 1980s, as revenues stagnated and endogenous mimetic competition increased the stakes, American households had no other choice than to overspend both for their basic needs and superfluous consumption. The alternative was to regress in the social pyramid. Reducing consumption in order to face other increasing expenses was sociologically impossible. Household debt was the logical recourse in order to solve this contradiction.

Inequalities and declining dynamism

If debt-driven consumerism is at the heart of the domestic and international flow of the dollar, inequalities should be considered as the potential difference driving the flow, much like in an electrical circuit. There is a general understanding that inequalities are better accepted in the United States than elsewhere. But the phenomena that have been described above would rather appear to indicate that they can trigger destabilizing dynamics of a particularly wide scope. Furthermore, several studies tend to show that Americans would prefer to live in a more equalitarian society. Norton and Ariely (2011) show that when asked about their preferences, Americans favor a fairly equalitarian model of wealth distribution, close to the Swedish pattern. The same study also shows that Americans dramatically underestimate the actual level of wealth inequalities in the United States, placing it in between the real level and their ideal model (Figure 4.13).

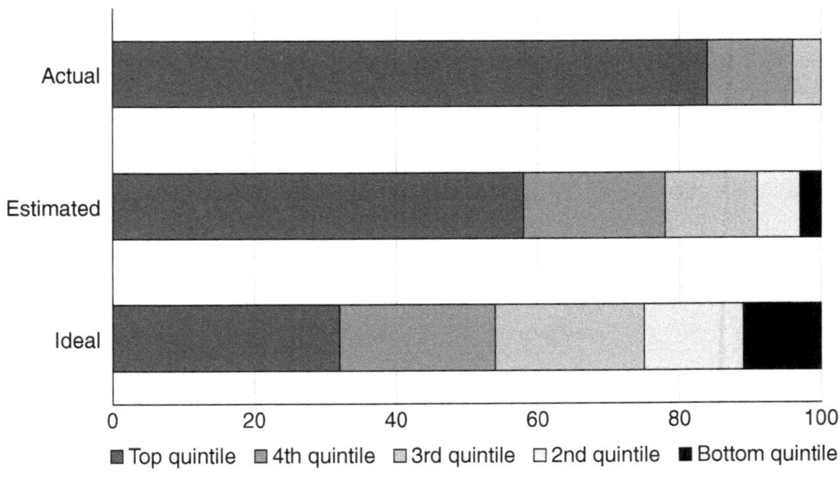

Figure 4.13 Distribution of wealth (source: Norton & Ariely, 2011).

Intriguingly, no explanation is given for this illusion. Why should Americans underestimate the real level of inequalities? One commonly accepted argument is that Americans have a dynamic perception of inequalities (Mistral, 2009). An initially high level of inequalities is acceptable as the nation's flexible social structure and dynamic economy provide relatively equal opportunities for social ascent. However, there are numerous indications that social mobility has fallen. Upward as well as downward mobility were at their highest after the war (Figure 4.14), but decreased rapidly before 1960 (Kopczuk *et al.*, 2007).

Also, intergenerational mobility seems to be comparatively low, much lower than in Nordic European countries, for instance (Winship, 2011). Forty-two percent of sons from households in the bottom quintile remained in the bottom quintile as adults. The percentage ranged between 23 and 30 for other countries in the same study.

What this might indicate is that increasing revenue inequalities fuel wealth inequalities, which in turn provide disproportionate advantages to those in the higher ranks of the social pyramid, to the point of crippling the dynamics of social mobility. This is particularly problematic for at least two reasons. (1) The phenomenon feeds on itself: wealth is reinvested, thus producing new streams of revenues, while debt taken by those experiencing revenue stagnation produces the opposite. (2) The reduction of social mobility endangers some of the most fundamental American beliefs which both underlie social stability and fuel US economic dynamism. According to a Pew Research Center study, 63 percent of Americans agreed that "most people who want to get ahead can make it if they

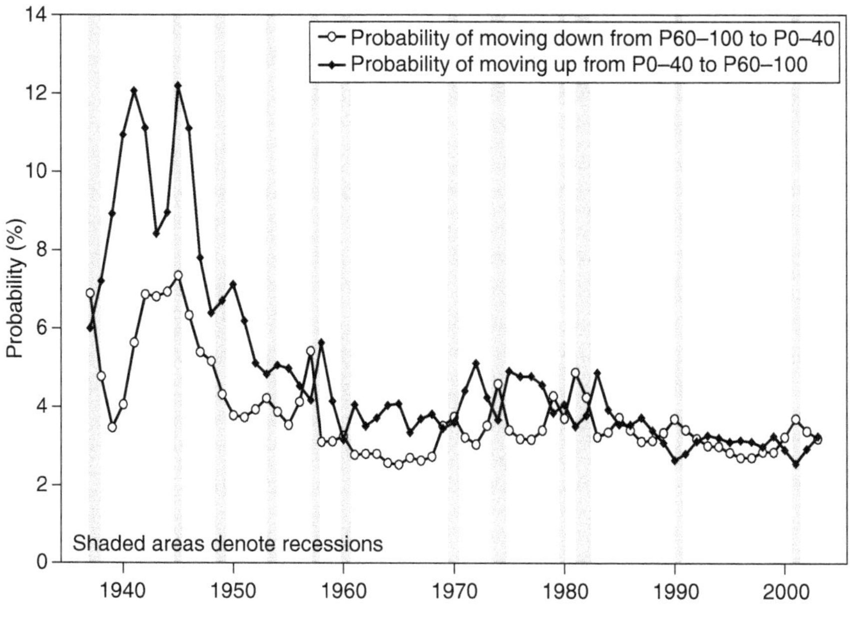

Figure 4.14 Downward and upward mobility (source: Kopczuk *et al.*, 2007).

are willing to work hard" in 2011, down from 74 percent in the late 1990s (Pew Research Center, 2012).

Another mobility which resonates with the American Dream also seems to be impaired: geographic mobility has been diminishing since 1980. The reasons for this decrease are unclear. Research so far can only produce hypotheses, including: multi-decade adjustments have finally come to an end; technological progress has made telecommuting easier, reducing the need for geographic mobility; locations have become less specialized in the types of goods and services produced; the availability of amenities has also become more homogeneous, reducing incentives to move (Molloy *et al.*, 2011). In comparison, intra-state mobility is flat, or has increased slightly in Europe, while remaining generally lower than interstate mobility in the United States. However, mobility between European countries increased in the 2000s.

Along with decreasing mobility, it seems that the reasons why some Americans wish to move are no longer related to the search for new economic opportunities. Over the first decade of the twenty-first century, half of the moves are related to housing (51 percent in 1998/1999, 47 percent in 2008/2009). Employment-related reasons represent only 17 percent in 2008/2009 (16 percent in 1998/1999). Among the housing-related reasons, looking for a cheaper house is sharply on the rise (from 6.2 percent to 11.4). On the other hand, moving related to a new job or job transfer drops from 9.2 percent (1998/1999) to 8.2 percent (2008/2009). Over the same period, moving to live closer to job location is up from 3.2 percent to 5.2 percent (Ihrke *et al.*, 2011).

These changes in the patterns of social and geographic mobility clearly contradict the American dream and consequently affect the social and cultural fabric of the United States. The dynamic nature of the American Dream has both justified and alleviated the existence of high initial inequalities. However, it may be assumed that inequalities have reached a level that now actually impairs the very dynamics that made them acceptable.

Another reason which may have caused Americans to disregard the true level of inequalities is easy credit. Households borrowed more and more in order to keep up with what they felt was the appropriate level of consumption. Mimetic competition and debt-driven consumerism increased financial imbalances, but at the same time produced the semblance of relatively homogeneous living standards. The difference between those who could keep up and those who were falling behind could not be made out from consumption patterns; it was in effect hidden within the intimacy of family accounts. It was the level of financial burden and risk taken by households that in effect materialized the growing inequalities. Debt-driven consumerism acted as a veil until it was torn by the subprime crisis. Personal bankruptcies and foreclosures revealed the extent of financial distress related to inequalities.

Conclusion

The vitality of the US economy has historically been fueled by a dynamic of imbalances: household debt, financial market excesses, and Schumpeterian shocks.

Speculation and overinvestment presided over the development of the railroad system at the end of the nineteenth century, as they did in the 1990s over the advent of the internet industry. The excesses of inequalities and indebtedness of the 2000s are reminiscent of those of the 1920s.

The ability of US society to sustain such sharp imbalances has played an important role – along with other more concrete factors such as the sheer size of the country, the amount of natural resources and a positive demography – in the ascent of the United States to its status of global economic leader. But this ongoing state of dynamic disequilibrium would not have been possible without a degree of acceptance on the part of the general public that is a consensus giving preference to risk-taking against security, a wider scope of opportunities against stability. This consensus is fueled by a number of sociocultural factors: a vision of the economy as an unlimited field offering unlimited individual opportunities; financial markets conceived as a dematerialized transposition of the Frontier, where the bold and the adventurous can risk it all and win big; the myth of the debt-driven entrepreneur reenacted as the debt-ridden consumer, flaunting the material symbols of the wealthy.

If structural imbalances historically mark the upward course of the US economy, should the current state of imbalance be a cause for concern? After all, isn't it just business as usual?

There are two objections to this reassuring perspective. First, it can be argued that beyond a certain threshold, imbalances lose their dynamic qualities and become highly destructive. This already happened once, in 1929. In some areas, the imbalances of the late 2000s bear disturbing similarities to those of the late 1920s, especially regarding social inequalities and the overextension of financial markets. Second, the imbalances of the 2000s are intertwined with monetary issues more than ever before. In many ways, the dual circulation of the dollar, as described in this chapter, propelled by national and international savings imbalances, is the monetary expression of this dynamics of imbalances.

What this implies is that, through the international role of the dollar, US imbalances are spreading to other countries where sociocultural tolerance to instability may be much lower. This causes an external risk that could very well boomerang back into the United States, using the same monetary channels. In that way too, US domestic imbalances have become a global issue. For example, the international flow of the dollar rests to some extent on rising inequalities in the US, as we have seen. Exporting countries are, however, also subject to the same phenomenon.

To maintain a strong positive balance, they have to keep salaries relatively low, in order to improve their competitiveness and moderate, in relative terms, the consumption of imported goods. Such moderation evidently weighs mostly on lower and middle incomes, hence increasing the differential between upper and lower revenues. In the past ten years, inequalities have increased both in Germany and China. The main difference with the United States is twofold: (1) these countries may not have the same sociocultural tolerance of sharp inequalities;[6] (2) they do not benefit from the phenomenon of debt-driven consumption which has veiled inequalities in the United States, making them more tolerable.

The events since 2008, in the United States and outside, seem to demonstrate that the imbalances which both feed and are stimulated by the dual flow of the dollar have reached a threshold beyond which their stimulative qualities no longer operate. Greater socioeconomic stability is needed and can only be achieved through progress in equality in the United States. This means reducing the revenue extremes, but also redefining the American Dream, establishing a representation of material success that is more homogeneous, more accessible, more equalitarian, in line – while not identical – with the model which successfully channeled consuming habits during the Golden Age. In the end, contrary to common wisdom, inequalities can be more disruptive in the United States than elsewhere, as the nation is broadly defined on the foundation of the economic prospects it opens to its citizens (Stiglitz, 2013).

But a return to greater relative equalitarian stability is hardly possible without revising the international role of the dollar. As long as the rest of the world uses the dollar as the reserve and exchange currency, the international flow of the dollar has to grow in line with the international needs of a growing global economy. As one of the mechanisms producing this flow, the trade deficit must continue, stimulating the growth of domestic imbalances and inequalities. In that sense, the international role of the dollar, once an exorbitant privilege, may by now have become an exorbitant duty, as the weight of the US economy in the world decreases in relative terms. It does serve the geopolitical objectives of the country, but it is also eating into its social, political and economic fabric.

Notes

1 The flow of the dollar can be seen as a full-circle process, in which dollars acquired by exporting countries through the sale of goods and services flow back into the United States as exporting countries buy US debt. The reason for this is twofold: (1) exporting countries need to keep dollar reserves – still the de facto international currency – for their foreign trade needs; (2) holding dollar-denominated securities rather than exchanging excess dollars into their local currency avoids pressure on foreign exchange markets that would cause less favorable exchange rates for exporting countries. Similarly, domestic inequalities cause a flow of debt and dollars between those enjoying excess savings and those compensating stagnant revenues with borrowing. Hence the term "dual flow."

2 Source: BEA – NIPA tables 5.1 & 1.1.5.

3 Source: FRB FFA B. 102 (non-financial corporation assets).

4 "Golden Age" here is taken from Giraud (1996), to characterize a period encompassing the post-war decades up to the crisis of the 1970, during which dynamic growth was fueled by technological progress, rapid productivity gains and consistent government intervention aiming at redistribution and full employment, in part due to the rapid development of services while agriculture and industry shed jobs through strong productivity gains. This period is often referred to as the "Fordist era," but the concept tends to overstate the technological factors against other elements, belonging to the sociopolitical realm, for instance.

5 This is not to say that in reality US society is devoid of classes, but what matters in the dynamics of a mimetic model is belief rather than objective reality.

6 Evidence of this can be seen in the numerous instances of protest in China, and the debate over a minimum salary in Germany in the wake of the 2013 election.

References

Arnaud, Pierre. (2015). La croissance sans limite: un paradigme américain proche de sa fin? In *Revue LISA, 13*(2). Retrieved from http://lisa.revues.org/8444.

Arrighi, G.. (2007). *Adam Smith in Beijing*. London: Verso.

Beatty, J. (2001). A riot of individualistic materialism. In Beatty, J. (ed.), *Colossus: How the corporation changed America*. New York: Broadway Books.

Boorstin, D. (2000). *The national experience*. London: Phoenix Press Paperback.

Bourguignat, H. (2003). Le retour des déficits jumeaux américains et le partage de l'épargne mondiale. In *Revue d'économie politique, 113*(4), 419–430.

Boyer, R. (1990). *The régulation school: A critical introduction*. New York: Columbia University Press.

Calder, L. (1999). *Financing the American dream: A cultural history of consumer credit*. Princeton, NJ: Princeton University Press.

Cohen, L. (2004). A consumers' republic: The politics of mass consumption in postwar America. *Journal of Consumer Research, 31*(1), 236–239.

Crook, J. & Hochguertel, S. (2007). US and European household debt and credit constraints. Tinburgen Institute. Retrieved from http://papers.ssrn.com/sol3/papers.cfm?abstract_id=1036002.

Cross, G. (2000). *An all-consuming century: Why commercialism won in modern America*. New York: Columbia University Press.

Dale, S. (2009). Separating facts from fiction: Household balance sheets and the economic outlook. Transcript of a speech given by Spencer Dale, Director and Chief Economist at the Bank of England Bank of England, September 24. Retrieved from www.bankofengland.co.uk/publications/news/2009/071.htm.

Durkin, T., Elliehausen, G., Staten, M.E. & Zywicki, T.J. (2014). *Consumer credit and the American economy*. New York: Oxford University Press.

Economist, The. (2009). When a flow becomes a flood. Retrieved from www.economist.com/node/12972083.

Forbes, K. (2008). Why do foreigners invest in the United States? NBER Working Paper Series, National Bureau of Economic Research. Retrieved from www.nber.org/papers/w13908.

Galbraith, J.K. (1967). *The new industrial state*. Boston, MA: Houghton Mifflin.

Giraud, P. (1996). *L'inégalité du monde: économie du monde contemporain*. Paris: Gallimard/Folio.

Ihrke, D.K., Faber, C.S. & Koerber, W.K. (2011). Geographical mobility: 2008 to 2009. US Census Bureau. Retrieved from www.census.gov/content/dam/Census/library/publications/2015/acs/acs-31.pdf.

Jorion, P. (2006). L'endettement excessif aux États-Unis et ses raisons historiques. *Revue du MAUSS*, 1(27), 322–342.

Kopczuk, W., Saez, E. & Song, J. (2007). Uncovering the American dream: Inequality and mobility in social security earnings data since 1973. NBER Working Paper Series, National Bureau of Economic Research. Retrieved from www.columbia.edu/~wk2110/bin/mobility-short.pdf.

Krippner, G.R. (2005). The financialization of the economy. *Socio-economic Review, 3*(2), 173–208.

Kumhof, M. & Rancière, R. (2010). Inequality, leverage and crises. IMF Working Paper *10*(268), International Monetary Fund. Retrieved from www.imf.org/external/pubs/ft/wp/2010/wp10268.pdf.

Mann, C.L. (2002). Perspectives on the US current account deficit and sustainability. *Journal of Economic Perspectives*, *16*(3), 131–152.
Mistral, J. (2009). *La troisième révolution américaine*. Paris: Perrin.
Molloy, R., Smith, R. & Wozniak, A. (2011). Internal migration in the United States. Discussion paper series//Forschungsinstitut zur Zukunft der Arbeit, No. 5903. Retrieved http://ftp.iza.org/dp5903.pdf.
Norton, M.I. & Ariely, D. (2011). Building a better America: one wealth quintile at a time. *Perspective on Psychological Science*, *6*(9). Retrieved from http://people.duke.edu/~dandan/Papers/Other/BuildingBetterAmerica.pdf.
Obstfeld, M. & Rogoff, K. (2000). Perspectives on OECD global integration: implications for US current account adjustment. Federal Reserve of Kansas City. Retrieved from www.kc.frb.org/publicat/sympos/2000/s00rogo.pdf.
Orléan, A. (2014). *The empire of value: A new foundation for economics*. Cambridge, MA: MIT Press.
Pew Research Center (2012). *Fewer, poorer, gloomier, the lost decade of the middle class.* Washington, DC: Pew Research Center. Retrieved from www.pewsocialtrends.org/2012/08/22/the-lost-decade-of-the-middle-class.
Piketty, T. (2014). *Capital in the twenty-first century*. Cambridge, MA: President & Fellows of Harvard College.
Piketty, T. & Saez, E. (2003). Income inequality in the United States, 1913–1998. *Quarterly Journal of Economics*. Retrieved from http://eml.berkeley.edu/~saez/pikettyqje.pdf.
Polanyi, K. (1944 [2001]). *The great transformation*. Boston, MA: Beacon Press.
Rifkin, J. (1995). *The end of work: The decline of the global labor force and the dawn of the post-market era*. New York: G.P. Putnam's Sons.
Rosanvallon, P. (2013). *The society of equals*. Cambridge, MA: Harvard University Press.
Ruben, M. (2009). Forgive us our trespasses? The rise of consumer debt in modern America. Proquest Discovery Guides
Saez, E. (2012). *Striking it richer: The evolution of top incomes in the United States* (Updated with 2009 & 2010 estimates), University of California, Department of Economics. Retrieved from http://eml.berkeley.edu/~saez/saez-UStopincomes-2010.pdf.
Sapir, J. (2009). From financial crisis to turning point: how the US subprime crisis turned into a world-wide one and will change the global economy. Library of the Friedrich Herbert Foundation. Retrieved from http://library.fes.de/pdf-files/ipg/ipg-2009-1/04_a_sapir_us.pdf.
Stiglitz, J.E. (2013). *The price of inequality: How today's divided society endangers our future*. New York: W.W. Norton.
Sullivan, T.A., Warren, E. & Westbrook, J.L. (2000). *The fragile middle class: Americans in debt.* New Haven, CT: Yale University Press.
Théret, B. (2012). From Keynesianism to libertarianism: the place of money in the transformations of the authorized economic knowledge. *Revue de la régulation, 10*(2). Retrieved from http://regulation.revues.org/9529.
Varoufakis, Y. (2013). *The global minotaur: America, Europe and the future of the global economy*. London: Zed Books/Economic Controversies.
Veblen, T. (1899). *Theory of the leisure class: An economic study in the evolution of institutions*. New York: Macmillan.
Warren, E. & Tyagi, A. (2005). What's hurting the middle class: the myth of overspending obscures the real problem. *Boston Review*, September–October 2005.

Retrieved from www.bostonreview.net/forum/what%E2%80%99s-hurting-middle-class.

Wills, J. (2003). Respectable mediocrity: the everyday life of an ordinary American striver, 1876–1890. *Journal of Social History*, *37*(2), 323–349.

Winship, S. (2011). Mobility impaired. *National Review*. Retrieved from www.nationalreview.com/article/282292/mobility-impaired-scott-winship.

Wolff, E.N. (2010). Recent trends in household wealth in the United States: rising debt and the middle-class squeeze – an update to 2007. Working Paper no. 589, Levy Economics Institute of Bard College. Retrieved from www.levyinstitute.org/pubs/wp_589.pdf.

Part II

Shifting paradigms, shifting scopes

Beyond the national crisis

5 A US national model of capitalism?

Lessons from the Great Recession

Martine Azuelos

The Great Recession and its aftermath have led to much questioning of the model on which US growth has been built historically. Indeed, while this model was still widely held as a paragon of economic efficiency across the world at the close of the twentieth century, more than eight years after the subprime crisis erupted, its image remains tarnished. As contagion of the US-born financial crisis spread instantaneously to financial markets across the globe (OECD, 2012), and from financial markets to the real economy, what began as a US recession rapidly turned into a global recession. The impact of this global recession on the real economy has been devastating, but has also led to a paradigm shift, reflecting the extent to which the American "model" in the normative sense of the word has become eroded.[1] Thus, while before 2007 the reality and desirability of "convergence" of national economies or "varieties of capitalism" towards the "best practices" associated with the American – or "Anglo-Saxon" – system might have been an object of dispute among economists (Coates, 2000; Hall & Soskice, 2001; Baumol *et al.*, 2007), more recently this system has mostly been blamed for its flaws, bringing the second *Pax Americana* to a close (Azuelos, 1999; Boyer, 2001).

To date, however, the validity of the American model as an ideal type in the Weberian sense[2] has hardly been questioned. Although economists have noted that the depth and duration of the Great Recession varied significantly across the US territory and that its impact was very uneven, this internal diversity has hardly been analyzed from a diversity-of-capitalism angle, in line with research conducted by Kratke (1997), Théret (1999) or Lane and Wood (2009). Thus, as an analytic tool, the national model is still commonly used to shed light on the fundamental features of the American economy in a comparative perspective.

The objective of this chapter is to see whether this analytical framework does full justice to the distinctiveness of American capitalism. Focusing on the Great Recession provides an interesting starting point because periods of crisis are not only periods of pain and trouble, or turning points, they are also periods when judgment becomes clearer, as the etymology of the word suggests.[3] We anticipate that analyzing the nature and impact of the Great Recession on the U.S. economy can help capture some of the defining features of American capitalism. To do so, the chapter is organized in three parts. The first argues that the classic characterization of American capitalism as the epitome of liberal market capitalism downplays the role of government intervention in the economy, and that the federal government's response to the Great Recession should not be seen as a departure from a "hands-off" government model but as a vivid illustration of a specific state–market nexus which has been an enduring feature throughout American history. The second part focuses on the regional and local impact of the Great Recession and suggests that the magnitude of variations that have been observed across the country should invite us to pay attention to the fact that in the United States the dynamics of economic change, growth or decline lie as much at the sub- or infra-national level as at the national level. Building on these empirical observations, the third part provides a tentative framework incorporating internal diversity in the broad picture of American capitalism. To do so it adopts a multi-scalar and cross-disciplinary approach to the state–market nexus that highlights the thickness and nestedness of its defining institutions.

Lesson 1: the state–market nexus is a defining feature of American capitalism

Characterization of American capitalism has been indebted to a variety of theoretical or disciplinary approaches, and shaped by the methodologies and research tools used by their followers. Thus, economic historians have tended to focus on its transformation from commercial to industrial capitalism from the colonial era to the post-Civil War decades, and described its modern avatar as "post-industrial," "financial" or "knowledge-based." In doing so they have focused on the dominant sphere accounting for growth and change at each stage of the development of the US economy over time. This analysis was long indebted to the dominant view among Western economists until the 1980s, i.e., that market economies follow the same development path over time, going through the same "stages of growth," although the chronology may differ from one nation to another (Rostow, 1962).[4] On the other hand, studies of "comparative economic systems" have rather focused on the modern era. During the Cold War they placed emphasis on the opposition between market economies (capitalism) and centrally planned economies (communism), and on the unity, rather than diversity, of each of the two systems.[5]

Following the collapse of the Soviet bloc and the conversion of the Chinese economy to state capitalism, attention shifted to the spatial diversity of capitalism and the dynamics of change within each model.[6] Indeed, since the 1990s, there has been growing emphasis on the differences in the organization of market/capitalist economies, with market mechanisms a far more determinant feature in some (dubbed "market-led," "liberal market" (LME) or "Anglo-Saxon" economies), and coordinating mechanisms more influential in others, dubbed "Rhine" (Albert, 1993) or "coordinated market" economies (Hall & Soskice, 2001).[7]

Whether it has been labeled "Anglo-Saxon" (Albert, 1993), "market-oriented" (Boyer, 2005), "market-based" (Amable, 2003) or characterized as the epitome of a "liberal market economy" (Hall & Soskice, 2001), the US model of capitalism has been primarily defined as a form of economic organization in which market forces are allowed to play freely, with particular emphasis being placed on competition and labor-market flexibility. The emergence of this model has also been associated with the "retreat of the state," or "neo-liberal turn," which began in the mid-1970s and paved the way for the emergence of a "finance-led" growth regime in the 1990s, at a time when globalization accelerated (Aglietta, 1998). Yet, as underlined in the introduction of this book, this emphasis on markets and finance in the characterization of contemporary US capitalism typically downplays the role of government intervention in the economy. Even Boyer (2005), whose characterization mentions the state, sees its role as limited by institutional fragmentation and competition. True, the separation of powers between the three branches of government, the existence of checks and balances, the division of authority between federal, state and local governments often lead to deadlocks and make public policies more complex to devise and implement than in many other Western democracies. Yet this should not obscure the size and scope of state intervention in the US economy, an issue which has kindled debates dating back to the American Revolution – when opposition between Jefferson and Hamilton on the subject framed political discourse and policy-making along lines that have remained alive to this day. Although, in the course of American history, the laissez-faire rhetoric dear to the former Founding Father has often been heard more loudly than echoes of the latter's interventionist doctrine, the size of government spending and the scope of its involvement in economic affairs have gradually made it one essential pillar of economic growth.

Support to the farming sector since the 1930s, or the existence of a "military–industrial complex"[8] since World War II are illustrations that immediately come to mind, but these are merely the tip of the iceberg. Even under Ronald Reagan's presidency – supposedly an age of government retreat – the massive defense build-up to defeat Soviet military power or the competitiveness policy devised to rise to Japan's economic challenge hardly chimed with the official tune that "in the present crisis, government [was] not the solution. Government [was] the problem" (Reagan, 1981). Deregulation implemented from the mid-1970s may have made markets more competitive for a while, only to foster concentration in most deregulated industries in the longer run. And the triple helix innovation system involving firms, universities and government has been a determining factor of US leadership in the knowledge economy (Etzkowitz & Leydesdorff, 1997, 2000; Etzkowitz, 2008).[9] Thus, in addition to its direct support to industries like farming and defense, the federal government's tax, fiscal and monetary policies powerfully impact not only the level of aggregate demand and supply, but also the strategies of private economic agents. One can only agree with Gertler (2010, p. 3) that the US economy is "the product of a panoply of nationally distinctive institutional forms through which the state defines ground rules, produces incentives, and transmits signals to economic actors, as well as redistributing income between individuals, social classes, and regions."

Against this backdrop, the Tea Party's outrage at President Obama's "socialist" policies[10] should be taken not only as a severe overstatement, but as a misreading of American history. Indeed, federal government spending may have reached 24.4 percent of GDP in 2009, but even before the outbreak of the financial crisis it stood at 19.1 percent in 2006, with state and local governments' expenditures accounting for a further 15.3 percent. Total public spending thus stood at over one-third of GDP (34.4 per cent), admittedly less than the OECD average (42 percent), but not altogether an insignificant share in an economy accounting for nearly one-quarter of global output.[11] Washington's swift and sweeping response to the financial crisis should therefore not be interpreted as a sudden departure from "neoliberal" policies which had become the rule since the 1970s, but as an illustration of the federal government's ability to muster massive public resources – even at the cost of increasing its debt to over 100 percent of GDP[12] – so as to bailout ailing industries,[13] pump-prime growth through lavish deficit spending[14] or massive injections of liquidity,[15] and reform the financial system.[16] Faced with similar difficulties, governments in most European "coordinated market" economies reacted far less forcefully.

Federal economic policies were in the limelight in much of 2008–2009, and rightfully so. The recession affected the whole nation's economy and required national remedies. The roots of the crisis lay in national institutions, reflecting the validity of the characterization of American contemporary capitalism as finance-led. The centrality of finance in the US economy, dynamic and largely unregulated innovation in this sector and central bank independence go a long way to explain why the financial crisis erupted in 2007–2008 (National Commission on the Causes of the Financial and Economic Crisis in the United States, 2011). Its starting point was the subprime crisis, itself the consequence of the bursting of a housing market bubble, the origin of which largely lay in the expansionary monetary policy implemented by the Federal Reserve from 2001 to 2004. This policy resulted in historically low interest rates on mortgages at a time when minority home ownership was encouraged in an attempt to revive the American Dream in the face of rising inequality and declining intergenerational economic mobility,[17] and when inadequate regulation and supervision of banking and finance combined with a failure to correctly assess the risks associated with securitization (Blundell-Wignall & Atkinson, 2008).

Thus, rather than reliance on competition and the free play of market forces, it is the prevalence of a complex web of state–market relations, itself the result of shifting socio-political compromises, which appears as a defining feature of American capitalism over time and a key factor of its distinctive capacity to get back on its feet and reinvent itself in the face of crisis.

Yet even if it was born in the United States, the financial crisis cannot be insulated from America's insertion in the world economy. It can arguably be traced back to such global developments as trade liberalization and financial globalization that accelerated from the 1990s (Obstfeld & Rogoff, 2009). Indeed, while trade liberalization resulted in massive current account surpluses in countries like China, greatly inflating the volume of international liquidity and putting downward pressure on interest rates, financial globalization and deregulation fueled a stellar rise of such innovations as securitization or derivatives in an era when the dogma of "efficient markets" made it appear riskless for credit institutions to lend to borrowers who could never be expected to repay their mortgages.[18] What this reveals is that the modalities of insertion in the global economy are also an important defining feature of American capitalism.

Another important feature is its internal diversity, which is reflected in the fact that although the effects of the Great Recession were felt nation-wide, they nevertheless differed markedly from one place to another. Keeping the lens focused on federal institutions and the nation-wide picture, as has often been done, may thus result in shedding only partial light on the system. As economic geographers have shown, "monoscalarity" may lead to "fetishizing the national scale" and virtually excluding all other scales of analysis (Peck & Theodore, 2007; Gertler, 2010). To see the picture in full we need to pay attention to local and regional diversity.

Lesson 2: internal diversity is another defining feature of American capitalism

The nation-wide recession that, according to the National Bureau of Economic Research Business Cycle Dating Committee, began in December 2007 and lasted until June 2009,[19] did not affect all the regions of the United States evenly. Its depth and duration varied markedly from one region to another, from one state to another and even from one county to another. Two commonly used indicators may be selected to illustrate this heterogeneity: the gross domestic product (GDP) real growth rate and the unemployment rate. The broad picture that emerges is that the recession was severest and longest in the Great Lakes and Far West regions, with real GDP contracting particularly severely in Michigan and Nevada in 2009, while the Southwest and Rocky Mountains fared much better: New Mexico even recorded positive growth in 2009 (see Table 5.1 and Map 5.1).[20] These geographical variations appear even more visible when one narrows the focus by choosing the metropolitan statistical area (MSA) scale (see Map 5.2).[21] In 2009, the worst year of the recession, real GDP declined in 292 of 366 (80 percent) MSAs, while it grew in 74 of them (20 percent). Geographically close areas were often impacted fairly differently. Thus, in California, the Los Angeles–Long Beach–Santa Ana metropolitan area, the second largest in the nation, shrank by 4.4 percent, while the neighboring MSAs of San Diego and Riverside shrank by 2.9 and 5.5 percent, respectively (see Map 5.2).[22]

Unemployment rates reflected these growth differentials (see Table 5.2, Maps 5.3 and 5.4). Thus, when unemployment peaked at the national average of 10.0 percent in October 2009, it reached 11.9 percent in California, 12.8 percent in Nevada, and 13.4 percent in Michigan, while North Dakota, Nebraska and Louisiana recorded rates well below average (at 3.2 percent, 4.5 percent and 6.7 percent, respectively). In 2007 the spread between the lowest and highest

Table 5.1 Real GDP growth by BEA region (2006–2012)

	2006	*2007*	*2008*	*2009*	*2010*	*2011*	*2012*
United States	2.7	1.8	–0.7	–3.8	3.1	1.4	2.1
New England	2.1	1.5	–0.8	–3.2	3.4	0.9	1.1
Mideast	2.8	1.3	–0.8	–2.9	3.3	0.9	2.0
Great Lakes	0.5	0.9	–2.8	–5.8	3.8	1.9	1.4
Plains	1.1	2.2	1.1	–3.3	3.4	2.1	2.0
Southeast	2.5	1.0	–1.1	–3.7	2.9	0.6	1.2
Southwest	5.1	4.4	0.5	–2.8	4.1	3.2	5.1
Rocky Mountains	3.8	3.3	1.5	–2.3	2.8	1.4	1.0
Far West	3.9	1.8	0.0	–4.3	2.0	1.4	2.2

Source: Bureau of Economic Analysis.

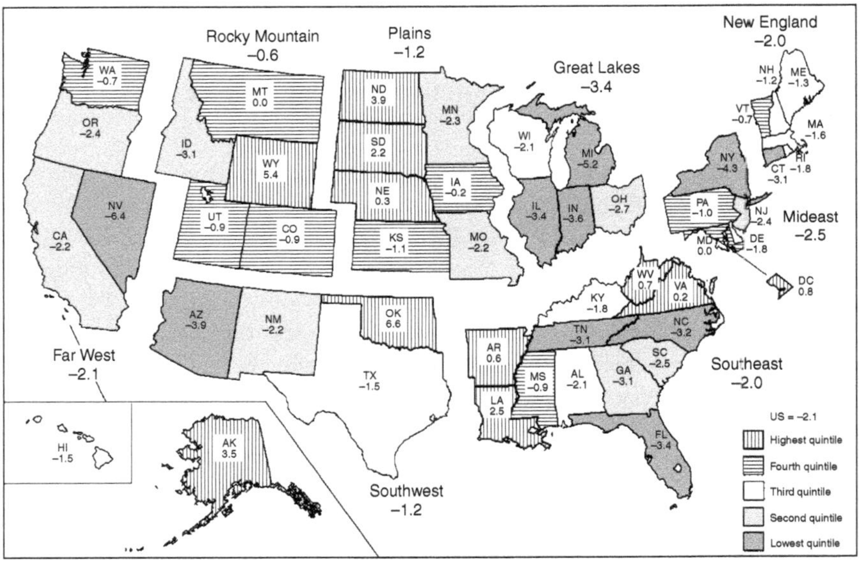

Map 5.1 Percentage change in real GDP by state and region (2009) (source: Bureau of Economic Analysis, Survey of Current Business, December 2010).

unemployment rate among the states was 4.6 percentage points. By October 2009 it had reached 10.2 percentage points. The spread at the MSA scale was even wider, at 27.6 percentage points, between El Centro, California (30.5 percent) and Bismarck, North Dakota (2.9 percent), with 15 MSAs recording jobless rates of at least 15.0 percent and 13 registering rates below 5.0 percent. Among the 15 areas with jobless rates of at least 15.0 percent, nine were located in California and three in Michigan (BLS, 2009, 2010). It was in the Far West that the increase in unemployment was steepest and longest, while the Plains weathered the impact of the Great Recession better than all other regions. But

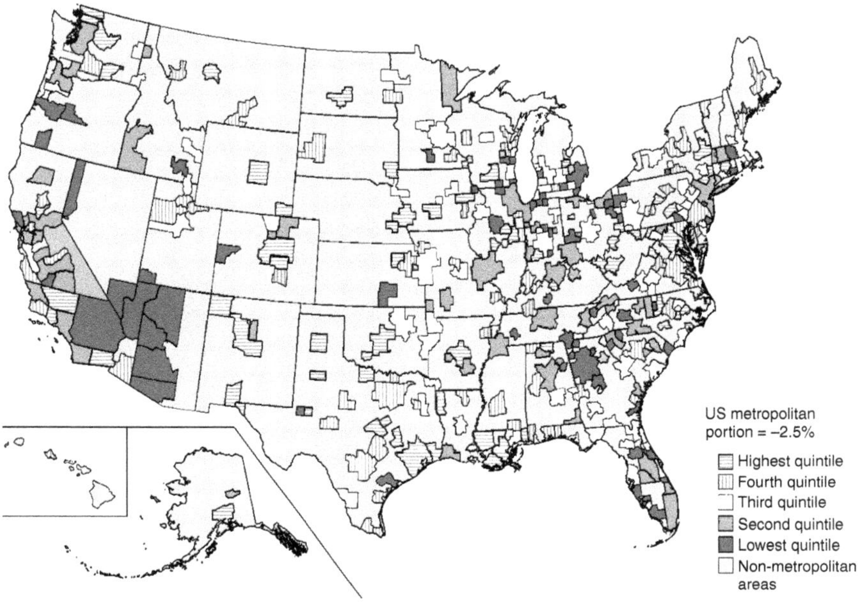

Map 5.2 Percentage change in real GDP by metropolitan statistical area (2009) (source: Bureau of Economic Analysis, Survey of Current Business, March 2011).

Table 5.2 Unemployment rates by BEA regions (2006–2012)

	2006	*2007*	*2008*	*2009*	*2010*	*2011*	*2012*
United States	4.6	4.6	5.8	9.3	9.6	8.9	8.1
New England	4.6	4.5	5.4	8.1	8.5	7.8	7.2
Mideast	4.5	4.3	5.3	8.2	8.7	8.3	8.3
Great Lakes	5.4	5.5	6.6	10.6	10.5	9.2	8.2
Plains	4.1	4.2	4.9	7.4	7.2	6.6	5.6
Southeast	4.4	4.4	5.9	9.6	9.9	9.3	8.2
Southwest	4.7	4.2	5.0	7.8	8.4	8.0	6.9
Rocky Mountains	3.6	3.3	4.4	7.7	8.4	7.8	7.0
Far West	4.8	5.1	6.9	10.9	11.8	11.2	9.9

Source: Bureau of Economic Analysis.

focusing on MSA or county data reveals wide differences between close neighbors, as Map 5.4 illustrates.[23]

Rather than appearing as a unified whole, as national averages may suggest, the United States can rather be pictured as a mosaic, a patchwork or a leopard skin. Internal diversity, rather than unity, appears as a major feature of US economic performance during the Great Recession. How can this empirical

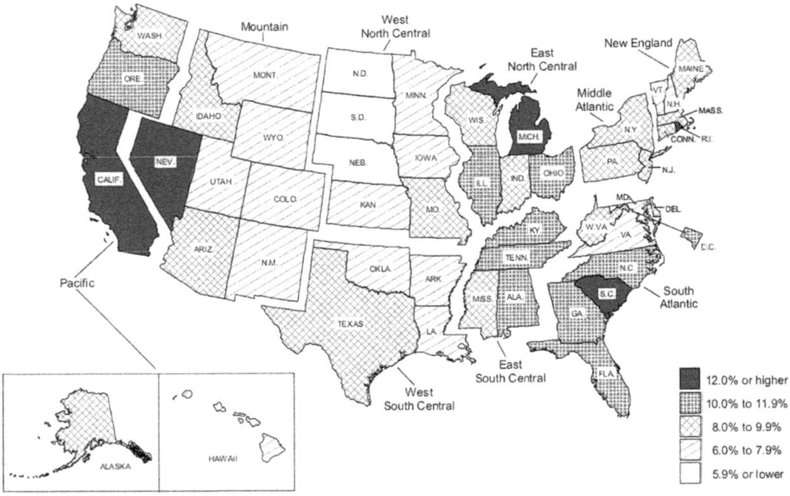

Map 5.3 State unemployment rate (October 2009) (percent) (source: Bureau of Labor Statistics, Economic News release, Regional and State Employment and Unemployment, October 2009).

Map 5.4 Unemployment rate by metropolitan statistical area (October 2009) (source: Bureau of Labor Statistics, News Release, Metropolitan Area Employment and Unemployment, October 2009).

reality be reconciled with the national model of capitalism outlined in the previous section?

Accounting for diversity: the role of economic structures

As this section shows, addressing the issue of internal diversity of economic performance during the Great Recession implies answering the following questions:

- What is the proper *spatial scale*? Should it be the "region", as defined by the BEA, the Bureau of the Census or the Federal Reserve?[24] Should it be the state? Or, given wide internal diversity observed at state and region level, should the lens focus on the metropolitan region – and then why not on the city or county?
- What concepts and theoretical framework(s) should one draw upon? To what extent may these concepts and theoretical frameworks be useful to move beyond exploration of the diversity of economic performance during the business cycle so as to shed light on the internal diversity of the model?

Economic theory offers conflicting answers as to whether economies that are part of an integrated whole, as is the case for states and regions of the United States, will converge over time. Standard neoclassical growth theory suggests that they should converge (Barro *et al.*, 1991), while endogenous growth theory (Romer, 1990) and new trade theory (Krugman, 1991a, 1991b) suggest that they should diverge in their growth paths, becoming more unequal over time.[25] Economic historians have, for their part, largely documented the diversity of regional economic performance over US history, and put forward the role of economic structures and incomes. Their work shows that regional economies first diverged in economic structures and incomes in the nineteenth century, due to differences in factor endowments and relative wages, and then converged in the twentieth, as the shift in industrial structure away from agriculture and manufacturing into services significantly reduced the importance of regional differences in land and resources, and as factors of production became more mobile (Kim, 1998; Caselli & Coleman, 2001). Recent literature on the subject, which covers recent history, suggests that regional convergence may have stabilized since the 1980s (Kane, 2001; Porter, 2003) or reversed (Gerolimetto & Magrini, 2014). In the past few decades the issue has attracted special interest on the part of economic geographers, who have increasingly relied on spatial econometric modeling to study regional diversity in economic performance (Siegel *et al.*, 1995), and spatial econometrics, which combines econometrics with a focus on sub-national spaces, has been a rapidly expanding field of research.[26] Thus differences in regional economic performance across the United States have been widely documented. "New economic geography" economists and economic geographers have thus focused on the causal factors underlying the development of successful regions, such as high-tech clusters, or "resilient" regions, vs. declining or stagnating regions (Martin & Sunley, 1998). In doing so, they have generally focused on the city-region, or metropolitan area or region. Since the early 1990s, there has been a resurgence of interest in the metropolitan region as the scale where "transformation takes place,"[27] leading to the emergence of a "new regionalism" (Wheeler, 2002).[28] Far from being limited to the United States, interest in metropolitan regions has become global, as underscored in the World Bank 2009 development report, entitled *Reshaping Geography*.

In response to these evolutions, US government agencies have increasingly collected and analyzed regional and sub-regional macro-economic data, in addition to national data.[29] Thus, measurement of economic performance at the metropolitan area scale has greatly improved, and statistical data can then be fed into econometric models based on regression techniques to identify factors accounting for variations in growth or employment across time and space.[30]

It will probably take a few years for comprehensive, in-depth studies of the local economic impact of the Great Recession to be published.[31] At the time the present chapter is being written, existing literature on the subject falls into three categories. The first includes accounts of monthly, quarterly or yearly changes in GDP and unemployment published by the BEA, the BLS or the Federal Reserve in its *Beige Books*. Typically, changes in economic outlook are related to a region's economic structure or industrial composition, as defined with reference to industrial classification (the NAICS).[32] Connaughton (2010) provides a descriptive synthesis of these news releases covering the whole recession period, while Connaughton and Madsen (2012) go a bit further in analyzing the recession's impact on local and state unemployment.

The second type of literature focuses on specific metropolitan regions (as Orlando and Buffalo in Cowell *et al.*, 2013; Hampton Roads, Virginia, in Koch, 2012) or states (as Texas in Anari, 2012; California in Bardhan & Walker, 2010; or Indiana and Michigan in Hicks & Kuhlman, 2011).

The third type of study identifies the regional or local differences observed when focusing on one particular aspect of the recession, such as increases in unemployment (Walden, 2012; Beyers, 2013), banking failures (Aubuchon & Wheelock, 2010), the collapse of the housing market (Martin, 2011; Cohen *et al.*, 2012) and subsequent foreclosures (Immergluck, 2011), the impact of state tax and budget policies (Jonas, 2012; Campbell & Sances, 2013) or degree of "resilience" to the shock.[33] After reading those studies, one comes to the conclusion that industrial structure matters, but does not tell the whole story.

Focusing on determinants of differences in unemployment rates, Walden (2012) interestingly concludes that if "industrial composition – specifically the share of state GDP (gross domestic product) in manufacturing – was strongly associated with greater labor market deterioration," so were, however, "larger declines in housing prices and bigger household in-migration." (p. 251). He also identifies three geographic groups of states – in the Far West, the Southeast and the Midwest – whose economic characteristics resulted in greater increases in unemployment rates. In each of the three groups a different factor accounted for the trend: a much higher-than-average decline in housing prices in the Far West;

a very high in-migration rate in the Southeast; and very high dependence on manufacturing in the Midwest.[34]

Industrial composition and diversification were indeed factors underpinning regional growth and unemployment differentials during the Great Recession. These findings are consistent with economic theory, which predicts that

> just as diversifying an investment portfolio can help reduce risk, the diversification of industries in a given region can help reduce volatility in growth rates. Thus regions specializing heavily in only one or two industries will be tied closely to the fate of those industries, a condition that may lead to large swings in employment growth and wage growth. If instead employment is spread across many industries, then when one industry stumbles, others may still fuel the region's overall economic performance and mitigate volatility in its growth rates.
>
> (Felix, 2012, p. 55)

What is more, regional specialization in relatively volatile sectors, such as manufacturing, finance, insurance and real estate, which have relatively high average wages, will also lead to higher-than-average incomes and growth in good times and lower them in bad times, thus increasing growth volatility over the business cycle. Evidence of this can be found in the experience of California, whose specialization in hyperactive finance – especially mortgage finance – home construction and real-estate lending and leasing made it particularly vulnerable to the hardships of the subprime crisis (Bardhan & Walker, 2010); or in that of Michigan, which was hard hit by the collapse of the automobile industry (Carnevale & Smith, 2011; Hicks & Kuhlman, 2011).

But economic structure does not tell the whole story, as the comparative analysis of Indiana and Michigan's experiences reveals. The variance in unemployment rates between these two neighboring, highly homogeneous, manufacturing-intensive and geographically similar states can only be explained by factors lying beyond the scope of economic structure and related to geography and institutions (Hicks & Kuhlman, 2011).

Lesson 3: the internal diversity of American capitalism is embedded in geography and institutions

As this section will show, geography and institutions are often intertwined. It is nevertheless useful to separate them conceptually to better understand their respective roles.

Geography

The first reason why geography matters here is because it largely determines a region's endowments in natural resources. These endowments played a significant part in the divergence of economic performance among regional economies in the nineteenth and early twentieth centuries (Kim, 1998), and although they gradually lost importance with America's transition to a "service," "post-industrial" or "knowledge-based" economy, recent developments have drawn renewed attention to their impact on local and regional performance. Indeed, with energy prices pushed up by the rise in global demand fueled by emerging nations' rapid growth, the "shale revolution" – the development of horizontal drilling and "fracking" techniques and shale oil/gas extraction – has led to regional booms in Louisiana, Alaska, North Dakota, Oklahoma and Wyoming. This easily explains, for example, why Bismarck, North Dakota, recorded positive output growth (1.6 percent) and the lowest metropolitan unemployment rate (2.9 per cent) in 2009 while the national economy was mired in recession.[35]

Regional and local variations in demographic and social structure, which are well documented by the US Census Bureau, also deeply impact economic conditions. Indeed, not only does a population's size and composition shape the supply side of the labor market, but its ethnic and socioeconomic composition largely determines its relative affluence or poverty. This is of particular relevance when one seeks to understand the local impacts of the subprime crisis, given that subprime mortgage lenders had targeted low income and poorly educated households (Martin, 2011, p. 603). Thus the local incidence of foreclosures was particularly severe in poor neighborhoods with a higher-than-average proportion of Hispanics,[36] as illustrated in the cases of the Riverside–San Bernardino–Ontario area or El Centro areas in California.[37] And while "the Great Recession had devastating impacts for families at every rung of the economic ladder," families in high-poverty neighborhoods were particularly hard-hit (Pew Charitable Trusts, 2012).

Third, geography also largely determines a region's openness to globalization. As Wallace *et al.* (2012) show, rather than being a "monolithic process" affecting all regions in the same way, globalization has differentiated regional effects across the United States. This can be illustrated by the case of the Los Angeles metropolitan area, which ranks first of 100 metropolitan areas on the value of its exports and is therefore strongly exposed to international trade forces. Exports account for about 11 percent of its gross product.[38] The drop in traffic caused the transportation and warehousing industry to lose 14,100 jobs, or 9.2 percent of its total employment, in the Los Angeles–Long Beach–Glendale metropolitan division between 2007 and 2009.[39] Given the role the two ports play in the local economy, the impact of this drop on local growth and employment was strong (Kyser *et al.*, 2010).

A fourth reason why geography matters has to do with industrial localization and clustering (Krugman, 1991a; Porter, 2003).[40] Industrial localization may be determined by the availability of natural resources,[41] but in traded industries[42] the key determinant factor is positive externalities.[43] Indeed, when industries are geographically concentrated, firms benefit from "agglomeration economies," and because they result in increasing returns to scale, these externalities largely determine regional advantage and competitiveness.[44] Thus, as emphasized by Porter (2003: 549), "[t]he performance of regional economies is strongly influenced by the strength of local clusters and the vitality and plurality of innovation." The implication is that regional development and growth are not only endogenous,[45] but also highly path-dependent.

The concept of path dependence has attracted considerable attention on the part of economists and geographers. It sheds light on the impact of history and institutions on regional economic specialization and performance (Martin & Sunley, 2006a, 2006b). In stressing the role of agglomeration economies, economists have shown that they generate a self-reinforcing tendency for particular activities to concentrate in particular areas. Following North (1990), they have also shown that institutional frameworks are another important source of the externalities that shape local economic path dependence. Geographers have used this concept to capture the way in which "small, historically contingent events can set off self-reinforcing mechanisms and processes that 'lock in' particular structures and pathways of development," especially at the regional level (Martin & Sunley, 2006a, p. 5). And they have argued that although the "canonical" path dependence model stresses continuity rather than change, it may also "incorporate mechanisms by which institutions change over time" and to allow "their development to be open, rather than constrained to inevitable stabilization" (Martin, 2010, p. 13). This leaves room for agency, as the introduction to this volume suggests, although location plays a fundamental role.

Thus, when considering global cities (Sassen, 2001, 2005) like Los Angeles or New York, we may observe that location was the determinant factor historically. In the case of New York, "[t]hanks to the strategic location of the island of Manhattan, New York became the port of choice for British merchants to auction their goods" (Global Cities Initiative, 2013a). But patterns of economic specialization subsequently became "locked in" through self-reinforcing effects and externalities.[46] Thus, "[i]n the first half of the 19th century, New York monopolized the country's financial institutions and became practically the only port of entry for immigrants, most of whom settled in the city" (ibid.). The city's present international dimension owes just as much to geography as it does to history, and to institutions. The same can be said of Los Angeles, despite the fact that its globalization trajectory followed a completely different path (Global Cities Initiative, 2013b) In the same way, Silicon Valley's success as a high-technology cluster had to do with its location close to San Francisco, the financial capital of the west coast, and to a top research university – Stanford – that benefited from lavish federal government defense contracts during World War II and the Cold War. But as Saxenian (1994, 2006) emphasizes, other key factors were industrial structure, corporate organization, the "brain circulation" of immigrant professionals, and local institutions and culture.

Institutions

Economists have also paid growing attention to the influence of institutions on economic development. North (1990) was a pioneer in arguing that institutions are "the underlying determinant of the long-run performance of economies"

(p. 107) but Rodrik *et al.* (2004) have gone even further in concluding that the quality of institutions "trumps" other factors, such as trade or geography, in determining levels of income and growth prospects. As Rodríguez-Pose (2013) underlines, most economic geographers would also agree with Martin (2000, p. 79) that "although institutions are unlikely to be the sole 'cause' of geographically uneven development, they enable, constrain, and refract economic development in spatially differentiated ways" (Martin, 2000, p. 79). Saxenian's study of the contrast between Silicon Valley and Route 128 in the Boston area illustrates the extent to which informal or tacit institutions matter in building regional advantage, and other studies have focused on the role of local/regional public policy and formal institutions. Both formal and informal institutions create subnational "rules of the game," i.e., institutional environments which constitute the framework within which markets function, resulting in a diversity of economic "ecosystems." Studying the impact of informal institutions across the United States is beyond the scope of this chapter, although it may offer potentially fruitful avenues for future research with a view to re-embedding the economy in culture, as suggested in the introduction to this volume. Focusing on a number of key formal institutions may be an easier path here, although what follows does not intend at presenting a comprehensive study.

The fact that the United States is a federal republic with autonomous state and local governments means that tax and fiscal policy, as well as labor laws and the quality of the educational system and infrastructures, vary significantly across the nation, which impacts local and regional economic ecosystems significantly. The concept of "institutional thickness," which economic geographers use to capture this multi-layering of institutional spheres within a given nation, seems particularly relevant here. Equally relevant is the concept of "institutional nestedness," first used by Boyer and Hollingsworth (1997) to shed light on the fact that (1) there is a hierarchy of institutional spaces ranging from the supranational to the national and the regional and local; and (2) the combination, interaction and mode of articulation of these institutional spaces varies from place to place, resulting in different "local institutional regimes." Thus, as Martin (2000, p. 87) puts it "as we move from one area to another within a national economic space, not only may the specifics of institutional nestedness change but also the interactions within that ensemble."

Tax and fiscal policies

The tax and fiscal institutional environment is a first source of regionally diverse institutions. Indeed, as taxing authority is shared between the federal, states and municipal governments, the types of tax imposed at each level of government vary. Thus, customs duties are only levied by the federal government, while income taxes (on individuals and corporations) are levied by the federal government and by most states. Taxes on property are imposed only at the local level (but the same property may be taxed by several local jurisdictions), and sales taxes are levied by most states and by many local governments. As tax rates implemented by state and local governments differ significantly, tax burdens on individuals and corporations differ from one area to another.[47] Thus, California has the top sales tax rate (7.5 percent), followed by Tennessee (7.0 percent) and Washington (6.5 percent), and five states do not impose any sales tax (Alaska, Delaware, Montana, New Hampshire, Oregon). In addition, localities may charge sales taxes, and nationally these vary from 0 to 8.5 percent, so that, all-in-all, tax rates may vary between 0 percent (in Delaware) and 12.5 percent in some localities of Alabama.

Property tax is another interesting case in point. Thus, after it adopted Proposition 13 in 1978 California cut its rate to a maximum of 1 percent of house value, and many other states followed suit. Today, rates vary substantially across regions and across counties. They are especially high in the Northeast and parts of the Midwest, and range from 0.2 percent in Maui County, Hawaii, to 3.1 percent in Wayne County, New York. Most of the variation is due to differences across rather than within states, with the highest rates in counties located in New York and New Jersey, and the lowest in those located in Alabama and Louisiana (Harris & Moore, 2013). As the Tax Foundation (2013) observes,

> [w]hile California's property taxes are lower than New Jersey, New York, and even Texas, it remains a high tax state. It has the third worst business climate in the country, the highest top marginal income tax rate in the country at 13.3 percent, a corporate income tax of 8.84 percent, and the highest statewide sales tax in the country at 7.5 percent. In 1978, California had the fourth highest overall tax burden, and today the state still has the fourth highest burden.

That this high tax burden has not discouraged entrepreneurship, immigration and in-migration, however, shows that there is more to a "business climate" than what may appear at first sight.

Together with federal grants, the level of state and local tax receipts determines the level of funding of these sub-national governments' operations – their primary responsibility being for investments in education, social services and infrastructure.[48] Not surprisingly, receipts fluctuate widely with economic activity, and the Great Recession caused the largest collapse in state revenues on record (Gordon, 2012, p. 3). The recession also increased spending pressures, as state and local governments' obligations rose. In particular, enrollments climbed for Medicaid, unemployment insurance and higher education. As a result of these pressures and revenue declines, most state and local governments were confronted with large budget gaps.

Another rule was then of the utmost importance to understand the policies they implemented: unlike the federal government, they are generally prohibited from running deficits, so that typically when their receipts fall they must raise revenues, cut spending or draw down reserves to balance their budgets.[49] This explains why most of them cut spending (mostly on education, health and social services), reduced their payrolls and why some also raised taxes.[50]

The impact of the Great Recession on state and local governments' finances was far from even, however. California was particularly hard-hit, but so were Arizona, Florida, Illinois, Michigan, Nevada, New Jersey, Oregon, Rhode Island and Wisconsin (Pew Center on States, 2009). And as an IMF study concludes, highlighting the importance of referring to state policies to understand the dynamics of American capitalism, "[t]he impact of the crisis on tax collection in individual states during the crisis was diverse, reflecting both the heterogeneity of tax systems and of the state economies and their varied exposure to financial and economic shocks" (Jonas, 2012, p. 16).

Rules governing the labor market

Employment rules are also part of the institutional environment impacting an economy's ability to weather financial and economic shocks. Standard economic theory argues that flexible labor markets are a source of advantage in that they favor adjustments to economic shocks. The US labor market is usually characterized as "flexible" but also as highly segmented. Indeed, an employee's terms of employment – including pay, healthcare, pensions and other benefits, hours, leave, job health and safety policies – are generally defined by his contract, and unless the contract contains provisions to the contrary, employment is generally "at will," which means it can be terminated at any time and for any reason so long as no law is violated. Federal labor laws provide a general framework of minimal rules, giving firms and states considerable leeway in implementing them, and flexibility varies depending on a number of provisions applying at the firm and/or state level. There is also considerable diversity in employment rules across the United States. Thus, in firms where a labor union has been "certified," collective bargaining can take place, and terms of employment are then negotiated and applied collectively. This is the exception rather than the rule, however. Although some three-quarters of private-sector workers and two-thirds of public employees have the right to collective bargaining, only 8 million private-sector workers and 8.5 million public-sector workers, i.e., 10 percent of the US labor force, are actually covered by collective bargaining agreements.[51] The share of workers represented by unions, which has declined significantly since the 1950s, varies significantly across states, with rates significantly lower in "right-to-work states." In 2012, when the national rate was 11.3 percent, it reached a minimum of 3.7 percent in Arkansas and a maximum of 24.9 in New York.[52] On the other hand, some federal laws do not apply to all types of businesses, as in the case of the Family and Medical Leave Act, which only requires employers of 50 or more employees to give up to 12 weeks of unpaid, job-protected leave to eligible employees for the birth or adoption of a child or for the serious illness of the employee or a spouse, child or parent. Again, eligibility criteria are often determined at state level, as in the case of unemployment insurance benefits. Indeed, although Unemployment Insurance was instituted by the federal government, it is administered by state governments (within guidelines established by federal law), and the benefits paid to unemployed workers vary from one state to another. Each state determines eligibility criteria, benefit amounts and the length of time benefits are available. In the majority of states, benefit funding is based solely on a tax imposed on employers, but three states (Alaska, New Jersey and Pennsylvania) also levy a tax on workers (US DOL, 2013).

State laws may also be more beneficial to workers than federal legislation, as in the case of minimum wages.[53] The federal rule, instituted by the Fair Labor Standards Act, is that employers are required to pay eligible employees at least the federal minimum wage and overtime pay of 1.5 times the regular rate of pay. But states also enact their own minimum wage laws. Thus, the federal minimum wage rate of $7.25 per hour effective as of July 2009 was applied in 29 states, while 21 states enacted higher rates, up to $9.10 in Oregon and $9.32 in Washington.[54] The fact that several states opted to reject the expanded Medicaid coverage provided for by the Patient Protection and Affordable Care Act which was enacted in 2010 and established state-based health insurance exchanges is a reminder of the spatial "nestedness" of many US institutions (Hollingworth & Boyer, 1998).

Education, training and the production and diffusion of knowledge

The educational system is another constituent of the institutional environment impacting regional economies. The positive contribution of a well-trained workforce to economic development and growth has been studied from a variety of theoretical perspectives in the past two decades, both at the national and regional scales (Martin & Sunley, 1998; Gennaioli *et al.*, 2013). As local skill bases are a key constituent of local economies, geographic disparities regarding the quality of primary and secondary (K–12) education[55] reinforce socioeconomic inequalities and contribute to varying local economic performance across the United States (Goldin & Katz, 2009). Although the comparative mobility of the US labor force (Molloy *et al.*, 2011) and the attractiveness of the United States for high-skilled immigrants ensure that economically dynamic localities will attract skilled labor, further reinforcing their growth potential, conversely a locality's poor educational results will contribute to low economic performance and even lead to a "brain drain" of its educated workforce, as parts of the Midwest and the South illustrate (Carnevale & Smith, 2011, 2012). States like Alabama, Mississippi and West Virginia lost young college graduates during the Great Recession because opportunity existed elsewhere. Thus investment "in K–12 and especially postsecondary education is not the magic pill, but it certainly is a key stepping stone towards the type of economic development which lifts [a] region out of prolonged stagnation" (Carnevale & Smith, 2012, p. 5).

The role of technological innovation in shaping the changing fortunes of regional and local economies has also been widely studied, with emphasis on the importance of the institutional setting within which innovation takes place, and the emergence and development of clusters of technologically based activity. As knowledge spillovers are important to the geography of innovation (Audretsch & Feldman, 2004), the role of research universities in knowledge-based, innovation-driven economies and regional innovation systems is now well established (Etzkowicz & Leydesdorff, 1997, 2000; Etzkowitz, 2008; Florida & Cohen, 1999; Bramwell & Wolfe, 2008).[56] The regional knowledge-based economies are attractive to domestic and foreign capital and domestic and foreign skilled labor and are therefore increasingly dependent on the global economy.

Conclusion

Our empirical study of the impact of the Great Recession on the American economy leads us to conclude that to fully capture the characteristics of American capitalism one should adopt both a multi-scale focus and a multi- or rather cross-disciplinary approach. Indeed, as we have seen, the dynamics of growth and change in the US economy are fundamentally driven by a web of local, regional, national, as well as global forces that, in addition to fostering social inequalities, also foster spatial inequalities. Because these forces relate to spheres that are the specific object of study of different scholarly disciplines (mostly economics, politics, sociology, history and geography) they cannot be understood unless one borrows from these various disciplines' literatures to underline the complementarities – and often mutually reinforcing nature – of these forces.

Nationally, the American model of capitalism appears to be characterized not so much by its reliance on markets and finance, but by a specific state–market nexus. But the fact that the United States is a federal republic makes institutions particularly "thick" and "nested." Thus the "state" should be understood not only as a synonym for the "federal government," but as relating to governments at the national, state and local levels. As we have seen, these governments set rules, produce incentives, transmit signals to economic actors, and redistribute income between individuals, social classes, and regions. And just as there is not one model but many national models of capitalism, with each model embedded in different nationally specific institutional environments, the American model of capitalism is therefore characterized by institutional thickness and nestedness, which, together with economic structure and geography, largely account for significant variations in economic performance and spatial inequalities between regions and localities. Thus, as Martin (2012) argues, how a specific region or community will resist, respond or recover from an economic shock can be explained by a number of factors which vary regionally and locally. These include economic structure; the ability of firms to innovate, compete and build networks with suppliers and customers nationally and internationally; the skills and culture of workers; and "economic governance arrangements." But resilience is also about political economy: "not only about how the region's firms and industries react and adjust, but also about how local institutional, cultural and political conditions mediate and respond to those reactions, about how national policy may help or hinder a region's recovery" (Martin, 2012, p. 13). Indeed, state and regional dynamics can either (1) reinforce dynamics or processes set at the federal/national level; (2) fill out a gap; or (3) neutralize or trump federal policies. In doing so they play a role in exacerbating or mitigating social, economic and educational disparities, thus explaining why some regions may be more "resilient," more "creative" or simply better at fostering innovation than others.

To gain insight into a region's specific ability to respond to changing market conditions one should not therefore only focus on its economic structure, but also factor in geography, institutions and institutional complementarities. But to characterize American capitalism, one should also bear in mind that in the nation's motto – *E pluribus Unum* – the *many* are just as important as the *one*. Given the size and complexity of the US economy and its relations to the global economy, local and regional differences are likely to persist in the years to come. This should, hopefully, caution future researchers against "fetishizing the national scale," and encourage them to adopt a cross-disciplinary, multi-dimensional and regionally contextualized approach to American capitalism.

Notes

1 As *The Economist* (2009) acknowledged,

> For years leaders in continental Europe have been told by the Americans, the British and even this newspaper that their economies are sclerotic, overregulated and too state-dominated, and that to prosper in true Anglo-Saxon style they need a dose of free-market reform. But the global economic meltdown has given them the satisfying triple whammy of exposing the risks in deregulation, giving the state a more important role and (best of all) laying low *les Anglo-Saxons*.

2 As defined by Max Weber (1997, p. 90),

> [a]n ideal type is formed by the one-sided accentuation of one or more points of view and by the synthesis of a great many diffuse, discrete, more or less present and occasionally absent concrete individual phenomena, which are arranged according to those one-sidedly emphasized viewpoints into a unified analytical construct.

3 In Ancient Greek, the word κρίσις means a separation, or the power of distinguishing, or a decision, a choice, a judgment.
4 This was in keeping with the neoclassical paradigm, in which market economies obey the same law of supply and demand.
5 One notable exception was Shonfield (1965), whose seminal work on capitalism described three models – liberalism, typical of Britain; statism, typical of France; and corporatism, typical of Germany.
6 "Model" is used here in the sense of ideal type or paradigm. A model does not describe an empirical reality, it is a mental construct which, when confronted with empirical reality, sheds light on it.
7 On theoretical approaches to capitalism, refer to the introduction of this book.
8 Even after the United States had withdrawn its troops from Iraq and downscaled its presence in Afghanistan, defense spending still accounted for 4.2 percent of GDP in 2012 (see Council of Economic Advisers (2014, Appendix B, Tables B-2 and B-21).
9 See the respective contributions of Velut and Coste in this volume.
10 See, for example, the Tea Party's website at www.teaparty.org/americas-fraud-president.
11 See Council of Economic Advisers (2014, Appendix B, Tables B-2, B-21, and B-24); OECD (2009, IMF database).

12 Gross federal debt reached 100.6 percent of GDP in 2013. See Council of Economic Advisers (2014, Appendix B, Table B-20).

13 The banking sector was salvaged by TARP, the Toxic Assets Relief Program passed by Congress and signed into law by President G.W. Bush on October 3, 2008, only two weeks after the Lehman Brothers bankruptcy. General Motors and Ford were rescued from the brink of bankruptcy by the Obama Administration in January 2009.

14 The American Recovery and Reinvestment Act of 2009 was passed by Congress and signed into law by President Barack Obama within a month of his inauguration.

15 After slashing interest rates aggressively from 2007, the Fed began resorting to quantitative easing (QE) from November 2008.

16 The Dodd–Frank Wall Street Reform and Consumer Protection Act was signed into law by President Barack Obama in July 2010.

17 As Saez shows, the top 1 percent income group saw its real income grow by 61.8 percent during the Bush expansion (2002–2007) while real income of the bottom 99 percent rose by a mere 6.8 percent (2013, p. 7). On declining intergenerational mobility, see Mazumder (2012).

18 As Alan Greenspan (2005) commented,

> As we reflect on the evolution of consumer credit in the United States, we must conclude that innovation and structural change in the financial services industry have been critical to providing expanded access to credit for the vast majority of consumers, including those of limited means. Without these forces, it would have been impossible for lower income consumers to have the degree of access to credit markets that they now have.

19 See NBER at www.nber.org/cycles.html.

20 For revised figures of percentage change in real GDP by region and state from 2007 to 2010, see BEA (2012).

21 The MSAs used by the Bureau of Economic Analysis for its entire series of GDP statistics are the county-based definitions developed by the Office of Management and Budget (OMB) for federal statistical purposes. OMB's general concept of a metropolitan area is that of a geographic area consisting of a large population nucleus together with adjacent communities having a high degree of economic and social integration with the nucleus.

22 See BEA (2011, table 2).

23 For a closer look at local differences in unemployment rates across the state of California, see the maps released by the Labor Market Information Division of the California Employment Development Department in September 2010, retrieved from mapswww.calmis.ca.gov/file/lfhist/aaurmap.pdf.

24 "Regions" bear different names and have different boundaries depending on the source on official information. The BEA regions are those outlined in Map 5.1. For a map of the Census regions, see www.census.gov/geo/maps-data/maps/pdfs/reference/us_regdiv.pdf. A map of the 12 Federal Reserve districts appears at www.federalreserve.gov/otherfrb.htm.

25 For a summary of these theories, see Kane (2001).

26 See LeSage and Pace (2009). The two key concepts in spatial econometrics are spatial dependence, or spatial autocorrelation ("near things are more related than distant things"), and spatial heterogeneity.

27 See the website of the U.C. Berkeley Institute of Government Studies Building Resilient Regions network at http://brr.berkeley.edu/about-us. Metropolitan areas are defined as a "collection of cities, suburbs and rural areas that house two thirds of America's population." This is where 96 percent of innovations occur.

28 The question of what proper scale should be chosen to study the dynamics of economic development and growth is not new and has been raised and widely debated by American geographers since Daniel Burnham's 1909 *Plan for Chicago* stressed the

need for infrastructure improvements and transportation investments at the regional rather than urban scale (Pastor *et al.*, 2009).

29 Thus, the Bureau of Economic Analysis, the major national official source of information on the US economy, measures GDP growth at the national, state or local level. Its basic tools are the national income and product accounts (NIPAs), as well as the North American Industry Classification System (NAICS). The Bureau of Labor Statistics publishes national data on the labor force and unemployment obtained from the Current Population Survey (CPS), a sample survey of households that is conducted by the US Census Bureau. It also publishes labor force and unemployment data for census regions and divisions, states, and selected sub-state areas thanks to its Local Area Unemployment Statistics (LAUS) program, which measures employment and unemployment on a place-of-residence basis. See BLS (2015).

30 In addition to national macro-economic multipliers, regional input–output (I–O) multipliers, which account for inter-industry relationships within regions, have been developed by the BEA to deal more specifically with the impact of a specific change or shock on a specific area. See *Regional Multipliers: A User Handbook for the Regional Input–Output Modeling System (RIMS II)*, March 1997 at www.bea.gov/scb/pdf/regional/perinc/meth/rims2.pdf?. RIMS II is based on an accounting framework called an I–O table. For each industry, an I–O table shows the distribution of the inputs purchased and the outputs sold.

31 Thus, it was only in 2008 that a working paper seeking to understand the determinants of economic change in metropolitan areas from 1990 to 2000 was released (Blumenthal *et al.*, 2008).

32 The BEA news release dated February 23, 2011 offers an illustration of this. It included the map reproduced here as Map 5.2.

33 Resilience is generally understood as "the ability of a local socio-economic system to recover from a shock or disruption." For a detailed analysis see Martin (2012).

34 The Midwest is the census region corresponding to the Plains and Great Lakes BEA regions. The rise in unemployment rates was particularly large in Michigan, Illinois and Indiana, where manufacturing accounts for a higher-than-average share of output.

35 See BLS, 2009 and 2010.

36 Hispanics, who represented 17.1 percent of the population in 2012, accounted for 29.3 percent of the poor (Gabe, 2013).

37 As Martin (2011) explains,

> The case of El Centro in southern California highlights how the "subprime" crisis has impacted on the local economy. El Centro had one of the highest rates of "subprime" lending, some 40% of the locality's borrowers purchased homes with this form of finance, often in the new housing developments that sprung up there in the boom. When the housing bubble burst, house prices fell, and foreclosures rose dramatically, housing construction ceased, with intense knock-on effects on employment in that sector of the local economy and on other local activities, and it now has one of the highest unemployment rates (23%) in the USA. (p. 605).

38 See the Brookings Institution's Export Nation website at www.brookings.edu/research/interactives/export-nation.

39 This is based on BLS and State of California, Employment Development Department data. In 2009 the transportation and warehousing industry accounted for 3.6 percent of total employment in the Los Angeles–Long Beach–Glendale metropolitan division. Directly and indirectly the two ports employ about 7 percent of the metropolitan division's labor force, which stood at close to four million in 2009.

40 Clusters are defined as "geographic concentrations of linked industries" (Porter, 2003, p. 562).

41 This is the case for resource-dependent industries. Thus, Houston is a center for the oil industry because of the vast oil fields located in east Texas.

42 Traded industries sell product and services across regions and to foreign countries.

43 An externality is the consequence of an economic activity that is external to the firm. Geographically concentrated industries result in positive externalities because they can support specialized suppliers, provide labor with specialized technical skills, and facilitate knowledge spillovers that benefit the firms settled in the area.

44 See the interactive maps provided by the US Cluster Mapping Project developed by Porter and the Harvard Business School's Institute for Strategy and Competitiveness at http://clustermapping.us/home.

45 Endogenous growth theory treats as endogenous to the growth process factors that the neoclassical growth model treats as exogenous, in particular technological change and human capital. It is based on the existence of positive externalities and increasing returns. This is of particular interest to account for regional growth in that it highlights "the significance and possible spatial consequences of increasing returns and externalities; the role played by endogenous human capital development in regional economies; and the importance of both technology innovation and technology transfer" (Martin & Sunley, 1998, p. 221).

46 The Global Cities Initiative, a joint project of the Brookings Institution and JP Morgan Chase, provides interesting material on the subject.

47 See Tax Foundation (2012).

48 In addition to their own tax receipts, state and local governments receive grants from the federal government, which allocates 17 percent of its budget to state and local grants. All-in-all, state and local government spending represented 15 percent of GDP before the Great Recession began. The American Recovery and Reinvestment Act of 2009 directed unprecedented fiscal relief to states and localities. It appropriated $145 billion to help states fill their budget gaps, and provided additional payments for highways and other infrastructure as well as education (Gordon, 2012).

49 The stringency of balanced budget requirements varies greatly from state to state. For detailed information, see National Conference of State Legislatures (2010).

50 See also the contribution of Cormier in the present volume.

51 For information resources on collective bargaining, see Cornell University's legal information website at www.law.cornell.edu/wex/collective_bargaining. For the history and present-day reality of collective bargaining, see the AFL-CIO's website at www.aflcio.org/Learn-About-Unions/Collective-Bargaining/Collective-Bargaining-Fact-Sheet.

52 See the map in the BLS news release, January 23 2013, at www.bls.gov/news.release/pdf/union2.pdf.

53 Five states require no minimum wage, and four require less than federal minimum wages. See US DOL (n.d.).

54 See details on the United States Department of Labor's website at www.dol.gov/whd/minwage/america.htm.

55 Local governments pay the lion's share of the cost of K–12 public education, although states also contribute a significant portion, with the federal government covering approximately 10 percent of the costs. The quality of K–12 education is therefore correlated with the wealth of localities as higher spending per student is correlated with higher test scores and lower dropout rates.

56 For further discussion, see the contributions of Velut and Coste in the present volume.

References

Aglietta, M. (1998). *Le capitalisme de demain*, Notes de la Fondation Saint-Simon, 101.

Albert, M. (1993). *Capitalism vs. Capitalism*. New York: Four Walls Eight Windows.

Amable, B. (2003). *The diversity of capitalism*. New York: Oxford University Press.

Anari, A. (2012, January). The Great Recession. Why Intensity and Duration Varied. *Monthly Rewiew of the Texas Economy*. http://recenter.tamu.edu/pdf/1989.pdf.

Aubuchon, C.P. & Wheelock, D.C. (2010). The Geographic Distribution and Characteristics of US Bank Failures, 2007–2010: Do Bank Failures Still Reflect Local Economic Conditions? *Federal Reserve Bank of St. Louis Review*, *92*(5), 395–415.

Audretsch, D.B. & Feldman, M.P. (2004). Knowledge Spillovers and the Geography of Innovation. *Handbook of Regional and Urban Economics*, Vol. 4. Amsterdam: Elsevier, pp. 2713–2739.

Azuelos, M. (ed.). (1999). *Pax Americana: de l'hégémonie au leadership économique*. Paris: Presses de la Sorbonne Nouvelle.

Bardhan, A. & Walker, R.A. (2010, March). California, Pivot of the Great Recession. Working Paper, Institute for Research on Labor and Employment, University of California, Berkeley.

Barro, R.J., Sala-I-Martin, X., Blanchard, O. & Hall, R.E. (1991). Convergence Across States and Regions. Brookings Papers on Economic Activity, 107–182.

Baumol, W.J., Litan, R. & Schramm, C.E. (2007). *Good capitalism: Bad capitalism and the economics of growth and prosperity*. New Haven, CT: Yale University Press.

BEA (Bureau of Economic Analysis) (2011, September 13). News release. Retrieved from www.bea.gov/newsreleases/regional/gdp_metro/2011b/gdp_metro0211b.htm.

BEA (2012, June 5). News release. Retrieved from www.bea.gov/newsreleases/regional/gdp_state/2012/pdf/gsp0612.pdf.

Beyers, W.B. (2013). The Great Recession and State Unemployment Trends. *Economic Development Quarterly*, *27*(2), 114–123.

BLS (Bureau of Labor Statistics) (2009, December 2). News release. Retrieved from www.bls.gov/news.release/archives/metro_12072010.pdf.

BLS (2010, December 7). News release. Retrieved from www.bls.gov/news.release/archives/metro_12072010.pdf.

BLS (2015) Regional and State Employment and Unemployment Technical Note. Retrieved from www.bls.gov/news.release/laus.tn.htm.

Blumenthal, P., Hill, E.W. & Wolman, H. (2008). Understanding the Economic Performance of Metropolitan Areas in the United States. Working Paper Number 032. George Washington Institute of Public Policy (GWIPP).

Blundell-Wignall, A. & Atkinson, P. (2008). The Sub-prime Crisis: Causal Distortions and Regulatory Reform. In P. Bloxham & C. Kent (eds.), *Lessons from the Financial Turmoil of 2007 and 2008*. Sydney: Reserve Bank of Australia, pp. 55–102. Retrieved from http://gem.sciences-po.fr/content/publications/pdf/Atkinson-Blundell_Subprime-Crisis032010.pdf.

Boyer, R. (2001). De la première à la seconde *pax Americana*. In R. Boyer & P.-F. Souyri (eds.), *Mondialisation et régulations. Europe et Japon face à la singularité américaine*. Paris: La Découverte, pp. 31–43.

Boyer, R. (2005). How and Why Capitalisms Differ. Max Planck Institute for the Study of Societies, MPIfG Discussion Paper 05/4. Retrieved from www.mpifg.de/pu/mpifg_dp/dp05-4.pdf.

Boyer, R. & Hollingsworth, J. Rogers (1997). From National Embeddedness to Spatial and Institutional Nestedness. In J. Rogers Hollingsworth & R. Boyer (eds.), *Contemporary capitalism: The embeddedness of institutions*. Cambridge, MA: Cambridge University Press, pp. 433–484.

Bramwell, A. & Wolfe, D.A. (2008). Universities and Regional Economic Development: The Entrepreneurial University of Waterloo. *Research Policy*, *37*(8), 1175–1187.

Campbell, A.L. & Sances, M.W. (2013). State Fiscal Policy during the Great Recession Budgetary Impacts and Policy Responses. *The Annals of the American Academy of Political and Social Science*, *650*(1), 252–273.

Carnevale, A.P. & Smith, N. (2011). *The Midwest challenge: Matching jobs with education in the post-recession economy*. Washington, DC: Georgetown University Center on Education and the Workforce.

Carnevale, A.P. & Smith, N. (2012). *A decade behind: Breaking out of the low-skill trap in the southern economy*. Washington, DC: Center on Education and the Workforce. Georgetown University.

Caselli, F. & Coleman II, W.J. (2001). The US Structural Transformation and Regional Convergence: A Reinterpretation. *Journal of Political Economy*, *109*(3), 584–616.

Coates, D. (2000). *Models of capitalism: Growth and stagnation in the modern era*. London: Polity Press

Cohen, J.P., Coughlin, C.C. & Lopez, D.A. (2012). The Boom and Bust of US Housing Prices from Various Geographic Perspectives. *Federal Reserve Bank of St. Louis Review*, *94*(5), 341–367.

Connaughton, J.E. (2010). Local Economic Impact of the Great Recession of 2008/2009. *The Review of Regional Studies*, *40*(1), 1–4.

Connaughton, J.E. & Madsen, R.A. (2012). US State and Regional Economic Impact of the 2008/2009 Recession. *Journal of Regional Analysis and Policy*, *42*(3), 177–186.

Council of Economic Advisers (2014). *Economic Report of the President*. Washington, DC. Retrieved from www.whitehouse.gov/sites/default/files/docs/full_2014_economic_report_of_the_president.pdf.

Cowell, M., Gainsborough, J. & Lowe, K. (2013, May 31). Homogenized Diversity: Economic Visions in the Great Recession. MacArthur Foundation Network on Building Resilient Regions, University of California, Berkeley. Working Paper presented at the Building Resilient Regions closing symposium at the Urban Institute, Washington, DC.

Economist, The. (2009, May 7). A New Pecking Order. Retrieved from www.economist.com/node/13610767/print?story_id=13610767.

Etzkowicz, H. (2008). *The triple helix: University–industry–government innovation in action*. New York: Routedge.

Etzkowitz, H. & Leydesdorff, L. (eds.). (1997). *Universities and the global knowledge economy: A triple helix of university–industry–government relations*. London: Pinter.

Etzkowitz, H. & Leydesdorff, L. (2000). The Dynamics of Innovation: From National Systems and "Mode 2" to a Triple Helix of University–Industry–Government Relations. *Research Policy*, *29*, 109–123.

Felix, A. (2012). Industrial Diversity, Growth, and Volatility in the Seven States of the Tenth District. Federal Reserve Bank of Kansas City, *Economic Review*, *4*, 55–76.

Florida, R. & Cohen, W.M. (1999). Engine or Infrastructure? The University Role in Economic Development. In L. Branscomb, F. Kodama & R.L. Florida (eds.), *Industrializing knowledge: University industry linkages in Japan and the United States*. Cambridge, MA: MIT Press, pp. 589–610.

Gabe, G. (2013, November 13). *Poverty in the United States: 2012*. Washington, DC: Congressional Research Service.

Gennaioli, N., La Porta, R., Lopez-de-Silanes, F. & Shleifer, A. (2013). Human Capital and Regional Development. *The Quarterly Journal of Economics*, *128*(1), 105–164.

Gerolimetto, M. & Magrini, S. (2014). A Novel Look at Long-run Convergence Dynamics in the United States. *International Regional Science Review*, DOI: 10.1177/0160017614550081.

Gertler, M.S. (2010). Rules of the Game: The Place of Institutions in Regional Economic Change. *Regional Studies*, *44*(1), 1–15.

Global Cities Initiative (2013a). The Ten Traits of Globally Influent Metro Areas: New York. Retrieved from www.brookings.edu/~/media/Multimedia/Interactives/2013/ten-traits/New_York.pdf.

Global Cities Initiative (2013b). The Ten Traits of Globally Influent Metro Areas: Los Angeles. Retrieved from www.brookings.edu/~/media/Multimedia/Interactives/2013/tentraits/Los_Angeles.pdf.

Goldin, C.D. & Katz, L.F. (2009). *The race between education and technology*. Cambridge, MA: Harvard University Press.

Gordon, T. (2012, December). State and Local Budgets and the Great Recession. The Russell Sage Foundation and the Stanford Center on Poverty and Inequality, Brookings Institution. Retrieved from www.brookings.edu/research/articles/2012/12/state-local-budgets-gordon#.

Greenspan, A. (2005). Remarks by Chairman Alan Greenspan at the Federal Reserve System's Fourth Annual Community Affairs Research Conference, Washington, DC, April 8. Retrieved from www.federalreserve.gov/BoardDocs/speeches/2005/20050408.

Hall, P.A. & Soskice, D.W. (eds.). (2001). *Varieties of capitalism*. Oxford: Oxford University Press.

Harris, B.H. & Moore, B.D. (2013, November 18). Residential Property Taxes in the United States. Urban-Brookings Tax Policy Center.

Hicks, M.J. & Kuhlman, K.F. (2011). The Puzzle of Indiana's Economy through the Great Recession. Sagamore Institute Working Paper. Retrieved from http://cms.bsu.edu/-/media/WWW/DepartmentalContent/MillerCollegeofBusiness/BBR/Publications/SagamoreMIINRecession091611.pdf.

Hollingsworth, J. Rogers & Boyer, R. (eds.). (1998). *Contemporary capitalism: The embeddedness of institutions*. Cambridge: Cambridge University Press.

Immergluck, D. (2011). The Local Wreckage of Global Capital: The Subprime Crisis, Federal Policy and High-Foreclosure Neighborhoods in the US. *International Journal of Urban and Regional Research*, *35*(1), 130–146.

Jonas, J. (2012). Great Recession and Fiscal Squeeze at US Subnational Government Level. IMF Working Paper Number 184.

Kane, R. (2001). Investigating Convergence of the U.S. Regions: A Time-Series Analysis. Paper presented at the Annual Conference of the Mid-Continent Regional Science Association, Duluth, MN June 31–July 2. Retrieved from www.bea.gov/papers/pdf/kanepaper.pdf.

Kim, S. (1998). Economic Integration and Convergence: US Regions, 1840–1987. *The Journal of Economic History*, *58*(3), 659–683.

Koch, J.V. (2012). Regional Economic Impacts of the World-Wide Recession: A Case Study of Hampton Roads, Virginia. *International Advances in Economic Research*, *18*(2), 163–176.

Kratke, S. (1997). Une approche régulationniste des études régionales. *L'Année de la régulation*, *1*, 263–296.

Krugman, P. (1991a). *Geography and trade*. Cambridge, MA: MIT Press.

Krugman, P. (1991b). Increasing returns and economic geography. *Journal of Political Economy*, *99*, 483–499.

Kyser, J., Sidhu, N.D., Ritter, K. & Guerra, F. (2010) 2010–2011 Economic Forecast and Industry Outlook. Los Angeles County Development Corporation, Kyser Center for Economic Research Los Angeles.

Lane, C. & Wood, G. (2009). Capitalist Diversity and Diversity within Capitalism. *Economy and Society*, *38*(4), 531–551.

LeSage, J.P. & Pace, R.K. (2009). *Introduction to spatial econometrics*. Boca Raton, FL: CRC Press.

Martin, R. (2000). Institutional Approaches in Economic Geography. In E. Sheppard & T.J. Barnes (eds.), *A companion to economic geography*. Oxford: Blackwell, pp. 77–94.

Martin, R. (2010). Roepke Lecture in Economic Geography: Rethinking Regional Path Dependence – Beyond Lock-in to Evolution. *Economic Geography*, *86*(1), 1–27.

Martin, R. (2011). The Local Geographies of the Financial Crisis: From the Housing Bubble to Economic Recession and Beyond. *Journal of Economic Geography*, *11*(4), 587–618.

Martin, R. (2012). Regional Economic Resilience, Hysteresis and Recessionary Shocks. *Journal of Economic Geography*, *12*(1), 1–32.

Martin, R. & Sunley, P. (1998). Slow Convergence? The New Endogenous Growth Theory and Regional Development. *Economic Geography*, *74*(3), 201–227.

Martin, R. & Sunley, P. (2006a). Path Dependence and Regional Economic Evolution. Paper prepared for the European Science Foundation Exploratory Workshop on Evolutionary Economic Geography, Saint Catherine's College, University of Cambridge, April 3–5.

Martin, R. & Sunley P. (2006b). Path Dependence and Regional Economic Evolution. *Journal of Economic Geography*, *6*(4), 395–437.

Mazumder, B. (2012, April). Is Intergenerational Economic Mobility Lower Now Than in the Past? *Chicago Fed Letter*, 297.

Molloy, R., Smith, C.L. & Wozniak, A.K. (2011). *Internal migration in the United States*. Washington, DC: National Bureau of Economic Research.

National Commission on the Causes of the Financial and Economic Crisis in the United States (2011). *The Financial Crisis Enquiry Report*. Washington: United States Government Printing Office.

National Conference of State Legislatures (2010, October). *NCSL Fiscal Brief: State Balanced Budget Provisions*. Retrieved from www.ncsl.org/research/fiscal-policy/state-balanced-budget-requirements-provisions-and.aspx.

North, D.C. (1990). *Institutions, institutional change and economic performance*. New York: Cambridge University Press.

Obstfeld, M. & Rogoff, K.S. (2009). *Global imbalances and the financial crisis: Products of common causes*. London: Centre for Economic Policy Research.

OECD (2012). Financial Contagion in the Era of Globalised Banking. *OECD Economics Department Policy Notes*, 14.

Pastor, M., Lester, T.W. & Scoggins, J. (2009). Why Regions? Why Now? Who Cares? *Journal of Urban Affairs*, *31*(3), 269–296.

Peck, J. & Theodore, N. (2007). Variegated Capitalism. *Progress in Human Geography*, *31*, 731–772.

Pew Center on States (2009, November). Beyond California: States in Fiscal Peril. Retrieved from www.pewstates.org/research/reports/beyond-california-85899376504.

Pew Charitable Trusts (2012, November 14). *Weathering the Great Recession: Did High-Poverty Neighborhoods Fare Worse?* Economic Mobility Project Issue Brief.

Porter, M. (2003). The Economic Performance of Regions. *Regional studies*, *37*(6–7), 549–578.

Reagan, R. (1981, January 20). Inaugural Address, Washington, DC.

Rodríguez-Pose, A. (2013). Do Institutions Matter for Regional Development? *Regional Studies*, *47*(7), 1034–1047.

Rodrik, D., Subramanian, F. & Trebbi, F. (2004). Institutions Rule: The Primacy of Institutions Over Geography and Integration in Economic Development. *Journal of Economic Growth, 9*, 131–165.

Romer, P.M. (1990). Endogenous Technological Change. *Journal of Political Economy, 98*, 71–102.

Rostow, W.W. (1962). *The stages of economic growth.* Cambridge: Cambridge University Press.

Saez, E. (2013). Striking it Richer: The Evolution of Top Incomes in the United States (Updated with 2011 estimates). University of California, Berkeley, Working Paper.

Sassen, S. (2001). *The global city: New York, London, Tokyo.* Princeton, NJ: Princeton University Press.

Sassen, S. (2005). When National Territory is Home to the Global: Old Borders to Novel Borderings. *New Political Economy, 10*(4), 523–541.

Saxenian, A. (1994). *Regional advantage: Culture and competition in Silicon Valley and Route 128.* Cambridge, MA: Harvard University Press.

Saxenian, A. (2006). *The new Argonauts: Regional advantage in a global economy.* Cambridge, MA: Harvard University Press.

Shonfield, A. (1965). *Modern capitalism: The changing balance of public and private power*. Oxford: Oxford University Press.

Siegel, P.B., Johnson, T.G., & Alwang, J. (1995). Regional Economic Diversity and Diversification. *Growth and Change, 26*(2), 261–284.

Tax Foundation (2012). *Location Matters: A Comparative Analysis of State Tax Costs on Business.* Retrieved from http://taxfoundation.org/article/location-matters.

Tax Foundation (2013). Blog on “Prop 13 in California, 35 Years Later.” Retrieved from http://taxfoundation.org/blog/prop-13-california-35-years-later.

Théret. B. (1999). Regionalism and Federalism: A Comparative Analysis of the Regulation of Economic Tensions between Regions by Canadian and American Federal Intergovernmental Transfer Programmes. *International Journal of Urban and Regional Research, 23*(3), 479–512.

US Department of Labor (DOL) (n.d.). Summary of the Major Laws of the Department of Labor. Retrieved from www.dol.gov/opa/aboutdol/lawsprog.htm.

US DOL (2013). Comparison of State Unemployment Laws. Retrieved from http://workforcesecurity.doleta.gov/unemploy/comparison2013.asp.

Walden, M.L. (2012). Explaining Differences in State Unemployment Rates During the Great Recession. *Journal of Regional Analysis and Policy, 42*(3), 251–257.

Wallace, M., Gauchat, G. & Fullerton, A.S. (2012). Globalization and Earnings Inequality in Metropolitan Areas: Evidence from the USA. *Cambridge Journal of Regions, Economy and Society, 5*(3), 377–396.

Weber, M. (1997). *The methodology of the social sciences* (translated by Edward A. Shils and Henry A. Finch). New York: Free Press.

Wheeler, S.M. (2002). The New Regionalism: Key Characteristics of an Emerging Movement. *Journal of the American Planning Association, 68*(3), 267–278.

6 Who's left to sink or swim?*

Practices and policies of the "submerged state" at the subnational level in the wake of the economic recession

Cécile Cormier

As of 2013, states and localities were still trying to grapple with major fiscal challenges and many were struggling to avoid financial meltdown. Indeed, by impacting their residents, the weak economy and rampant unemployment diminished states' and localities' fiscal revenues while at the same time increasing the need for public services and social assistance. States, for the most part, and contrary to the federal government, are bound to balance their operating budgets. So faced with mounting expenditures, dwindling local revenues and the end of the 2009 federal stimulus package, state and local governments massively opted to cut into public spending and services in healthcare, education, social services and public safety, suppressing whole programs, slashing jobs and attacking public employees' benefits. Yet, while state and local governments failed in their duty to deliver public services to their residents, they have made good on their bonds' ratings as safe investments and kept servicing their municipal securities by unfailingly paying out interests to their bondholders.

The neoliberal market regime pursued in the United States since the 1980s seems to be in turmoil and the 2009 stimulus package and the new regulations introduced at the federal level in the wake of the Recession might signal a shift back toward a form of Keynesianism. In sharp contrast meanwhile, at the subnational level, neoliberal practices have been ubiquitous. Indeed the major cuts imposed by state and local governments in public employment, services and social provision in the name of fiscal austerity have exposed larger segments of the American population to pauperization and have worsened social inequality – "a universal tendency" of neoliberalization, according to David Harvey (2005, p. 118). Moreover, the systematic prioritization of bondholders' returns over the integrity of public services and the welfare of all residents could constitute a significant development in the neoliberal project in the United States by attacking "the various forms of common property rights" (Harvey, 2005, p. 160), notably the local bastions protecting public employees' benefits and pension rights.

Interestingly, the deleterious effects of neoliberal practices on social inequality have been intensified by the regressive effects of "submerged state" policies introduced both at the federal and subnational state levels. Coined by Suzanne Mettler, a political scientist, "the submerged state" refers to a set of public policies in the form of indirect subsidies and benefits, introduced by federal policy-makers in such a way that they remain largely invisible to most Americans, beneficiaries notwithstanding (Mettler, 2010, 2011). The aim of submerged government policies can vary from helping to encourage home-buying through the deductibility of mortgage-interest payments, to supporting job creation through the tax-exemption for employer-provided health and retirement benefits, or to contributing to promotion of private investment in state or local government projects through the deduction of municipal bond-interest payments from federal income taxation. The 2009 federal economic stimulus package pushed by the first Obama Administration to alleviate the impact of the recession was a recent addition to the submerged state that consisted primarily of stimulating the economy by lowering tax bills through tax breaks (Mettler, 2010, pp. 810–811). Mettler contends that not only most of its beneficiaries are little aware of the submerged state, but many of its policies favor the most affluent Americans in a regressive and disproportionate way at the expense of foregone tax revenues that could have been used for direct social program expenditure. This chapter inquires how salient the concept of "the submerged state" could be when applied to subnational levels of government. More precisely, I will examine how state and local governments struggling with operating budget deficits and large amounts of debt aggravated by the downturn in the national economy have resorted to outright spending cuts and tax hikes, but also to more insidious and invisible submerged state practices with the same "upwardly redistributive bias" as the federal submerged state (Mettler, 2010, p. 809).

The primary purpose of this chapter is thus to provide an insight into the states' and localities' budgetary situation and trade-offs, and to question the fairness and validity of some recent decisions which, although generally presented as financially sound and socially acceptable, epitomize neoliberal practices through a regressive redistribution of wealth by gutting social programs and preserving the financial interests of bondholders. I will first show that the state and local governments' financial predicament did not originate with the 2008 financial crash, but was aggravated by its economic and social impact as states and localities had long been suffering from pension plan underfunding and bond indebtedness. I will then examine how, faced with plummeting revenues that are insufficient to cover mounting budget needs and long-term liabilities, state and local governments have resorted to severe spending cuts and tax increases that affect all their residents. Meanwhile, submerged state policies have kept preserving local bondholders' interests and tax benefits. Finally, I offer an overview of bondholders and of the latest submerged state developments in some states that establish bondholders' prevalence over local residents and public employees to preserve the local governments' ability to raise money for public purposes and induce investment through the US municipal bond market.

States in dire straits

How infrequent bankruptcies and defaults really are?

According to Meredith Whitney, the banking analyst who made a name for herself by forecasting the banking meltdown, state and local governments' finances could be the source of the next financial crisis as she predicts a "wave of muni defaults" (Whitney, 2010) which, combined to local government bankruptcies, could once again shatter the US economy. So far, even though there has been a lot of media attention on the dismal fate of some American cities and counties, defaults on municipal securities have remained rare. Indeed, according to Moody's Investors Service, even if the 5.5 average of defaults per year for 2010 and 2011 reveals an increase from a 2.7 average over the 1970–2009 period, the number of defaults remains "low in absolute terms" (Medioli *et al.*, 2012). Yet, an analysis conducted by economists at the Federal Reserve Bank of New York reports this number to be as high as 2,521 (Appleson *et al.*, 2012), while Moody's Investors Service estimates the number of municipal bond defaults to be 71 from 1970 to 2011 (Medioli *et al.*, 2012). This discrepancy is accounted for by the inclusion in the total number of municipal bonds of unrated bonds whose credit quality is lower and default rate higher. The economists underscore the necessity to distinguish between general obligation (GO) bonds on the municipal market – secured by the GO pledge of a state or local government and backed by its taxing power to meet debt service requirements – and revenue bonds – backed solely by the revenue generated by the project (toll bridge, highway, local sewer system, etc.) financed by the bond issue. They show that GO bonds are rated and rarely default, whereas unrated bonds are to be found among revenue bonds and exhibit a higher frequency of defaults. Moreover, they point out the evolution of the municipal bond market over the past 20 years, with an ever-increasing number of revenue bonds being issued.

As for municipal bankruptcy filings, their number has increased since the beginning of the economic crisis, but not considerably, and it remains "very rare" (Hoene, 2010, 2011) as shown by Figure 6.1.

What is more, the data collected by Spiotto (2012) reveal that among the 264 municipal bankruptcies that have been filed since 1980, only 49 were filed by a city or a county, while the majority were filed by municipal utilities and special districts (Figure 6.2).

These figures make clear that special-purpose governments are much more likely to seek bankruptcy protection by filing under Chapter 9 of the Bankruptcy Code than general-purpose governments.[1] Interestingly, they also indirectly correlate those of the Federal Bank of New York on the higher default rate of revenue bonds: revenue bonds are mainly issued by special-purpose districts.[2] What is more, the number of special district governments has increased by 18 percent over the past 20 years as state and local governments, in accordance with the neoliberalization of the state apparatus, have increasingly resorted to the creation of special districts as a way to devolve the provision of some services they

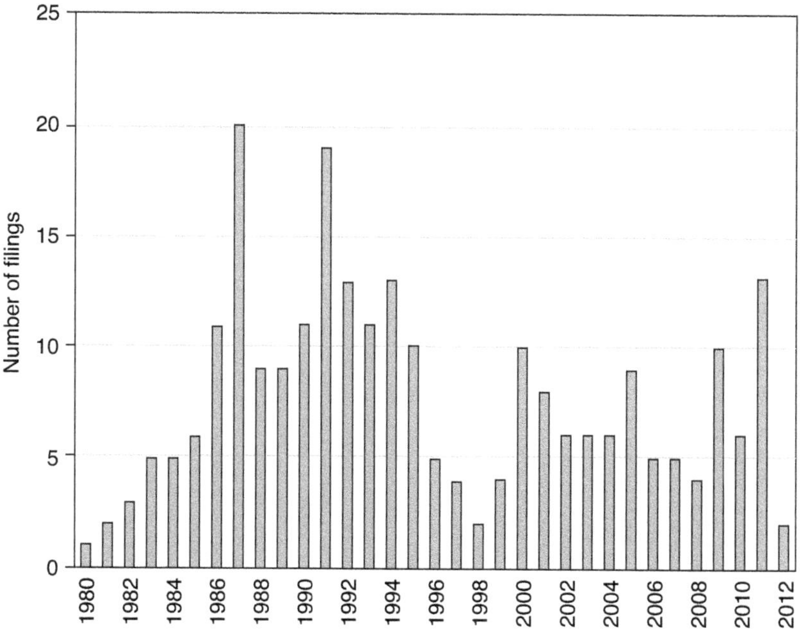

Figure 6.1 Number of Chapter 9 filings by year (1980–2012) (source: Spiotto, 2012: app.C-2).

Note
Data as of January 31, 2012.

no longer wanted to provide directly (US Census Bureau, 2012c).[3] The ability of the newly created special districts to raise money by issuing bonds is a way for state and local governments to remove all or most of the costs related to particular service provisions from their budgets as well as to circumvent their own restrictions on direct debt issuance and their constituents' aversion to higher taxation.

But the relatively rare occurrence of local government bankruptcies should not obscure the fact that even if federal law permits all local governments to file for Chapter 9 protection, state laws greatly differ on that point as more than half of the states restrict, bar or do not specifically allow Chapter 9 filings (Spiotto, 2012, app. D). One may wonder whether the infrequent instances of Chapter 9 cases are not the tip of the iceberg of financially distressed local governments. Indeed, 264 municipal bankruptcies were filed between 1980 and 2012 in the 33 states where they are not overtly prohibited, and more than half occurred in only four states (namely Nebraska, California, Texas and Colorado) that specifically or conditionally authorize Chapter 9 filings (ibid., app. C-2). Furthermore, as mentioned earlier, most Chapter 9 cases involve municipal utilities and special districts (which mainly issue revenue bonds) and more seldom large municipalities

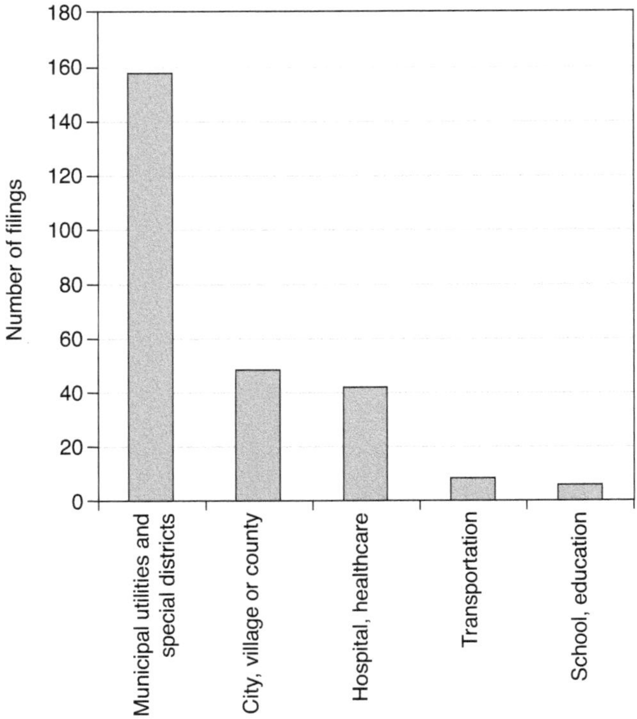

Figure 6.2 Number of Chapter 9 filings by type (1980–2012) (source: Spiotto, 2012: app.C-3).

Note
Data as of January 31, 2012.

(which issue both GO and revenue bonds) even though the latter receive much more media attention. To better grasp the actual magnitude of the "iceberg," we can consider the causes of past defaults and bankruptcies as identified by Spiotto and see how pervasive they could be throughout all local governments. Indeed, to explain the failure of some local governments to meet municipal obligations as they become due, Spiotto points to a series of factors which, for the most part, can be encountered in all local governments: the deteriorating state of public works and facilities that require significant repair and capital improvement spending; the growing budgetary weight of public employees' benefits and pensions on municipal finances; taxpayers' reluctance toward higher taxation; inflation; and the economic crisis (ibid., 7).

The combination of most of these factors can cause default or bankruptcy, especially when they are associated with yet an additional factor: enduring mismanagement. If we take the examples of Jefferson County, AL, or Harrisburg, PA, or more recently Central Falls, RI, it appears that their plight was not triggered, but rather aggravated, by the economic crisis. Indeed, analysis of these particular bankruptcies points to "years of financial mismanagement and political dysfunction" that paved the way to financial failure (*The Economist*, 2011a). The current crisis only precipitated the process of those localities' financial deterioration (de Angelis & Tian 2013). Indeed, Howell-Moroney and Hall (2011) have shown in their detailed analysis of the financial demise of Jefferson County that it resulted from a lack of transparency and accountability combined with defective local government oversight, mismanagement and inconsiderate reliance on risky and complex financing arrangements. In the case of the city of Harrisburg, an investigation was launched to determine how the modernization of the city-owned rubbish incinerator into a state-of-the-art device that was supposed to pay for itself pushed the city toward bankruptcy (*The Economist*, 2011b). As for Central Falls, the root of its financial woes lies in its choice to operate its own pension fund for police officers and firefighters (rather than relying on the state-run pension system), its commitment, despite its very modest size and financial means, to offer retirement benefits as generous as those provided by better-off states or municipalities, and its inability to fund its growing pension costs (*The Economist*, 2012b; Walsh & Goodnough, 2011).[4]

The crisis has worsened the already difficult financial situation of many local governments, including those located in the 17 states that do not allow local governments to file for bankruptcy. These financially distressed local governments share the same economic conditions and often present the same "default-factors" as those which can resort to Chapter 9 filing, which implies that a probably greater number of local governments are under severe financial duress and are forced into tough budgetary choices so as to meet their debt obligations. But hard figures on how many local governments actually face this predicament are rare. To fathom the scale of the problem, we need to turn to state and local government budgets.

Budgetary challenges

The grim and permeating image conveyed in the media of high-profile though infrequent municipal bankruptcies should not eclipse the current and relative improvement in the general fiscal condition of state and local governments. Indeed, the data provided by the US Census Bureau for its annual state tax collection reports from FY2005 to FY2011 (Figure 6.3) show that states' total tax revenues rebounded in 2011 after a two-year decline since FY 2008.

The rebound in tax revenues is largely due to the increase in income tax collections and sales tax receipts. But this general upward trend results from different situations locally, some states having increased their income tax base, others enjoying lower unemployment, and some a combination of the two.[5] Yet this slight improvement in states' tax revenues does not mean that states are no longer facing fiscal hardship. Indeed, though definitely perceptible, the recovery as of 2013 is both modest as some states are still far from their pre-recession fiscal condition and fragile as a combination of aggravating factors threatens to jeopardize this upward trend in fiscal year 2012 and beyond.

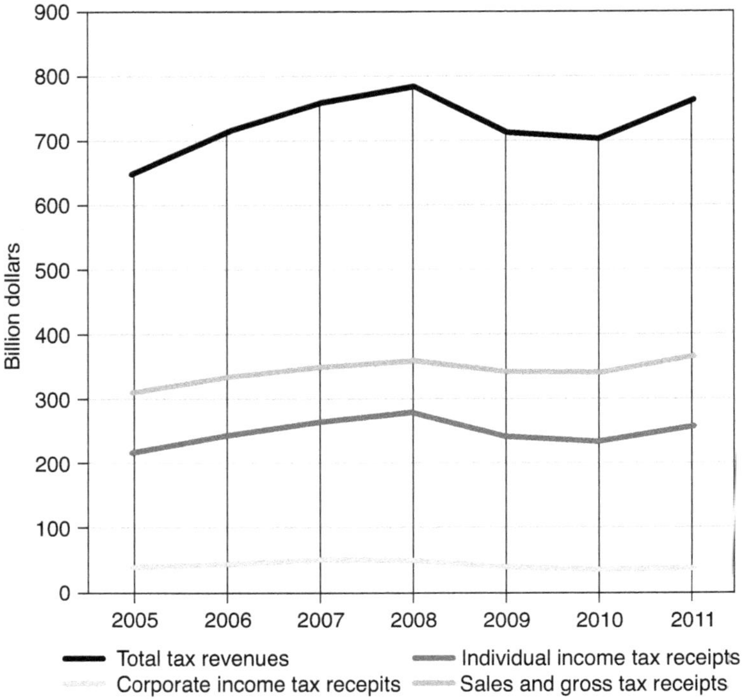

Figure 6.3 State government tax collections (FY2005–2011) ($ billion) (source: based on data from the US Census Bureau).

State and local governments' fiscal condition is still convalescent and there are serious risks of a relapse looming ahead. To start with, the economic buffers that enabled states and localities to reduce the damaging impact of the recession on their budgets are nearing depletion. Indeed, faced with huge state budgetary shortfalls in the 2009, 2010 and 2011 fiscal years[6] due to plummeting tax revenues and mounting public services and social assistance expenditures, states were able to fill part of the gap (between 30 and 40 percent) thanks to the American Recovery and Reinvestment Act (ARRA, also known as the Recovery Act or the stimulus package), enacted in 2009 (McNichol *et al.*, 2012, p. 7). Though extended to June 2011, the stimulus program is now over and will no longer be instrumental in helping states bridge their budget gaps (Figure 6.4). In addition to this temporary federal assistance, state and local governments have been resorting to their rainy-day funds to compensate for their fiscal shortfalls, but these financial reserves are running dry.[7]

To make things worse on the revenue side of budget shortfalls, the National League of Cities (NLC) predicts that in the 2012 fiscal year and beyond, local property tax collections will further diminish, a decline that affected most states

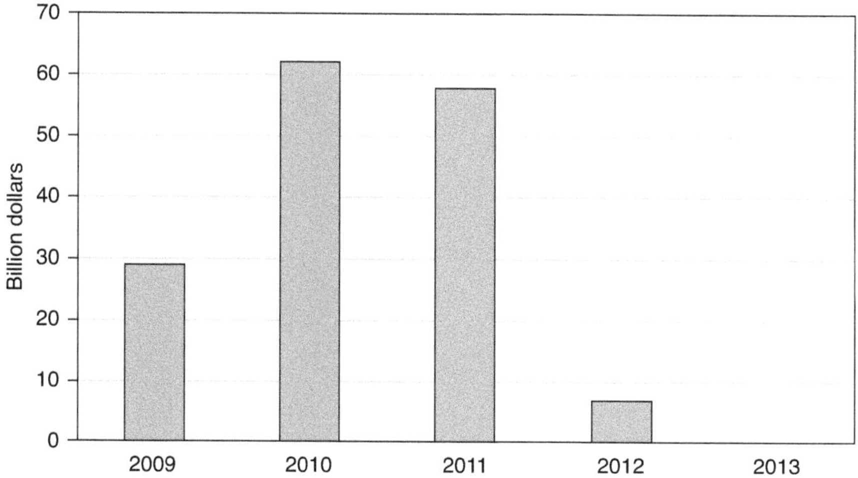

Figure 6.4 Recovery Act funds available to states ($ billion) (source: Center on Budget and Policy Priority).

from FY2010 to FY2011 (by more than 50 percent in Florida or even 80 percent in Indiana and Nebraska).[8] This on-going drop in property tax receipts results from the combined effects of the slow-down in new construction and the downturn in real-estate values, whose delayed impact is due to the time lag (from 18 months to several years) between the real-estate market conditions and the assessment of the value of property by local governments for tax collection (Hoene & Pagano, 2011, p. 4). This is bad news for local governments for which property tax represents the largest source of general revenue to finance schools and security services. Moreover, this likely loss in property tax receipts for local governments will be compounded by the on-going reduction of intergovernmental revenues (payments and grants transferred by the state to local governments).[9]

On the expenditure side, state and local governments are facing escalating demand for Medicaid and other social services as their residents have lost jobs, income and health insurance.

The Recovery Act of 2009 was meant to address this issue and most of the federal fiscal relief to state and local governments went to additional Medicaid funding and education (Figure 6.5).[10] But, as mentioned earlier, this federal aid program came to an end in June 2011 despite students' and citizens' greater social needs in times of economic sluggishness. Indeed, in 2012 both the school and higher education population[11] and the number of people eligible for Medicaid[12] were expected to grow. Moreover, the US Government Accountability Office (GAO) predicts that the implementation of the Patient Protection and Affordable Care Act (PPACA, also known as Obamacare) will raise state outlays

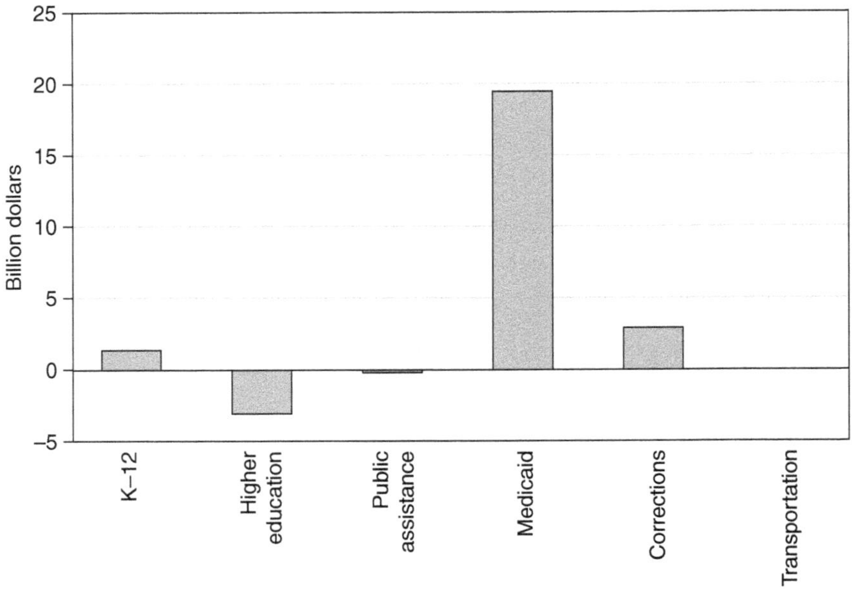

Figure 6.5 Changes in general fund spending by category between FY2011 and FY2012 ($ billion) (source: National Association of State Budget Officers).

in states currently offering less healthcare protection through Medicaid than required by the new healthcare reform (GAO, 2012a, p. 7).

Another major cause for fiscal pressure on state and local governments is the funding and payment of state and local pensions for their current employees and retirees. Today more than 27 million employees and beneficiaries are covered by pension plans sponsored by state or local governments, but the funded status of those pension schemes has declined significantly from 88 percent in 2007 to 75 percent in 2011 according to the Center for Retirement Research[13] (Munnell *et al.*, 2012, p. 2) (Figure 6.6). The GAO admits that most pension plans are largely underfunded (GAO, 2009, 2012b), and explains the down-trend of the funded ratios by the investment losses incurred by the recent financial market crisis, and by governments' budgetary inability to fund rising sponsor contribution rates.

The GAO points to the fiscal challenge to provide adequate contributions, and the Center for Retirement Research raises concerns about small pension plans, more likely to suffer from severe underfunding (below 60 percent) as illustrated by the above-mentioned example of Central Falls' pension scheme or other towns in the state of Rhode Island, whose pension shortfalls are abysmal (Munnell *et al.*, 2012, p. 3).

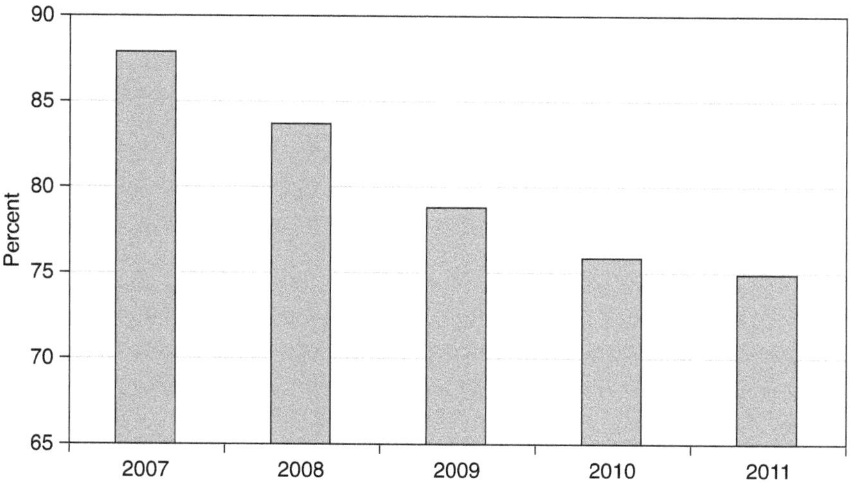

Figure 6.6 State and local pension funded ratios (2007–2011) (source: Center for Retirement Research at Boston College).

Budgetary shortfalls and trade-offs

Budgetary alternatives

Since unlike the federal government, state – with the exception of Vermont – and local governments cannot run budget deficits; fiscally distressed states and localities have to deal with their budget shortfalls by increasing revenues and raising taxes and/or reducing expenditures and cutting services and benefit payments to citizens. According to the Center on Budget and Policy Priorities (CBPP), since 2008 and up to fiscal year 2011, "more than 30 states have raised taxes to at least some degree, in some cases quite significantly," while 46 states opted for a reduction in "services for their residents, including some of their most vulnerable families and individuals" (McNichol *et al.*, 2012, p. 6), notably low-income households, children, the elderly and disabled residents. So, up to fiscal year 2011, states and localities resorted to a combination of federal relief funds, reserve funds, spending reductions and tax increases to compensate for their diminished revenues and increased needs for public and social services so as to bridge their budget gaps and meet their balanced budget requirements. Today the slight improvement in state revenues will not be sufficient to pay for needed expenditure. Indeed, the data collected by the CBPP show that for fiscal year 2012, "at least ten states have seen new shortfalls open in their budgets" and, "30 states have projected or have addressed shortfalls" for fiscal year 2013 (ibid., pp. 2–6). To close those shortfalls, since the buffer funds are exhausted, states are left with only two options: additional taxes or further cuts.

Revenue increases

Tax receipts represent the largest source of general revenues for states and local governments (Figure 6.7).

Many budget staffers in city and county governments are currently considering compensating their expected budget gaps for FY2013 by relying even more on property tax by raising the tax rate (Figure 6.8). But in most states, any property tax rate increase is capped and constrained by state law and should decision-makers exceed the limit, residents could petition for an election to confine the increase.

As for states (Figure 6.9), since they derive most of their general revenue from taxes and charges (77 percent in FY2009, the remainder coming from intergovernmental grants), their only income-raising option is to raise their own-source revenue (Urban Institute-Brookings Institution Tax Policy Center, 2009).

According to the Center on Budget and Policy Priorities, more than 30 states have resorted to raising their own-source revenues, and more than ten have enacted packages of substantial tax changes, including temporary increase of sales tax, excise tax and the extension of sales tax to a selection of services and to internet sales (Johnson *et al.*, 2011, p. 5). Even if it cannot be denied that more taxation will affect the local economy by reducing the amount of residents' disposable income, tax increases, if aimed at upper-income households, are less

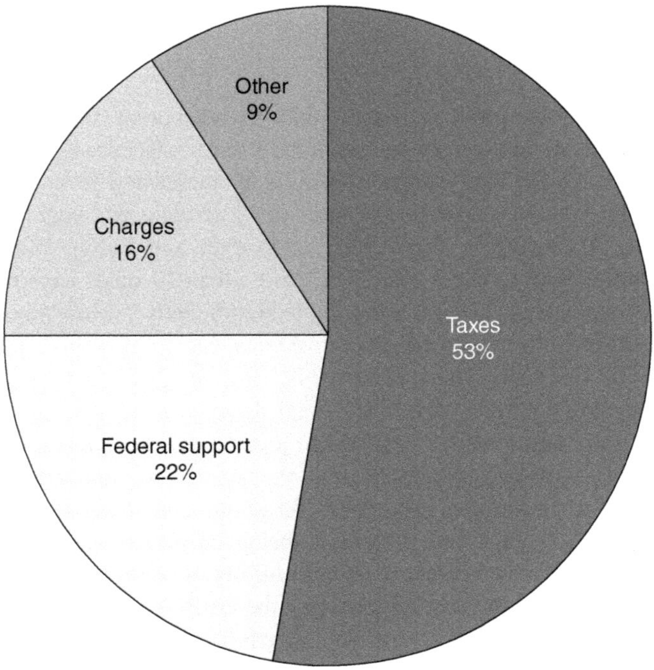

Figure 6.7 Source of state and local government revenues (2009) (source: US Census Bureau, 2011c).

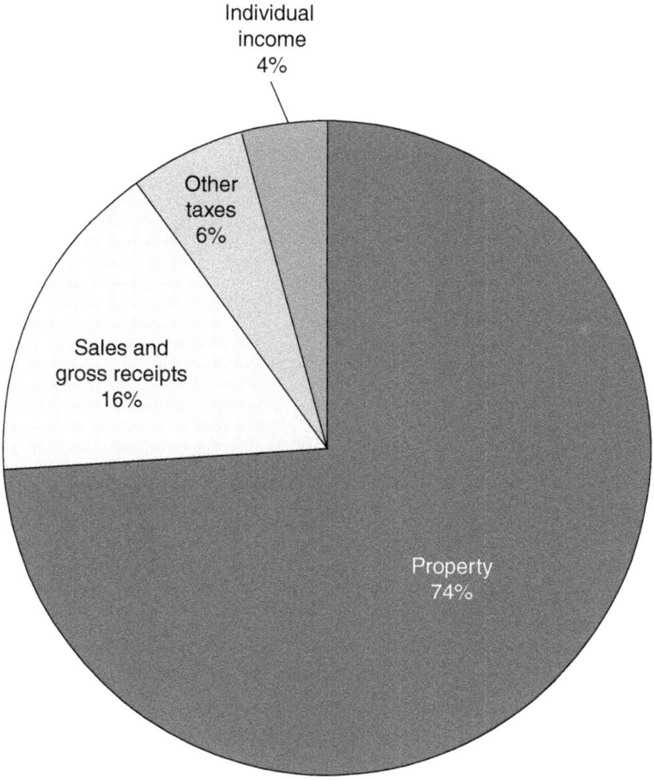

Figure 6.8 Local government tax collections (2009) (source: based on data from the US Census Bureau).

damaging than cutbacks on state expenditures for the local economy and for the state's population at large.

Spending cuts

As mentioned earlier, from FY2008 to FY2011, 46 states resorted to cuts in their operating budgets to bridge their budget gaps. But if we consider state expenditure by category, it appears that some categories have been hit particularly hard, notably human services, education and the public sector workforce, while one, the debt service, stands out as unscathed.

The CBPP report (Johnson *et al.*, 2011) counts all the states that have enacted cuts in their funding of the areas of public health (31 states), the elderly and the disabled (29 plus DC), K–12 and early education (34 and DC), higher education (43) and the state workforce (44 plus DC) (Figure 6.10). The details provided by the report for each state reveal common trends in the way states have been

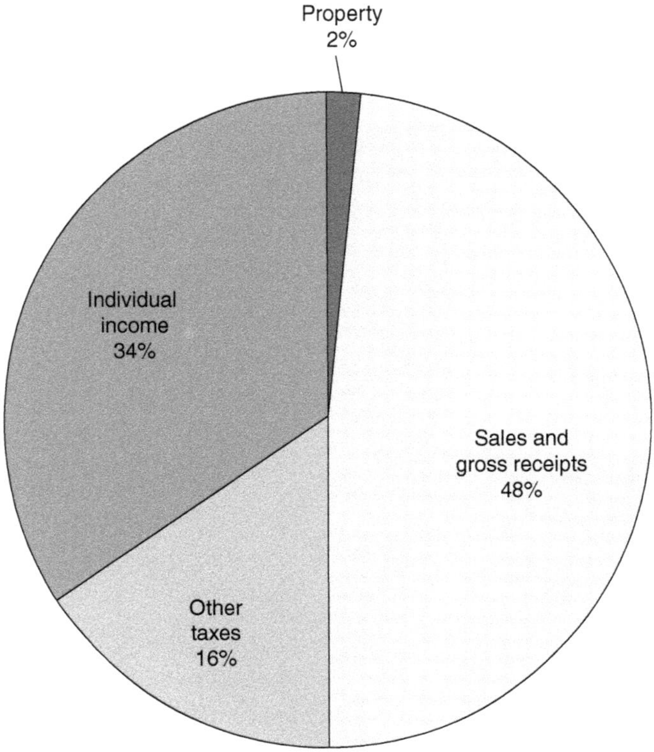

Figure 6.9 State government tax collections (2009) (source: based on data from US Census Bureau).

cutting back funding in those areas. For public health programs and programs for the elderly and disabled, there has been a general reduction both in the range of healthcare and home care services and in the eligibility for access and coverage. The residents who are the most affected by these changes are low-income adults, elderly adults and children (Medicaid and CHIP recipients), HIV/AIDS patients and individuals with disabilities. For K–12 and early education programs, the general reduction in state aid has resulted in the suspension of specific programs (like class-size reduction or special-needs students), as well as decreasing funds transferred to local governments and school districts. The combined effects of declining state educational funds and transfers and declining revenues derived from property taxes on which local governments depend to finance schools have forced them to lay off teaching staff, leaving behind unemployed teachers and students squeezed into overcrowded classes. For higher education programs, the reduction of state funding has led to widespread tuition increases (sometimes up to 30 percent), reductions of student financial aid, and restructuring plans involving furloughs, layoffs and higher education employee

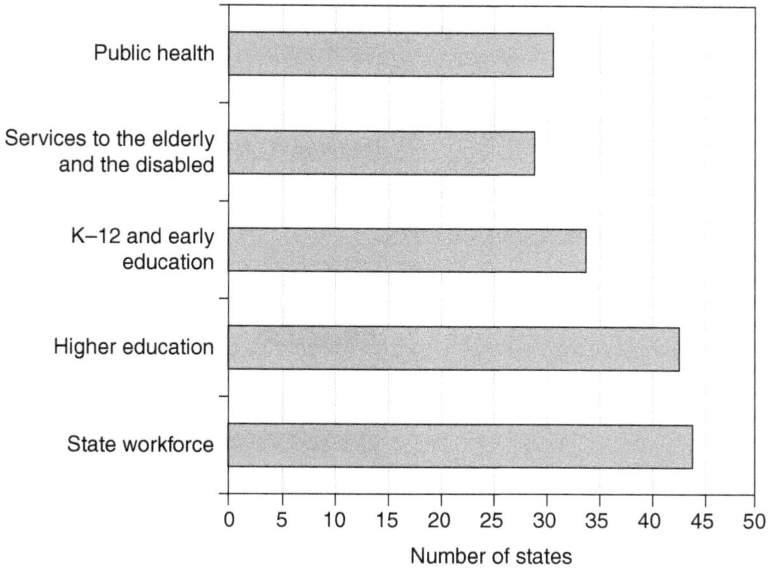

Figure 6.10 Number of states having enacted cuts since 2008 by service areas (source: based on data from the Center on Budget and Policy Priorities).

workloads. As for the public sector workforce at large, state and local governments have shed jobs massively since 2009 (about 100,000 workers for states and more than half a million for local governments, most of them in education (Figure 6.11) (*The Economist*, 2012a).

These severe public job cuts in the public sector worsened unemployment locally, seriously deteriorated the delivery of public service and even deprived residents of essential services like a locally based 24/7 fully operational fire department.[14]

In addition to cutting public jobs, states have backed down from their pension promises to their current, separated or retired employees. Indeed, many states and localities have implemented pension reforms by reducing pension benefits and increasing service requirements (generally for future employees), by increasing employee contributions, and for some states by introducing a defined-contribution plan component to the traditional defined-benefit system (Munnell *et al.*, 2012, pp. 5–6) (Figure 6.12).

These changes are mainly at the expense of public employees as a larger share of pension costs and more investment risk are now shifted to them, whereas their pension benefits are being trimmed. From a budgetary point of view, those changes have contributed to reducing the growth in pension liabilities, but according to the Center for Retirement Research this is a "one-shot" effect and "liability growth is likely to pick up somewhat in coming years"

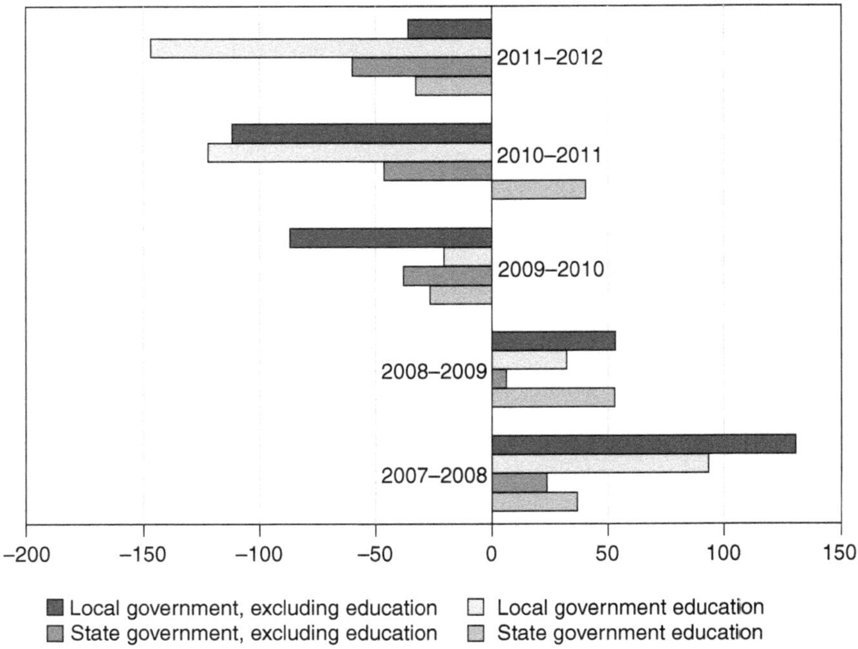

Figure 6.11 Year-on-year employment change in selected governments from 2007 to 2012 (in thousands) (source: based on data from the Bureau of Labor Statistics, Current Employment Statistics).

(Munnell *et al.*, 2012, p. 6). Novy-Marx and Rauh (2009, p. 195) believe that if a state or local government were to renege on the promised payments to its current retirees and defaulted on its pension obligations because of underfunding, pensioners would not be left holding the bag as the federal government would step in for a bailout. This remains to be seen. More likely scenarios would consist of future and current public retirees being compelled to agree to scale down their pension benefits, or having taxpayers foot the bill for shortfalls through tax hikes, or redirecting part of general expenditure towards pension obligations to the detriment of other social benefits or services to the community.

On the whole, education and public welfare account for the two largest expenditure items for state and local governments (Figure 6.13), and public welfare spending in the period 2009–2010 rose by 5.7 percent (US Census Bureau, 2012b, p. 4). Yet, this increase is mainly due to the rise in health costs and in Medicaid enrollments, and should not overshadow the severe cuts in benefits and services that have affected Americans in their everyday lives.

It is noteworthy that the broad "Insurance trust expenditure" category comprises unemployment compensation as well as employee retirement and that funding pension plans represents 6.6 percent of total expenditure. The even

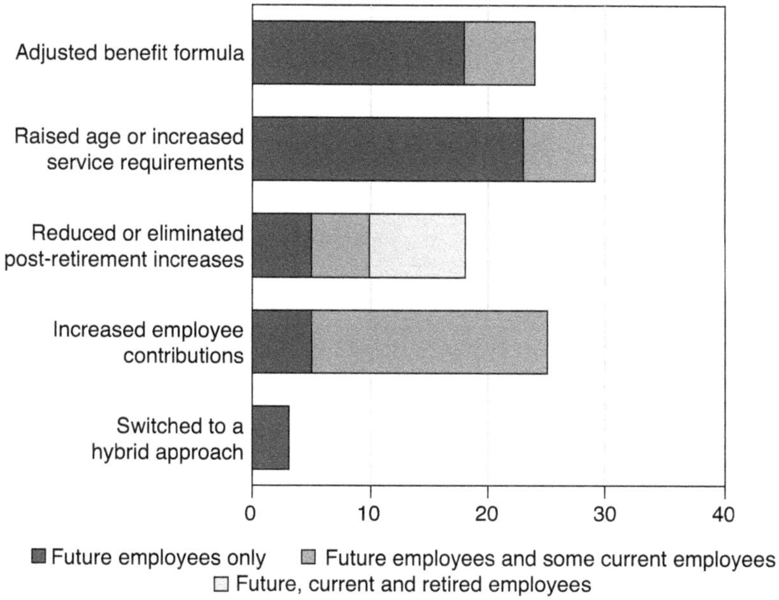

Figure 6.12 Number of states reducing benefits in state-sponsored pension plans (January 2008–June 2011) (source: US Census Bureau, 2012b, p. 19)).

broader "Other" category includes police and fire protection, which represents 4.4 percent of total expenditure. It also includes debt servicing interest which accounts for 3.8 percent of state and local government expenditure. But to grasp the importance of debt service relative to other expenditure items, we need to differentiate state from local governments.

If we look at the evolution of the share of interest payments compared to other expenditures or to state and local own-source revenues (Figure 6.14), it appears first that as state and local governments' own-source revenues decreased in the wake of the crisis, the share of debt service to own-source revenues has logically increased; and second, that debt service payments weigh more heavily on local governments' budgets. Indeed, in 2010, out of the $2.8 trillion outstanding debt, local governments' share amounted to more than 60 percent. In 2007, when the US Census Bureau conducted its last detailed census for local governments for which data are available, most local government outstanding debt had been largely incurred by county and municipal governments (through GO and revenue bond issuance), and no less than 20 percent had been incurred by special district governments (mainly through revenue bond issuance). But special districts' levels of indebtedness were nearly twice as high as local governments' in general as debt service represented 7.3 percent of their expenditure and 14 percent of their own-source revenues (US Census Bureau, 2011d, Table 2), which explains why most default and Chapter 9 filing cases are to be found

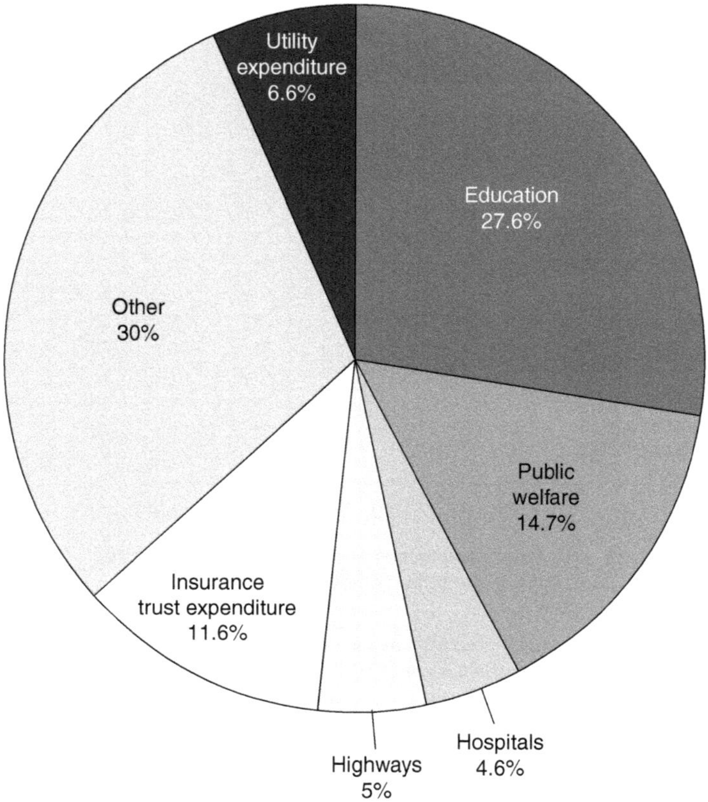

Figure 6.13 State and local government expenditures (2010) (source: US Census Bureau, 2011b).

among special districts as mentioned earlier. This also sheds light on the transfer of debt from state or local governments to special-purpose entities for the delivery of devolved services, as well as the prevalence of interest payment for the revenue bonds issued to finance the provision of devolved services, over the quality and sometimes even the availability of the very services they were meant to deliver in the first place. Indeed, while some local governments opted for severely scaling down fire protection services as mentioned above, others slashed into the budgets allocated to services devolved to special districts like housing and community development, sewerage or solid waste management, sometimes with double-digit cuts running over two budget years.[15]

Citizens and public employees are being deprived of social benefits and public services in the name of budgetary balance, whereas expenditures for debt service have not been concerned by budget reductions. The degradation of the social safety net of residents and of their standard of living, as well as the transfer on the part of some states and localities of more responsibility to each

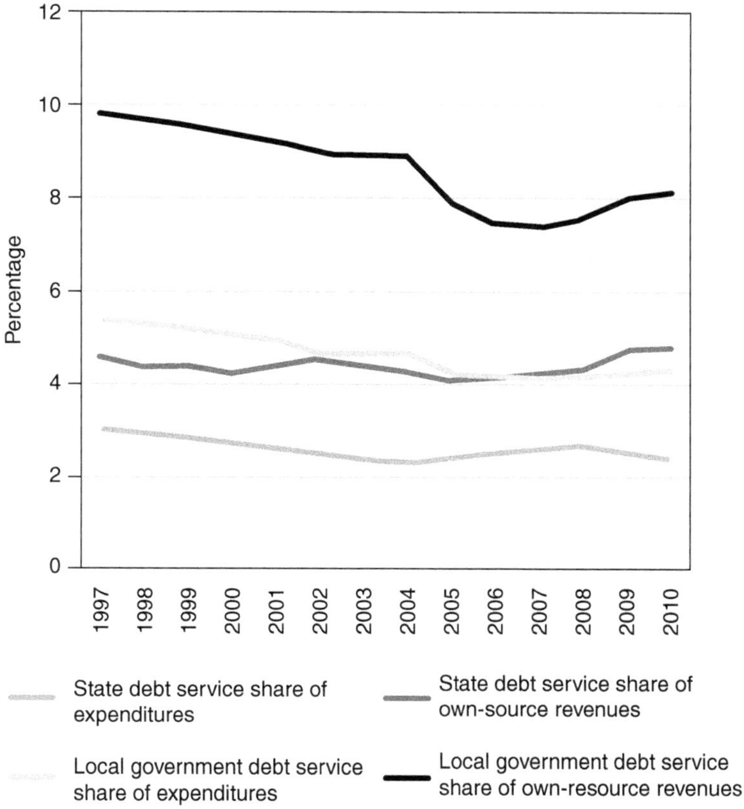

Figure 6.14 State and local government debt service ratios (1997–2010) (source: based on data from the US Census Bureau, State and Local Government Finance, 1997–2010).

public employee for his/her public pension provision are typical consequences of neoliberal practices (Harvey, 2005). Meanwhile, municipal bondholders have continued to be paid interests and to enjoy the corresponding submerged state tax-exemption, a preferential treatment to which the next section turns.

Bondholders vs. local citizens and public employees?

Who are bondholders?

To finance capital-intensive infrastructures like roads, water distribution or educational facilities, state and local governments generally resort to long-term borrowing, mainly by issuing municipal bonds which investors can purchase in exchange for a stream of interest payments and the repayment of the principal at maturity. As we saw earlier, states, counties and municipalities can issue GO

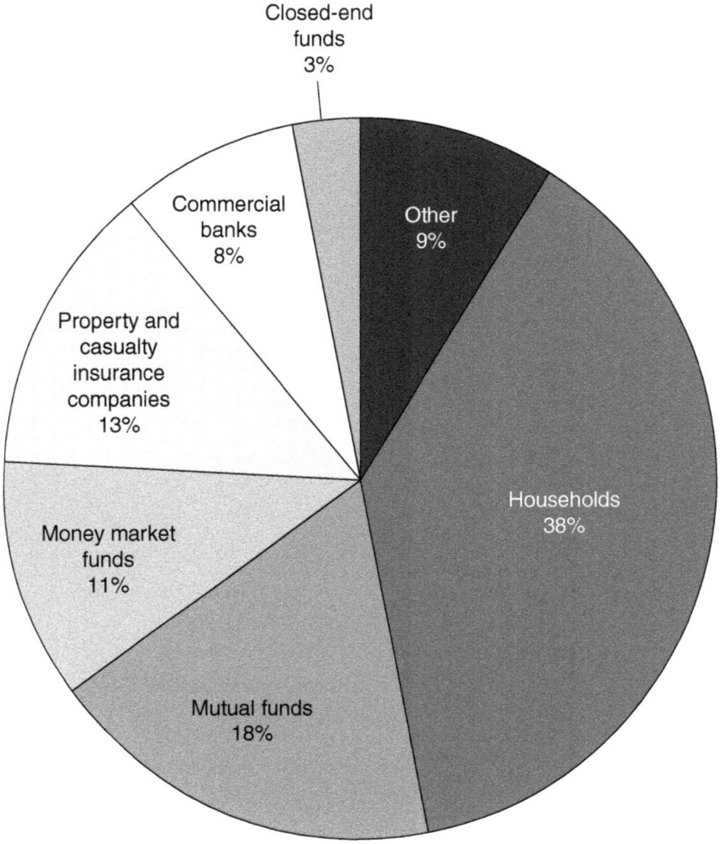

Figure 6.15 Holders of US municipal bonds (source: US Federal Reserve Board).

and revenue bonds while special districts generally rely on the issuance of revenue bonds to raise financing. According to the data provided by the Federal Reserve Board for 2010 (Figure 6.15), domestic households represented the largest category of bondholders, and if we combine households, mutual funds and money markets, it appears that holdings owned by individuals account for nearly two-thirds of holders of municipal debt.

Munis constitute an attractive investment because they are rather safe and because they are "submerged" government financial instruments operating both at the federal and local levels. Indeed, they come with a federal income tax exemption on interest payments, combined to a state and local income tax exemption when the bondholder resides in the state of issuance. So they are particularly appealing to taxpayers with high personal income tax rates who can thus realize a substantial profit by paying nothing on the additional stream of income they receive from interest payments.

In the event of a local government's financial shipwreck, who's left to sink or swim?

Offering federal income tax-exemption to attract investors amounts to subsidizing state and local government debt by indirectly reducing the interest rate paid by states and localities, as well as bondholders' investment by exempting interest payments from taxation. The US Office of Management and Budget estimates that between FY2012 and FY2016 this exemption will cost $230 billion in foregone revenue to the federal budget (Gordon, 2011, p. 5). The magnitude of federal tax expenditure has led some to question the economic efficiency of transferring federal resources to state and local governments in such a way (Maguire, 2011, p. 16), and of providing tax preference to high-income taxpayers. Indeed, according to a study based on the 2009 US Congressional Budget Office and Joint Committee on Taxation, "high-bracket taxpayers receive a higher subsidy to purchase muni bonds" (Gordon, 2011, p. 5). The exemption's economic efficiency can further be disputed when bondholders reside in the state of issuance as in that case the exemption is extended to state and local income taxes. Although the federal "submerged state" tax-exemption contributes to states and localities being granted lower interest rates, the local "submerged state" tax-exemption has an adverse and dual effect on localities' budgets in the present context of fiscal pressure: on the one hand, it deprives states of much needed income tax revenues and accordingly reduces the amount of tax revenue, which constitutes the largest source of general revenues used to finance general expenditure; on the other hand, it crowds out other items in the list of general expenditure as spending cuts have been imposed to social and public services, educational programs, public workforce or public employees' compensations and pension plan funding while the payment of interest to bondholders has been preserved.

The budgetary arbitrations in favor of bondholders over non-bondholders, among whom we find public employees and needy residents, are usually justified by two arguments. First, the share of the debt service in states' expenditure is deemed minimal; and second, attacking bondholders' interests would result in destabilizing the bond market, damaging states' financial creditworthiness and increasing the cost of borrowing (Lav & Nichols, 2011, pp. 7–10). Yet we saw that the share of debt service in localities' expenditure is not negligible (Figure 6.14) and becomes even higher in the case of special districts. Moreover, as previously mentioned, states cannot default on bond debt and file for bankruptcy; hence bond interest payments are given the first call on revenues. As for localities, they can declare bankruptcy provided they are specifically authorized and deemed eligible to file under Chapter 9 of the Bankruptcy Code by their state government. In a bankruptcy case, bondholders are not incontrovertibly given priority of payments – it all depends on the type of bond they hold. GO bonds issued by states, counties, municipalities or school districts to finance public-purpose projects that benefit the common good (roads, courthouses, schools, etc.) are pledged to the taxing power of the issuer, whose revenues are used to service the bonds. GO bonds are rated as safe investment, but in a Chapter 9 proceeding they are "unsecured," meaning that GO bondholders' claims fall in the "unsecured claims" category along with public employees' compensation and pension liabilities (Spiotto, 2012, p. 32). The claims of holders of GO bonds can obtain priority of payment over all "unsecured claims," when they are secured by a statutory lien (ibid., p. 30). Revenue bonds, like GO bonds, can be issued by general-purpose governments, and increasingly by special-purpose districts (excluding school districts) to finance the construction or improvement of facilities, like water, sewer or utility services, whose revenues and fees are pledged for the repayment of the bonds. Revenue bonds are more likely to default than GO bonds, but should the issuer file for bankruptcy, bondholders' claims will be "secured" and met in full provided the payment of the "necessary operating expenses" of the facility is ensured.[16] Furthermore, in the event of default on the part of the revenue bond issuer, bondholders' claims will stop with the end of the stream of revenues that secured the bond and cannot be extended to non-pledged revenues.

Until recently, bondholders, public workers and pensioners have generally fared according to the statutory nature of their claims when involved in a Chapter 9 proceeding, with the latter's pension rights being protected so consistently that they even appear to be "the most senior of all unsecured" debt (Novy-Marx & Raugh, 2009, p. 195) and "free of risk" (Brown & Wilcox, 2009, p. 539). Indeed public pension benefits are protected by constitutional provisions in most states of the Union. But in 2010, the Colorado Legislature passed a bill that unilaterally modified the contractual pension benefits for public employees and retirees, notably by eliminating the annual cost-of-living adjustment (COLA, of vital importance for low-income pensioners in case of inflation). The rationale for altering the state's contractual obligations to its employees lies in the severity of the financial situation which imposed efforts to stem budgetary and pension deficits. The fact that Colorado does not rank among the most indebted states (its debt and pension liability to GDP amounts to 3.8 percent) (*Barron's*, 2010) has prompted Colorado's public employees and retirees to denounce the spuriousness of the recession justification and to sue the state for breach of contract (Cloud, 2011). The district court upheld the state's decision, but in 2012 the Court of Appeals reversed the trial court and recognized the COLA contractual rights but remanded the case to determine whether the impairment to those rights could not be justified as "reasonable and necessary to serve a significant and legitimate public purpose."[17] Other states have followed suit (Arizona, Maine, Minnesota, New Jersey, Rhode Island, South Dakota) and suits have followed with mixed results so far.[18]

Besides, in 2011 Rhode Island passed another groundbreaking piece of legislation that moves bondholders to the top of the priority list for payments by providing bondholders with a statutory lien on all revenue sources of the issuer (Spiotto, 2012, pp. 44–45). It implies that in case of default, revenue bondholders will also have access to the issuer's tax revenues and general funds, and that revenue and GO bondholders will have priority of payment over all other claims, including public employees and retirees. The rationale behind this important change is primarily to maintain the state and local governments' access to the financial market by improving their credibility (Rhode Island ranks among the most indebted states)[19] and by reassuring potential bond investors. All these recent local decisions and developments constitute corroborative evidence of what Stephen Gill sees as a general tendency of neoliberalism "to subject the majority of the population to the power of market forces whilst preserving social protection for the strong" (Gill, 1995, p. 407); or more precisely of what Harvey identifies as a principle of neoliberalism: "in the event of a conflict between the integrity of financial institutions and bondholders' returns, on the one hand, and the well-being of the citizens on the other, the former [are] to be privileged" (Harvey, 2005, p. 48).

Municipal bonds and government pension plans are both legally binding obligations for governments, as bond issuers to their bondholders, and as pension scheme sponsors to their employees and retirees. Yet the recent legislative modifications of public employees' and retirees' impaired pension benefits and the bondholders' upgraded claim statute are evidence that in the eyes of some state law-makers, the contractual rights of public employees are not as rock solid as bondholders'. The neoliberal rationale behind some state and local government budgetary decisions is embedded in submerged state policies that grant priority to bondholders. Designed to ensure further access to the municipal debt market to finance public purpose projects and facilities, these policies result in the downgrading of public services and social programs. The validity of sacrificing public services to borrow money and finance public projects certainly needs to be challenged on logical and economic grounds. But the net result is that some citizens in distress are left to sink while others who know how to swim and are already wearing a life-jacket are provided with an inflatable boat.

Notes

* Parts of this chapter appeared in Cormier, Cécile (2014) Servicing Bondholders and Defaulting on Basic Public Services. *Studies in Political Economy*, 93, 53–80.

1 Special-purpose governments provide specific services (like fire protection, sewerage, water supply, electric power or gas utilities, etc.) that are not supplied by general-purpose governments, such as counties, municipal governments or townships, which provide general government services. For more information on the difference between special-purpose governments and general-purpose governments, see the US Census Bureau (2012a, 2012b).

2 Except school districts, which are not allowed to issue such bonds.

3 It should be noted that for the first time since 1942 the number of special districts has stalled and might be shifting to a downward trend as it decreased by 0.5 percent over the 2007–2012 period.

4 The funding ratio amounts only to 34 percent.

5 Data on unemployment by state are from the Bureau of Labor Statistics.

6 Budget shortfalls were the largest on record according to the Center on Budget and Policy Priority. See McNichol *et al.* (2012, figure 2).

7 For the levels of cities' ending balances, see Hoene and Pagano (2011, p. 8).

8 Though the bulk of property taxes is usually levied by local governments, most states

(except Colorado., Connecticut, Delaware, Hawaii, Idaho, Iowa, New York, North Carolina, Ohio, Oklahoma, South Dakota, Tennessee, Texas, Utah) levy property taxes. For precise data on property tax collection by states for FY2010 and FY2011, see the "Annual Survey of State Government Tax Collections" and the "Summary Table" issued by the US Census Bureau. For further discussion, see also Azuelos in the present volume.

9 According to the US Census Bureau, "Total intergovernmental expenditures (payments and grants to local governments) showed a decrease of 1.1 percent from 2009, totaling $481.2 billion in 2010, compared with $486.5 billion in 2009" (US Census Bureau, 2011a, p. 5).

10 The purposes of the Recovery Act are enunciated in §3 and read as follows:

> (1) To preserve and create jobs and promote economic recovery. (2) To assist those most impacted by the recession. (3) To provide investments needed to increase economic efficiency by spurring technological advances in science and health. (4) To invest in transportation, environmental protection, and other infrastructure that will provide long-term economic benefits. (5) To stabilize State and local government budgets, in order to minimize and avoid reductions in essential services and counterproductive state and local tax increases.

The text of the full bill is available at www.gpo.gov/fdsys/pkg/BILLS-111hr1enr/pdf/BILLS-111hr1enr.pdf.

11 According to the Center on Budget and Policy Priorities, "states expect to educate 350,000 more K–12 students and 1.7 million more public college and university students in the upcoming school year than in 2007–2008" (McNichol *et al.*, 2012, p. 1).

12 "Some 5.6 million more people are projected to be eligible for subsidized health insurance through Medicaid in 2012 than were enrolled in 2008, as employers have cancelled their coverage and people have lost jobs and wages" (ibid., p. 1)

13 There has been some debate among financial economists as to the true magnitude of public pension liabilities. For details, see Wilshire Consulting (2012) and Rauh (2011).

14 As was the case in Baltimore, see CBS Baltimore (2012).

15 The deepest cuts were imposed on sewerage and solid waste management (with a 56 percent decrease in Oklahoma in 2010, and two-year cuts ranging from 20 to more than 30 percent in Delaware, Montana and Michigan). The local governments that inflicted the most substantial and comprehensive budget reductions from 2008 to 2010 in these three service areas were located in California, Colorado, Michigan and West Virginia. Calculations based on US Census Bureau, State and local summary tables by level of government (2008, 2009, 2010).

16 As stated in §928(b) of the Bankruptcy Code. But no court so far has clearly determined what "necessary operating expenses" are (for more detail, see Spiotto, 2012, pp. 22–23, and app. F-1).

17 More detailed information is available on the website of Save PERA COLA (2010).

18 In Arizona, one judge ruled the suspension of COLA unconstitutional (Kiefer, 2012). Maine and New Jersey upheld the state's decision (see, respectively, National Conference of State Legislatures (2011) and National Association of State Retirement Administrators (2011a)). Finally, three states dismissed the lawsuits: Colorado, but the court's decision was reversed (National Association of State Retirement Administrators, 2012; Public Employees' Retirement Association of Colorado, 2011); Minnesota (National Association of State Retirement Administrators, 2011b; *New York Times*, 2011); and South Dakota (National Association of State Retirement Administrators, 2011c; State Budget Solutions, 2012).

19 Its debt and pension liability represents 13 percent of its GDP (*Barron's*, 2010).

References

Appleson, J., Parsons, E. & Haughwout, A. (2012). The Untold Story of Municipal Bond Defaults. Liberty Street Economics, Federal Reserve Bank of New York. Retrieved from www.libertystreeteconomics.newyorkfed.org/2012/08/the-untold-story-of-municipal-bond-defaults.html.

Barron's (2010). The Best and the Worst. Retrieved from www.online.barrons.com/article/SB50001424053111904881404577603301566976164.html#articleTabs_article%3D1.

Brown, J. & Wilcox, D. (2009). Discounting State and Local Pension Liabilities. *American Economic Review, 99*(2), 538–542.

CBS Baltimore (2012, June 29). Baltimore to Shut Down 3 Fire Companies: Residents Concerned about Emergency Response. Retrieved from http://baltimore.cbslocal.com/2012/06/29/baltimore-to-shut-down-3-fire-companies-residents-concerned-about-emergency-response/.

Cloud, W. (2011, June). State Pension Deficits, the Recession, and a Modern View of the Contracts Clause. *Yale Law Journal, 120*(8), 2199–2212.

de Angelis, M. & Tian, X. (2013). US: Chapter 9 Municipal Bankruptcy – Utilization, Avoidance and Impact. In O. Canuto & L. Liu (eds.), *Until debt do us part* (pp. 328–330). Washington, DC: World Bank.

Economist, The (2011a, December 3). American Municipal Finances: The Sewers of Jefferson County. Retrieved from www.economist.com/node/21541053.

Economist, The (2011b, October 29). Harrisburg's Bankruptcy: Money up in Smoke.

Economist, The (2012a, May 12). Unequal Pain: The Public Sector Is Still Hobbling the Economy, 39–40.

Economist, The (2012b, May 5). Bankruptcy in Rhode Island: Improvident, 44–45. Retrieved from www.economist.com/node/21534811.

GAO (Government Accountability Office) (2009). State and Local Governments Retiree Health Benefits: Largely Underfunded, but Some Governments are Taking Action. GAO-10-61. Retrieved from www.gao.gov/products/GAO-10-61.

GAO (2012a, April). State and Fiscal Outlook, GAO-12-523SP. Retrieved from www.gao.gov/products/GAO-12-523SP.

GAO (2012b, March). State and Local Government Pension Plans: Economic Downturn Spurs Efforts to Address Costs and Sustainability. GAO-12-322. Retrieved from www.gao.gov/products/GAO-12-322.

Gill, S. (1995). Globalization, Market Civilization and Disciplinary Neoliberalism. *Millennium, 24*(3), 399–423.

Gordon, T. (2011, September 19). Buy and Hold (On Tight): The Recent Muni Bond Rollercoaster and What It Means for Cities. Brookings Institution. Retrieved from www.brookings.edu/~/media/Files/rc/papers/2011/0919_muni_bonds_gordon/0919_muni_bonds_gordon.pdf.

Harvey, D. (2005). *A brief history of neoliberalism*. Oxford: Oxford University Press.

Hoene, C.W. (2010, December). Crying Wolf about Municipal Defaults. National League of Cities Blog. Retrieved from http://citiesspeak.org.

Hoene, C.W. (2011, October 29). Interview with *The Economist.* Harrisburg's Bankruptcy: Money Up in Smoke. Retrieved from www.economist.com/node/21534811.

Hoene, C.W. & Pagano, M.A (2011, September). Research Brief on America's Cities: City Fiscal Conditions in 2011. National League of Cities. Retrieved from www.nlc.org/file%20library/find%20city%20solutions/research%20innovation/economic%20development/state-of-americas-cities-workforce-development-rpt-11.pdf.

Howell-Moroney, M. & Hall, J. (2011, March/April). Waste in the Sewer: The Collapse of Accountability and Transparency in Public Finance in Jefferson County Alabama. *Public Administration Review*, *71*(2), 232–242.

Johnson, N., Oliff, P. & Williams, E. (2011, February). An Update on State Budget Cuts: At Least 46 States Have Imposed Cuts that Hurt Vulnerable Residents and Cause Job Loss. Center on Budget and Policy Priorities. Retrieved from www.cbpp.org/cms/index.cfm?fa=view&id=1214.

Kiefer, M. (2012, May 29). Maricopa Judge: Halting Pension Raises Unconstitutional. *The Arizona Republic*. Retrieved from www.azcentral.com/arizonarepublic/local/articles/2012/05/29/20120529maricopa-judge-pension-raises.html.

Lav, I.J. & Nichols, E. (2011, January 20). Misunderstandings Regarding State Debt, Pensions, and Retiree Health Costs Create Unnecessary Alarm. Center on Budget and Policy Priorities. Retrieved from www.cbpp.org/cms/index.cfm?fa=view&id=3372.

Maguire, S. (2011, April 14). State and Local Government Debt: An Analysis. Congressional Research Service. Retrieved from www.fas.org/sgp/crs/misc/R41735.pdf.

McNichol, E., Oliff, P. & Johnson, N. (2012, March 21). States Continue to Feel Recession's Impact. Center on Budget and Policy Priorities. Retrieved from www.cbpp.org/files/2-8-08sfp.pdf.

Medioli, A., Tudela, M. & Van Praagh, A. (2012, March 7). Special Comment: U.S. Municipal Bond Defaults and Recoveries, 1970–2011. Moody's Investors Service, Report No. 140114. Retrieved from www.nhhefa.com/documents/moodysMunicipal-DefaultStudy1970-2011.pdf.

Mettler, S. (2010). Reconstituting the Submerged State: The Challenges of Social Policy Reform in the Obama Era. *Perspectives on Politics*, *8*(3), 803–824.

Mettler, S. (2011), *The submerged state: How invisible government policies undermine American democracy*. Chicago, IL: University of Chicago Press.

Munnell, A., Aubry, J.P., Hurwitz, J., Medenica, M. & Quinby, L. (2012, May). The Funding of State and Local Pensions: 2011–2015. *State and Local Pension Plans*, 24. Center for Retirement Research at Boston College. Retrieved from www.crr.bc.edu/wp-content/uploads/2012/05/slp_24-508.pdf.

National Association of State Budget Officers (2011, November 28). Summary: Fall 2011 Fiscal Survey of States. Retrieved from www.nasbo.org/sites/default/files/Fall%202011%20Fiscal%20Survey%20-%20Summary.pdf.

National Association of State Retirement Administrators (2011a). New Jersey. Retrieved from www.nasra.org/nj.

National Association of State Retirement Administrators (2011b). Minnesota. Retrieved from www.nasra.org/mn.

National Association of State Retirement Administrators (2011c). South Dakota. Retrieved from www.nasra.org/sd.

National Association of State Retirement Administrators (2012). Colorado. Retrieved from www.nasra.org/co.

National Conference of State Legislatures (2011). 2011 Pension and Retirement Enacted Legislations. Retrieved from www.ncsl.org/research/fiscal-policy/2011-pension-and-retirement-enacted-legislation.aspx.

New York Times (2011). Swanson v. PERA. Retrieved from http://graphics8.nytimes.com/packages/pdf/business/20110701pension/swansonPera.PDF.

Novy-Marx, R. & Rauh, J. (2009). The Liabilities and Risk of State-Sponsored Pension Plans. *Journal of Economic Perspectives*, *23*(4), 191–210.

Public Employees' Retirement Association of Colorado (2011). Justus v. PERA. Retrieved from www.copera.org/pdf/Misc/06-29-11Order.pdf.
Rauh, J. (2011, October 5). Shortfall for State and Local Pension Systems Today: Over $4 Trillion. Kellogg's School Finance Department. Retrieved from http://kelloggfinance.wordpress.com/2011/10/06/shortfall-for-stateand-local-pension-systems-today-over-4-trillion/.
Save PERA COLA (2010). Fighting for Retirees' Annual Benefit Increases. Retrieved from http://saveperacola.com.
Spiotto, J. (2012). Primer on Municipal Debt Adjustment: Chapter 9, the Last Resort for Financially Distressed Municipalities. Chapman and Cutler LLP. Retrieved from www.afgi.org/resources/Bankruptcy_Primer.pdf.
State Budget Solutions (2012). December State Pension Litigation Update. Retrieved from www.statebudgetsolutions.org/publications/detail/december-state-pension-litigation-update.
Urban Institute-Brookings Institution Tax Policy Center (2009). State & Local Government Finance Data Query System. Retrieved from http://slfdqs.taxpolicycenter.org.
US Bureau of Labor Statistics (2012, May), Current Employment Statistics Highlights. Retrieved from www.bls.gov/web/empsit/ceshighlights.pdf.
US Census Bureau (2011a). State Government Finances Summary. Retrieved from www.census.gov/prod/2011pubs/g10-asfin.pdf.
US Census Bureau (2011b, December). State Government Finances Summary: 2010. Retrieved from www2.census.gov/govs/state/10statesummaryreport.pdf.
US Census Bureau (2011c, October). State and Local Government Finances Summary: 2009. Retrieved from www2.census.gov/govs/pubs/state_loc_gov/state_loc_gov_2009.pdf.
US Census Bureau (2011d, October). 2007 Census of Governments, Table 2. Local Government Finances by Type of Government and State. Retrieved from www.census.gov//govs/local/historical_data_2007.html.
US Census Bureau (2011e, March). 2010 Annual Survey of State Government Tax Collections. Retrieved from www.census.gov/govs/statetax/historical_data_2010.html.
US Census Bureau (2012a, May). Population of Interest: Special Districts. Retrieved from www.census.gov/govs/go/special_district_governments.html.
US Census Bureau (2012b). Definitions: Local General Purpose Governments. Retrieved from www.census.gov/newsroom/cspan/govts/20120301_cspan_govts_def_3.pdf.
US Census Bureau (2012c). 2012 Census of Governments: Preliminary Count of Local Governments by Type and State: 2012. Retrieved from www.census.gov/govs/cog/2012/.
US Census Bureau (2012d, September 12). State and Local Government Finances Summary: 2010. Retrieved from www2.census.gov/govs/local/summary_report.pdf.
US Census Bureau (2012e, April). 2011 Annual Survey of State Government Tax Collections. Retrieved from www.census.gov/govs/statetax/.
US Federal Reserve Board (2010). Flow of Funds Accounts. Fourth Quarter 2010. Retrieved from www.federalreserve.gov.
Whitney, M. (2010). Interview with CNBS. Wave of Muni Defaults to Spur Layoffs. Retrieved from www.cnbc.com/id/40769692/Wave_of_Muni_Defaults_to_Spur_Layoffs_Social_Unrest_Whitney.
Walsh, M.W. & Goodnough, A. (2011, July 11). A Small City's Depleted Pension Fund Rattles Rhode Island. *New York Times*. Retrieved from www.nytimes.com/2011/07/12/business/central-falls-ri-faces-bankruptcy-over-pension-promises.html.
Wilshire Consulting (2012). 2012 Wilshire Report on State Retirement Systems: Funding Levels and Asset Allocation. Retrieved from www.wikipension.com/images/6/6e/Wilshire_2011.pdf.

7 The subprime crisis

A multiscalar issue challenging the American Dream

Cynthia Ghorra-Gobin

Analyzing the foundations of the subprime crisis going back to 2007 may be an interesting way of looking at American capitalism, since it reveals some aspects that are often hidden, such as the indirect role of the federal state in housing mortgage lending. American capitalism may not be the free market economy that some have described (Hall & Soskice, 2001). Banks that used to finance mortgage lending through the deposits they received from their customers have moved to a new model in which they sell on mortgages to the bond market. Given the dynamism of the bond market, banks did not really carefully check the financial capacity of American borrowers. They were also encouraged to increase mortgage lending under the Community Reinvestment Act (1977),[1] as part of a government effort to fight against redlining in ethnic and racial neighborhoods. Useful to remember is the fact that in 2007 the mortgage bond market represented $6 trillion and was the largest single part of the whole $27 trillion US bond market, bigger even than Treasury bonds (BBC News, 2007).

Though the role the federal state may have played in the housing mortgage system addresses a main concern of the editors of the present volume – that of the reductive conception of state capacities – the involvement of Freddie Mac and Fannie Mae has been delved into at length (Aalbers, 2012). This chapter has a different objective and specifically responds to the editors' claim in their introduction that a too narrow focus on the national level of policy-making has blinded observers to the subnational level. The purpose here is twofold.

The first purpose is to shed some light on the link between urbanization and financialization and thus stress the urban and local roots of the global financial crisis. The subprime crisis was not limited to deprived inner cities; it also included suburban and exurban areas, and still does. Based on this interpretation, one can say that the fate of urban homeowners was somewhat intertwined with the opaque dealings of financial institutions working in a borderless world. The subprime crisis is a multiscalar issue: it concerns the local (people), the national (legislation) and the global (financial stability).

The second objective is to contribute to the assumption that the subprime crisis is not only a financial crisis but a crisis revealing to some extent the collapse of the American Dream, and one of its tenets, the ownership of a house surrounded by a garden. In that respect, this chapter follows the editors' invitation to consider to what extent the crisis may foster a shift in American "civilization" (Swedberg, 2010). A new generation of urban planners see the American (national) model as being outmoded and no longer adequate with the rise of middle classes in emerging countries and with the global environmental concerns if the latter were to live according to the American way of life. The point is not to merely criticize a model of national housing mortgages sold to the bond market that is going global. It is to seize the opportunity of a financial crisis to challenge the traditional housing model of the American national dream, which also involves a right to ownership.

The spatial and social geography of the subprime crisis

The subprime crisis is an American crisis that concerns localities (inner cities and suburbs) while disrupting the wider financial order around mortgages. The subprime crisis, despite being a national issue, has both roots in localities and global impacts. It is a multiscalar question. It is about working-class households living in poor neighborhoods or in suburban areas, while reflecting the dynamics of the bond market in the United States and in some parts of the world, given the interdependency of the financial system.

A local issue affecting inner cities as well as suburbs

The subprime crisis, which has had a severe local and urban impact, is not limited to one specific part of the metropolitan area. It affected inner-city areas in Cleveland (OH) as well as suburbs in Southern California, Arizona, Nevada and in metropolitan areas ranging from Washington, DC to New York City and Louisville (KY). However, in both areas it concerned individual houses and not housing units in buildings (Leinberger, 2008).

The documentary "Cleveland vs. Wall Street" by Jean-Stephane Bron (2010) gives an idea of the complexity of the subprime crisis, which involved mortgage brokers as well as fragile homeowners. It tells the story of a lawyer hired by the city of Cleveland to file a lawsuit against 21 banks, which were held accountable for the wave of foreclosures that had left their city in ruins. This fiction is the story of that trial in which the facts, the participants and their testimonies are all real: the judge, lawyers, witnesses, even the members of the jury – asked to give their verdict – play their own roles. One witness after another, the film, a universal fable about capitalism, takes apart, from a local and human perspective, the mechanisms of subprime mortgage loans, a system that sent the world economy reeling. The system worked as long as market prices were rising. The whole system collapsed when the prices of the housing market fell down.

For many years, Cleveland was a poor, working-class city located in the rust-belt region that happened to be the subprime capital of America. Between 1980 and 2000, the city lost one-sixth of its population. In 2010, according to the census, its population reached 396,815 compared to 478,403 in 2000, 505,616 in 1990 and 573,822 in 1980. More than half of its population is African-American (53 percent), while the white population represents 37 percent. As revealed by the film, mortgage brokers sold subprime mortgages in working-class black neighborhoods where many households had achieved some form of home ownership. They were told they could get cash by refinancing their homes but were rarely warned that the new subprime mortgages would be reset after two years at double the interest rate.

In 2005, according to a BBC News report, one in five mortgages was subprime and they were also popular among recent immigrants trying to buy a home for the first time in the suburbs. House prices were increasing, and it was difficult to become an owner-occupied without moving to the very edge of the metropolitan area in exurbs. A telling example of a suburban area is Moreno Valley in Riverside County, a suburban county located in the metropolitan area of Los Angeles. During the last decade, Moreno Valley was recognized as the fastest-growing area in America. Its population represented 193,365 inhabitants in 2010 compared to 142,381 in 2000. Its growth rate was 35.8 percent, a little less than the growth rate of Riverside County, which reached 41.7% between 2000 and 2010. Its population was 18 percent white, 18 percent black and 54.4 percent Hispanic. Moreno Valley lies in the Inland Empire, whose population increased from 2.6 million to 4.1 million between 1990 and 2007 – a demographic growth equivalent to the entire population of the city of Philadelphia. In Moreno Valley, entire neighborhoods sprung up, encouraged by easy access to credit, which translated into luxurious villas for the middle class (*The Economist*, 2008).

But in the neighborhood of Camino del Rey, sumptuous houses are now empty. The population is starting to decrease in Moreno Valley, as revealed by falling high-school enrollment, vacant units in strip malls or Pentecostal churches occupying former stores (ibid.).

The subprime crisis is not limited to neighborhoods in the urban core. As in the case of Louisville (Kentucky) and Moreno Valley (California), suburban zip codes exhibited a high rate of foreclosures. As for suburban areas, the neighborhoods with longer commutes to the workplace were likely to have more foreclosures (Leinberger, 2008).

The national picture of foreclosures and underwater homes

According to RealtyTrac, the largest US database of foreclosed properties, foreclosures reached three million units in 2010. In normal times, new foreclosures run at fewer than one million per year. This figure for 2010 was high despite ramped-up efforts by the Obama Administration to bolster loan modifications, which yielded mixed results. One in every 418 US households received a foreclosure filing in 2010. According to Standard and Poor's Case-Shiller index, home prices in the largest 20 cities were down 3.1 percent, with some cities such as Las Vegas still experiencing a 20.6 percent annual decline. But overall, many homeowners were still stuck with underwater mortgages – with the value of their loans higher than the value of their homes. On February 18 of that same year, the federal government pledged $75 billion to reduce the mortgage payments of homeowners at risk of default (Politi & Kapner, 2010).

One may ask the following questions concerning foreclosures. Was it because homeowners could not afford to pay? Or did they decline to do so because their homes were now worth less than their mortgages (negative equity)? Some economists think that, even in cases of negative equity, most homeowners will not default if they can afford the payment. For instance, the Federal Reserve Bank of Boston found that when home prices fell 23 percent in Massachusetts between 1988 and 1993, only 6.4 percent of borrowers with negative equity ended up in foreclosure. The study concluded that most such borrowers felt what they got from their home was still worth the payment. Others believe that once the home is worth less than the mortgage, homeowners have a significant incentive to walk away even if they can make the payment, since in many states lenders cannot litigate them for the shortfall.

It was only five years after the crash that the American housing market began to show signs of recovery. The share of underwater homeowners started to improve in 2012. According to the real-estate website Zillow, of all homeowners, 15.3 million (30.9 percent) remained underwater in 2012, a figure which was down from 15.7 million or 31.4 percent in the first quarter (Florida, 2012).

Underwater homes were concentrated in the Sunbelt, with Florida and California showing especially high concentrations. In Las Vegas, more than two-thirds of homeowners remained underwater. This figure was about 50 percent in places like Atlanta, Orlando and Riverside.

Among the many communities around the nation, black neighborhoods were hit the hardest. According to the Center for Responsible Lending, 8 percent of African-American and Latino families lost their homes to foreclosure, compared to 4.5 percent of white families (Gilderbloom *et al.*, 2012). This raises the question of what accounts for the concentration of subprime lending and foreclosures in minority neighborhoods. According to Gilderbloom *et al.*, the number of foreclosures per census tract was nearly twice as high in black communities (39) as in white neighborhoods (20). There were also around 15 foreclosures on properties owned by investors rather than owner-occupants in black communities, but only two foreclosures in white areas. It seems, then, at least in Louisville, that investors seeking a quick profit – not homeowners – were part of the real problem in black neighborhoods. In some cases, white owners of foreclosed properties in black neighborhoods lived miles away, in suburbs. In the case of Louisville, the problem was due to investors, not owner-occupants, whose properties in black neighborhoods were lost to foreclosure, again to the detriment of all who live and work in those communities. In other words, federal policies that increased responsible lending in low-income and minority communities were not the culprits. It was investors who did not live in, understand or appreciate the black communities they were tearing apart, who were at the heart of the problem (Gilderbloom *et al.*, 2012).

The probability of a shift: how the crash will reshape America

Most planners involved in the Congress of New Urbanism (CNU)[2] think the crisis was an opportunity for reshaping the American Dream based on the model of the detached single-family house and for working on a more compact design of subdivisions (Dunham-Jones, 2011). They see the crisis as an opportunity for accelerating the change in terms of design without challenging the ideal of access to ownership.

Reshaping the suburbs

In spite of the gloom created by the subprime crisis, some remained unexpectedly cheerful. Planners, engineers and researchers close to the CNU seized upon the crisis in far-flung regions like the Inland Empire (CA) as evidence that sprawl is no longer viable. They think that the American myth of a frontier of endless mobility is closing (Dunham-Jones, 2011; Gallagher, 2014).

The Great Recession challenged not only the economics of homebuilding, but also the essence of the suburban dream. For the CNU, it is important that once the economy has fully revived, the country will not return to home-building-as-usual. Planners and architects think that a crisis may become an opportunity for rethinking suburban housing in order to make it responsive, not to dated demographics and wishful economics, but rather to the actual needs of a diversifying and dynamic population. They are also bringing back the idea of renting instead of ownership. A new housing market should be sensible not only to traditional households but also to the growing numbers of those who prefer to rent rather than buy, who either can't afford or don't want a 2,000-square-foot-plus detached house, who are retired and living on fixed incomes and maybe driving less, who want granny or nanny flats, who want to pay less for utilities and reduce their carbon footprint, etc.

Christopher B. Leinberger, known for his 2009 book *Investing in a New American Dream*, wrote in a 2008 *Atlantic* article that the subprime crisis was just the "tip of the iceberg." For him, profound changes are taking place in American civilization. For 60 years, Americans have pushed steadily into the suburbs, leaving cities behind. But the pendulum is swinging back toward more urban living. Leinberger sees low-density suburbs and McMansion subdivisions as the future inner cities of the 1960s and 1970s slums. Based on housing prices per square foot, urban residential neighborhood space goes from 40 percent to 200 percent more than traditional suburban space in areas as diverse as New York City, Portland, Oregon, Seattle and Washington, DC. Consumers prefer to live in walkable urban places, whether they are located in cities or in suburbs. There is a preference for urban amenities rather than suburban amenities. In this perspective, conventional suburban living may not be much of a bargain in the future. In fringe counties of metropolitan areas, the tax base dependent on housing values and new development may deteriorate and in turn create budget deficits. Leinberger foresees the division of neighborhood houses into rental units that in turn will attract the poor in suburbs. Of course, not all suburbs will suffer this fate. Those that are affluent and relatively close to central cities are likely to remain in high demand. However, suburbs that are poorly served by public transport will suffer from decline. In other words the crisis will not be limited to subprime areas. And those suburbs will become magnets for poverty, crime and social dysfunction (Leinberger, 2008; Gallagher, 2014).

This argument on the decline of traditional suburbs is shared by an expert on the housing market, Leigh Gallagher. In a recent book she wrote that we are seeing the end of the single-family house, given the rising demand for urbanity by the "creative class" and the aging suburban and wealthy population. Gallagher writes that the American Dream is moving and will no longer be related to the suburbs. Elderly people don't see the opportunity of living in a large house while the creative class is looking for urban amenities. There is an increasing demand for walkable communities. This "back to the city" trend in American society is also stressed by urban planner Alan Ehrenhalt (2013). According to him, the twenty-first century will see an "inversion" of the American model. Upper middle-class residents will live in cities while low-income households will live in suburbs. American cities will look more like European cities. It follows from the arguments of Leinberger, Gallagher and Ehrenhalt concerning the transformations of suburbs after the subprime crisis, that gentrification processes will take place across cities and that middle-class households will be displaced.

The foreclosure crisis has made it painfully clear that Americans are at a pivotal moment, when thousands of neighborhoods will need to adapt in order to accommodate current realities and correct deficiencies in the housing market. For progressive planners, resilient environments should always be adapting. Traditional suburbs should not become obsolescent. The local crisis is the appropriate time for architects, landscape architects and urban designers to collaborate with developers, builders, economists, engineers, ecologists, homeowners and homebuyers, with the collective goal of reimagining the suburban single-family residence and reversing the decline of so many suburbs. And through these urban design and planning processes, the deeper issues of housing affordability and suburban sprawl should then be fully addressed.

From ownership to rentership

The US Census Bureau reported in its 2010 census brief, *Housing Characteristics*, that the homeownership rate decreased by 1.1 percent to 65.1 percent in 2010. The decrease is the largest since the 1930–1940 period. For African-Americans, it fell from 49.4 percent to 47.5 percent. Latinos, native and foreign-born together, had a longer period of growth, with homeownership rising to 49.8 percent in 2006 before falling to 48.9 percent in 2009 (Mazur & Wilson, 2011).

While homeowners were the majority in most of the nation's metro areas, they were outnumbered by renters in many of the country's largest cities, including the four most populous cities. In New York, renters made up 69 percent of households; in Los Angeles, 61 percent; in Chicago, 55 percent; and in Houston, 54 percent (ibid.).

For some observers, Americans are slowly getting used to the idea of renting the good life, from cars to homes. For Daniel Gross, Americans are getting over the idea of owning the American Dream; they are increasingly opting for renting. For him, Americans are gradually getting used to the idea of giving up the stability of being an owner for the flexibility of being a renter. These new realities of an increasingly mobile economy make it more likely to help the transition from an ownership society to what might be called a "rentership" society. Consumers should learn to consume more intelligently. The vast mortgage–political–financial complex valued homeownership as a good in its own right. During the boom, homeownership grew steadily, peaking at a record 69 percent in 2006 to fall back to 65.4 percent in 2010. But those gains were short-lived and came at a truly massive cost (Gross, 2012).

Renting used to be understood as something one does when they have failed as a homeowner or are not yet ready to be one. But the rise of rentership is a sign of a system adapting to new realities. According to the *Wall Street Journal*, there is indeed a correlation between high local unemployment rates and high levels of homeownership (ibid.).

According to Daniel Gross, the Census Bureau indicated that in the first quarter of 2012, starts of multifamily housing structures increased by 27 percent, while single-family starts increased by only 16.7 percent. Somewhat surprisingly, builders of these structures were more likely to rent them out. In 2007, only 62 percent of the housing units in buildings with two or more units were built for rent, a number that rose to 84 percent in 2009, before reaching 91 percent in 2011 (Gross, 2012).[3]

The rising popularity of rentership is not limited to the housing market. Indeed, it has spurred the creation of innovative businesses in a number of other realms, like car ownership. The Bureau of Labor Statistics says that private transportation – owning and running a car – is the second largest cost for a typical American household, accounting for 16 percent of expenditures. Factoring in financial costs, depreciation, repairs, insurance, taxes and gas, the AAA (American Automobile Association) calculates that an owner of a mid-size car who drives 15,000 miles per year spends $8,588 each year on his or her car. Since 2000, the auto-sharing firm Zipcar has grown in cities and college campuses. The company uses information technology to manage its fleet and control access (people get cards that let them into garages where cars are kept, and into the cars themselves). Zipcar's membership went up as the American economy went down, growing from 225,000 members in 2008 to 650,000 members in November 2011. It went public in 2011 and has rapidly expanded in big cities like Boston, New York and San Francisco, as well as on college campuses and in smaller cities like Providence and Portland. In response to Zipcar's rise, large rental agencies like Enterprise and Avis have developed similar services.

The same renting orientation has spread to college textbooks, which are becoming rental goods. Students buy them at retail, use them for four months, and then resell them to the campus store or a used-book dealer. In 2010, the US college-textbook market was worth about $4.5 billion, according to the American Association of Publishers. The question is, then: why buy textbooks when you can spend less and rent them? Chegg.com, founded in 2001, is aiming to replace the college bookstore by offering students to rent instead of buying textbooks. As the *Wall Street Journal* notes, this trend is likely to grow as more students come to campus with e-readers.

These two examples point to a shift from an ownership to a rentership society, a different form of consumption emerging from America's mass market. This process is also at play in the housing sector, as witnessed by the growing acceptance of home and apartment rental. This marks a significant departure from the pre-crisis era, when people used house mortgages for refinancing and believed that the homes would return profit once they were sold. Today this economic model is questioned, along with the individualistic civilization it was rooted in (ibid).

Conclusion

The subprime crisis is certainly a remarkable example of the way the American capitalist system has been functioning over the years and its reliance on the bond industry. It also underlines the link between rampant urbanization and the financialization of the capitalist system (Aalbers, 2012). The subprime crisis is intricately linked to the way the national system of mortgage functions, but it indicates how price depreciation in the housing market at the local level has suddenly led to a dramatic wave of foreclosures and a widespread phenomenon of negative equity in a global crisis often qualified as *Made in America*. The subprime crisis is not only a local and national one: it became rapidly a global issue because of the interdependency between financial institutions located in different parts of the world. In the case of the subprime crisis, European banks were not spared. The negative impact of the subprime crisis was not confined to localities such as Cleveland and Moreno and not limited to one racial or ethnic group. The crisis affected different neighborhoods across many metropolitan areas. It concerned inner cities largely inhabited by African-American households as well as suburban fringes populated by white and Latino populations. The subprime crisis may then be understood as a multiscalar crisis that tells us about the essence of American civilization, a complex multi-level paradigm where institutional, sociocultural and spatial dynamics intersect.

The most striking fact caused by the subprime crisis is no doubt the awareness of planners, architects and economists denouncing the limit of what has been described as the epitome of the American Dream: owning a single-family house. Since the 1990s, urban sprawl has been criticized for its negative impacts on resources and land conversion, water and sewer infrastructure, local public-service costs and real-estate development costs (Burchell *et al.*, 2002). The subprime crisis may then be understood as a catastrophic event, a breaking point that may eventually reduce urban sprawl. Today, behind the smokescreen provoked by the subprime crisis, suburbia seems to be weakening the American economy instead of propping it up. The question is: what will replace suburbia as the engine of the American economy, and to some extent, the backbone of an American way of life? For real-estate theorist Christopher Leinberger (2009) and the planner Alan Ehrenhalt (2013), the answer is in the rising demand for walkable urbanism. Americans seem to be asking for sweeping new development at just the moment when they are looking for some new sources to power the economy.

This policy in favor of walkable urbanism may bring a significant change to the traditional American way of life and is not limited to empowering America: it will also be a response to the coming over the next two decades of three billion people projected to join the global middle class. One billion did this in the past 20 years. Their emergence will, of course, be one of the great success stories of the twenty-first century, while at the same time causing tremendous resource strain across the world. This is the international challenge America will have to navigate, and it ties back to two other direct benefits that walkable neighborhoods can offer. First, they will reduce the demand for oil. Walkable development is both the means to drive the economy and the product that enables all of us to live more sustainably. In this perspective one can say that the subprime crisis may have been an opportunity for America to lead on sustainability – and help the world get there with minimal conflict – although that will require a host of other policy changes. Thus, it seems that reinventing the American Dream may after all be congruent with fulfilling the needs of the rest of the world. One may conclude by saying that the crisis of American capitalism as seen through the lenses of the subprime crisis not only informs us about the way the mortgage industry used to work, but also deals with some central aspects of American civilization (Swedberg, 2010). It may be that the crisis of American capitalism is also redefining the American Dream and the American way of life – a shift away from the twentieth-century ideal of suburban comfort (Dunham-Jones, 2011; Florida, 2009).

Notes

1 According to the Federal Reserve, "the Community Reinvestment Act is intended to encourage depository institutions to help meet the credit needs of the communities in which they operate, including low- and moderate-income neighborhoods, consistent with safe and sound operations" with an aim of reducing redlining. (www.federalreserve.gov/communitydev/cra_about.htm).
2 See www.cnu.org.
3 The next three paragraphs borrow from Gross (2012).

References

Aalbers, M. (ed.). (2012). *Subprime cities: The political economy of mortgage markets.* London: Wiley-Blackwell.

BBC News (2007, November 21). The Downturn in Facts and Figures. Retrieved from http://news.bbc.co.uk/2/hi/business/7073131.stm.

Bron, J.S. (Director). (2010). Cleveland vs. Wall Street (Motion Picture). France: Saga Productions.
Burchell, R. *et al.* (2002). *Costs of sprawl*. Washington, DC: Transportation Research Board.
Dunham-Jones, E. (2011). *Retrofitting suburbia: Urban design solutions for redesigning suburbs*. Chichester: Wiley.
Economist, The (2008, August 14). Cities and Housing: The End of the Dream. Retrieved from www.economist.com/node/11920735.
Ehrenhalt, A. (2013). *The great inversion and the future of the city*. New York: Vintage.
Florida, R. (2009, March). How the Crash Will Reshape America. *The Atlantic*. Retrieved from www.theatlantic.com/magazine/archive/2009/03/how-the-crash-will-reshape-america/307293.
Florida, R. (2012, August 23). The Geography of Underwater Homes. *The Atlantic*. Retrieved from www.citylab.com/housing/2012/08/geography-underwater-homes/3034.
Gallagher, L. (2014). *The end of suburbs: Where the American dream is moving*. New York: Portfolio.
Gilderbloom, J., Ambrosius, J.D., Squires, G.D., Hanka, M.J. & Kenitzer, Z. (2012). Investors: The Missing Piece in the Foreclosure Racial Gap Debate. *Journal of Urban Affairs*, *34*(5), 559–582.
Gross, D. (2012, May 4). Renting Prosperity. *Wall Street Journal*. Retrieved from http://online.wsj.com/news/articles/SB10001424052702304746604577382321021920372.
Hall, P.A. & Soskice, D. (eds.) (2001). *Varieties of capitalism: The institutional foundations of comparative advantage*. Oxford: Oxford University Press.
Leinberger, C. (2008, March). The Next Slum? *The Atlantic*. Retrieved from www.theatlantic.com/magazine/archive/2008/03/the-next-slum/306653.
Leinberger, C. (2009). *The option of urbanism: Investing in a new American dream*. New York: Island Press.
Mazur, C. & Wilson, E. (2011). Housing Characteristics: 2010. U.S. Census Bureau. Retrieved from www.census.gov/prod/cen2010/briefs/c2010br-07.pdf.
Politi, J. & Kapner, Z. (2010, March 11). US Foreclosures Take their Toll on Homeowners. *Financial Times*. Retrieved from www.ft.com/intl/cms/s/0/418919a4-2d3c-11df-9c5b-00144feabdc0.html#axzz3YaNutg00.
Swedberg, R. (2010). A Note on Civilizations and Economics. *European Journal of Social Theory*, *13*(1), 15–30.

8 Transcending boundaries*

America's hybrid and multiscalar response to the competitive challenge of globalization

Jean-Baptiste Velut

At the intersection between the public and private spheres, the notion of competitiveness policy epitomizes the structural transformations of the American model of capitalism over the past few decades. It can be broadly defined as the set of policy tools used by local, state and federal governments to promote, sustain or restore US economic leadership in an increasingly competitive and global economy. From a cultural perspective, this concept lies at the crossroads between two ideological traditions: (1) the Hamiltonian tradition that favors the pursuit of a national economic strategy; (2) the Jeffersonian ideal of a "wise and frugal government," a form of "market-preserving federalism" that confines government intervention to the protection of free enterprise and property rights (Weingast, 1995).

But beyond ideological conflicts between "big," "small" or "smart government" (Clinton, 2011), American competitiveness policy is the complex product of institutional factors and power struggles that are inherent to any "political economic regime" at a specific time in history (Eisner, 2011). Whereas these dynamics are before all embedded within the American cultural-institutional context, they have also been redefined under the forces of globalization, which has accelerated and intensified the circulation of goods, services and knowledge, thereby altering the balance of power among American policy stakeholders (consumers and producers, employees and employers, etc.) and redefining traditional boundaries between local, regional, national and global spaces.

This chapter will study the mutations of America's state–market nexus before and after the 2008–2009 crisis through the prism of its competitive strategy. To do so, it will examine three pillars of US competitiveness: innovation policy, military–industrial programs and trade diplomacy.[1] It will examine the interests, ideas and institutions – Peter Hall's three "Is" of economic policy-making (Hall, 1997) – that have determined America's response to the challenges of globalization, from the early debates on industrial policy under the Reagan Administration, to Obama's promises to "out-innovate, out-educate and outbuild the rest of the world" (Obama, 2011).

From a theoretical standpoint, this chapter aims to analyze the resilience and mutations of America's model of capitalism during a period shaped by dramatic transformations in the global economy. In order to shed light on the change and continuity of American capitalism, I will seek to transcend the state–market dichotomy and reveal the complex modalities of state intervention and the interpenetration of public and private spheres. As Evans (1995) noted 20 years ago, the challenge is not to determine "how much" state intervention takes place in the economy but "what kind" of political action is implemented and to what effect for the overarching political economic structure.

The ghost of American industrial policy

Although political debates on the scope of government intervention in the economy are as old as the US Constitution, contemporary debates on the proper strategy that Washington should adopt in the face of emerging economic powers can be traced back to the Carter and Reagan presidencies. Officially, the very idea of devising a national industrial policy – known today as competitiveness policy – was abandoned owing to internecine conflicts within the Democratic Party and to the uncompromising stance of the Reagan Administration, who had vowed to unleash "the magic of the market." Thus, in 1986, the economist R.D. Norton was already writing a requiem for an "idea with a brief career" (Norton, 1986, p. 1). But while the conservative revolution was indeed a historical turning point toward a more restrictive conception of government intervention, a peculiar form of competitive strategy took shape throughout the 1980s (Azuelos, 1997). This contained or repressed form of industrial policy rested upon three pillars: military research, innovation policy and trade diplomacy.

The first policy starkly contrasts with Ronald Reagan's free market ideology and consists of the substantial military investment undertaken by the Republican Administration. Military spending was by no means confined to the strategic objectives of the Cold War: the tremendous financial support granted to the Defense Advanced Research Project Agency[2] was a sign that decision-makers had no qualms about using military research for commercial purposes. In a study of military R&D, Fong (2000) draws a typology of DARPA's main research programs based on their military and/or commercial objectives. He concludes that DARPA began a process of "strategic reorientation" toward dual-use programs during the 1980s.

Given its fiscal prerogatives, the Democratic Congress played a crucial part in what Ezkowitz (1998) describes as the "civilianization" of military research. DARPA even borrowed from the Japanese playbook to support the semiconductor sector by financing half of the *Sematech* consortium, a form of public–private partnership that seemed at odds with America's free market tradition (Nester, 1997). Admittedly, Ronald Reagan and his successor George H.W. Bush were both ambivalent about adopting such interventionist measures. Yet, in effect, they contributed to the strategic reorientation of American military research.

Beyond the myths of free enterprise, local and regional governments also implemented sectoral initiatives that strikingly resembled meso-level industrial policies. Confronted by factory closures and budgetary restrictions in the late

1970s to early 1980s, state governments developed an array of competitive measures in the hope of replicating the success story of competitive clusters like Silicon Valley and Route 128 in the Boston area (Eisinger, 1988).

This decentralizing trend in innovation policy might be interpreted as the essence of a political economic model where a wise and frugal federal government chooses inaction over interference to nurture private initiatives. Yet, during the 1980s, federal agencies actively participated in this process through a triple function of deregulation, investment and brokerage. The first function began at the end of the Carter presidency and consisted, on the one hand, of facilitating technology transfers from public universities to the private sector (Bayh–Dole Act of 1980, Stevenson Wydler Act of 1986), and on the other, of loosening antitrust laws to allow new forms of business partnerships like *Sematech* (e.g., National Cooperative Research Act in 1984). This deregulating process was not akin to retrenchment as the federal government launched several investment programs to face the new competitive challenges of emerging economies in Europe and Asia. Thus, the federal government propped up its support to small businesses by allocating 2 percent of its federal research budget to the Small Business Innovation Research (1982). Paradoxically, the Reagan Administration did not oppose the creation of what a Cambridge scholar has described as "the largest seed capital fund in the world" (Connell, n.d.), even if it initially opposed the Omnibus Trade and Competitiveness Act of 1988 supported by the Democratic Party. This legislation revealed that economic interventionism was not anathema to the American political economy. Through the creation of the Manufacturing Extension Program and the Advanced Technology Program (ATP), the federal government performed a critical brokerage function between public and private actors, initiating new hybrid forms of partnerships structured through a decentralized and flexible innovation system that would flourish in the following decades (Block, 2008).[3]

The third pillar of America's competitiveness policy in the 1980s was the emergence of a more aggressive trade diplomacy. Although the Reagan Administration was initially reluctant to intervene on behalf of American manufacturing producers, it made a signature of its "aggressive unilateralism," i.e., the systematic use of protectionist sanctions to pry open foreign markets (Baghwati & Patrick, 1990). Thus, export promotion became an integral part of a more assertive trade diplomacy model that began to crystallize with bilateral US–Japanese trade relations,[4] through the development of the first free trade agreements with Israel and Canada, to culminate in the launch of the Uruguay Round within the GATT (1986–1994). Beyond trade policy, the Plaza Accord of 1985, by putting an end to the strong dollar policy, had probably the most significant impact on the international competitiveness of American businesses (Nester, 1997).

This emerging global strategy on behalf of American business interests reflected shifting grounds within the American political economy. Globalization reshuffled the power game to the benefit of internationalist or "anti-protection" interests, among which were multinational corporations and large retailers

(Destler & Odell, 1987). The latter used America's system of trade advisory committees to push trade negotiators to expand the scope of negotiations in new territories, such as investment protection and intellectual property rights. This new driving force of US international economic policy propelled the negotiations of the North American Free Trade Agreement (NAFTA) under the Bush Administration. By venturing in new policy areas (investor rights, services trade, government procurement, etc.), NAFTA incarnated a new "variety of global capitalism" that would serve as a template for US trade diplomacy for the next two decades.

Hence, the competitive pressures of globalization transformed the US political economy at the local, regional, federal and global levels. This multiscalar response to America's economic challenges spawned new public–private partnerships, i.e., hybrid forms of governance that would become ever more common in the following decades.

Bringing the state out of the shadows

If the 1980s saw the emergence of new forms of industrial policies, the White House did not officially embrace economic interventionism until the Clinton Administration. The Democratic president's unabashed support for a coherent competitive policy partly owed to the context of the 1992 presidential campaign, when Bill Clinton famously castigated his Republican rival for his political inertia in a period of economic sluggishness – "It's the economy, stupid!"

Influenced by his long-time friend and secretary of labor, Robert Reich – who had participated in the debates on industrial policy a decade earlier – Clinton promised to put in place a comprehensive economic strategy that would allow the United States to "compete, not retreat" in the face of increasing international pressures (Clinton, 1993). His competitive policy had both domestic and international components. At the international level, the Clinton Administration vowed to pry open new markets and thereby rally the business community behind the New Democrats' political agenda. On the domestic front, the federal government would support private and public investments in infrastructure, education and training (Shoch, 2001; Hughes, 2005). This dual approach to the challenges of globalization was perhaps what distinguished the Democrats' competitive policy from the policy framework established by their Republican predecessors. If Clinton's uninhibited approach to industrial policy contrasted with the disguised or perfunctory actions of the Reagan and Bush Administrations, the modalities of his competitive policy were, for the most part, a logical continuation of ongoing transformations of the state–market nexus.

The end of the Cold War confirmed the merits of the strategic reorientation of military research. Clinton reinforced this process of civilianization by capitalizing on the synergy effects of new public–private partnerships. One example of this hybrid approach was the $1 billion investment-matching fund provided by the Technology Reinvestment Project that led to civilian spin-offs like infra-red night-vision technologies and high-density data storage devices (Weiss, 2007).

The DARPA model, a network of high-skilled researchers in both public and private sectors, inspired other agencies like the CIA, which developed its own venture capital funds (In-Q-Tel), before being adopted by the Army (OnPoint) and NASA (Red Planet Capital), both of which have long experimented with public–private partnerships and dual use.[5]

Within the realm of innovation policy, Bill Clinton adopted the three-pronged strategy implemented under the Reagan and Bush Administrations. Deregulation and brokerage were also inherent to his approach, as witnessed by his efforts to relax the rules regulating business partnerships (National Cooperative Research Act of 1993) and his belated initiative to facilitate the transfer of intellectual property rights between federal agencies and corporations (Technology Transfer Commercialization Act of 2000) (Schacht, 2012). Perhaps more idiosyncratic was his strong commitment to boost federal investment. Despite the failure of his 1993 investment plan, Clinton renewed his efforts to support federal research programs like the Manufacturing Extension Partnership or the ATP (Etzkowitz, 1998). Monitoring these programs and assisting in the civilianization of military research, the Department of Commerce became a crucial organ in the design of American innovation policy (Hughes, 2005). Bill Clinton also oversaw the implementation of new investment programs in information and communication technology (Information Superhighway), the automobile sector (Partnership for a New Generation of Vehicles) and in nanotechnology (National Nanotechnology Initiative) (Nester, 1997).

Bill Clinton's efforts to build a more coherent competitive policy framework were not exempt from partisan debates on the size of the federal government. After its victory at the midterm elections of 1994, the new Republican majority led by Newt Gringrich launched an assault against several federal agencies and programs, some of which were part of Clinton's innovation strategy. The new "Contract with America" put the White House on the defensive by targeting federal programs.[6] Partisan conflicts and Clintonian triangulation did not, however, derail the trajectory of America's multipronged strategic response to economic globalization. In fact, in the trade policy sphere, the Republican majority turned into a valuable ally for the Clinton Administration that partly offset the Democratic Party's divisions over trade liberalization.

The most significant legacy of Bill Clinton's national economic strategy was arguably his foreign economic policy. It rested first on a more comprehensive approach to export promotion through the creation of the Trade Promotion Coordinating Committee and the International Trade Administration Advocacy Center (under the Department of Commerce), which improved access to financial, technical and diplomatic assistance for American exporting firms (Weiss, 2007). The Clinton Administration also institutionalized the practice of "competitive liberalization" under which Washington used bilateral, regional and multilateral trade agreements to open new markets to US business interests. Over the opposition of "Old" Democrats and their union backers, Clinton managed to secure the passage of NAFTA, concluded the Uruguay Round and normalized trade relations with China, thereby enabling its entry to the WTO. Like innovation policy, trade agreements were also the product of close collaboration between public and private actors in which the executive branch played a leading role, not only before trade negotiations (e.g., trade advisory committees) but also after the negotiations in order to rally legislative support in Congress. The close collaboration between economic and political elites raised controversies on the governance of American trade policy and explains why labor unions, environmentalists and consumer advocates like Public Citizen, who had little access to the policy process, fiercely opposed trade agreements. Thus, over the course of the 1990s, all subnational, national and international tools were mobilized to make economic competitiveness a central objective of America's national interests. This gave birth to new forms of private–public partnerships that contributed to preserve America's competitive leadership, despite the dislocating effects that competitive pressures exerted on certain segments of the US workforce.

George W. Bush and the Reaganite illusion

At first sight, the evolution of American competitiveness policy under the Bush Administration mirrors Ronald Reagan's strategy in many regards. First, like his conservative forebear, George W. Bush was initially equivocal about adopting a national economic strategy. Instead, he favored a macroeconomic approach centered on tax cuts, thereby renewing the supply-side economics of the "Great Communicator." Second, beyond his laissez-faire rhetoric, George W. Bush also adopted a form of industrial policy that, like his conservative predecessor, became more coherent during his second term. Third, the 9/11 terror attacks brought national security back to the top of the White House's political agenda and prompted the Bush Administration to embrace the type of military Keynesianism on which Ronald Reagan had built his political legacy.

The new security imperatives of the "War on Terror" reinvigorated military research, as witnessed by the 49 percent growth of DARPA's budget between 2001 and 2005.[7] While military R&D had already proved its economic virtues during the Cold War, the potential spin-offs of the new "security–industrial complex" are equally clear (Mills, 2004). For instance, scanners and geospatial technology (e.g., GPS) have already transformed the medical, transportation and IT sectors, while the development of civilian applications for unmanned aerial vehicles (i.e., drones) also promises to create new business opportunities. Here again, America's military–industrial policy relies on a network of private and public actors like universities. However, the Bush Administration altered DARPA's *modus operandi* in two significant ways: first, by prioritizing research programs with more direct commercial potential to the detriment of radical innovation projects that had shaped DARPA's reputation; second, by disrupting the public–private balance to transfer more resources and authority toward businesses (Patterson, 2009; Markoff, 2009).

In the sphere of innovation policy, the legacy of the Bush Administration is similarly mixed. At the outset, George W. Bush's military priorities, his inclination toward macroeconomic solutions, his defensive approach to sectoral issues (airline bailouts, steel tariffs) and his distant relationship with the scientific community all augured poorly for the fate of American competitiveness policy (Hughes, 2005; Schacht, 2012). Yet, regardless of their proclivities for market mechanisms, both the White House and the Republican majority in Congress continued to support federal intervention on behalf of innovation. Thus, the National Nanotechnology Initiative saw its budget triple under the Bush presidency (Sargent, 2012). Furthermore, during his 2006 State of the Union address, George W. Bush announced the launch of the American Competitiveness Initiative, which planned to double basic research funding within ten years under the purview of the National Science Foundation and the Departments of Energy and Commerce. The US Congress followed the president's call with the America COMPETES Act of 2007, a rare bipartisan law in a context of political polarization. In a sense, the American COMPETES Act of 2007 incarnates the Bush Administration's ambivalence about implementing a national competitive strategy. Admittedly, this program dramatically raised the budget allocated to research and STEM (science, technology, engineering and mathematics) education. It also created a new research agency inspired by the DARPA model within the Department of Energy: ARPA-E. The latter would paradoxically become the Republicans' *bête noire* within Barack Obama's stimulus package.[8] On the other hand, the America COMPETES Act not only undermined the coordination of US technology policy by abolishing the position of undersecretary for technology, created in 1989 under the Department of Commerce, but as for DARPA, transferred authority to the business sector (Schacht, 2012).[9]

Finally, as far as trade diplomacy is concerned, the Bush Administration generally followed in the footsteps of his predecessor. By conducting negotiations for myriad free trade agreements at the bilateral and regional levels, George W. Bush institutionalized the strategy of competitive liberalization undertaken by Bill Clinton (Velut, 2010). Yet, if the latter had provided few opportunities for civil society representatives to participate in the policy process, President Bush completely excluded labor unions and non-governmental organizations from decision-making, leaving large firms free to shape Washington's trade policy objectives (Velut, 2009).

Thus, whether in the realm of military–industrial policy, innovation or trade diplomacy, the Bush Administration worked to reconfigure the state–market nexus by shifting the cursor to market actors, without necessarily depriving the federal government of its investment and brokerage functions. This reveals that beyond policy legacies, institutional rigidities and path dependence, political and ideological factors can affect the trajectory of a model of capitalism often deemed immutable. Barack Obama's attempt to shape a competitive strategy in the aftermath of the crisis would confirm the conflictual and malleable character of the American political economy.

Plus ça change, plus c'est la même chose?

Barack Obama's election in the midst of the 2008 global financial meltdown meant that the new Democratic president would build his policies in contradistinction with his predecessor's political legacy. Despite the relative continuity in the immediate management of the crisis – most notably the financial and auto bailouts – Barack Obama vowed to reassert the role of the federal government in the pursuit of economic competitiveness, and thereby renewed with a Clintonian approach to national economic strategy. Within the military–industrial sphere, the White House sought to restore confidence with the scientific community through the nomination of Regina Dugan (2009–2012), businesswoman, inventor and technology developer. Dugan also worked to veer away from the security trope of the Bush Administration and extend DARPA's research programs to robotics, nanotechnology or vaccines (Markoff, 2010). Cybersecurity research programs like the National Cyber Range were also renewed under the Obama Administration, with both security and commercial objectives (Lynn, 2010).[10] Another example of the blurred line between civilian and military research was the participation of DARPA in the Brain Research through Advancing Innovative Neurotechnologies (BRAIN) initiative alongside civilian agencies like the National Science Foundation and the National Institute of Health. This program was endowed with $100 million in 2014 and showcased as a "paradigm shifting" research endeavor comparable to the Human Genome Project jointly undertaken by the Department of Energy and the National Institute of Health (Markoff & Gorman, 2013).[11]

Likewise, Obama's innovation policy conferred a greater role to federal intervention in economic competitiveness than was traditionally acknowledged in American politics:

> Our free enterprise system is what drives innovation. But because it's not always profitable for companies to invest in basic research, throughout our history, our government has provided cutting-edge scientists and inventors with the support that they need. That's what planted the seeds for the Internet. That's what helped make possible things like computer chips and GPS.
>
> (Obama, 2011)

Ideological affinities with Clintonomics notwithstanding, Obama's conception of governmental action as a creative force for innovation was arguably influenced by the context of the global economy. Indeed, the financial crisis had discredited laissez-faire and renewed decision-makers' interests in Keynesianism, as illustrated by the flurry of post-crisis recovery programs and industrial policies (*The Economist*, 2010). Additionally, the rise of Chinese state capitalism and its resilience to the financial collapse seemed to summon greater intervention in the economy. If George W. Bush had responded to the 2000–2001 dotcom crisis with a combination of macroeconomic solutions and sectoral bailouts, the Obama Administration saw in the Great Recession an opportunity to design a new industrial policy. "You never want a serious crisis to go to waste" declared White House chief of staff Rahm Emanuel in 2008. The American Recovery and Reinvestment Act (ARRA) brought these words to life.

At a total cost of $831 billion, ARRA stands as the most expensive law in American history, dwarfing the Louisiana Purchase, the Marshall Plan and even Roosevelt's New Deal. Often reduced to a countercyclical economic policy, the so-called stimulus was also a bold attempt to reorient America's energy policy toward sustainable solutions, at a time when renewable energy like wind power was declining. Obama's unprecedented investment in clean technologies (wind and solar power, smart grid, retrofitting, electric vehicles, etc.) – from a few billion dollars annually to $90 billion – may have allowed this infant industry to reach critical mass (Grundwald, 2012). This innovative process was emblematic of a submerged model of US competitiveness policy, whereby federal, state and local programs subsidized clean energy through preferential loans and research grants, before being relayed by the competitive pressures of the market.

Partisan politics and media coverage reduced ARPA-E's large-scale investment program in advanced clean technology to the story of Solyndra, a solar panel producer that went bankrupt two years after obtaining a $535-million federal grant from the Department of Energy. The new Republican majority used this example as a symbol of Obama's "big government" approach to economics, an opportunity to bury industrial policy debates under the pretense that the state should never pick "winners." This paradox epitomizes the contradictions of the American state–market nexus. As Surowiecki (2011) aptly notes, while risks and bankruptcies have always been an integral part of capitalism, failure cannot be tolerated if the federal government is involved.

In many respects, however, "Solyndragate" was a distorted representation of the innovative process. First, to use academic parlance, it was a classic fallacy of hasty generalization based on an unrepresentative sample. Indeed, two years after ARPA-E deployed its financial clout, business failures like Solyndra represented only a small fraction of the more than $20 billion preferential loans granted to clean energy projects (Surowiecki, 2011). Second, and perhaps more ironically, the travails of the solar power industry in the United States and Europe were as much the product of market pressures as they were the result of state intervention – but state intervention *from China* and more specifically, the overcapacity resulting from its heavily subsidized solar panel industry (Anderlini, 2013). Third, as mentioned earlier, ARPA-E was not created out of thin air by the Obama Administration but rested upon pre-existing innovative programs created under the America COMPETES Act passed under the Bush presidency. And without downplaying the innovative spirit and the business acumen of clean tech entrepreneurs, the resilience of the renewable energy sector and its growing ability to compete with conventional energy sources also partly owe to persistent shadow forms of state intervention like tax credits and preferential loans (Cardwell, 2014). In short, bitter partisan politics have obscured both the effective intervention of the federal government in the creative dynamics of American capitalism, as well as the institutional resilience of US competitiveness policy over the decades.

Emphasizing the institutional legacies of US neo-industrial policies does not mean that the political sphere should be dismissed. Although partisan politics might distort the true nature of the US model of capitalism, political factors remain vital to understanding its dynamics. As in the mid-1990s, when Bill Clinton was compelled to adapt his national economic strategy to the demands of the Republican majority, Barack Obama also had to reconsider his political strategy after the Democrats' "shellacking" in the 2010 midterm elections. To begin with, amidst controversies surrounding the Solyndra scandal, ARPA-E's budget was halved (Surowiecki, 2011). Furthermore, the America COMPETES Act – a legacy of the Bush Administration – was reapproved only after bitter partisan conflicts in Congress. Last, but not least, the return to a divided government also buried Obama's cap and trade project,[12] which might have strengthened clean technology investments by providing a long-term regulatory framework favorable to renewables.

This political inertia has encouraged local and state governments to take the lead. Since the Great Recession, American cities from New York City to Denver have developed innovative strategies to diversify their local economies and stimulate the development of competitive clusters (Katz & Bradley, 2013). This "Metropolitan Revolution" is a groundbreaking process in name only to the extent that it builds upon the decentralizing forces under play since the 1980s. What is new is the emergence of networks of global cities that intend to play a leading role not only in innovation, but also in social and environmental reforms. One example is the C40 Climate Leadership Group, a network of cities that aim to surpass – or bypass – national climate actions undertaken within the multilateral forum after Kyoto. This confirms that the creative processes inherent to the dynamics of American capitalism – whether merely competitive or socially and environmentally oriented – takes place at multiple levels and can no longer be captured by clean hierarchies of power (Sassen, 2004).

Political polarization and decentralizing trends have not, however, stopped the president's efforts from reorienting American competitiveness policy toward a more sustainable path. Throughout his presidency, Barack Obama has widely resorted to executive power under the 1970 Clean Air Act to define new regulatory standards (from CO_2 to ozone emissions, soot and mercury) via the Environmental Protection Agency (Davenport, 2014). Combined with ARRA's large investments in clean technology and with Obama's recent environmental diplomacy with China, this series of regulatory measures are constitutive of an emerging national climate change strategy that has the potential to reshape entire sectors of the US economy.

Although denounced as an abuse of executive power by Republican critics, this green variety of industrial policy cannot be reduced to a top-down process. Here again, it is emblematic of the multiscalar nature of American competitiveness policy. The new EPA rules provide states with ample leeway to design emission-cutting plans adapted to their regional economies. Like the Affordable Care Act (ACA) and the "Race to the Top" education reform, this policy therefore instantiates a decentralized approach to economic policy whereby states are expected to operate as laboratories of innovation (Davenport & Baker, 2014).[13] Additionally, and despite the failure of cap-and-trade reform at the federal level, 14 states, representing nearly one-third of the US population, have formed regional cap-and-trade programs like the Western Climate Initiative (AZ, CA, NM, OR and WA) and the Regional Greenhouse Gas Initiative (CT, DE, ME, MD, MA, NH, NY, RI, VT). As of this writing, 34 states have designed or are developing climate action plans, which reveals that with environmental as well as competitiveness policy, subnational initiatives are as important to the dynamics of US capitalism as federal programs.[14]

Finally, although the proliferation of local and state initiatives demonstrate that political action needs not be pursued by the federal government, the latter has remained a central actor of trade diplomacy, the stakes of which are nothing less than the definition of the regulatory contours of globalization. In this realm, President Obama has not fundamentally departed from the precepts of his predecessors. First, his National Export Initiative, which sought to double US exports within five years,[15] along with the creation of a new Export Promotion Cabinet, mirrored the national export strategy adopted by the Clinton Administration. Second, President Obama only marginally altered the content of the bilateral free trade agreements negotiated under the Bush Administration (with South Korea, Panama and Colombia) before requesting their ratification in Congress in 2011, capitalizing, for once, on Republican legislative support. What distinguished Obama's trade diplomacy from the Bush Administration's was the scope of the cross-regional "mega" trade agreements undertaken on both sides of the United States: the Transpacific Partnership (TPP) and the Transatlantic Trade and Investment Partnership (TTIP). The former aims to liberalize trade and investment and harmonize regulatory standards between 12 countries on both sides of the Pacific Ocean,[16] while the latter brings together the United States and the European Union through a similar approach. Both agreements are considered to be "next generation" accords owing to the very broad scope of the negotiations – services liberalization, regulatory coherence, state-owned enterprises, etc. By venturing "behind the borders" – i.e., beyond conventional tariff barriers – trade diplomacy has been taking an ever-greater role in the promotion of US economic interests. The ultimate objective of this latest phase of competitive liberalization consists of creating rules amenable to international businesses, particularly in sectors where the United States has a competitive advantage. This reveals that the dynamics of American competitive policy, and to a greater extent, of the US variety of capitalism, are not only driven by market forces but are also considerably shaped by state intervention at the local, national and international levels.

Conclusion

Analyzing the evolution of American competitiveness policy over the past three decades reveals the dynamic and complex nature of the US variety of capitalism. This convoluted, conflicted political economy challenges conventional representations of the free-market model and the state–market dichotomy to shed light on the subtle modalities under which the state intervenes in the US economy. At first sight, the federal government appears to have delegated or subcontracted some of its functions to local and regional actors and/or the private sector. Yet, far from yielding to the forces of globalization, state capacities have fundamentally reinvented themselves from the 1980s. The relative decline of American economic power has prompted the US government to gradually develop a strategic competitiveness policy that rests upon three pillars. First, the Reagan and Bush Administrations heralded a slow process of strategic reorientation of military research, the final objectives of which have become more and more commercial. Second, from the 1980s, the state has implemented a complete renewal of innovation policy through three policy tools: deregulation, brokerage and investment. Far from retreating from its functions, the federal government has played an active role in decentralizing and flexibilizing innovation policies, as witnessed by the series of research programs launched from the Reagan to the Obama Administrations. Third, since the mid-1980s, Washington has developed a vigorous – some might say aggressive – trade diplomacy designed to open foreign markets through export promotion and the negotiation of free trade agreements. These three developments demonstrate that the "Reagan revolution" was never a return to laissez-faire, to the extent that both government intervention and market forces have been instrumental in shaping America's response to increasing international competition.

Through the emergence of a three-pronged competitiveness policy, the state has played an important role in defending US business interests at the local, national and international levels. One major point of convergence between the three axes of US competitiveness policy is the hybridization of the public and private spheres displayed through the increasing collaboration of public and corporate actors in developing military research, fostering innovation, as well as designing global regulatory standards as part of international trade negotiations. This constitutes perhaps the common thread of American competitive strategy in the face of increasing international competition.

What are the driving forces of this strategic response? Whereas the rise of Japanese competition served as a catalyst for prominent debates on industrial policy and concealed forms of policy action in the 1980s, the growing power of emerging economies, most notably China, has renewed controversies on the role that the state should play in the dynamics of US competitiveness. Beyond external factors, three internal variables have shaped American competitiveness policy over the past three decades. First, the emergence of a coherent institutional framework – never devoid of inconsistencies and redundancies – has nonetheless served to stabilize American competitiveness policy through institutional layering and path-dependent processes. Additionally, America's idiosyncratic cultural tradition, especially regarding the role of the federal government in society, explains for a large part the tribulations of American competitive strategy, which, like all policy spheres, remains contingent upon electoral politics. Partisan battles can shift the cursor of the state–market spectrum toward one end or another and "big events" like the financial crisis of 2007–2009 may disrupt institutional equilibriums. Finally, the politicization and mobilization of business interests since the 1970s has contributed to the hybridization phenomenon inherent to the dynamics of contemporary American capitalism. This shows that beyond institutional rigidities and structural constraints, politics retains a crucial role in shaping the American political economy, whether decision-makers aim to retain a competitive edge in the global economy or aspire to make this competitive model fairer. This echoes the editors' call to reaffirm the embeddedness of American political economy in the political, social and cultural sphere. While this chapter has focused on the dynamics of competitiveness policy, the creative processes inherent to American capitalism cannot be dissociated from its social ramifications, which are addressed at greater length in other chapters of the current volume.

Notes

* Parts of this chapter appeared in French in Jean-Baptiste Velut (2015). "We need to [...] Out-innovate the world": les tribulations de la politique de compétitivité américaine, in Martine Azuelos (ed.), *Capitalisme anglo-saxon et monde(s) anglophone(s): des paradigmes en question*, *Revue LISA/LISA e-journal*, vol. 13(2): http://lisa.revues.org/8311.

1 Trade diplomacy is understood here as the arsenal of measures developed by the government to defend US economic interests within the framework of international trade negotiations.

2 DARPA or ARPA was created in 1958 by President Eisenhower and has since engendered a cornucopia of radical innovations in various sectors such as electronics, medicine, information technology, etc.

3 For more information on the incremental transformations of the US national system of innovation, see Coste's contribution to the present volume.

4 Ronald Reagan first imposed "voluntary" restraint agreements on Japan's steel and auto sectors, before sanctioning its electronic industry with tariff hikes in 1987.

5 For more details, see Weiss (2007). Block (2008) describes the DARPA model as a "developmental network state."

6 One obvious example is the welfare reform of 1996, which restricted assistance to the poor, thereby exacerbating competitive pressures on the lower class.

7 Author's calculation based on figures from DARPA and the Department of Defense.

8 See discussion below.

9 Unlike its predecessor, the Advisory Board with the new Technology Innovation replacing the Advanced Technology Program (ATP) was composed of only private sector members.

10 Launched at the end of the Bush presidency, the National Cyber Range consists of creating a parallel internet network with the aim of simulating cyberattacks and testing the Pentagon's capacity to protect government computer systems.

11 Initiated by the US government and funded at $135 million dollars annually, the Human Genome Project is another example of federal research leading to significant technological innovation and commercial applications. For a discussion, see Block (2008).

12 After passing the House of Representatives in 2009, the cap-and-trade bill failed in the Senate in 2010.

13 Like Medicaid expansion (as part of Obamacare), this approach is likely to face political opposition, as hyperpartisanship is no longer confined to the federal government. For a discussion on the declining function of states as laboratories, see Chatterji (2015).

14 See the website of the Center for Climate and Energy Solutions: www.c2es.org/us-states-regions/policy-maps/climate-action-plans.
15 Five years after the launch of the National Export Initiative, US Census Foreign Trade Statistics show that exports have increased by only 48 percent, a remarkable development that falls, however, short of Obama's promises.
16 TPP negotiating parties include Australia, Brunei, Canada, Chile, Japan, Malaysia, Mexico, New Zealand, Peru, Singapore, the United States and Vietnam.

References

Anderlini, J. (2013, June 16). Chinese Industry: Ambitions in Excess. *Financial Times*.

Azuelos, M. (1997). Les États-Unis et la mondialisation: de l'ébranlement de la puissance nationale à l'émergence d'un nouveau défi américain. In M.C. Esposito & M. Azuelos (eds.), *Mondialisation et domination économique: la dynamique anglo-saxonne* (pp. 143–167). Paris: Economica.

Bhagwati, J. & Patrick H. (eds.). (1990). *Aggressive unilateralism: America's 301 trade policy and the world trading system.* Ann Arbor, MI: University of Michigan Press.

Block, F. (2008). Swimming Against the Current: The Rise of a Hidden Developmental State in the United States. *Politics & Society*, *36*(2), 169–206.

Cardwell, D. (2014, November 23). Solar and Wind Energy Start to Win on Price vs. Conventional Fuels. *New York Times*. Retrieved from www.nytimes.com/2014/11/24/business/energy-environment/solar-and-wind-energy-start-to-win-on-price-vs-conventional-fuels.html.

Chatterji, A. (2015, January 12). Don't Look to States for New Ideas. *New York Times*. Retrieved from www.nytimes.com/2015/01/12/opinion/dont-look-to-states-for-new-ideas.html.

Clinton, B. (1993, February 26). Speech at the American University Centennial. Washington, DC. Retrieved from www1.media.American.edu/speeches/1993centennial.htm.

Clinton, B. (2011). *Back to work: Why we need smart government for a strong economy.* New York: Alfred A. Knopf.

Connell, D. (n.d.). Secrets of the World's Largest Seed Capital Fund. Center for Business Research, University of Cambridge. Retrieved from www.cbr.cam.ac.uk/pdf/SBIR%20Full%20Report.pdf.

Davenport, C. (2014, November 26). Obama Builds Environmental Legacy with 1970 Law. *New York Times*. Retrieved from www.nytimes.com/2014/11/27/us/without-passing-a-single-law-obama-crafts-bold-enviornmental-policy.html.

Davenport, C. & Baker, P. (2014, June 2). Taking Page From Health Care Act, Obama Climate Plan Relies on States. *New York Times*. Retrieved from www.nytimes.com/2014/06/03/us/politics/obama-epa-rule-coal-carbon-pollution-power-plants.html.

Department of Commerce (2010, September). Report to the President on the National Export Initiative: The Export Promotion Cabinet's Plan for Doubling U.S. Exports in Five Years. Retrieved from www.whitehouse.gov/sites/default/files/nei_report_9-16-10_full.pdf.

Destler, I.M. & Odell, J. (1987). *Anti-protection: Changing forces in United States trade politics*. Washington, DC: Institute for International Economics.

Economist, The (2010, August 9–10). Leviathan Inc. Retrieved from www.economist.com/node/16743343.

Eisinger, P. (1988). *The rise of the entrepreneurial state*. Madison, IW: University of Wisconsin Press.

Eisner, M. (2011). *The American political economy: Institutional evolution of market and state*. New York and London: Routledge.

Etzkowitz, H. (1998). The Triple Helix of Academia–Industry–Government: The U.S. National Innovation System. In R. Anderson, T. Cohn, C. Day, M. Howlett & C. Murray (eds.), *Innovation systems in a global context* (pp. 127–147). Montreal: McGill-Queen's University Press.

Evans, P. (1995). *Embedded autonomy: States and industrial transformation*. Princeton, NJ: Princeton University Press.

Fong, G. (2000). Breaking New Ground or Breaking the Rules: Strategic Reorientation in U.S. Industrial Policy. *International Security*, *25*(2), 152–186.

Grunwald, M. (2012). *The new New Deal: The hidden story of change in the Obama era*. New York: Simon & Schuster.

Hall, P. (1997). The Role of Interests, Institutions, and Ideas in the Comparative Political Economy of the Industrialized Nations. In M. Lichbach & A. Zuckerman (eds.), *Comparative politics: Rationality, culture and structure* (pp. 174–207). Cambridge: Cambridge University Press.

Hughes, K. (2005). *Building the next American century. The past and future of American economic competitiveness*. Washington, DC: Woodrow Wilson Center Press.

Katz, B. & Bradley, J. (2013). *The metropolitan revolution*. Washington, DC: Brookings Institution Press.

Lynn, W. (2010). Defending a New Domain. *Foreign Affairs*, *89*(5), 97–108.

Markoff, J. (2009, October 6). Pentagon Research Director Visits Universities in Bid to Re-energize Partnerships. *New York Times*. Retrieved from www.nytimes.com/2009/10/07/science/07darpa.html.

Markoff, J. (2010, April 12). New Force Behind Agency of Wonder. *New York Times*. Retrieved from www.nytimes.com/2010/04/13/science/13prof.html.

Markoff, J. & Gorman, J. (2013, April 2). Obama to Unveil Initiative to Map the Human Brain. *New York Times*. Retrieved from www.nytimes.com/2013/04/02/science/obama-to-unveil-initiative-to-map-the-human-brain.html.

Mills, M. (2004, November 29). The Security–Industrial Complex. *Forbes*. Retrieved from www.forbes.com/forbes/2004/1129/044.html.

Nester, W. (1997). *American industrial policy: Free or managed markets*? New York: St. Martin's Press.

Norton, R.D. (1986, March). Industrial Policy and American Renewal. *Journal of Economic Literature*, *24*, 1–40.

Obama, B.H. (2011, January 25). State of the Union Address, Washington, DC. Retrieved from www.whitehouse.gov/the-press-office/2011/01/25/remarks-president-state-union-address.

Patterson, D. (2009, November 3). Revamping DARPA is Vital to Preserving the U.S. Lead in IT. *Harvard Business Review*. Retrieved from https://hbr.org/2009/11/restoring-darpa-is-the-key-to/.

Sargent, J. (2012, December 16). The National Nanotechnology Initiative: Overview, Reauthorization, and Appropriations Issues. Congressional Research Service. Retrieved from www.fas.org/sgp/crs/misc/RL34401.pdf.

Sassen, S. (2004). Local Actors in Global Politics. *Current Sociology*, *52*(4), 649–670.

Schacht, W. (2012, December 3). Industrial Competitiveness and Technological Advancement: Debate Over Government Policy. Congressional Research Service. Retrieved from www.fas.org/sgp/crs/misc/RL33528.pdf.

Shoch, J. (2001). *Trading blows. Party competition and U.S. trade policy in a globalizing era*. Chapell Hill and London: University of North Carolina Press.

Surowiecki, J. (2011, October 10). A Waste of Energy. *The New Yorker*. Retrieved from www.newyorker.com/talk/financial/2011/10/10/111010ta_talk_surowiecki.

Velut, J.B. (2009). Free or Fair Trade? The Battle for the Rules of American Trade Policy from NAFTA to CAFTA. PhD dissertation, Université Sorbonne Nouvelle/City University of New York.

Velut, J.B. (2010). La Politique Commerciale de George W. Bush: rupture ou continuité? *La Revue LISA/LISA e-journal*, *8*(1), 153–166.

Weingast, B. (1995). The Economic Role of Political Institutions: Market-Preserving Federalism and Economic Development. *Journal of Law, Economics & Organization*, *20*(1), 1–31.

Weiss, L. (2007, August 5). Governing the Market in America. Conference organized by the Ford Foundation/Politics & Society, City University of New York.

Part III

Disruptive and creative agency

The dynamics of cultural resilience and renewal

9 The evolutions of the US innovation system as a political economy paradigm

From systemic governance to innovation policy-making?

Jacques-Henri Coste

The United States has long been praised for the dynamism and resilience of its "national system of innovation" (NSI). A shifting but distinctive institutional framework has enabled innovators and institutions to produce and commercialize novelty, inventions and research within and across national borders. The resulting open innovation paradigm has helped identify the driving force of the innovation process as the outcome of successful interactions that occur under specific historical, cultural and socioeconomic conditions between entrepreneurs, organizations, universities, the state and markets (Freeman, 1995; Lundvall, 1992; Mowery, 1998; Etzkowitz & Leydesdorff, 2000). The American NSI and its successive adaptations have played a crucial role in the vibrancy of the US political economy model and the primacy of its "liberal-market economy" over other varieties of capitalism (Hall & Soskice, 2001; Amable, 2003).

A complex web of interrelated factors, institutions and actors nested in interacting environments would have spawned numerous innovations and spurred job creation as well as long-term national growth (Nelson, 2005, 2010; Phelps, 2006; Baumol, 2007). By combining small and large firm capitalism, selecting a legitimate mix of government involvement, activating Schumpeterian disruptive forms of entrepreneurship, fostering key linkages between private research and academic institutions, developing proactive civil society associations and globalized regional networks, the American innovation model has constantly transformed itself. It has often redesigned its various configurations and boundaries to suit economic and political cycles and its various stakeholders' expectations.

Today, an emerging system assumes a "soft" form of regulation and governance of innovation in which the optimal role of the state and markets is not fixed, but continues, as in previous times, to be a major topic of debate and confrontation between spheres and actors. The American innovation system that was formalized around a dual (university/firms) then triple interstructuration (government/academia/business) has recently evolved into a multi-level, adaptive and apparently self-organizing ecosystem in permanent tension and transition toward a stabilized but provisional innovation regime in order to better respond to the complex dynamics of regional and global markets and the challenges of renewed competitiveness.

The US innovation system appears as a paradoxical but powerful integration mechanism for competing but largely interdependent economic, political and social spheres: a hybrid but highly versatile economic and political framework that strives to address both the demands of economic globalization and the domestic constraints of a multiscalar federal structure fostering competition between states. Built on intrinsically American norms and values, it remains strongly embedded in a pluralist polity and a wider cultural political economy predominantly structured around agency power and a changing and unstable market–state nexus arrangement. It is part and parcel of an American economic civilization that endlessly opposes and momentarily reconciles pervasive market-led beliefs with more mercantilist and federalist growth-promoting policies.

The NSI acts as an "intermediary" institution operating at macro- and micro-levels, between order and disorder, incremental and radical change: "on the edge of chaos." The ecosystem model often serves as an implicit form of market-preserving federalism (Weingast, 1995) and a shadow regulation mechanism against direct state interventionism. It has become a discreet but efficient countervailing power for staunch opponents to interfering forms of industrial policy and, conversely, a consensual and useful political metaphor for national and local governmental policy-makers. As a consequence, the US NSI assumes a "subpolitical" role (Beck, 1992) but also provides a sustainable and flexible innovation compromise between actors and institutions that is based on decentralization, interaction and also policy confrontation principles.

The present chapter analyzes innovation as a governance system, a socioeconomic paradigm, and a political economy construct at the core of the American variety of capitalism. It traces the development path of the US NSI and the legacy of successive innovation regimes before considering the current strengths and weaknesses of an open governance and collaborative innovation model that has emerged in the wake of its successive transformations (from closed/linear science model to regional cluster theory, from triple helix, to the biological metaphor of the ecosystem). The trajectory of the US innovation model and the unraveling of its intrinsic contradictions are assessed before considering its redevelopment path. We reflect on the resilience, coevolution, possible hybridization of former innovation matrixes and the extension of a contingent, decentralized, "natural" innovation ecosystem framework geared toward market logics through ad hoc strategies led by coalitions of private rather than public stakeholders. The new configuration tends to underplay and often veil the persistence of former models and the new developmental and entrepreneurial role of the federal and local states and more subnational institutions in the governance system of the innovation process. Systemic and multiscalar governance is more openly preferred to top-down policies.

Innovation as a pervasive socioeconomic paradigm and a resilient political economy construct

One must note the permanence and remanence of a risk and innovation culture in the United States (Turner, 1920; Boorstin, 1974; Giddens, 1991; Shah *et al.*, 2015) whose hallmark is a tradition of enterprising experiments, a frontier spirit and strong beliefs in markets. This mentality expresses itself first in a transatlantic, colonial and entrepreneurial experience, then in numerous commercial, technological and social ventures, but also in institutional innovations like the Constitution and its patent clause or the successive creation of dedicated agencies and changing innovation policies characteristic of a democratic society in constant evolution.

Since the early colonial adventure and the Young Republic, the inception of the Hamiltonian American system of manufactures and the twentieth-century expansion of its large-scaled firms (Chandler, 1977), via today's world-class science parks, down to the development of a small business economy in knowledge-based clusters led by high-growth start-ups, the very business and pride of America has been the technologically and financially successful experiment and translation of new ideas into commercialized applications. Such focus on the creation of socioeconomic value, ceaseless technological change through a wide range of scientific, business initiatives and innovation policies has launched a strong entrepreneurial and institutional dynamic of interactions between private and public spheres. The short- and long-term production of radical and incremental innovations soon required linkages and complementarities between initial individual agency and supportive institutions and also more systemic, collaborative and hybrid "solutions" between a wide array of actors and institutions.

Yet, the disembedding and disruptive power of technological progress and business enterprise that are novelty-focused and forward-looking has constantly brought to the fore and valorized the "heroic" role of inventors and entrepreneurs as major cycle activators and "change makers" within a relatively uncoordinated US political economy (Schumpeter, 1934). The forces of technology and agency have also been shaped in their joint trajectory by a multiplicity of contexts and events (wars, markets development, creation of agencies, radical inventions, etc.) and partly constrained and channeled by political institutions, federal and state policies, socio-political "infrasystems," and implicit but potent political objectives and cultural values. The innovative activity of independent entrepreneurs and companies, the leadership of a constantly renewed entrepreneurial and creative class have always been seen as a "natural" process, "a fact of life" in capitalist economies (Schumpeter, 1942; Florida, 2002) and the major driver of the great American free-market machine whose primary product is economic growth and upward mobility (Baumol, 2002; Sheshinski *et al.*, 2007). "After all, innovation is what America has always been about," President Obama (2012) enthused in an address to the nation destined to revive stronger faith in the American Dream and after his administration had launched a series of federal programs designed to jumpstart a stalling innovation system challenged by newcomers, the Great Recession and eroded competitiveness.[1]

The 2008 collapse of the financial system and the subsequent bailout of major banks and firms by the American government have first questioned a long-standing free-enterprise and self-regulating market stances and a more traditional Jeffersonian and neoconservative anti-statist visions. A neo-Hamiltonian conception of the national interest and government intervention has been reasserted when national security and the fabric of the economic system were threatened. Such radical policy was soon toned down by recurrent forms of market-preserving federalism limiting the interventionist power of the state and extolling the boundless capabilities of a networked civil society. The 2009 American Recovery and Reinvestment Act (ARRA), Obama's first stimulus package with its small $97 billion portion dedicated to supporting commercialization of energy-efficient technologies, along with successive incentive programs, have not really dented an implicit innovation laissez-faire paradigm anchored in a pervasive neoliberal paradigm and a self-governing philosophy privileging business enterprise, the individual–opportunity nexus and the quest for fast-paced technological development and commercial adoption. The growing diversity and multi-faceted nature of a pluralist US innovation system that is currently concerned with finding a quick path from idea to product through knowledge spillovers has sped up the "delinearization" of top-down innovation processes entailed by the post-war translation of science and technology inventions into applied research and commercial developments. The recent deregulation, privatization and internationalization of R&D has reinforced the networked dimension and serendipity of a fairly proactive model at the expense of a clearer orientation and more vocal innovation policies. More recently, it has entrenched the Republican and Democratic parties behind antagonistic policy views and left innovation actors to play an increasingly interactive, competitive and collaborative game without many strings attached, but reduced private and public funding. Hence the surge for knowledge sharing and the race for network externalities exploitation that are seen as remedying budgetary cuts in research and development.

Nevertheless, the resilience of a market–state dichotomy within a highly interactive and collaborative innovation system generally understood as an open "opportunity structure" and an "ecosystem," calls for a re-examination of the new role of the state and a broader understanding of the intrinsic relationship between markets and public institutions in such a hybrid and co-evolutionary regulatory device. This chapter views the dramatic shifts in the locus of innovation and the various forms of regulations and policies that have occurred in the past decades through the lens of the successive strategies, policies and institutional arrangements that have been set up to boost, govern and regulate the complex dynamics of "creative destruction" and "incremental innovation."

The governance of innovation systems and the promotion of an acceptable form of policy-making and desirable open governance model are, indeed, economic, but also political and cultural issues in the United States, as testified by the historical trajectory of the innovation system that balances between forms of closed and open innovation, straightforward or submerged state interventions. The recent lack of bipartisan compromise on industrial policy and the Congress budget wars incessantly waged against Obama's "mission-oriented" innovation initiatives have recently tested and challenged a long-standing bipartisan innovation compromise. The series of budget caps and "sequestrations" put up by a Republican Congress dead set on cutting federal R&D funding on all sectors but defense procurements show that infrastructural systems and previous political mind frames may slow or even block transformative and innovation transitions. Innovation gridlock may create regime lock-in embedded in ideological preferences and paralyzing cultural worldviews.

The recurring debates on either "simplifying" or "strengthening innovation" through extended deregulation or a startup and manufacturing renaissance (Pisano & Shih, 2012), the search for more multiscalar, less fragmented but better coordinated innovation policies highlight the relative structural erosion of a legitimate type of systemic and interactive governance (Etzkowitz's triple-helix innovation) that had characterized the past three decades. It had successfully recombined former linear and regional models into collaborative and flexible transnational network arrangements suited to the internationalization of research and development and the globalization of innovation systems (Miotti & Sachwald, 2003).

Reconciling radical and incremental innovation while capturing their joint value, coping with fierce global competitors while producing more indigenous innovations may require rejuvenating a multi-layered, modestly "federalist" innovation model and formulating broader but compatible framework policies between interconnected and competing spheres (Wessner & Wolff, 2012). Rising to the challenge of an innovation-led economy implies reaching a new national innovation consensus in times of fiscal, budget and resource contraction. The implementation of new policies goes beyond the traditional state approach of only fixing market failures or providing ad hoc infrastructure investment (Stiglitz, in Todeva 2013). Reinventing a new technological leadership also rests on the elaboration of a more responsive, legitimate and coherent model in consonance and resonance with the American society and polity contradictions and aspirations.

To do so, the current American open governance model has extended and delegated the funding and execution of research to a large group of stakeholders within increasingly decentralized ecosystems. It seems to assign a backseat to state intervention policy and even former managerial closed innovation. It places networked private firms and entrepreneurial actors on top of the governance list while attributing a critical ideological role to a forum of interest groups, think-tanks and organizations often able to capture knowledge spillovers, state or federal policy-making but also structuring the public agenda. Open innovation policies and entrepreneurial discourses may, however, continue to shape a pragmatic and legitimate compromise that fits both open neoliberal market principles and more submerged mercantilist and federalist policy-making principles.

Is the Obama Administration's policy an attempt to re-energize market–state nexus relations in which government is not simply seen as a facilitator, a promoter but also as a catalyzer and coordinator of resources and competencies in a complex but redesigned multi-scalar governance process of innovation? Does the return of a national innovation system issue on the political agenda testify to the current absence, the invisibility or structural impossibility of a directing line and societal agreement on an acceptable form of industrial policy? Does it signal the emergence of an entrepreneurial role of government or a more submerged developmental one within a reconfigured political economy around free-enterprise, entrepreneurship and knowledge network externalities?

We hypothesize that the NSI paradigm and the innovation ecosystem metaphor, notably, are "boundary objects" that serve as hybrid institutional arrangements and complex innovation opportunity structures embedding knowledge and stabilizing practices in a shared paradigm while possibly controlling the role of the state within a pluralist but largely privatized stakeholder model. Such collaborative space and cross-boundary loci produce pools of knowledge and discursive compromise devices for both the innovation stakeholders and the American polity at large. In times of crisis and scarce growth, the open innovation model (Chesbrough, 2003) and the entrepreneurial ecosystem paradigm appear as pragmatically effective economic and political options. This multiscalar political economy construct offers a legitimate open governance innovation regime that thrives on exploiting extensive linkages, institutional complementarities and the driving force of agency and unresolved contradictions that are deeply embedded in a resilient political, cultural and civilizational context increasingly in transaction with the unruly forces of globalization.

The national innovation system as a shifting economic and policy paradigm

The NSI construct also rests on a series of premises and discourses that have formalized and textualized innovations, trends and practices into a structured but complex political economy paradigm laden with contradictions and antinomies.

Mainstream economists explain US growth performance and innovation emergence by favorable circumstances, technological advance (Solow, 1956) and endogenous factors within the economic system (Romer, 1994; Aghion & Howitt, 1998). Free-enterprise advocates extol the primacy of agency, e.g., the innovative power of actors to operate independently of the determining constraints of structures and to break away from path-dependent routines and traditional value systems. Cluster and regional innovation theoreticians (Krugman, 1991; Porter, 1998; Saxenian, 2006; Eisingerich *et al.* 2010) consider that the interaction between multiple actors and diverse public and private institutions at the local level help to tap network externalities, share common pools of knowledge and trigger spillovers and innovation processes that are re-embedded in more localized business ventures and autonomous governance structures such as private–public partnerships or policy subsystems like regional clusters. Loose innovation frameworks would partly inhibit the intrusive and regulatory role of government and make it subservient to technological schemes, business interests and entrepreneurial communities of practices. Since the 1980s, innovation stakeholders and deregulation policies have rather constrained federal institutions toward the legal and macro-economic stimulation of innovation and growth through favorable legislation, R&D funding and sectoral initiatives rather than the adoption of top-down industrial policies or mission-oriented programs.

The microeconomic and regional governance of innovation devolved to local actors and the private sector is often viewed as more efficient, conducive to radical innovation, upward mobility and swift social change. Reliance on market forces and a revivified spirit of enterprise have fostered a cultural form of rugged and heroic individualism best exemplified today by the "animal spirits" (Akerlof & Shiller, 2009) and the ingenuous passions for sociotechnical innovations of successful high-tech and internet entrepreneurs like Bill Gates, Steve Jobs or Mark Zuckerberg, all willing to change and "save the world."

A risk-friendly and pragmatist behavior, availability of venture capital and skills, quick business formation, flexible employment relations, new organizational and financial tools and tailored but bounded governmental support seemed to have been instrumental in the permanent reinvention and reactivation of the innovation and business cycle in the United States until the recent economic crisis. A pervasive competitive market culture and the power of agency rather than a strong interventionist state would have fueled the development logic of the American brand of innovation and financial capitalism (Baumol, 2002).

A growing body of scholarly research first based in evolutionary economics (Freeman, 1995; Lundvall, 1992; Nelson, 1993), the French regulation theory (Aglietta, 1979; Boyer and Saillard, 2001; Hollingworth & Boyer, 1997), the variety of capitalism school (Hall & Soskice, 2001; Amable, 2003) and socio-institutionalism (Werle, 2012) has contested this synchronic and ahistorical approach of entrepreneurial innovation that premises an "uncoordinated" form of market-led capitalism popped out of a Hayekian "spontaneous order," Schumpeterian "creative destruction" or Knightian uncertainty. This relatively simple conception of entrepreneurial capitalism and canonization of markets as the "one best way" mode of innovation emergence and governance is still a distinctive trait of American public discourse and microeconomic theory. It is, however, mitigated, in real life, by the effective role of government and subnational institutions in protecting market conditions or enabling a more mixed governing structure. In many cases, the American state remains a leading participant and funder of the innovative process (Weiss, 1998) and a major initiator of new legislation.

Thus, many political economists (Eisner, 2011b; Block & Keller, 2011; Mazzucato, 2013a, 2013b) have gone beyond this narrow focus on markets and actors. It underplays the current developmental and indirect policy-making role of the federal state and the hidden coordination of more decentralized structures such as federal agencies, local networks in regional clusters or more globalized ecosystems (Wade, 2012). More critical theorists have also unveiled the ideological representations of a presumed market–state divide impeding innovation development. They consider that innovation flows from fruitful dynamic interrelations between agency and structure, organizations and institutions as they evolve over time. They place greater emphasis on the centrality and efficiency of complex interactive innovation systems that stabilize and orient an accumulation regime characteristic of a late form of American capitalism predominantly thriving on knowledge, finance and entrepreneurship. They analyze the tangled economic, political and cultural nature and development trajectory of an enduring but changing institutional arrangement named the "National System of Innovation."

Originally defined as a "network of institutions in the public and private sectors whose activities and interactions initiate, import, modify and diffuse new technologies" (Freeman, 1995, p. 1), the concept of the "national innovation system" was also characterized as "the nation's institutions and policies governing the invention, development, and adoption of new technologies" (Mowery, 1998, p. 640). The American NSI is also strongly embedded in past and present American sociocultural values, norms and policy frameworks, as well as conflicting narratives over the role of the state and the business world at large. Innovation systems are not simply value creation and appropriation mechanisms, but also complex institutional assemblages whose driving power lies in the legitimacy of their core principles and their transformative power. These autonomous subsystems may be seen first as best coordinated by "post-state actors," yet many state-sponsored programs and government policies continue to impact and also orient the trajectory of the American innovation system. A stabilized innovation system must produce coordinative mechanisms for innovation stakeholders and communicative discourses for policy-makers and the general public. They serve as shared beliefs, communities of practices, sub-political mode of integration and sense-making processes (Weick, 1995) in the decisions that inform policy-making and institutional change (North, 2005; Borrás & Seabrooke, 2015).

Policy-makers, politicians, experts and members of think-tanks also play a major role in the selection of principles and doctrines that coalesce into dominant paradigms. Conflicting institutional discourses re-emerge in debates that justify or inform Congressional budget decisions over research development funding and execution. Shared representations by a majority of actors legitimize a selected "innovation policy mix" apt to enact coherent, relevant and "politically correct" innovation system models. Such worldviews shape interactions among subnational and transnational actors, but also condition systemic evolutions towards more open and deterritorialized "ecosystems." This complex and variegated coordinating mechanism relies mostly on the creation of "complementarities" but also the acceptance of changing political compromises between various innovation stakeholders, interacting institutions and organizations.

Successive business cycles and innovation regimes have thus required renewed intricate connections between private and public initiatives and the invention of hybridized modes of governance that embed compatible forms of competition and cooperation in sustainable institutional forms while maintaining the promotion of an individual ethos dear to innovators and entrepreneurs. Power relations within and outside the innovation system have consequently been impacted. They have determined co-adaptation between competing spheres and co-evolution ("changing together") within common opportunity structures.

The development path of the US innovation system and its socioeconomic legacies

Innovation systems undergo historical transformations over time and morph into hybridized and stabilized innovation regimes until the next crisis. They are embedded in a national political economy history and polity, but shape, in turn, as they evolve, the fabric of a larger American economic civilization (Braudel, 1993). "History matters" in explaining innovation emergence, cultural imprinting and perennial beliefs as well as the dialectics of institutional stability and systemic governance. Technological and institutional evolutions result from this constant interplay between action and structures in specific relational-temporal contexts. Path dependency analysis (David, 1994; North, 1990) provides a relevant diachronic approach to understanding the origins and transformations of innovation processes in the short and the *longue durée*. They reveal the changing structure of the US NIS over time (Mowery, 1998) and important breaks and turning points in the innovation regime. Two structural regimes must be distinguished: a long dominant open innovation regime that spans centuries, which is interrupted by a shorter but powerful closed innovation regime that only spans a few decades. Emerging innovation regimes were initiated by radical Schumpeterian innovators whose disruptive innovations were soon appropriated by large firms and universities, then stabilized and channeled into incremental trends by government policies and powerful federal agencies. The establishment of institutionalized relation patterns helped re-embed the exogenous dynamic of entrepreneurial and spontaneous innovation into cumulative innovations. They were developed within industrial organizations in collaboration with a growing number of state research agencies and federal laboratories. The Great Depression, two World Wars, a long Cold War, major technical breakthroughs that required massive public funding (nuclear and space programs), weakened the primacy of agency power and entrepreneurial capitalism that serves the interest of a "small but artful and enterprising community," to quote Washington's phrase (1796). As a result, the early trajectory of market-led and firm-led innovations was strongly affected and controlled by the top-down coordination and regulatory power of the federal state until the mid-1970s.

The US NIS has thus evolved along temporal dynamics and stochastic events that have first restructured pioneering entrepreneurial practices into closed institutionalized arrangements. Innovation history has come full circle in the past three decades. A new focus on entrepreneurial innovation has revived and adapted the initial US "spontaneous innovation" matrix, adding a collaborative turn to its intrinsic disruptive dynamic. Open innovation developments in the 1980s, based on new economic cycles and neoliberal political compromises, finally tilted the postwar market–state compromise toward a new interactive innovation mix that became the legitimate development path in the mid-1990s. Universities and research agencies, regional clusters and entrepreneurial networks, regulatory policies and governmental institutions have been working more synergistically since to provide an open environment conducive to more co-produced and ad hoc innovation (Atkinson, 2014).

With the privilege of hindsight, the American system of innovation results from a series of sociocultural and institutional socio-political transformations grounded in: (1) a shared commercial and business culture and a strong work ethic; (2) a common individualistic and rationalist "psyche" combining an entrepreneurial spirit and "Yankee ingenuity"; (3) a democratic and institutional context in the making. A passion for inventive activity has led individuals into entrepreneurial quests for technological knowledge, material wealth, and social success as early as the foundations of the American Republic. The "search for novelty" (Boorstin, 1974) soon turned into the Nation's political project, "a Great experiment for promoting happiness" (Washington, 1796) thanks to a "nation of joiners" (Neem, 2008). Later, entrepreneurship and innovative ventures became part of a perennial national identity and power search: an "endless frontier" toward economic sovereignty and world leadership through the invention, production, patenting and commercialization of technology and the incessant creation of business enterprises and innovative ventures.

The history of innovation in its early mode of governance is linked, on the one hand, to the spontaneous emergence of tinkerers and inventors like Benjamin Franklin and, a century later, "wizards" like Edison, who turned into a professional researcher and business entrepreneur and, on the other hand, to the rapid development of "intermediary" institutions: large-scale Chandlerian firms that acquired economic efficiency and political sovereignty in the nineteenth century. As urbanization and industrialization gained momentum, the "visible hand of management" provided an organizational structure and technical support for these inventors in the relative absence of a strong federal government and national innovation policy. The "American system of manufactures" envisaged by the mercantilist Hamilton in his 1791 "Essay on Manufactures" took shape as a fully fledged "American system" thanks to the interchangeable part systems implemented by the gun manufacturer Colt and developed during the Civil War, the rationalization of work by Taylor's scientific management at the turn of the twentieth century and the generalization of Fordist assembly-line production later on. Former entrepreneurial and business norms and a technological and organizational ability to innovate became associated with early railways and industrial firms and the American system of mass production that required a new type of hierarchical, functional multi-unit type of firm apt to conduct more complex research and wide-ranging activities on a continental and international scale.

In the interwar period, big managerial organizations reinforced the institutionalization of scientific and technological innovation. They internalized its process in integrated industrial and university research laboratories thanks to their early close links to university training and research fields. Until World War II, big firms and their science laboratories made up the largest part of incremental innovation soon known as R&D. Private research was mostly geared toward the improvement of products and internal organizations. The "invention of the method of invention" had first taken place in industrial enterprises and in-house research departments, but also occurred in parallel with the emergence of applied engineering disciplines taught in technical universities such as MIT that were created in the wake of the Morill–Land Grant acts (1862 and 1890). Only local states funded public higher education and public universities that set up early research facilities, implementing the first mixed private/public innovation policies. When US manufacturing firms operating in science-based industries such as chemical, electrical engineering and metallurgy merged into monopolies at the end of the Gilded Age, they developed internal and external strategies to capture innovations and protect them with patents, thus retaining their market power and avoiding antitrust actions until the Progressive Age (Mowery & Rosenberg, 2000).

The US innovation trajectory first shows that the original heroic, independent, spontaneous, disruptive entrepreneurial model of innovation (open entrepreneurial mode 1: 1740–1880) was superseded by a first closed and linear innovation model during the era of managerial and organizational capitalism (closed mode 2: 1880–1940). To acquire scale, two interlocked actors like universities and firms developed inventions and cooperated within the same locale. Large corporations like Bell internalized innovation in their research departments and appropriated it within their organization as a strategic specific asset thanks to a closed type of research and patenting systems. Interdependent sequences of events and major turning points, like World War II, interrupted this applied science trend and reordered university/business cooperation around "big science" and military objectives under the supervision and leadership of the federal state (Federal innovation: mode 3: 1941–1970). The entrepreneurial and managerial orientations of the pre-war innovation system were then put in the service of the national war effort and Cold War rearmament. A militarized *Pax Americana* absorbed more than 80 percent of federal spending that was mostly defense-related (Bauer, 2012). The science-based system of innovation, first legitimized by Vannevar Bush (1945), was dominated by massive federal funding for basic science in research universities and the development of defense technologies in national laboratories. Numerous breakthrough technologies originally developed for military purposes – such as the computer, the radar, the transistor, the semiconductor – had dual uses once they were transferred into industries like electronics and aerospace. Federal government funding took over as state and industry funding declined until the early 1980s, when the closed innovation cycle led by government transitioned into a more mixed public/private innovation regime focusing on commercialization rather than big science. The closed innovation trend would then be fully reversed into open innovation by the mid-1990s, and globalized ecosystems in the twenty-first century (Coste, 2006). Yet, it is to be noted that the promotion of economic objectives had, indeed, been systematically rejected during the Kennedy, Johnson and Nixon Administrations by Congress, in spite of federal efforts to push for more commercial innovations.

The statist and military model of university–industry–government relations characteristic of the 1950 military–industrial complex expanded nonetheless until the early 1980s. Simultaneously, it generated, as of the 1960s and 1970s, a new but common knowledge infrastructure between the three overlapping spheres. This interactive model entailed growing decentralization of the federal research system and extensive systemic exchanges (interactive mode 4: 1970–1980). In this nascent interactive and open innovation model – soon to be characterized as the triple-helix model (Etzkowitz & Leydesdorff, 2000, 2001) – linear R&D was no longer on the cards since each autonomous entity became more or less interchangeable and could assume the role of the other. The construction of this new transaction space required bringing respective organizations, state agencies and users into common acceptance of a shared network perspective. Different views and objectives were then confronted in an interactive and iterative innovation process. The public/private divide was not as clear-cut nor was the locus of control anchored in a specific sphere. Power and action slowly shifted from federal government and its interlocking power elite (Mills, 1957) to an extended and fluid coalition of decision-makers belonging to different institutions or organizations. In this blurred configuration that cut across traditional sector divides, the new network model opened windows of opportunity for universities and local regional clusters that became autonomous "islands of innovation" relying on their local resources and inter-linkages. Geography and proximity had comparative advantages, too. Universities funded more basic research and also started to perform applied research while training future researchers into would-be entrepreneurs and patent owners as soon as a legal framework for property rights would be enacted. New firms and research universities started playing a prominent role in the commercialization of technological advances.

Faced with fierce and mounting international competition, persistent stagflation, a declining Keynesian macroeconomic model, and the threats of a lingering cold war, the closed national innovation system reached its limits at the end of the 1970s. A third turning point happened in the early 1980s. Major policy and legal changes in the innovation regime shifted the former top-down industrial policies toward more bottom-up innovation policies (mode 5: 1980–1990). The US government took very proactive and landmark policy measures designed to both stimulate traditional defense spending and quickly hybridize federal innovation policy with more private orientations (Block & Keller, 2011). Influenced by a market philosophy that regarded deregulation and privatization as the key to growth, government mobilized public resources and a strong legislative process to facilitate the interaction and growing interdependence between spheres. It reduced federal research funding and abandoned vocal industrial policy as had previously been the case with the post-war top-down federal policies.

Bipartisan policy initiatives under Carter, Reagan and Bush Sr. were undertaken to speed technology transfers and facilitate commercialization. The 1980 Stevenson–Wydler Technology Innovation Act established technology offices and funds aimed at strengthening civilian technology through the transfer of technology originating from public labs. The Bayh–Dole Patent and Trademark Amendments Act facilitated the dissemination of scientific research produced in federal labs and gave licenses to small businesses and universities with ownership of inventions made with federal funding. The 1981 Economy Recovery Tax Act granted tax credits to business research and experimentation programs. The 1982 Small Business Innovation Development Act (SBIR) administered by a pilot agency called Small Business Administration (SBA) provided set aside funds for small business R&D. The 1984 Cooperative Research Act eliminated antitrust-violation threats. Firms, universities and federal labs could more readily engage in joint pre-competitive research. The 1986 Federal Technology Transfer Act authorized national labs to negotiate cooperative R&D licensing agreement (CRADAs).

Despite the claimed "non-interventionist" orientation of the Reagan government, a very impressive number of acts reorganized the rules and norms governing the "dual" and "triple helix" interactive innovation regimes. Paradoxically, it was the state that planned the new deregulated and decentralized innovation framework through extensive legal regulations designed to foster more innovation capabilities and more market-led research. Old innovation trends persisted for a decade, with high military research spending that was rekindled with Reagan's Star Wars programs. Such a dramatic policy shift considerably altered the legal and regulatory centralized federal-led innovation framework that was subsequently transformed into a favorable regime for innovators and entrepreneurs encouraged to take risks, start small businesses and take up patents. The legal reconfiguration of the US innovation system was rather "indirect" and "submerged." No real and vocal industrial policy was openly claimed. Framework reconfiguration was huge and targeted. Very few experts and commentators at the time realized the magnitude of the policy shift that had implemented decentralized framework policies focused on intellectual property, tax policy and easier access to procurement and finance, and paved the way for the emergence and primacy of a new innovation governance mechanism.

In the Clinton years, the innovation context significantly changed. It opened even more to private, financial and market logics as the globalization of the world economy accelerated and the importance of a form of "competitive-based innovation" became more than instrumental in the reaffirmation of the technological leadership of the United States. The Administration openly called for extended federal support to civilian and dual-use technology and promoted public–private partnerships as a true strategy but also as a sort of political mantra apt to capture bipartisan support. The political end result of this new developmental approach that manifested a new form of subdued economic interventionism was mixed. There was broad political agreement, however, that rapid technological development in the manufacturing and high-tech sector was necessary to regain a declining technological edge. Yet, the reallocation of defense funding to more commercial purposes first met with Republican opposition and elicited a politicized debate in Congress. In a 1993 report on technology policy entitled *Technology for America's Economic Growth*, President

Clinton reflected on the sweeping changes and the new pro-innovation policies to be implemented:

> American technology must move in a new direction to build economic strength and spur economic growth. The traditional federal role in technology development has been limited to support of basic science and mission-oriented research in the Defense Department, NASA, and other agencies. This strategy was appropriate for a previous generation but not for today's profound challenges. We cannot rely on the serendipitous application of defense technology to the private sector. We must aim directly at these new challenges and focus our efforts on the new opportunities before us, recognizing that government can play a key role helping private firms develop and profit from innovations.

A series of federal programs were implemented that testifies that major evolutions between the private and the public sectors had already taken place and would make policy change acceptable. An innovation policy consensus had been partly reached, although Clinton had lost majority in Congress in 1994. In 1996, the 105th Congress consented to the developmental policies and budgetary measures taken by the Administration. Such innovation policies were not considered as "corporate welfare" or intrusive industrial policy by the Republican majority. The new innovation policy seemed to be finally in step with society's values, the new global market paradigm and the expected strategy from a modern, responsive and entrepreneurial state. The Advanced Technology Program (ATP) provided funds for firms and consortia at pre-commercial stages, the Manufacturing Extension Partnership (MEP) helped small firms use new tools. The Commerce department became a major innovation agency promoting standards and providing support to small and medium firms when the economy was becoming export-led and major agreements like NAFTA were signed. Modernized information highways would boost the fast-developing ICT sector. The divide between basic and applied science waned. The delinearization and decentralization of the vertical R&D architectures, the growing privatization of public research advances, and the new conception of a more horizontal form of innovation flowing from civil society and an open and inter-institutional system rapidly generated political agreement but also large economic gains.

Spin-offs from big companies and universities grew in numbers as the internet revolution was rising; Silicon Valley and other high-tech clusters in the Boston region became technology powerhouses. Innovation clusters emerged from the interaction between the private sector and research universities that had initially received important federal funding. The new competitive landscape launched local states and cities into a race for talents, investment and knowledge-intensive industries. Quick delivery of commercial applications to the markets and a renewed interest in former entrepreneurial paradigms enthralled start-up founders until the dot-com bubble burst in 1999. It also brought about major shifts in public and private R&D spending and performance while creating an increased division of labor in the US innovation system. Basic research continued to be predominantly financed by federal agencies, but to a lesser extent. Universities began assuming a larger share. Industry took up a greater portion of applied research, but more and more tapped new sources of knowledge outside the usual boundaries of its firms and through their international networks. Experiments and joint-collaboration between states, federal agencies and regional authorities and dynamic business communities helped forge a new non-partisan innovation consensus and cluster development. The "New Economy" that thrived on venture capital and business angels strengthened the new innovation regime of shared knowledge around cluster dynamics and a rejuvenated entrepreneurial culture. Entrepreneurial, financial and technological communities in close collaboration with local agencies helped spur the development of many regional clusters in the United States. They thrived on geographical proximity, the aggregation of dispersed resources, shared knowledge learning and inter-firm collaboration. Information technology entered into a new phase, with more powerful microchips, broadband telecommunication networks, internet platforms and marketed applications produced by corporations such as Intel, Microsoft and Apple. The IT trend started developing more deterritorialized and virtual ecosystems enabled by the rapid development of internet technology and finance. A conceptual shift turned technology-development into innovation-based growth. The unrelenting search for innovation was seen as the key driver for competitiveness and the new political economy frontier.

When Republican President Bush came to power in 2001, R&D intensity had somewhat fallen and US competitiveness sagged. The Bush Administration partly rejected the former Clinton Administration proactive industrial polices and appeared more supportive of modest ad hoc strategies such as tax incentives, intellectual property protection or antitrust laws that fostered technology innovation in small businesses. The preferred modes of innovation policy were private sector funding when it came to applied research and public funding only for basic research that would not rival the market sector. An implicit neoliberal paradigm and market–state nexus framework may have governed policy choices when increased funding for basic research and decreased direct federal funding for private sector technology were selected options:

> The role of government is not to create wealth; the role of our government is to create an environment in which the entrepreneur can flourish, in which minds can expand, in which technologies can reach new frontiers.
>
> (Bush, 2002)

In spite of the 9/11 attacks that brought back national security concerns and a direct form of industrial policy geared toward military procurements, the US "civilian" policy for technology development followed a more indirect and incremental path aimed at facilitating rather than steering technological advancement. In 2003, the 21st Century Nanotechnology Research and Development Act authorized coordination of expenditures between involved agencies and provided new forms of social and public engagement in the technological development process. However, two costly wars in Afghanistan and Iraq and the creation of a new security agency (Homeland Security Agency) boosted defense research spending and reactivated previous state-led military–industrial policies that paralleled Reagan's and were also reminiscent of Eisenhower's old military–industrial complex. Former federalist practices that drew from the old linear innovation model were reactivated with defense innovations. A traditional federalist state-guided form of capitalism coupled to big firm involvement was recombined into an entrepreneurial type of innovation-led capitalism that called for the involvement of large number of actors in the production and commercialization of innovation. In 2006, President Bush announced the "American Competitiveness Initiative" and signed into law the 2007 American Creating Opportunities to Meaningfully Promote Excellence in Technology, Education, and Science Act (COMPETES Act), supporting the role of federal agencies in advanced technologies, increasing funding, setting up units to promote and disseminate innovation, giving prizes and allowing for better coordination of education in science and mathematics (STEM). Interestingly enough, the Act was reauthorized in 2010 and signed into law in January 2011 by President Obama. Innovation policies that enhanced moderate public interventions, market opportunities and entrepreneurial capabilities had become bipartisan solutions once again.

Whither the US innovation system? The conflicting dynamics of policy rejuvenation and cultural embeddedness

Following the magnitude of the 2008 financial crisis and the Great Recession, the pace of innovation has slowed and America's position as the source of the world's global innovation has been eroded. With the emergence of a more competitive knowledge-based economy, the increased internationalization of R&D, the rise of fierce and inventive foreign competitors and the violence of the current economic crisis, the efficacy of the former national innovation model has been seriously challenged and contested. The vitality and pre-eminence of a decentralized US innovation system that had long been unrivaled has been partly lost, undermining multi-level governance assumptions that had guided policy-making and anchored innovation processes in evolving but fairly stable market-led regimes. Although the US remains the largest world investor in R&D, with 30 percent of the global total in 2011, the country has experienced significant decline in the last decade in its share of global R&D, which has continued to shrink. US federal spending on basic research as a percentage of GDP has been going down since the early 1960s and is strongly impacted by current fiscal pressures. University funding has also suffered from severe cuts due to budgetary constraints. There has been a downward trend in US patents applications and student performance, which are key indicators, along with academic R&D produced by research universities, which has also stagnated. Early-stage finance like venture capital and business angel investment, key drivers of entrepreneurial growth, have fallen sharply, affecting start-ups generation and destabilizing the development of innovation ecosystems. Attracting foreign high-skilled scientists from around the world to universities and research centers has proved difficult – a sign that a kind of relative reverse brain drain had been going on since the 9/11 events.

Since the 2007 publication of *Rising Above the Gathering Storm* (2007), which detailed the major innovation inputs to be dramatically improved, Congress and the Administration have had to take a series of measures to try to contain the decline in science, technology and business creation. The weak innovation performance has been aggravated by the offshoring of important segments of the R&D value chain, radical entrepreneurial forms of "destructive creation" that have destroyed jobs in labor-intensive unprofitable sectors and the lingering budget crisis that has limited focused federal intervention. The loss of high-tech and manufacturing competitive advantages because of offshored core capabilities and lack of incremental innovation has also been a cause of great concern, as Susan Berger (2013) revealed in her book, *Making in America.*

President Obama released a "Strategy for American Innovation" (White House, 2011) to formulate a high-tech and innovation strategy and suggest a new policy agenda likely to revive the long-term success of the national innovation system. In his January 2011 State of the Union Address he spoke of a broad range of policy decisions to "out-innovate, out-build, out-compete, and out-educate" the rest of the world. President Obama, in a piece of glorious oratory, struck the cultural cord of exceptionalism and national pride while acknowledging the "inherent ingenuity of the American people," "the central importance of the private sector as the engine of innovation" and the nurturing and supporting role of government in starting new businesses or financing public research through preserved budgets. The rejuvenation of industrial policy was to be achieved thanks to a new innovation policy mix. It would be founded on the "building blocks of American innovation" that help educate a world-class workforce, strengthen research leadership and build adequate infrastructures. "Promoting market-based innovations" thanks to tax credit, intellectual property enforcement, high-growth entrepreneurship and embracing market competition would "catalyze breakthroughs for national priorities" and finally provide "sustainable growth and quality jobs."

Obama's resilient innovation strategy over the past years has acknowledged the fissures in the model and attempted to revitalize the dynamism of the innovation system by adopting a pragmatically middle-of-the road approach. Avoiding direct interventionist policies and laissez-faire extremes, the White House innovation strategy steers a middle course that balances the respective functions of the public and the private sectors and ascribes an "appropriate" role for government while providing an eminent part to entrepreneurs and business, considered as the driving force of the economy:

> Entrepreneurs embody the promise of America: the idea that if you have a good idea and are willing to work hard and see it through, you can succeed

> in this country. And in fulfilling this promise, entrepreneurs also play a critical role in expanding our economy and creating jobs.
>
> (Obama, 2011)

Building complementarities between past innovation regime traditions and former Administration policies, combining modest but focused federal innovation policies with strong individual initiative while maintaining strong leanings toward market logics has not always calmed partisan differences. Yet, such a stand has partly been successful in lifting the spending caps known as "sequestration," which were set up in 2011 by a Republican Congress that has agreed to ease the 2014 and 2015 caps and expressed relative interest in ending limits on defense spending.

The persistence of a debate on the proper role of the federal government and the lack of consensus on the direction of a national innovation policy is not simply the mark of a dysfunctional political system nor the absence of an agency in charge of innovation policy. It must be interpreted as a paradoxical but pluralistic, multi-faceted type of meta-governance characteristic of a federal system. It retains strong faith in unfettered markets and requires bipartisan agreement among innovation stakeholders. All the more so when major policies are to be enacted outside the current canon of market primacy and the dominant cultural framework of a specific innovation regime that revolves around competitive advantage and the creation of economic value. The US federal system requires in-built governance mechanisms testing and discussing policies across subsections of the US economy and the polity. Similarly, the US NIS mirrors the same diversity of levels and the same ambivalent relationship of its constituents with the need for a national innovation strategy that is often described as unwanted government intervention into free markets. The dialectics of open/closed innovation and market/institutions governance explains the constant discussion and reconfiguration of the market–state nexus and the tangled role of private and public interests in such a political economy and representation process.

Innovation policy-making highly depends on an incremental and ad hoc compromise that does limit the prospect of a planned industrial policy. It must follow legitimate and acceptable trajectories that remain extremely complex because they are structured in non-linear ways by conflicting coalitions. Future policies are the result of a diversity of interactions and inter-structured institutional environments that a multiplicity of actors try to control and capture. This subpolitical process makes innovation strategy by deliberate design difficult, if not impossible when openly posited as a top-down decision. The successful collaboration and interaction of government with the private sector revolves around the type of governance that strengthens or weakens framework conditions and nurtures innovations.

Today, the innovation process is mediated and co-produced by a vast array of enterprises, entrepreneurs, universities, government agencies and research institutes. This open-ended configuration and pluralist political economic device is still seen as the most efficient and legitimate innovation architecture conducive to flexible and adaptive strategies. This innovation policy mix gives, per se, coherence and acceptability to innovation practices and discourses, and provides a spontaneous form of multiscalar type of governance meeting the demands of a globalized market-based economy and the perennial spirit of Americans. The innovative performance of the United States depends largely on how these actors and sovereign but autonomous entities quickly interact and network with each other to produce, use and exploit the generated collective flow of knowledge and applications. In such a vision, the NIS is often considered as the great "black box" of the US political economy: a "natural order" led by the self-correcting market's invisible hand and the final harmony of private and public interests.

However, the social, cultural and political underpinnings of such an innovation model must be evidenced and deeply situated in an American political economy context and its cultural milieu. Such bottom-up and loose coupling between actors emanating from the US civil society and tangled institutions remains the great American way of implementing an efficient but hidden industrial policy within a neoliberal regime. The NIS paradigm that has morphed into the ecosystem paradigm acts as a substitute for voluntary policy-making and a self-fulfilling metaphor in times of dissensus over industrial policy. In such a decentralized, pluralistic and seemingly democratic system, there is no central plan for innovation nor permanent dominant player. Various agencies and actors compete for influence and successive leadership in a multi-dimensional opportunity and governance structure that must be constantly reinvented and legitimized as it evolves.

In times of crisis and declining world leadership, more institutional vision and policy are called forth to rejuvenate the existing US model around new principles that recombine "horizontal" institutional complementarities and "vertical" complementarities, as well as radical and incremental forms of innovation into a newly coordinated regime. Re-assembling public institutions and private agents into a larger inclusive ecosystem creates more productive and sustainable complementarities at the local, regional, state and federal levels.

The road is, however, narrow as the mitigated success of Obama's innovation policy initiatives have showed when they were confronted with Congress votes and a crumbling bipartisan political system that pits opposite strategies against each other. As a result, the debate on government intervention and the regulation of innovation policy-making that is framed in the context of an interventionist or a developmental state is surfacing again. Neo- and post-Keynesian economists and leaders will envisage renewed forms of industrial policy-making so as to strike a new political economy compromise more amenable to innovation stakeholders. Staunch opponents will defend a contrasting laissez-faire and open innovation regime that allows surfing and governing the waves of creative destruction. The law of motion of US capitalism may lie in this unresolved contradiction between agency, institutions and culture that has played a major role in the successive transformations of American capitalism. The recent legislative drama and innovation policy gridlock (Binder, 2014) may raise the hot but relevant question: "Polarized we govern?"

Note

1 For a broader overview of the multi-faceted forms of American state intervention on behalf of national competitiveness, see Velut's contribution to the present volume.

Bibliography

Aghion, P. & Howitt, P. (1998). *Endogenous growth theory*. Cambridge: MIT Press.

Aglietta, M. (1979). *A theory of capitalist regulation: The US experience*. London: Verso.

Akerlof, G.A. & Shiller, R.J. (2009). *Animal spirits: How human psychology drives the economy, and why it matters for global capitalism*. Princeton, NJ: Princeton University Press.

Amable, B. (2003). *The diversity of capitalism*. New York: Oxford University Press.

Arora, A. & Bokhari, F.A. (2007). Open versus closed firms and the dynamics of industry evolution. *Journal of Industrial Economics*, *55*(3), pp. 499–527.

Atkinson, R.D. (2014). Understanding the US national innovation system. Information Technology & Innovation Foundation. Retrieved from www2.itif.org/2014-understanding-us-innovation-system.pdf.

Atkinson, R.D. (2015). American innovation under structural erosion and global pressures. Information Technology & Innovation Foundation. Retrieved from www2.itif.org/2015-innovation-structural-erosion.pdf.

Balleisen, E. & Moss, D. (eds.) (2012). *Government and markets: Towards a new theory of regulation*. Cambridge: Cambridge University Press.

Bauer, J.M. (2012). Entrepreneurship and government in US high-tech policy. In *Innovation policy and governance in high-tech industries* (pp. 103–125). Heidelberg: Springer-Verlag.

Baumol, W.J. (2002). *The free-market innovation machine: Analysing the growth miracle of capitalism*. Princeton, NJ: Princeton University Press.

Baumol, W., Litan, R. & Schramm, C.E. (2007). *Good capitalism, bad capitalism and the economics of growth and prosperity*. New Haven, CT: Yale University Press.

Beck, U. (1992). *Risk society: Towards a new modernity*. London: Sage Publications.

Berger, S. (2013). *Making in America, from innovation to market*. Cambridge, MA: MIT Press.

Binder, S. (2014). Polarized we govern? Brookings. Retrieved from www.brookings.edu/research/papers/2014/05/27-polarized-we-govern-congress-legislative-gridlock-polarized-binder.

Blien, U. & Maier, G. (eds.) (2008). *The economics of regional clusters: Networks, technology and policy*, Cheltenham: Edward Elgar Publishing.

Block, F. & Keller, M.R. (2011), *State of innovation: The US government's role in technology development*. Boulder, CO: Paradigm Publishers.

Boorstin, D. (1974). *The Americans: The democratic experience*. New York: Vintage.

Borrás, S. & Seebrooke, L. (2015). *Sources of national industrial competitiveness: Sense-making in institutional change*. Oxford: Oxford University Press.

Boyer, R. & Saillard, Y. (eds.) (2001). *Régulation theory: The state of the art*. London: Routledge.

Braudel, F. (1995). *A history of civilizations*. New York: Penguin Harper [Originally published as *Grammaire des civilisations*. Flammarion, 1987].

Breznitz, D. (2007). *Innovation and the state, political choices and strategies for growth in Israel, Taiwan, and Ireland*. New Haven, CT: Yale University Press.

Bush, G.W. (2002). Promoting innovation and competitiveness. President Bush's Technology agenda. Retrieved from http://gcrio.org/OnLnDoc/pdf/technology_agenda.pdf.

Bush, V. (1945). *Science, the endless frontier*. Washington, DC: Government Printing Office.

Carayannis, E.G., Barth, T.D., Campbell, D.F. (2012). The Quintuple Helix innovation model: global warming as a challenge and driver for innovation. *Journal of Innovation and Entrepreneurship, 1*(1), 1–12.

Carey, D., Hill, C. & Kahin, B. (2012). *Strengthening innovation in the United States*. Paris: OECD.

Chandler, A.D. (1977). *The visible hand: The managerial revolution in American business*. Cambridge, MA: Harvard University Press.

Chesbrough, H. (2003). *Open innovation: The new imperative for creating and profiting from technology*. Boston, MA: Harvard Business School Publishing.

Clinton, B. & Gore, A. (1993). *Technology for America's economic growth: A new direction to build economic strength*. Retrieved from http://ntl.bts.gov/lib/jpodocs/briefing/7423.pdf.

Coste, J.H. (2006). La dynamique de la recherche et développement aux Etats-Unis: origines et évolution du système d'innovation américain. *LISA e-journal, 4*(1), 11–28. Retrieved from http://lisa.revues.org/2117.

David, P.A. (1994). Why are institutions the "carriers of history"? Path dependence and the evolution of conventions, organizations and institutions. *Structural Change and Economic Dynamics*, *5*(2), 205–220.

Edquist, C. (1997). *Systems of innovation: Technologies, institutions and organizations*. London: Pinter.

Eisner, M. (2011a). Beyond the logic of the market: toward an institutional analysis of regulatory reforms. In D. Levi-Faur (ed.), *Handbook on the politics of regulation*. Cheltenham: Elgar.

Eisner, M. (2011b). Markets in the shadow of the state: an appraisal of deregulation and implications for future research. In E. Balleisen & D. Moss (eds.) (2012), *Government and markets: Towards a new theory of regulation* (pp. 512–537). Cambridge: Cambridge University Press.

Eisner, M. (2011c). *The American political economy: Institutional evolution of market and state*. New York: Routledge.

Eisingerich, A.B., Bell, S.J. & Tracey, P. (2010). How can clusters sustain performance? The role of network strength, network openness, and environmental uncertainty. *Research Policy*, *39*(2), 239–253.

Etzkowitz, H. & Leydesdorff, L. (2000). The dynamics of innovation: from national systems and "mode 2" to a triple helix of university–industry–government relations. *Research Policy*, *29*(2), 109–123.

Etzkowitz, H. & Leydesdorff, L. (2001). The transformations of university–industry–government relations. *Electronic Journal of Sociology*, *5*(4). Retrieved from http://arizona.openrepository.com/arizona/bitstream/10150/106531/3/th.html.

Florida, R. (2002). *The rise of the creative class: And how it's transforming work, leisure, community and everyday life*. New York: Perseus Book Group.

Freeman, C. (1995). The national system of innovation in historical perspective. *Cambridge Journal of Economics*, *19*, 5–24.

Furner, M.O. (2012). From "state interference" to the "return to the market": the rhetoric of economic regulation from the Gilded Age to the new. In E. Balleisen & D. Moss (eds.), *Government and markets: towards a new theory of regulation* (pp. 92–141). Cambridge: Cambridge University Press.

Giddens, A. (1991). *Modernity and self-identity: Self and society in the late modern age*. Stanford, CA: Stanford University Press.

Hall, P.A. & Soskice, D. (eds.) (2001). *Varieties of capitalism: The institutional foundations of comparative advantage*. Oxford: Oxford University Press.

Hollingsworth, J. Rogers & Boyer, R. (1997). *Contemporary capitalism: The embeddedness of institutions*. Cambridge: Cambridge University Press.

Keller, M.R. & Block, F. (2011). Explaining the transformation in the US innovation system: the impact of a small government program. *Socioeconomic Review, 11*(4), pp. 629–656.

Krugman, P. (1991). Increasing returns and economic geography. *Journal of Political Economy, 99*, 483–499.

Law, M.T. & Kim, S. (2011). The rise of the American regulatory state: a view from the Progressive era. In Levi-Faur, D. (ed.). *Handbook on the politics of regulation* (pp. 113–127). Cheltenham: Elgar.

Levi-Faur, D. (ed.). (2011). *Handbook on the politics of regulation*. Cheltenham: Elgar.

Levinson, M. (2013). *U.S. manufacturing in international perspective*. Washington, DC: Congressional Research Service.

Locke, R.M & Wellhausen, R.L. (2014). *Production in the innovation economy*. Cambridge, MA: MIT Press.

Lundvall, B.A. (1992). *National systems of innovation: Towards a theory of innovation and interactive learning*. London: Frances Pinter.

Mazzucato, M. (2013a). *The entrepreneurial state: Debunking the public vs. private myth in risk and innovation*. London: Anthem.

Mazzucato, M. (2013b). Financing innovation: creative destruction vs. destructive creation. *Industrial & Corporate Change, 22*(4), 851–867.

Mazzucato, M. & Shipman, A. (2014). Accounting for productive investment and value creation. *Industrial and Corporate Change, 23*(4), 1059–1085.

Mills, C.W. (1957). *The power elite*. New York: Oxford University Press.

Miotti, L. & Sachwald, F. (2003). Co-operative R&D: why and with whom? An integrated framework of analysis. *Research Policy, 32*, 1481–1499.

Mowery, D.C. (1998). The changing structure of the US national innovation system: implications for international conflict and cooperation in R&D. *Research Policy, 27*(6), 639–654. In C. Kaysen (ed.), *The American corporation today*.

Mowery, D.C. & Nelson, R.R. (1998). The U.S. corporation and technical progress. In *The American corporation today* (pp. 187–241). New York: Oxford University Press.

Mowery, D.C. & Rosenberg, N. (2000). Twentieth-century technological change. In S.L. Engerman & R.E. Gallman (eds.), *The Cambridge economic history of the United States* (pp. 803–925). Cambridge: Cambridge University Press.

National Science Academy. (2007). *Rising above the gathering storm: Energizing and employing America for a brighter economic future*. National Academies Press. Retrieved from www.sandia.gov/NINE/documents/RisingAbove.pdf

Neem, J.N. (2008). *Creating a nation of joiners, democracy and civil society in early national Massachusetts*. Cambridge, MA: Harvard University Press.

Nelson, R.R. (ed.) (1993). *National innovation systems: A comparative analysis*. Oxford: Oxford University Press.

Nelson, R.R. (ed.) (2005). *The limits of market organization*. New York: Russell Sage.

Nelson, R.R. (2010, June). Capitalism as a mixed economic system. Working Paper no. 59. Center on Capitalism and Society, Columbia University. Retrieved from http://capitalism.columbia.edu/files/ccs/CCSWP59_Nelson.pdf.

North, D.C. (1990). *Institutions, institutional change and economic performance*. Cambridge: Cambridge University Press.

North, D.C. (2005). *Understanding the process of economic change*. Princeton, NJ: Princeton University Press.

Obama, B. (2011). Startup America. Retrieved from www.whitehouse.gov/economy/business/startup-america.

Obama, B. (2012, January 24). Remarks by the President in State of the Union Address. Retrieved from www.whitehouse.gov/the-press-office/2012/01/24/remarks-president-state-union-address.

Phelps, E.S. (2006). *Toward a model of innovation and performance along the lines of Knight, Keynes, Hayek and Polanyi*. New York: Center on Capitalism and Society.

Pisano, G.P. & Shih, W.C. (2012), *Producing prosperity: Why America needs a manufacturing renaissance*. Cambridge, MA: Harvard Business Review Press.

Porter, M.E. (1998). Clusters and the new economics of competition. *Harvard Business Review, 76*(6), 77–90.

Romer, P.M. (1990). Endogenous technological change. *Journal of Political Economy, 98*(5), S71–102.

Romer, P.M. (1994). The origins of endogenous growth. *Journal of Economic Perspectives, 8*(1), 3–22.

Rosenau, J.N. & Czempiel, E.O. (1992). *Governance without government: Order and change in world politics*. Cambridge: Cambridge University Press.

Saxenian, A.L. (2006). *The New Argonauts: Regional advantage in the global economy*. Harvard, MA: Harvard University Press.

Schumpeter, J.A. (1934). *The theory of economic development*. Cambridge, MA: Harvard Economic Studies.

Schumpeter, J.A. (1942 [2000]). *Capitalism, socialism and democracy*. London: Routledge.

Shah, R., Gao, Z. & Mittal, H. (2015). *Innovation, entrepreneurship, and the economy in the US, China, and India*. London: Elsevier.

Sheshinski, E., Strom, R.J. & Baumol, W.J. (2007). *Entrepreneurship, innovation and the growth mechanism of the free-enterprise economies*. Princeton, NJ: Princeton University Press.

Shiller, R. (2000). *Irrational exuberance*. Princeton, NJ: Princeton University Press.

Solow, R. (1956). A contribution to the theory of economic growth. *Quarterly Journal of Economics, 70*(1), 65–94.

Todeva, E. (2013). Governance of innovation and intermediation in the triple helix interactions. *Industry and Higher Education, 27*(2), 263–278.

Turner, F.J. (1920). *The frontier in American history*. New York: Krieger.

von Hippel, E. (2005). *Democratizing innovation*. Cambridge, MA and London: MIT Press.

Wade, R.H. (2012). The mystery of US industrial policy: the developmental state in disguise. Working paper retrieved from www.eastforum.it/EastForum2012/documenti/RWADE_US%20industrial%20policies_UNCTAD%20_2_.pdwade.

Washington, G. (1796). Farewell address. Retrieved from http://en.wikisource.org/wiki/Washington%27s_Farewell_Address#1.

Weick, K. (1995). *Sensemaking in organization*. London: Sage.

Weingast, B.R. (1995). The economic role of political institutions: market-preserving federalism and economic development, *Journal of Law, Economics, & Organization, 11*(1), 1–31.

Weiss, L. (1998), *The myth of the powerless state*. Cambridge: Polity Press.

Werle, R. (2012). Institutions and systems: Analysing technical innovation from an institutional perspective. In J.M. Bauer, A. Lang, & V. Schneider (eds.), *Innovation policy and governance in high-tech industries*. Heidelberg: Springer-Verlag.

Wessner C.W. & Wolff, A.W. (2012). *Rising to the challenge: US innovation policy for the global economy.* Washington, DC: National Research Council, National Academies Press.

White House. (2011). *Strategy for American innovation, securing our economic growth and prosperity*. Retrieved from www.whitehouse.gov/innovation/strategy.

10 US labor market institutions and employment dynamics

A turning point?

Catherine Sauviat

Introduction

The highly flexible US labor market has always been considered an inherent strength of the US economy. The level of workers' legal protection is well below that of other developed countries. Hiring and firing are less restricted and the latter also less costly, making layoff a much easier option than in many other countries. Unionization rates and minimum wages are lower, and unemployment benefits are less generous. The weakness (and the continuous weakening) of the main labor institutions affecting wage setting have given more room than elsewhere to the domination of market forces and to the prevalence of employers' prerogatives at the expense of workers' protection. Moreover in a consistent way with economic liberalism, the involvement of the US state in labor market policy is low by comparative standards, although it is strong in terms of macroeconomic and monetary policies. The United States spends considerably less than other developed countries on labor market policies, both as a share of GDP and per labor market participant.

This model has been presented as a benchmark in Europe, despite its cultural, and historical specificities and despite its weak performance during the recent recovery, along with negative externalities for society. Flexibility has not prevented the US labor market from experiencing substantial and persistent increases in unemployment, notably long-term unemployment. The slow recovery since the official end of the Great Recession illustrates the gradual trend of increasingly "jobless recoveries" over the last three recessions (2001, 1981–1982, 1990–1991) that contrasts sharply with previous US experience. And this despite the intensive intervention of the US state (the two-shot fiscal stimulus with the TARP in 2008, and the ARRA in 2009)[1] to sustain economic growth, coupled with a very active role played by the Federal Reserve Bank to stimulate the economy through strong unconventional policy since 2008.

The first part of this chapter seeks to characterize the initial weakness of US labor market institutions and the way some of them have been weakened further. The second part addresses the question of the recent "jobless recovery." It points out the main features of this recovery compared to previous ones. It then explores the possible explanations of persistent weakness and whether they are economic, social or cultural. Finally, it questions the famous "Great job machine" and its capacity to deliver a superior outcome in terms of employment level and quality, wellbeing and social mobility.

The initial weakness and the erosion of main US labor market institutions

The "New Deal" that followed the Great Depression in the 1930s allowed the setting up of several core labor market institutions that helped to regulate the U.S. employment relationship. It contributed to legitimating a strong involvement of the federal state in the economy. It also created the conditions for the emergence of a powerful industrial unionism as well as new wage-earner protections against unemployment, old-age and economic insecurity. This process opened the way for the development of a "middle-class society" in a context of sustained growth and relative social mobility. The labor institutions inherited from this period, considered as exceptional in the long run of capitalism, have been progressively weakened. What, then, are the specificities of US labor market institutions, particularly of employment protection legislation (EPL), of trade unions, of the minimum wage and of unemployment insurance?

Labor rights vs. employee rights

The OECD index of EPL strictness for individual and collective dismissal shows the United States to have the lowest score of all OECD countries in 2013. This fits with the conventional wisdom of a highly flexible labor market where state intervention is very limited (OECD, 2013). Even if the pertinence of this index is questionable for interpreting the strictness of EPL in a country governed by common law (Kirat, 2006), the United States is undoubtedly the country where the relationship between employer and employee clearly and strongly favors the former. Since the last half of the nineteenth century, the principle of "at-will" employment prevails, in harmony with the ideology of laissez-faire and individualism. This principle was later limited in scope by the emergence of labor law and the development of jurisprudence and state laws.[2]

The specificity of US labor rights is that they have developed from two different legal sources that have grown separately: traditional labor law, which regulates collective workers' labor rights (rights of representation, right of collective bargaining) and employee rights in the workplace, more individually focused and enforceable against corporations in the courts. This situation is very different from the one which prevails in most European countries, where the first type of regulatory source is dominant.

The dilution of collective labor rights

The complexity of US labor law per se is that it comes from different sources: federal, state, jurisprudence from the Common Law, as well as collective bargaining. The labor law of federal origin emerged during the 1930s, aimed at limiting the power of employers in the workplace, particularly for workers represented by a union. With the exception of the Fair Labor Standards Act (FLSA) enacted in 1938, an inheritance of the New Deal, which set up minimum standards concerning wages (minimum wage) and work duration for individual workers (payment of overtime over a ceiling of 40 hours per week), the employment laws came later during the 1960s. These laws are focused on protecting individual workers' rights in the workplace (discrimination, etc.), encouraging employees to claim their rights to government or judiciary bodies, and shifting away from traditional organized labor. As a result, employment laws have expanded and strengthened at the expense of labor laws, thus weakening trade union representation. Consequently the US worker has been increasingly protected by federal legislation as an employee with specific characteristics (as female, Black, disabled) rather than as a unionized employee with collective rights in the workplace.

This process occurred because labor law was weakened all along the second part of the twentieth century. The major labor law, the National Labor Relations Act (NLRA, also known as the Wagner Act), was enacted in 1935 under the Roosevelt presidency to restore the balance in the employer–labor relationship. It set up the legal basis of union representation and collective bargaining, from which, however, a number of workers had been originally or later excluded.[3] It established a permanent National Labor Relations Bureau (NLRB), an independent federal agency charged with interpreting, administering and enforcing the NLRA.[4] In 1947, through the Labor-Management Relations Act (called the Taft–Hartley Act), then in 1959 through the Landrum–Griffith Act, several amendments were enacted that severely restricted the collective rights conceded by the NLRA. These forbid closed shop, require 60 days' notice for strikes, exclude supervisors from unionizing and collective bargaining coverage, allow states to pass right-to-work (RTW) laws[5] and put unions' financial resources under strict control. After that, US courts (including the Supreme Court) continuously weakened the content and scope of the NLRA. Since the penalties against employers were and remain negligible and weakly deterrent, the labor law has been frequently violated.

The NLRB itself participated in this process, partly because of the inability or unwillingness of Congress to change labor law during the 1980s. Gaining importance in labor regulation because of the inaction of Congress, it became less and less neutral and arbitrated increasingly in favor of employers in labor disputes. Since the election of President Obama, the authority of NLRB has been strongly contested[6] in a context where Obama has been unable or unwilling to push for the enactment of the new labor law he promised during his campaign to facilitate union representation.[7] More recently, a US Court of Appeal overturned a 2012 NLRB decision that would have outlawed arbitration agreements bearing on working conditions. The Court ruled that employers can require their workers to sign such agreements, limiting legal exposure and costs of class action lawsuits over workplace rules violation.[8]

The surge of individual employee rights

The weakening of collective labor rights has, however, been accompanied by the increasing passage of employment laws in the 1930s and again since the 1960s (Heckscher, 1996). Two kinds of laws have been developed to protect employee rights in the workplace: one concerning basic employee rights (wage rate, hours of work, pension benefits, leave for family and medical reasons, advance notice for mass layoff or plant closing, safe and healthy working conditions); the other that proscribe all kinds of discrimination (race, color, religion, sex, national origin, age). However, most of the time these laws exclude from their scope of action workers that do not work minimal hours or those that belong to small business enterprises. So their protection is far from being universal.

At the federal level, a number of laws have also set minimal standards with which employers have to comply in the workplace.[9] Let us take the example of the FLSA enacted in 1938, which establishes basic employee rights with respect to rates of pay, hours of work and overtime. Here, the notion of employee is central to the entitlement to legal protections and a number of workers were excluded from the start.[10] Furthermore, employers are responsible for determining the status of their own workers (either an employee or an independent contractor) and declaring them at the Department of labor and at the Internal Revenue Service (Department of the Treasury). There is of course some incentive for employers to mischaracterize their workers, in order to lower labor costs (wages and benefits). The most famous example is *Vizcaino* v. *Microsoft*, where workers were hired by the software company as independent contractors and used as employees and recognized as such by a Court of Appeal. The investigation by the Internal Revenue Service required Microsoft to reclassify its workers. The company lost the appeal and in 2000 had to settle the case for S97 million of taxes and penalties (Muhl, 2002). Other examples are the employment discrimination laws enacted from the 1960s to the 1990s. A specific administration, the Equal Employment Opportunity Commission (EEOC), is responsible for enforcing these laws that gave impetus for a strong push in individual legal actions (Befort, 2002; Oyer and Schaeffer, 2000).

If we turn now to the state level, a number of state courts and legislatures started in the late 1950s and mainly in the 1980s to recognize exceptions to the prevailing employment-at-will doctrine, as developed in common law. Muhl (2001) describes three major exceptions: the first and most widespread is state policy that protects workers from terminations in some cases (injuries, etc.); the second is the existence of an implied contract between an employer and an employee; the third and much less common among states rests on a covenant of good faith and fair dealing in the employment relationship, or the requirement of a "just cause" to terminate a contract. However, this common law is not without serious deficiencies, notably for rank-and-file workers (St Antoine, 1993, 1994). That is why the Model Employment Termination Act (META) was proposed by some lawyers in 1991 to prohibit the termination of most full-time workers without a "good cause." But up to now, no state has enacted such a legislative proposal. This reveals that when it comes to labor rights, America's variety of capitalism cannot be reduced to its national dimension, but must take into consideration the importance of state decisions.

Finally, if the at-will doctrine has been eroded along the last decades, the extension of employee rights has developed at the expense of collective bargaining rights, resulting in a reduced power of unions as organizations.

A declining union environment

US trade unionism has developed in a particularly hostile political and legal context. It never really succeeded in acquiring the dimension of mass unionism, except for rare exceptions in its history. Its leaders chose quite early to focus on collective bargaining for the exclusive benefit of union members and, therefore, at the expense of broader solidarities. This kind of "business unionism" condemning itself to a very unequal face-to-face with employers, without any support in social, economic or political institutions. The continuous decline in membership, notably in the private sector, has increasingly reduced its range of action in the field of collective bargaining. Moreover, the outcome of collective bargaining is ever less in favor of unions or reduced to minimal wage agreements and benefits for an ever more restricted number of unionized workers. Since the 1980s, concession bargaining at the shop level has developed in the private sector – that is downsizing wages and benefits against the promise of protecting jobs (or with the hope of saving jobs). When the Great Recession confronted state governments with a deep fiscal crisis, concession bargaining spread to the public sector. Public sector workers have seen their wages and benefits lowered in several states. In 2011 their rights to bargain collectively and strike were under massive attack, particularly in Midwestern manufacturing states like Wisconsin, which had been one of the first states to extend those rights to public sectors workers, and Ohio.[11] Over the last years, Indiana and Michigan, two Midwestern states where there are still the Big Three carmakers, passed a right-to-work legislation (RTW). Then Wisconsin followed suit, leading to a total of 25 RTW states today. There had been no such new legislation for more than a decade. Once again, the regional dimension of American capitalism must not be neglected in a country where federalism has granted states with significant powers.

The drop in union membership

The constant fall of unionization since the mid-1950s is well documented. Union membership has decreased for several reasons: decline in manufacturing employment where workers used to be organized; shift of manufacturing firms from traditional unionized Midwestern industrial states to RTW states, mainly located in the South; weakened or broken labor law as mentioned above, coupled with a growing anti-union behavior of American business employers to exploit its lacunae and push forward anti-union policies of the Reagan and Bush Administrations;

skill-biased technology changes that transformed workplaces; globalization that permitted American business to benefit from a cheap reserve workforce (or labor supply),[12] either by shifting production abroad or by offering immigration temporary visas to Indian and Chinese workers, at the mercy of their US employers during the validity of their visa. By contrast to some European countries (France, for example), the degree of unionization in the United States determines precisely the degree of collective bargaining coverage: one needs to be unionized to benefit from collective agreement outcomes.

The last figures issued by the Department of Labor confirm the declining trend of unionization rate since the beginning of the Great Recession. The percentage of workers belonging to a union has dropped to a historical post-war low in 2014, to 11.1 – from 12.4 percent in 2008. In 1983, the first year for which comprehensive data are available, 20.3 percent of American workers were union members. If the public sector remains heavily organized (35.7 percent in 2014), more than five times higher than for private sector workers (6.6 percent),[13] public sector unions also lost membership between 2008 and 2014. The reason for this decline is that over the last years, public sector jobs were unusually hit by the crisis, which deteriorated state fiscal resources and pushed governors and mayors to downsize public services and cut jobs in public administration, education and police, among others. Since 2010, many workers have also dropped their union membership in states where trade unionism was under assault from newly elected Republican governors. In Wisconsin, union membership fell to 306,000 workers in 2014 from 355,000 in 2010 (or a 2.5 percentage points decline) (US BLS, 2015). In Michigan, union membership declined to 585,000 in 2014 from 627,000 in 2010 (or a 2 percentage points drop). Local governments suffered the most from job losses, with the elimination of 390,000 jobs between December 2007 and December 2014, of which more than two-thirds took place in the education sector (–258,000 jobs).[14]

Nevertheless, the advantages of unionization are still high. Unions in 2014 maintained a 27 percent wage advantage and were four times more likely to benefit from pension plans and to take advantage of other social benefits, as shown in Table 10.1.

Table 10.1 The union advantage in 2013

	Union members	*Non-union members*
Median weekly earnings ($)	950	750
Participants in retirement benefits (%)	86	48
Recipients of job-provided health insurance (%)	79	49
Recipients of paid holidays (%)	81	74
Recipients of paid sick leave (%)	83	62

Source: Union members – 2013, US BLS, January 24, 2014; and National Compensation Survey, Employee benefits in the US, March 2014, US BLS, July 25, 2014.

The decreasing outcome of collective bargaining

In the United States, collective bargaining is highly decentralized. American business negotiates very little at the industry level, let alone at the national level, since no employer organization is entitled to bargain. No coordination mechanism exists to homogenize working conditions and wages, except pattern bargaining in use between big corporations but on the decline today.[15] A first cycle of concession bargaining was inaugurated by Chrysler in 1979 where UAW conceded wage cuts to the firm on the brink of bankruptcy. In the 1980s, such concessions spread to several industries under deregulation (steel, aerospace) and also to traditional industries facing new competition from Japanese and European (automobile) firms. In the private sector, unions agreed to real wage freezes or cuts, notably for new hires, in the hope of maintaining the level of employment. During the two decades of 1990–2010, big corporations orchestrated an assault on fringe benefits. Representing roughly one-quarter of workers' compensation, health insurance was particularly targeted because of its weight in total contributions (35 percent). But defined benefit pension plans were also under attack, because manufacturing companies support the bulk of contributions in that case. During the last decade, the rate of health insurance coverage among workers aged less than 65 decreased to 58.6 from 69.2 percent, while the rate of retirement benefits coverage dropped to 42.8 from 48.3 percent (Mishel *et al.*, 2012).

The Great Recession offered the opportunity of inaugurating a third and sharp round of concession bargaining. In new collective agreements, unions faced with mass unemployment gave most of the time priority to jobs at the expense of wages. The automobile industry is a good example. In 2007, just before the official start of the Great Recession, the new round of collective bargaining at the Big Three prefigured the American business' offensive against workers (Sauviat, 2008), which was to spread to other industries (wage freeze or cut, introduction of a two-tier wage system with half the hourly standard rate for new hires). In 2009, General Motors (GM) and Chrysler received a financial aid package from the US government through the Troubled Asset Relief Program: more than $50 billion for GM, $10.9 billion for Chrysler. In exchange, the government obtained strong restructuring by the two companies[16] and major concessions from UAW.[17] The new collective bargaining agreement of 2011 amplifies the concessions obtained from UAW in 2007: wages and benefits were sacrificed in the name of competitiveness and new hires paid around half the hourly rate legacy workers make ($10–15, against $28 an hour) for an unlimited duration (Sauviat, 2012a). Other big manufacturing companies have followed suit, like General Electric. But the real novelty is the general assault over public sector workers' status, from state and local governments. From 2009 to 2011, fringe benefits were downsized by a huge majority of states for teachers, police officers and firefighters.

The minimum wage, a poor instrument of income protection

In the United States the federal minimum wage was introduced in 1938 by the FLSA, although several states had enacted minimum wages well before, applicable to women (Skocpol, 1995). Compared to main European countries, the federal minimum wage rate remains very low ($7.25 to date). Depending on Congress decisions, its level, non-inflation adjusted, does not offer a strong protection against economic insecurity. It is so low that fewer than 2 percent of hourly paid workers in the United States are still beneficiaries.[18] This is why, from the start, states took earlier action and enacted minimum wage legislation that guarantees a better protection than the federal minimum wage.[19] That is also why local governments, under growing pressure from unions and community groups, have enacted "living wages" since the 1990s, with which employers are required to comply.[20]

The eroding value of the minimum wage as a labor standard

The federal minimum wage has been frozen during long periods in recent decades, victim of Congress inertia. It was the case during the Reagan era in the 1980s, then during the Bush era in the 2000s. The last federal minimum wage's raise was enacted in 2007, which led in 2009 to its current level, representing a 40 percent increase. But its real value has decreased since and represents only 35 percent of the real average wage in December 2014 dollars, much lower than US historical levels of the 1950s and 1960s, which peaked around 50 percent.

With the sluggish job recovery, the political and academic controversies surrounding the impact of minimum wage increases on employment level and growth persist, although adverse effects, when they are found, appear to be small according to most recent studies.[21] At a time of growing income inequality and rising poverty (more than 45 million people living at or below the poverty line in 2013), the option of raising the minimum wage to $10.10 by 2015 (The Fair Minimum Wage Act of 2013)[22] and adjusting it for the cost of living is supported by a majority of Americans. The White House has backed the Democratic proposal, coupled with some exemptions for small businesses. Initiatives from states and municipalities to raise the minimum wage have intensified across the country. In 2013, four state governments passed laws progressively raising the hourly minimum wage during their legislature (California, New York, Rhode Island and New Jersey); in 2014, ten states (Connecticut, Delaware, Hawaïi, Maryland, Massachusetts, Michigan, Minnesota, Rhode Island, Vermont, West Virginia) and DC had followed the same way,[23] along with several big cities (Seattle, San Francisco, San Diego) (NCSL, 2014). This option has also been at the forefront of an ongoing movement of fast-food strikes which started in autumn 2012[24] asking for the reform of the minimum wage to a living wage, with cost of living adjustment of $15 an hour (called "Fight for Fifteen").

Income inequalities and labor market polarization

The eroding value of the minimum wage and the fact that minimum wage workers rarely hold full-time, year-round positions contributed to rising inequality and labor market polarization – a trend exacerbated by explosive wages, bonuses and stock options at the top. US economists have documented trends in income inequality and academic and non-partisan studies are recurrent on this topic. Picketty and Saez (2003), then Kopczuk *et al.* (2007), have offered a long-term perspective of the growing wage and income dispersion process since the late 1970s and early 1980s, with dramatic increases at the very top of income distribution and the emergence today of a "working rich" class by contrast with the traditional "rentier" class. Lazonick (2009), among others, has stressed the exorbitant pay of US corporate executives obtained through forms of stock-price manipulation to boost their stock options when exercised, in relation with the financialization of US firms since the 1980s.

Since 1975, the 90th to 10th percentile household income ratio grew almost 40 percent, from 8.53 to 10.93.[25] If we consider the top 1 percent of the US population, it received about one-fifth of household income in 2012, an amount extraordinarily high by historical standards. According to the Congressional Budget Office (CBO), this very small minority saw its average real after-tax household income grow by 275 percent between 1979 and 2007.[26] The increase in income concentration for the top percentile (and within it) as measured by CBO came to a larger extent from rising labor income (wages and other forms of labor compensation) and an advantageous tax and transfer system that both widen income inequality.

Tolerance to inequalities has to a large extent always been higher in the United States than elsewhere, in particular in European countries. It was so because there was (and there is still today) a strong belief that social mobility is possible for individuals ready to work hard and make whatever effort is needed to realize the "American Dream." This conviction continues to feed large immigration flows from all over the world to "America." However, recent polls have revealed increasing public concern about social mobility.[27] At the end of 2013, President Obama described the widening income gap as "the defining challenge of our time" (Obama, 2013). It seems that they are right to worry. A study shows that US upward economic mobility as measured by rising in the distribution of income rank from birth to adult age is much more limited for the bottom quintile than other quintiles (Bengali & Daly, 2013).

But even for the United States there seems to exist a limit to this tolerance. It was probably reached and was illustrated when Occupy Wall Street emerged in 2011 with its slogan: "We are the 99 percent." This proclamation recognized the threat of inequalities as a major economic and political problem and thus a public policy concern. Rising inequality implies that US households take on more debts to maintain their standard of living,[28] a process at the origin of the financial meltdown. Increased spending by the top 1 percent has also entailed what Franck (2007) called "expenditure cascades," by raising proportionally for middle-class families "the cost of achieving many basic goals" through indebtedness. Too much income disparity not only tends to feed financial crisis and harm aggregate demand and potential growth. It also undermines democracy and the commitment to the common good in US society, thus threatening the ideological foundations of American capitalism.

The loopholes of unemployment insurance

The US unemployment insurance (UI) system has been shaped outside of any social compromise, as an outcome of academic expertise and earlier state experiences (Becker, 1973; Baicker *et al.*, 1997). That is why it remained mostly designed and managed by individual states, under a few federal standards, however. Unions, although initially opposed to compulsory UI, never really contested the system. They were able to negotiate seniority systems and supplementary UI company schemes for their members in firm-level collective agreements, which made layoffs an acceptable option for them. The US UI system was designed mainly for people with strong links within the labor market (as male breadwinner unionized workers typically used to be),[29] possibly victims of seasonal unemployment resulting from business cycles (people laid off temporarily). Thus labor market changes since the 1980s have made the UI system a less and less effective tool to protect the bulk of US workers from cyclical downturns.

A decentralized system, immune to potential adverse effects

As a federal country, the United States has a relatively decentralized UI system. The 50 states of the federation offer regular jobless benefits up to a maximum of 26 weeks under the Unemployment Compensation (UC) program, a duration that can be extended between 13 and 20 weeks, depending on state laws and unemployment rates.[30] Beyond, the federal government takes over under a program named the "Emergency Unemployment Compensation (EUC) program." Thus the system offers potentially broad flexibility. Since the last recession, the US Congress has allowed continuous extension of available UI compensation up to a maximum of 99 weeks for most eligible job seekers.[31]

Within the guidelines of federal law, states determine who is eligible to receive UI benefits and how much they receive. The experience rating system is operating in most states, making the employer contribution depend on the company's layoff record over the previous three to five working years. This has not dissuaded US employers from turning to layoffs as a quite easy and cheap option[32] to adjust to downturns. The US system was mainly conceived in order to avoid "disincentives to work" and to limit so-called "moral hazard" effects. Thus, it offers low and short-term benefits compared with UI systems in other developed countries.

Nationwide, UI benefits corresponded to 46 percent of workers' previous wages in 2010. As compared to most industrialized countries, the level of benefits offered under the US UI system and its potential duration have been substantially lower. It was so even during the Great Recession, when temporary benefit programs were available (Burtless, 2009).

Many unemployed exhaust UI benefits before finding a job. This maintains a strong pressure to find jobs quickly. In 2012, the exhaustion rate was at 46.4 percent. The rise of the UI exhaustion rate during the Great Recession (55.7 percent at its peak in March 2010) partly reveals the inadequacy of the UI program.

A system less and less consistent with labor market changes

The regular UI program was not designed to address permanent job separations. It was rather set up to provide temporary income support to jobless workers impacted by business cycles. There has been, however, a significant and accelerating increase of permanent as opposed to temporary layoffs since the 1980s. It was caused by a new wave of manufacturing plant restructurings associated with mass layoffs, prompted by the new axiom of "maximizing shareholder value" (Lazonick & O'Sullivan, 2000). During the Great Recession and its aftermath, this phenomenon was to accelerate.[33] Employers seem to be much less inclined than in the past to operate temporary layoffs (Katz, 2010).

Demographic changes in the labor market also occurred, notably the rising participation rate of women since 1970. Women are more likely to work part-time and to leave their jobs to care for dependent family members. They are particularly vulnerable to unemployment without generally meeting the criteria entitling them to benefits. The UI system is also particularly ineffective in helping people, mostly women, who have just left the Temporary Assistance to Needy Families program. The social safety net was redesigned in 1996 from Welfare to Workfare and tightened conditions for eligibility. Women that exit the program after a maximum of five years without a job are usually unable to meet the criteria for being eligible for UI benefits because of low past earnings and intermittent employment records.

Following these changes, the scope and level of UI benefits has shrunk, sometimes leading more vulnerable individuals to turn to the Social Security Disability Insurance (SSDI) program for which eligibility criteria have been relaxed. Since the 1980s, as stressed by Autor and Dugan (2006), the SSDI program acted partly as a substitute for the failing UI system. This has also been the case during the Great Recession, where a clear correlation between the rise of unemployment and the rise of disability filings has been observed by recent economic literature.[34] Addressing the question of persistent jobless recoveries, Coibon *et al.* (2013) suggest that the main explanation might be a cultural one that is a decline in social trust in the form of individuals finding it increasingly justifiable to claim for government benefits rather than looking for jobs. Because of the Great Recession, work might no longer be what the US culture venerates as a moral imperative.

As seen in the first part of this chapter, all US labor market institutions were designed so as not to dissuade or discourage employers from hiring and workers looking for jobs, leaving the initiative to individual US states to set them up and handle their day-to-day management. The passage of the Full Employment Act in 1946, enacted under President Truman, gave the federal government the responsibility "to promote maximum employment, production, and purchasing power." This is reflected in the Fed's dual mandate – maximum employment and stable prices – a responsibility that J. Yellen, the president of the Fed, recalled in her statement before the US Senatorial Committee on Banking, Housing and Urban Affairs, on November 14, 2013.

However, the succession of jobless recoveries since the early 1980s suggests that structural changes in employment have occurred, putting into question the "great US job machine." The US economy officially exited from recession in June 2009. This has not generated a quick and robust job recovery, despite a strong return of the federal government into the economy and an extensive reliance on active and accommodative monetary policies.[35] What is really occurring since the official end of the Great Recession?

What is at stake behind the fragile last recovery?

The conventional wisdom in labor economics is that labor markets with very flexible institutions and policies favor employment creation. As a result, the highly flexible US labor market should have been quick to recover from the Great Recession, with the largest fiscal stimulus and the most expansive monetary policy in history. That has not exactly happened. On the contrary, five years after the 2007–2009 recession officially ended, employment has just recovered to its pre-crisis peak level, but this is mainly due to a decline in the labor participation rate, reaching its lowest level in more than three decades. Therefore, the declining ability of the US labor market to create jobs seems "to be more than a short-term cyclical problem," as argued by the OECD (2014).

The main features of the last recovery

The job deficit from the last recession has been much larger than those in any previous ones. Job losses and recovery are bleak in the US labor market, when compared to other recent recessions.

The Great Recession started by far the longest and most severe of the jobless recoveries that took place since the beginning of the 1980s. Not only did the US labor market take 76 months to surpass the previous employment peak of January 2008 (x-axis of Figure 10.1), but the drop in employment was also much sharper than in other recessions (y-axis). Even if notable improvements have been registered in 2014, some labor market indicators remain a cause for concern. It was only in May 2014 that the level of non-farm employment recovered from what it was in December 2007, when the recession started. The employment-to-population ratio (58.9 percent) was still far closer to this trough in 2010–2011 than its pre-recession level (around 63 percent), and prime-age workers (those between ages 25 and 54) have been hit especially hard (–3.1

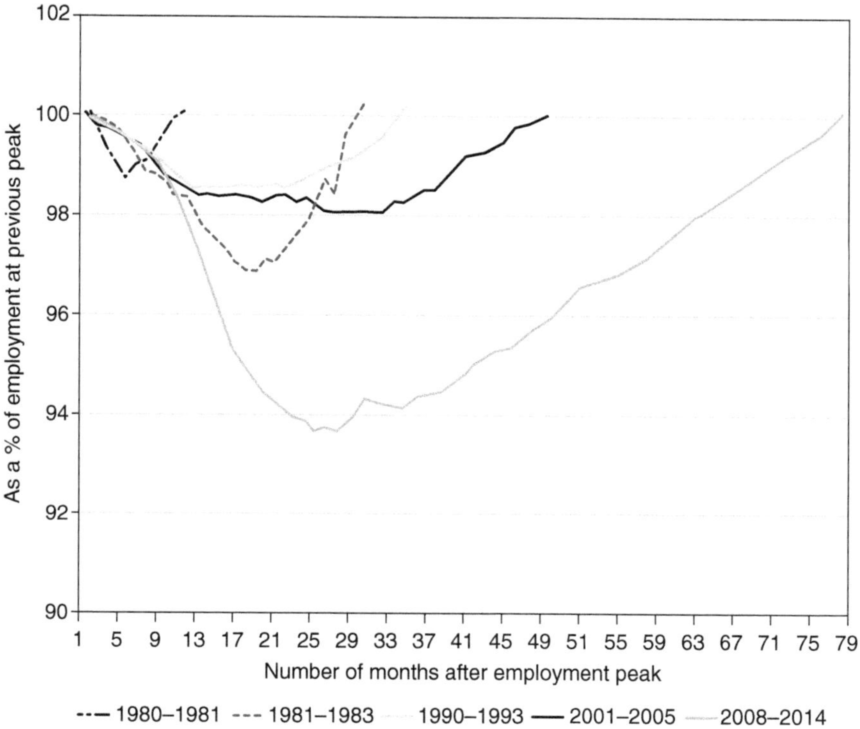

Figure 10.1 Job changes in the last business cycles as a share of employment at previous peaks (source: C. Rample, Comparing Job Recessions and Recoveries, *NYT Economix*, May 13, 2013, updated by the author).

percentage points from December 2007 to July 2014). Unemployment rose far more than in previous recessions, although it has decreased to 6.2 percent in July 2014. The long-term unemployment level and duration are still historically high, while the recession is disproportionally affecting men, younger workers and black workers (US Congress Joint Economic Committee, 2013). In July 2014, one-third of labor force participants have been unemployed for more than six months and over one-quarter have been out of work for a year or more (the definition of the very-long-term unemployed in the United States). Even if the average length of unemployment has come down from its peak of nearly 41 weeks in 2011, it has remained at a significant level of 32.4 weeks in July 2014. It is still more than 16 weeks longer compared to pre-recession levels.

However, the unemployment rate, whether short term or long term, may not be the best barometer of US labor market conditions, or at least an incomplete one, not to mention its likely underestimation as recently pointed out by Krueger *et al.* (2014).[36] The US labor market has actually experienced a continued exodus of individuals leaving the labor force, rather than entering employment. The percentage of people in the labor force (or participation rate) fell in July 2014 to its lowest level since March 1978 (62.9 percent), the largest declines affecting states with the largest falls in employment. Because many discouraged Americans are dropped out of the labor force, they are no longer counted as unemployed, a phenomenon that illustrates a path of unemployment to inactivity (Bengali *et al.*, 2013). This is particularly true for prime-age workers, whose participation in the labor force fell to a 30-year low of 80.8 percent in July 2014. Aaronson *et al.* (2014) found that besides the influence of the aging population (the retirement of baby boomers), the polarization of the labor market and the subsequent decline in labor demand for middle-skill jobs is an important reason explaining the decline in labor force participation. Therefore, the recent decline in unemployment has been driven more by continuous declining labor force participation (and shorter unemployment insurance benefits) than by improvement in job creation.

The other noticeable trend, which reflects the weakness of the recovery, has been the rise of part-time work (those who work fewer than 35 hours according to the US Bureau of Labor Statistics), a burden that is no longer borne by the young, but is shifted to older people. Compared with December 2007, there are 3.1 million fewer Americans working full-time and 3.3 million more working part-time (in July 2014). The current share of workers with part-time jobs, after a peak of 19.9 percent in 2009, stayed at high levels (around 18.9 percent). Among them, more than one-quarter is working part-time for economic reasons. That is the reason why the standard unemployment rate probably understates the extent of underemployment,[37] as pointed out by the Federal Reserve chairwoman, J. Yellen, in a speech in Chicago at the end of March 2014.

Moffit (2012) has also pointed to a steady decline in the employment population ratio for both sexes since 2000,[38] which might indicate cultural changes in the use of time among given sociodemographic groups.[39] These changes influence the age distribution, particularly at its extremes (the younger, notably).

Unemployment has also failed to decrease in inverse relation to the increase in job vacancies, causing a deviation of the Beveridge curve from its historical pattern, more or less pronounced across industries.[40] Despite the fact that there were 4.7 million job openings in July 2014 (against 2.1 million in July 2009 at this trough), there were still more than double this number looking for work (9.7 million) (US BLS, 2014). The other labor market concern among economists has been the decoupling of employment and GDP, questioning another well-known economic law, the Okun law. This law shows a close (negative) relationship between unemployment rate and real output growth. This was the case until the 1980s, when this trend was reversed for the first time and continued to be so during the three following recessions (Basu & Foley, 2011), and notably during the last Great Recession (Rothstein, 2012). Even if Daly *et al.* (2014) dispute these findings, they nevertheless question to what extent the Great Recession might have altered the fundamentals of the US economy. As Freeman (2013) pointed out, this measure of employment–output elasticity appeared to be exceptionally low by US standards from mid-2009 through 2012. This reversal might be due to structural shift in the US economy toward a "service economy" in the context of economic and financial globalization,[41] since employment–output elasticity in service industries is lower than non-service industries.

The deterioration in the quality of jobs

However, to have a more complete picture of US labor market conditions, it is worth focusing not only on the number of jobs offered, but also on their quality. In the United States, more than elsewhere, holding a permanent contract does not really differentiate jobs, because of the very high flexibility of the labor market. Schmitt (2007) has proposed a minimal definition of "good jobs," referring to three components: median hourly earnings of at least $19 (inflation-adjusted $2011) or $40,000 annually, with solid employer-sponsored retirement and health insurance plans. By this measure, Schmitt and Jones (2012) found that the share of workers with a "good job" has declined almost 3 percentage points, falling to 24.6 percent in 2010, from 27.4 percent in 1979.

This trend is an expression of industry shifts, a proxy of how the jobs distribution between "bad jobs" and "good jobs" has changed. Between 1980 and 2014, goods-producing employment as a share of total non-farm employment fell to 13.8 percent from 26.8 percent, while private service-producing employment grew to 70.4 percent from 55.1 percent (Table 10.2). The growing share of service industries in total employment has fed the development of "bad jobs" along with the disappearance of existing middle-class jobs from manufacturing. Today, new job growth across the country remains disproportionally concentrated in private-service industries. The cuts in government jobs because of the budget crisis and long-term outsourcing to the private sector have clearly amplified the downward trend of "good jobs." Budget cuts have reduced public sector payrolls by 599,000 since the economy recovered (from July 2009 to July 2014). While the public sector had a countercyclical role in the US economy in the recession, on the contrary, now job losses from 2010 onwards due to austerity in public spending have seriously impaired economic recovery.

The current recovery has been weak by historical standards. Except for healthcare and professional and business services, employment gains have been concentrated mainly in low-wage industries in its aftermath (accommodation and food services, retail trade and employment services, i.e., temporary jobs), as shown in Table 10.3.

Table 10.2 Employment changes among industries as a share of total non-farm employment (percentage)

	Private-service provided	*Construction*	*Manufacturing*	*Government*
1980 (%)	55.1	4.9	20.7	18.1
2013 (%)	70.3	6.4	8.8	16.0

Source: Current Employment Survey, BLS.

Table 10.3 The largest employment gains among industries since the recovery (July 2009–July 2014), and by hourly wage

NAICS	*Industry*	*Job gains*	*Hourly wage ($)*
54	Professional and business services, of which	+2,856,000	29.20
541	• *Professional and technical services*	*+913,400*	37.77
56	Administrative and waste management services, of which	+1,659,000	18.68
561	• *Administrative and support services, of*	*+1,626,300*	18.35
5613	*which*		
56132	• *Employment services, of which*	*+1,211,900*	N.A.
	• *Temporary help services*	*+1,131,700*	N.A.
62	Healthcare and social assistance, of which	+1,617, 800	24.84
621	• *Ambulatory healthcare services, of which*	*+894,300*	23.93
624	• *Social assistance*	*+438,800*	15.33
72	Accommodation and food services, of	+1,370, 400	12.86
722	which		
	• *Food services and drinking places*	*+1,243,200*	*12.35*
44+45	Retail trade	+891,200	17.03

Source: Current Employment Survey, BLS.

Table 10.4 The top five major occupations by employment gains and by median hourly wage (from May 2010 to May 2013)

Major occupations	*Employment gains*	*2013 median hourly wage ($)*
Food preparation and serving related occupations	887,250	9.15
Sales and related occupations	630,210	12.10
Business and financial operations occupations	567,180	30.67
Personal care	561,520	10.1
Production occupations	528,840	15.03

Source: Occupational Employment Statistics (May 2010 and May 2013), BLS.

The same is true for major low-wage occupations, where the bulk of job creation occurred since the recovery, with the exception of business and financial operations occupations (Table 10.4).

Given that labor productivity (output per hour) increased at a particularly strong pace in 2009, after a short decline in 2008, the divergence with real hourly compensation that dates back to the early 1970s has been reinforced. Hence, most gains in labor productivity have benefited firms through higher profits rather than workers through higher inflation-adjusted wages (Table 10.5).

Table 10.5 Labor productivity and compensation during the Great Recession and its aftermath (percentage change from the same quarter one year ago)

	2007 Q4	*2008 Q1*	*2008 Q2*	*2008 Q3*	*2008 Q4*	*2009 Q1*	*2009 Q2*	*2009 Q3*	*2009 Q4*	*2010 Q1*	*2010 Q2*	*2010 Q3*	*2010 Q4*
Labor productivity per hour	2.4	1.3	1.6	1.7	–0.4	1.3	2.3	3.6	5.5	5.1	3.5	2.6	1.9
Real hourly compensation	–0.1	–1.7	–1.7	–2.1	1.4	–0.3	2.9	3.4	–0.3	0.7	0.0	0.5	0.4

Source: BLS, Major sectors productivity and costs.

Table 10.6 The largest employment gains among states since the recovery (July 2009 to July 2014)

States	*Employment gains*	*Employed members of unions (%)*
Texas*	+1,355,800	4.8
California	+1,236,100	16.4
Florida*	+429,800	5.4
New York	+489,400	24.4
Michigan*	+331,200	16.3
Ohio	+258,300	12.6
North Carolina*	+254,700	3.0
Massachusetts	+233,400	13.7
Georgia*	+229,700	5.3
Indiana*	+229,400	9.3

Source: Current Employment Survey, and Union members, 2013, BLS.

Note
* Right-to-work states.

This downward trend in wages is also driven by the spread of two-tier compensation systems among big manufacturing companies when collective agreements are renewed[42] and the shift of factory-job growth to less-unionized Sunbelt states, of which several RTW states are shown in Table 10.6.

The challenge of the labor market debate: structural change vs. lack of demand

There is an ongoing debate in the United States on whether the decline in employment dynamics is structural (i.e., skills mismatch) or due to shortfalls in the aggregate demand for labor. Several commentators have interpreted the deviation from the traditional Beveridge curve as a result of the first explanation. N. Kocherlakota, president of the Reserve Bank of Minneapolis, has argued for example that a number of factors impede workers from being as mobile as before, such as the housing and mortgage-debt crisis (with foreclosures that go with it). Mulligan (2011) has upheld that expansion in safety net programs (UI system, Supplemental Nutrition Assistance Program, Medicaid) over the recession could be a potential source of reducing incentives to work. According to these authors, such mismatches are not easily corrected through expansive monetary policy. They would be best addressed through policies aimed at improving labor supply, such as job training, mobility support, immigration or reductions in labor income taxes. On the other hand, authors like P. Krugman or J. Stiglitz argue that recent poor labor market performances are primarily the result of a shortfall in aggregate demand. Goldman Sachs US economics analysts reinforce this thesis, attributing the persistent underperformance of the labor market to the weakness in aggregate demand.[43] Thus, a stimulus of appropriate magnitude along with further unconventional monetary policy would be necessary to boost effective demand. More recently, Diamond and Sahin (2014) questioned the two theses by undertaking a detailed examination of outward shifts in the Beveridge curve along eight business cycles. Rather than suggesting a deterioration in the matching process, their results show that the return of unemployment rate to pre-recession level (or possibly below) depends much on the duration of the expansion preceding the recession than on the weakness in the demand for goods and services.

But whatever the right explanation is, the skill gap evidence remains very questionable (Cappelli, 2014). As most economists would argue, a shortage of labor supply should have entailed wage increases for the workers concerned. However, this is not what the numbers tell us: on the contrary, real hourly wage gains have been weak on average since the official recovery, after adjusting for inflation, meaning that the bargaining power of workers relative to employers has not improved significantly.

Conclusion

The dynamism of the US labor market is essential to the very working of the US variety of capitalism. Based mainly on market forces and meritocracy, and lightly regulated, it is however strongly supported by active macroeconomic policies. There is also significant intervention by the US federal government and states, which as the editors underline in the introductory chapter, is often hidden or not fully recognized. This feature contrasts with traditional representations of laissez-faire in the US economy.

The Great Recession contributed to accelerating the erosion of some core labor market institutions (unionism and collective bargaining, along with minimum wage). By doing so, the Janus face of the very flexible US market in terms of inequality and poverty has accentuated, with a return to levels reminiscent of the "roaring twenties." The Great Recession also had a deep impact on economic and labor market performances as we have seen, exacerbating long-term labor market trends like the decline in the labor force participation rate or the polarization of the labor market, while possibly breaking core US cultural or social values, notably work as a moral duty.

The trends studied in this chapter raise also fundamental questions on whether the decline in labor market dynamism is cyclical or has taken a more structural pattern affecting the very essence and capacity or ability of the US employment model to regenerate and renew with vibrant job creation. Because over the long-term, these labor market trends are likely to undermine the growth rate of GDP, alongside the slowdown in the pace of innovation.

At the same time, the massive federal government and Federal Reserve Bank involvement in the economy to try to dampen the impact of the Great Recession in the United States stressed once again the tiny relationship between American capitalism and its political and economic institutions. The very active role of the Fed during and after the recession, the extreme attention paid by the Federal Chairwoman, J. Yellen, to the evolution of labor market indicators in deciding whether interest rates should be kept near zero or raised are the expression of this intricate state–market nexus that characterizes the American variety of capitalism.

Finally, the Great Recession has illustrated the transformative power of crises. It has done so in two opposite directions. It has been on the one hand an opportunity for an unprecedented political offensive of private employers and Republican governors aiming at dismantling collective bargaining outcomes, whereas at the federal level, the Employee Free Choice Act aimed at easing union certification and collective agreement has not been passed. On the other hand, it has given impetus to a new form of social mobilization, Occupy Wall Street (OWS), a movement against the excess of financial capitalism tackling very sensitive issues of inequality and economic justice. Even if OWS did not last long, it had a major impact on public consciousness. It sounded as a warning, and in this regard the fight for a $15 minimum wage by workers of the fast-food industry all over the country today can be seen as a derivative outcome of OWS, and as a tolerance limit to inequalities and labor market polarization.

Notes

1 The Troubled Asset Relief Program (TARP) was signed into law by President G.W. Bush in 2008, allowing the US government to bailout big financial and industrial firms on the brink of bankruptcy. The American Recovery and Reinvestment Act (ARRA) was signed into law by his successor, President B. Obama, in 2009. It aimed at stimulating demand and at sustaining employment through major public investments.

2 Courts in some states have either limited the employer's ability to set contract terms unilaterally (Michigan, California, South Carolina) or laws have been enacted in other states that provided for just cause employment (Montana, Arizona) (see Dannin, 2007).

3 These are public sector workers, supervisors, agriculture workers, domestic workers, nurses, etc.

4 Its two principal functions are administering union representation elections through secret ballot, investigating and prosecuting unfair labor charges. The election procedure is quite lengthy and clearly favors employers: between the moment of the petition, when at least 30 percent of workers of a bargaining unit have to say their wish to be represented by a union and the holding of the election, when the union has to collect 50 percent of positive votes, anti-union campaigns can be (and are) run by employers with the help of anti-union consultants. The number of held elections declined 60 percent over 1997–2009, and those won by unions declined 48 percent (US BLS, 2010). Even if the union wins the exclusive representation of workers in a bargaining unit, there is sometimes a long time before the union can bargain collectively on a contract. The last organization campaign led by UAW at a VW factory in Tennessee is symptomatic of strong opposition to unions. It failed because instead of remaining neutral during the election period, the firm used a consultant to drive an anti-UAW campaign in local media, coupled with a flood of anti-union adverts that poured in from outside the state, see *Labor Notes*, October 28, 2013.

5 An RTW state enables workers belonging to an organized bargaining unit to opt out of paying union dues, thus reducing union power and union financial resources.

6 The Board, by statute, has five members who serve five-year terms. Their appointments are made by the president, but have to be confirmed by Congress. Until the 1970s, these nominations aimed at preserving a political balance between Democrats

and Republicans, whatever the party of the president and the balance of power in Congress. This neutral composition of the board started to be reversed under the presidency of R. Reagan during the 1980s and beyond. From 2008 to 2010, the Board had to act with only two members (one Republican and one Democrat) instead of five, because Congress, the Senate more particularly, made continuous partisan obstructionism to presidential nominations, using the filibuster to block nominees. In 2010, the Supreme Court ruled than the NLRB does not have the authority to act without a quorum of three members. As a result, the enforcement of hundreds of decisions concerning workplace disputes has been stopped and delayed. In November 2013, the US Senate voted to ban the use of the filibuster to block presidential nominees from being confirmed.

7 In 2009, US labor unions again tried to push legislation that would have legalized the card check process, recognizing a union through a majority of workers' signature of affiliation card. The Senate rejected the union-sponsored bill, called "Employee Free Choice Act," as it has been always the case from its start in 2003.

8 See "Courts Blocks Labor Board on Law Suits," *New York Times*, December 3, 2013.

9 Equal Pay Act, Civil Rights Act, Age Discrimination in Employment Act, ERISA, Occupational Safety and Health Act, Family Medical Leave Act, among others.

10 Agricultural workers, most of them black at that time, government workers who would be integrated later (1974), independent contractors, domestic service workers and tipped employees (Vinel, 2004).

11 In Ohio, voters succeeded in overturning the law.

12 There would have been an estimated 50 percent increase of new workers to the global supply of labor since the integration of large, emerging economies into the world economy (Ahearn, 2012).

13 The reasons for this divergence are well documented. Farber (2005) provides four kinds of explanations, related to different employment and competitive dynamics, and also to some differences in the role of unions and in the incentives employers are facing.

14 From Employment, Hours and Earnings from the CES Survey, Bureau of Labor Statistics (data seasonally adjusted, extracted on March 31, 2015).

15 Until the late 1970s, the pattern bargaining tradition was in broad use. In leading industries, the representative union targeted one firm to start negotiations and ended up with an agreement, which was mimicked by other firms of the industry.

16 More than 20 assembly and part facilities were closed and GM and Chrysler were divided between various stakeholders, included the US and Canadian governments and UAW.

17 What was at stake was achieving labor cost alignment with the non-union transplants.

18 As already said, a number of workers were excluded from eligibility by the FLSA. During the 1960s–1970s, some exemptions were eliminated but not all, and states had already covered a number of them under their own state laws. In 2013, the department of labor issued final regulations, effective January 2015, that apply the federal minimum wage and overtime protections of the FLSA to most home-care workers.

19 More than half the states are in this situation today.

20 However, a growing body of research documents a broad and worsening violation trend of the minimum wage in the United States; see NELP, "Winning Wage Justice," July 2013.

21 There is no or very little academic consensus on the adverse impacts of minimum wage on employment. The question of minimum wage effects remains certainly one of the oldest and most widely studied and debated among US labor economists (see, *inter alia*, Card & Krueger, 1995; Neumark & Washer, 2006; Dube *et al.*, 2010; Dube, 2013; Meer & West, 2013; Neumark *et al.*, 2013).

22 A Democratic legislative proposal, the Harkin–Miller Bill, was introduced in the US Senate in 2013 (S. 460).

23 www.ncsl.org/research/labor-and-employment/state-minimum-wage-chart.aspx.

24 The strike movement started in New York City in November 2012. In late July 2013, thousands of fast-food employees went on strike in seven US cities, demanding $15 an hour, which is more than twice the current federal minimum wage of $7.25.

25 See DeNavas-Walt *et al.* (2013, Table A2).

26 See the CBO's 2011"Trends in the Distribution of Household Income Between 1979 and 2007."

27 See "More and More People Express Uncertainty in Chance to Achieve the American Dream," *Washington Post*, September 29, 2013.

28 Total household debt peaked at 85 percent of GDP in the third quarter of 2008 and is down to 67 percent in the fourth quarter of 2014, according to Federal Reserve Bank of New York data. Mortgage debt continues to represent the bulk of it (69 percent), followed far behind by student loans (10 percent).

29 The unionized workforce has changed dramatically during the last three decades, being much less male-dominated than it used to be in the early 1980s (Schmitt & Warner, 2009).

30 Extended benefits are normally funded equally by the state and the federal government in all but exceptional recessions. During the Great Recession, the American Recovery and Reinvestment Act of 2009 provided for 100 percent of the financing for extended benefits paid in 2009 and the first few months of 2010, added 13–20 extra weeks under the permanent extended benefit program, depending on economic conditions in each state. States must choose whether to participate in the program or not.

31 The EUC program, entirely federally funded, was first authorized in 2008. It has been extended repeatedly until the end of 2013. It offers four tiers of benefits. The first two tiers are available in all states (34 additional weeks), while the second two tiers are only available in states with high unemployment (up to 19 additional weeks). The program provided for as many as 53 weeks of benefits for a total of 99 weeks when added to 26 weeks of regular benefits and 20 weeks of extended benefits.

32 Employers' costs concerning layoffs have been modulated by states. Thus, imperfect experience rating in most state UI systems created an implicit subsidy for employers.

33 Permanent layoffs as a share of unemployment reached 54.7 percent at their peak (November 2009), as opposed to 10.1 percent for temporary layoffs; see BLS, Table A-8, The Employment Situation, December 2009.

34 See Mueller & al. (2013) and Coibon & al. (2013).

35 Based on low interest rates and "quantitative easing."

36 The CPS has been redesigned since 1994 and a rise of non-response has been observed by Krueger *et al.* (2014), amplifying the technical bias inherent to the multiple-interviews-based survey.

37 The official US unemployment rate was 7.7 percent in October 2013, while the effective (or alternative) unemployment rate that counts part-time workers and those who have stopped looking for work was around 20 percent.

38 This ratio fell to 66 percent in 2011 from 74.1 percent in 2000, according to BLS data.

39 Women, for example, could be taking more responsibility for family care and household work.

40 Named after a British economist, William Beveridge, this curve relates the job openings rate to the unemployment rate, maintaining historically a negative relationship between the two metrics (see Barnichon *et al.*, 2012; Leduc & Liu, 2013; Diamond & Sahin, 2014).

41 Most workers who permanently lost their jobs through layoffs that involve outsourcing had been employed by manufacturers. By contrast, the magnitude of job losses from services offshoring appears to be relatively small in the aggregate, although concentrated in a few industries and occupations (CRS, 2012).

42 See Sauviat (2012b) and "Wages Stagnate as U.S. Manufacturers Reap Record Profits," *Bloomberg*, November 21, 2013.

43 See *Goldman Sachs Economics Analysts*, Issue 13/49, December 6, 2013.

Bibliography

Aaronson, S., Cajner, T., Fallick, B., Galbis-Reig, F., Smith, C. & Wascher, W. (2014, September). Labor force participation: Recent developments and future prospects. FEDS Working paper. Federal Reserve Bank of Cleveland.

Ahearn, R. (2012, February 27). Globalization, worker insecurity, and policy approaches. Congressional Research Service, February 27.

Associated Press. (2013, December 3). Courts Blocks Labor Board on Law Suits.

Autor, D. & Duggan, M. (2006). The growth in the social security disability rolls: A fiscal crisis unfolding. *Journal of Economic Perspectives*, *20*(3).

Baicker, K., Goldin, C. & Katz, L. (1997, January). A distinctive system: Origins and impact of US employment compensation. NBER Working Paper No. 5889.

Barnichon, R., Elsby, M. & Hobijin, B. (2012, June). Which industries are shifting the Beveridge curve? *Monthly Labor Review*.

Basu, D. & Foley, D. (2011). Dynamics of output and employment in the U.S. economy. University of Massachusetts, Economics Department Working Paper Series, paper 111.

Becker, J. (1973). *Experience rating in unemployment insurance: An experiment in competitive socialism*. Baltimore, MD: Johns Hopkins University Press.

Befort, S. (2002). Labor Rand Employment Law at the millennium: A historical review and critical assessment. *Boston College Law Review*, *43*(2).

Bengali, L. & Daly, M. (2013, March 4). U.S. economic mobility: the dream and the data? *FRBSF Economic Letter*.

Bengali, L., Daly, M. & Valetta, R. (2013, May 13). Will labor force participation bounce back. *FRBSF Economic Letter*.

Bureau of Labor Statistics, US Department of Labor. (2010a, January 8). The employment situation – December 2009.

Bureau of Labor Statistics, US Department of Labor. (2010b, July 9). Employee union representation elections – 1997–2009.

Bureau of Labor Statistics, US Department of Labor (2013a, January 23). Union members – 2012.

Bureau of Labor Statistics, US Department of Labor. (2013b, October 24). Jobs openings and labor turnover survey highlights – August 2013.

Bureau of Labor Statistics, US Department of Labor. (2014a, August 1). The employment situation – July 2014.

Bureau of Labor Statistics, US Department of Labor (2014b, August 1). Employment, hours and earnings – CES survey.

Burtless, G. (2009, September 15). Unemployment insurance for the Great Recession. *Testimony before the U.S. Senate Committee on Finance*.

Cappelli, P. (2014, August). Skill gaps, skill shortages and skill mismatches: Evidence for the US. NBER Working Paper No. 20382.

Card, D. & Krueger, A. (1995). *Myth and measurement: The new economics of the minimum wage*. Princeton, NJ: Princeton University Press.

Catts, T., Robison, P. & Kolet, I. (2013, November 21). Wages stagnate as US manufacturers reap record profits. *Business Bloomberg*.

CBO (Congressional Budget Office). (2011, October). Trends in the distribution of household income between 1979 and 2007.

Coibon, O., Gorodnichenko, Y. & Kostas, D. (2013, October). Amerisclerosis? The puzzle of rising U.S. unemployment persistence. NBER Working Paper No. 19600.

Daly, M.C., Fernald, J., Jordà, O. & Nechio, F. (2014, April 21). Interpreting deviations from Okun's Law. *FRBSF Economic Letter*.

Dannin, E. (2007). Why at-will employment is bad for employers and just cause is good for them? *Labor Law Journal*, *58*(5).

DeNavas-Walt, C., Proctor, B. & Smith, J. (2013, September). *Income, Poverty and Health Insurance Coverage in the United States*. Washington, DC: US Census Bureau.

Diamond, P. & Sahin, A. (2014, August). Shifts in the Beveridge. Federal Reserve Bank of New York Staff Report no. 687.

Dube, A. (2013, October). Minimum wages and aggregate job growth: Causal effect or statistical artifact. IZA Discussion Paper no. 7674.

Dube, A., Lester, W. & Reis, M. (2010). Minimum wage effects across state borders: Estimates using contiguous counties. *Review of Economics and Statistics*, *92*(4).

Farber, H. (2005, September). Union membership in the United States: The divergence between the public and private sectors. Working paper no. 503, Princeton University.

Franck, R. (2007, May 16). Falling behind: How rising income inequality harms the middle class. *Testimony before the House Financial Services Committee*.

Freeman, R.B. (2013, October). Failing the test? The flexible U.S. job market in the Great Recession. NBER Working Paper No. 19587.

Gordon, R. (2014, February). The demise of U.S. economic growth: Restatement, rebuttal, and reflections. NBER Working Paper No. 19895.

Heckscher, C. (1996). *The new unionism: Employee involvement in the changing corporation*. Ithaca, NY: Cornell University Press.

Katz, L.F. (2010, April 29). Long-term unemployment in the Great Recession. *Testimony before the Joint Economic Committee*.

Kirat, T. (2006). Les indicateurs de protection de l'emploi: la mesure du droit du travail en question? In Kirat, T. & Valentin J. (eds.), *La protection de l'emploi en question*. Economie et institutions.

Kopczuk, W., Saez, E. & Song, J. (2007, August). Uncovering the American Dream: Inequality and mobility in social security earnings data since 1937. NBER Working Paper No. 13345.

Krueger, A., Cramer, J. & Cho, D. (2014, March 10). Are the long-term unemployed on the margins of the labor market? Brookings Panel on Economic Activity, Final Conference Draft.

Lazonick, W. (2009). *Sustainable prosperity in the new economy? Business organization and high-tech employment in the United States*. Kalamazoo, MI: UpJohn Institute.

Lazonick, W. & O'Sullivan, M. (2000). Maximizing shareholder value: A new ideology of corporate governance. *Economy and Society*, *29*(1).

Leduc, S. & Liu, Z. (2013, July 22). Uncertainty and the slow labor market recovery. *FRBSF Economic Letter*.

Meer, J. & West, J. (2013, July). Effects of the minimum wage on employment dynamics. NBER Working Paper No. 19262.

Mishel, L., Bivens, J., Gould, E. & Shierholz, H. (2012). *The state of working America*, 12th edition. Ithaca, NY: Cornell University Press.

Moffit, R. (2012, November). The U.S. employment–population reversal in the 2000s: Facts and explanations. NBER Working Paper No. 18520.

Morello, C., Craighill, P.M. & and Clement, S. (2013, September 29). More and more people express uncertainty in chance to achieve the American Dream. *Washington Post.*

Mueller, A., Rothstein, J. & Von Wachter, T. (2013, September). Unemployment insurance and disability insurance during the Great Recession. Retrieved from http://gsppi.berkeley.edu/faculty/jrothstein/jesse-rothstein#wp.

Muhl, C. (2001, January). The employment-at-will doctrine: Three major exceptions. *Monthly Labor Review.*

Muhl, C. (2002, January). What is an employee? The answer depends on the federal law. *Monthly Labor Review.*

Mulligan, C. (2011, December). The expanding social safety net. NBER Working Paper No. 16654.

NCSL (National Conference of State Legislature). (2014). *State minimum wages.* Retrieved from www.ncsl.org/research/labor-and-employment/state-minimum-wage-chart.aspx.

NELP (National Employment Law Project). (2013, July). Winning wage justice. National Employment Law Project

Neumark, D. & Wascher, W. (2006, November). Minimum wage and employment: A review of evidence from the minimum wage research. NBER Working Paper No. 12663.

Neumark, D., Ian Salas, J.M. & Wascher, W. (2013, revised May). Revisiting the minimum-wage-employment debate: Throwing out the baby with the bathwater? NBER Working Paper No. 18681.

Obama, B. (2013, December 4). Remarks by the president on economic mobility, Washington, DC. Retrieved from www.whitehouse.gov/the-press-office/2013/12/04/remarks-president-economic-mobility.

OECD. (2013). *Employment Outlook 2013.* Paris: OECD Publishing.

OECD. (2014). *Employment and Skills Strategies in the United States.* Paris: OECD Publishing.

Oyer P. & Schaeffer S. (2000, summer). Layoffs and litigation. *Rand Journal of Economics, 31*(2).

Picketty, T. & Saez, E. (2003, February). Income inequality in the United States, 1913–1998. *Quarterly Journal of Economics, 118*(1).

Rothstein, J. (2012, March). The labor market four years into the crisis: Assessing structural explanations. NBER Working Paper No. 17966.

Sauviat, C. (2008, January). Restructurations et renouvelles des conventions collectives chez les trois grands de l'automobile: un véritable tournant. *Chronique internationale de l'Ires, 110.*

Sauviat, C. (2010). The U.S. unemployment benefit system: A degree of minimal protection, for "insiders" only. In Lefresne, F. (ed.), *Unemployment benefit systems in Europe and North America: Reforms and crisis.* Brussels: IRES/ETUI, ETUI.

Sauviat, C. (2012a, January). Renouvellement des conventions collectives chez General Motors, Ford et Chrysler: l'emploi contre les salaires. *Chronique internationale de l'Ires, 134.*

Sauviat, C. (2012b). L'emploi contre les salaires depuis les années 1980. *Revue de l'Ires,* no. spécial: 30 ans de salaire d'une crise à l'autre.

Schmitt, J. (2007, November). The good, the bad and the ugly: Job quality in the United States over the three most recent business cycles. Center for Economic and Policy Research.

Schmitt, J. & Jones, J. (2012, July). Where have all the good jobs gone. Center for Economic and Policy Research.

Schmitt, J. & Warner, C. (2009, November). The changing face of U.S. labor. Center for Economic and Policy Research.

Skocpol, T. (1995). *Social policies in the United States: Future possibilities in historical perspectives*. Princeton, NJ: Princeton University Press.

Slaughter, J. (2013, October 28). Auto workers try a new angle at Volkswagen. *Labor Notes*.

St Antoine, T. (1993, January 22–23). Employment-at-will: Is the model act the answer? Paper Delivered to the Eighth Annual National Conference on Labor and Employment Law: Critical Issues for 1993, Tampa, Florida.

St Antoine, T. (1994, April 6). Statement of Theodore J. St. Antoine before the Commission on the Future of Worker–Management Relations. *US Department of Labor, Key Workplace Documents*. Cornell University.

US Congress Joint Economic Committee. (April, 2013). Long-term unemployment in the United States.

Vinel, J.-C. (2004). Les avatars de l'employé: Itinéraire social et politique d'une catégorie juridique, 1867–1974, Thèse, Université Lyon 2.

11 Occupy Wall Street

Anything more than a fly in the ointment?

Marie-Christine Pauwels

The widening gap in economic inequalities and the increasing concentration of wealth within American society came to national attention during the fall and winter of 2011, as an increasingly mesmerized public witnessed the spreading protest of the *Occupy Wall Street* (OWS) movement, marveled or sniggered at its particular form of participative democracy and cheered at the vibrancy of its simple, alluring slogan – the 99 percent vs. the 1 percent.[1] While there is no disputing the disruptive potential of OWS and the number of small victories it was able to score, we may wonder in hindsight what were the real chances for the movement to bring about any kind of long-term substantial change, or to significantly alter the current power structure. This chapter posits that one of the main obstacles preventing this from happening was not so much the loose organization model favored by the protesters or their reluctance to morph from street action to a more structured activism, but rather the fact that they may ultimately have misjudged their target. Although it did challenge the status quo on a discursive level, as we shall see in a first part, the movement indeed may have fallen prey to the same shortsightedness of those theoreticians analyzing the sustainability of the US capitalist paradigm, who tend to "underplay the socio-political role of institutions in their interrelations with the market sphere and economic agents" (Introduction, this volume, p. 2) while also underestimating the potency of the cultural myths within which the American capitalist model is deeply embedded.

Shifting the conversation about inequality

Early on, in October 2011, the movement had an undeniable momentum. It scored several victories, among which was a $25 billion agreement settled between 49 state attorneys general and five large banks to help the victims of abusive foreclosures.[2] The following month, on November 5, dubbed "bank transfer day," 650,000 Americans chose to close their bank accounts and move their money to credit unions.[3] In December, Mario Cuomo, governor of New York state, endorsed the "millionaires' tax" on individuals earning over $200,000 per year, in a reversal of his previous position. In April 2012, following resolutions in Hawaii and New Mexico, Vermont called for an amendment to end corporate personhood, which holds that corporations have a First Amendment right to free speech (a move which was part of the fight to turn around the 2010 *Citizens United* ruling concerning campaign financing). The bill was an exact replica of a House bill introduced in November 2011 by Representative Ted Deutch (D-Fla), called "Outlawing Corporate Cash Undermining the Public Interest in our Elections and Democracy." Colloquially referred to as the OCCUPIED Amendment, it is the first piece of federal legislation to take its name from the OWS movement, thus acknowledging its influence in political circles. As the winter months drove their outside encampments indoors, OWS movements all over the country kept busy working on all sorts of projects, fighting against foreclosures, pushing for financial and electoral reform, demanding corporate accountability, etc. Without being as dismissive as the *New York Post* columnist who wrote in November 2011 that "the sum total of what *Occupy Wall Street* has accomplished is zero," and "inspiring chat around the national water-cooler is not an achievement" (Smith, 2011), it is true that these victories were rather small.

On another level altogether, other analysts contended that this narrow focus missed the point, that the most important achievement of OWS was in fact of a discursive nature, and that it had at last succeeded in shifting the national conversation about inequality by denouncing the economic and political disenfranchisement of many middle- and lower-class Americans. With a simple, easy catchphrase ("we are the 99 percent") which, as Paul Krugman said (2011), is a great slogan because it defines the issue as the middle class versus the elite as opposed to the middle class versus the poor, OWS put class back into the equation, forcing the media and politicians to speak out on economic justice, rising income inequality, jobs and unemployment, instead of falling back on their usual formulation of the crisis in terms of debt and deficits. Wealth and income inequalities are not this "necessary evil" that everyone tolerates more benignly in the United States than in Europe because the American social compact is built on a "rags-to-riches"/upward mobility mythology. Instead, protesters claimed, they are evidence that the current unregulated free-market economy, left to its own device and hijacked as it is today by the financial elites, will inevitably widen the gap and shortchange most citizens.

For several months, the message had traction. Mainstream media like *Time Magazine* devoted its cover to the topic in November, asking, "Can you Still Move Up in America?" The myriad problems of poverty, debt – especially student debt – unemployment, declining wages, etc. were spelled out in terms that struck a chord with many Americans. Isabel Sawhill (2011), from the Brookings Institution, sums up this shift in perspective:

> But what's emerging in the wake of all this bad economic news, I think, is the idea that America is no longer an opportunity society. As someone who has studied poverty, inequality, and social mobility for many years, I have always been fascinated by the apparent tolerance in the United States for a huge gap between rich and poor. Survey data from a few years ago show

> that this tolerance has been due to the American public's strong belief that you can be poor today but rich tomorrow, that your children will do better than you, and that anyone who works hard and has a certain amount of talent can make it in America. These attitudes have contrasted sharply with those in Europe, where the public has been much less optimistic about the role of individual effort and more willing to turn to government to help the less fortunate.

OWS undeniably shifted the conversation about inequality and raised the level of visibility about the rigidity of the American class structure. In January 2012, a Pew survey showed that about two-thirds of Americans now saw "strong conflicts" between rich and poor in the United States.[4]

But raising doubts about the validity of one of the leading American founding myths – that of America as a land of opportunities where anyone can make it if they play by the rules – is one thing. Identifying the real nature of the obstacles to social mobility and to wealth concentration in order to bring about meaningful change is another. At some point, both a clear vision and a clear strategy were needed. And on this score, OWS clearly missed the mark, even if, for a while, its alliance with organized labor seemed to reenergize unions and give a new impetus to the entire progressive movement.

A shot in the arm for the Left

Even if OWS claimed it was not a partisan movement and refused to avail itself of either the Left or the Right, its message clearly resonated with the Left, which until then had been more skillful at promoting social causes like legalizing same-sex marriage and protecting the environment than demanding millions of new jobs that pay a living wage. The radical Left in particular, bogged down over the past 30 years in a sterile debate pitting capitalism against socialism/communism, and trying ever since to justify and legitimate its very existence, saw the opportunity to recenter its focus on class issues while undertaking an in-depth self-examination as to its inability to make itself heard in the public debate. How and why it was sidelined for so long, how it lost its soul, or in the words of Jodi Dean (2012, p. 7), how it went "from the new Left to the no Left to the left behind."

For labor also, OWS was seen as a shot in the arm. Labor organizers across the country admitted that Occupiers could take risks that unions were unable or unwilling to, yet could indirectly benefit from. Robert Master, Northeast political director for the Communications Workers of America (over 500,000 telecommunications workers), acknowledged this influence:

> In three months, this movement succeeded in shifting political discourse more than labor had been able to accomplish with years of lobbying and electoral campaigns. I think there are going to be tremendous opportunities for labor and the Occupy movement to work together. We have different

> roles – as labor we are much more embedded in mainstream politics. But we understand that without the pressure of more radical direct-action tactics, the debate in this country won't change substantially.
>
> (Eckholm, 2012)

For a labor movement that some consider to be on life support today (with an 11.1 percent national unionization rate for 2014 according to the Department of Labor), this mobilization was unhoped for. Several alliances were formed during the movement's occupation of Zuccotti Park: in October, Mary Kay Henry, president of the Service Employees International Union (SEIU), declared her solidarity with the protesters while the Communications Workers of America gave OWS walkie-talkies, air mattresses and meeting rooms. Conversely, protesters joined the teamsters in their attacks on art auction house Sotheby's, which had locked out 43 teamster art handlers on July 29, after the union balked at its demands for sizable concessions.[5]

Both the slogans and the organizational tactics of OWS inspired unions, which started to consider alternatives to traditional picketing. Labor leaders, inspired by the Occupy protests, talked of mobilizing the rank and file to organize large, boisterous marches. The very simplicity of Occupy's message was also seen as something to learn from: in November 2011, the AFL-CIO sent out a memo recommending that unions use the Occupy message about inequality and the 99 percent slogan far more in their communications with members, employers and voters. This recommendation was followed in the battle between Verizon and the Communications Workers' union: picket signs accused Verizon and its highly paid chief executive of being part of the 1 percent, while the Verizon workers were presented as the 99 percent.

Expectedly, there were also some tensions, as Occupy tended to disrupt unions' usual modus operandi. The December 2011 West Coast port shutdowns organized by Occupy thus caused friction with leaders of the International Longshore and Warehouse Union, who opposed the blockade attempts. Yet, when the Occupy movement started organizing flying pickets to aid the ILWU in confronting agribusiness giant EGT, which was trying to freeze out the union workforce at the Port of Longview in Washington State, the corporation relented and struck a deal with the union.

At the time, then, new hopes were raised. It seemed that combining the radical voices of OWS and the mainstream tactics of organized labor might be able to challenge the power structure or at least change the terms of the debate on American capitalism by bringing back the notion of class with a new meaning, spelled out in simple, alluring terms (the 1 percent versus the 99 percent).

Can American capitalism really be challenged?

Street action and encampments can last only so long. As most of the country's attention was shifting to the electoral campaign in 2012, OWS's message started to lose momentum, in spite of all the sound advice of advocates like Frances Fox

Piven, who urged protesters to find ways to "spread the movement. Thinking of second, third, fourth, fifth phases. Other forms of disruptive protest that are punchier than occupying a square" (as cited in Engler, 2011).

During the winter months, OWS was gradually marginalized. The media lost interest, no clear course of action or leadership emerged out of the many subgroups that made up the movement, and its core message on rising inequalities was both diluted and reappropriated by popular culture, business and the political elite. As most camps had been dismantled by the end of 2011, the movement lost its novelty for the mainstream media and was no longer deemed headline material. A quick search on the Lexis-Nexis database shows that for the four leading papers (*New York Times*, *Washington Post*, *USA Today* and *LA Times*), mentions of "Occupy Wall Street" or "Occupy movement" dropped in early 2012, as well as mentions of "income inequality" and, to an even greater extent, "corporate greed." News programs on the major networks (ABC, CBS, NBC), cable (MSNBC, CNN, Fox News) and NPR all followed the same trend. The movement was gradually sidelined and OWS protesters were increasingly pictured as troublemakers, with confrontation stories taking the lead. During the Chicago NATO summit in May, coverage of OWS was restricted to the security measures taken by Rahm Emmanuel in anticipation of unrest:[6] the huge expenditures for police surveillance, the large fines for minor crimes, the time limits required for demonstrations, the advance registration of any objects to be carried, the size of signs, the amount of fines (between $200 and $1,000 and/or ten days behind bars) in case of violations, etc. The media were also quick to point out that both city governments of Tampa, Florida (where the Republican convention was to be held at the end of August) and Charlotte, North Carolina (which would host the Democratic Convention in early September) had stepped up their police protection. And the Department of Homeland Security kept a close watch on the movement.

One of the many pitfalls that awaited the movement was the alienation of the public. Almost all of the Occupy protesters remained committed to a non-violent form of protest even when faced with police brutality. Even so, given that public opinion eventually grows weary of disruptions to the social order, regardless of who initiated them, initial benevolence gave way to suspicion and annoyance. In January 2012, a majority of Americans were reportedly considering the movement as a public nuisance (Rasmussen Reports, 2012), and in April, an NBC News/*Wall Street Journal* poll found that 51 percent of respondents believed the movement had run its course.

The second type of marginalization the movement had to face was political. OWS prided itself on having no political structure/organization, no single cause, no central authority, no single ideology, no unified set of demands, and a horizontal structure which set it apart from the vertically organized political parties. It claimed to support neither candidate to the presidency, and apart from Elisabeth Warren, the front-runner for the Democratic nomination for the 2012 Senate election in Massachusetts, no political figure had OWS's favor. Which was probably just as well for Barack Obama anyway, who sensed trouble ahead if voters connected him too closely to the pessimistic "we're going after the rich and the top 1 percent" message, and only paid lip service to OWS in case it might compromise his candidacy.

Although the movement's grievances did focus on the corruption of the political elites, the unfair tax system, etc., its tactics were to stay out of institutional-electoral politics, a posture which failed to take into account the importance of the franchise at the root of the American democracy. Americans indeed firmly believe that legitimate change should occur through the ballot box. As Frances Fox Piven aptly remarked in her seminal work on Poor People's Movements (1979, p. xi), "obviously, protest movements are discredited in the dominant pluralistic tradition on the ground that there is ample opportunity for the working class to pursue its interests through democratic institutional channels." Hence the difficulty for an apolitical movement like OWS to wield influence in an election year such as 2012. But, of course, another point to take into consideration is the fact that the movement was not monolithic and made up instead of both radical and reformist factions which did not necessarily see eye to eye about the origins of the problems and the best solutions to implement. This made it all the harder for a unified leadership to emerge. As Judith Stein made very clear in October 2011, this "open source" positioning was bound to weaken its message over the long term:

> OWS operates less on politics than society. Participants have little faith in politics because they say the whole system is corrupt. Although they promise future demands, they spend their time attempting to create alternatives—democratic forums, alternative financial institutions, and so on. These kinds of endeavors have a long history in the United States—from the creation of utopian communities in the nineteenth century to the formation of communes in the 1960s and 1970s. But their track record as a vehicle for change is poor.... In short, political theater can capture the imagination at a time when politics seem bankrupt, but it cannot solve political problems or short-circuit political organizing.

This reluctance to enter the political arena for fear of being co-opted, and of "selling out," and to adopt instead the "I'd prefer not to" stance reminiscent of Melville's Bartleby's, was not only bound to be short-lived; it was also short-sighted, as Jodi Dean (2012, p. 4) painfully came to realize:

> A real problem is identifying the enemy, that is, what the movement opposes: is it capitalism or the state? Do we have a corrupt political system but a basically solid economic model? Or is the problem with the neoliberal model of capitalism, which has let inequality soar and banks and corporations exert undue influence in government? Or is it capitalism itself, encountering its limits—declining rate of profit, growing immiseration and proletarianization, impossibility of continued capital accumulation?

No clear answers were offered, but it seems that OWS somewhat misdiagnosed the sources of the problem, since it mostly directed its grievances at Big Business and Wall Street, and downplayed the responsibility of the state, which is also largely to blame for the rising inequalities (Hacker and Pierson, 2010). The dismantling of the welfare state, the financial deregulation policies undertaken since the Reagan years, a tax system geared toward the wealthy, and the widespread collusion between politicians and corporate elites took a back seat to the vilifying of big banks that were "too big to fail" and of corporations, guilty of "placing profit over people, self-interest over justice, and oppression over equality" (NYC General Assembly, 2011). Barack Obama clearly disappointed protesters, for example, yet he was not pictured as a villain. It was easier to illustrate the abuses of the system by conjuring up the image of the immoral stock exchange broker taking home obscene bonuses than by focusing on politicians like Robert Rubin, former director of Citigroup and former Treasury secretary under Bill Clinton, or Larry Summers, Ben Bernanke and Timothy Geithner, who all argued against increased regulation of financial markets and meanwhile played pivotal roles in the first Obama Administration. One of the main weaknesses of the movement, therefore, was to underplay the power of the state–market nexus, and to direct its anger at only one of these two forces. A phenomenon of "state denial" well analyzed by Australian professor Linda Weiss, who believes that in the face of increased globalization and economic integration, state capabilities will matter more rather than less in fostering social wellbeing and the creation of wealth (Weiss, 1998).

The final demise of OWS came in the form of cultural cooptation and political reappropriation, as the fate of counterculture movements is often to feed consumer culture (Heath & Potter, 2004), capitalism setting off its "reappropriation loops" to defuse and absorb protest movements (Boltanski & Chiapello, 1999). In yet another vivid illustration of how the advertising and marketing industry draws its inspiration from rebellious movements – recalling Thomas Frank's 1998 analysis of the reappropriation of the youthful 1960s rebellion in *The Conquest of Cool* – OWS slogans and idiosyncrasies were reincorporated into a form of "hip consumerism" (Frank, 1998). The first brand that took advantage of the protest movement was rap artist Jay-Z's Rocawear clothing company, which started selling "Occupy All Streets" T-shirts priced at $22 – without planning to transfer any of the profits to OWS; Miley Cyrus, a young teenage idol, followed suit and released her "Liberty Walk" clip with footage from Occupy movements around the globe. Swiss watchmaker Swatch then jumped on the bandwagon, releasing a green "Occupy" watch, with the word "occupy" written in bright orange on the wristband. The movement was then incorporated into popular sitcoms like *30 Rock* and *The Office*, and countless parodies sprouted in popular culture, from "Occupy Sesame Street" to an episode of *South Park* called "the 1%."

Even those who were vilified by OWS for their collusion with the financial elite got their own back with a vengeance: companies like *Interactive Brokers*, an online brokerage firm, released a commercial in March 2012 mocking the Occupy movement with colorful puppets jumping up and down outside Wall Street and brandishing posters that advertised "much lower commissions" and

"Join the 1 percent." The phrase "1 percent" was gradually diverted from its initial meaning and became a fixture of popular folklore, describing anything from recent lottery winners to consumers of expensive new gadgets. Reduced to being a simple buzzword, it ceased to have any connection to the way American capitalism produces and reproduces economic and social inequality.

Political reappropriation also took place as the Republicans completely turned around OWS's claims and used them to their advantage to get their own message across in the presidential race. Initially fearing in 2011 that the protest movement was moving public opinion, Republican pollster and communication strategist Frank Luntz told Republican governors during their annual conference in November 2011: "I'm so scared of this anti-Wall Street effort. I'm frightened to death. The OWS movement is having an impact on what the American people think of capitalism." He advised his audience to steer away from the word "capitalism," telling them to speak instead of "free-market economy" or "economic freedom." He thus adroitly moved the debate back into familiar territory by suggesting they hammer at one of the most potent founding myths of US democracy, since "freedom" and "free markets" are two of the definitions which undergird the American model of capitalism and not class struggles (Republican Governors' Conference, November 2011). Republicans soon learned to capitalize on the "protest" bandwagon and tap into today's protest culture in their efforts to "occupy" the White House: on December 28 Mitt Romney released a web video in which sullen-looking people were shown carrying cardboard placards with slogans typical of the "We are the 99 percent movement" (e.g., "nearly 25 million Americans are Unemployed, Underemployed, or Stopped Looking for Work"; "34 Straight Months of Unemployment Above 8%"; Romney, 2011). The anti-capitalist discourse was neutralized, reappropriated and framed as a short-term consequence of the recession and Obama's policies. Clearly, OWS was seen as a fly in the ointment, but not as a real threat.

Finally, the movement also had to deal with accusations of representativeness and legitimacy from a racial perspective, and charges that it was not really representative of the 99 percent. For if it did challenge the discourse on class, it failed to link class and race, another idiosyncratic puzzle of the US political economy. There were indeed few people of color who openly supported the movement, and little minority endorsement. Several prominent African-Americans such as Cornel West, Russell Simmons, Kanye West and Rep. John Lewis (D-Ga) did make appearances at OWS protests, but the main movement was over 80 percent white. According to a Fast Company survey (November 2011), blacks made up only 1.6 percent. Many blacks stayed out of the movement, not very optimistic that it would in any way help them, a position well summed up by Leslie Wilson, a professor of African-American history at Montclair State University (as cited in Patton, 2011), who wrote in the *Washington Post* in November:

> Occupy Wall Street cannot produce enough change to encourage certain types of black participation.... The church cannot get enough blacks out on the streets. Some students will go, but not the masses. Black folks, particularly

> older ones, do not think that this is going to lead to change.... This generation has already been beaten down and is hurting. They are not willing to risk what little they have for change. Those who are wealthier are not willing to risk and lose.

The author of the article, Stacey Patton (2011), adds:

> Why should they ally with whites who are just now experiencing the hardships that blacks have known for generations? Perhaps white Americans are now paying the psychic price for not answering the basic questions that blacks have long raised about income inequality.

She notes the sharp difference with past movements: in 1969, James Forman, former executive secretary of the Student Nonviolent Coordinating Committee (SNCC), a civil rights organization, called on blacks not to perpetuate capitalism or contribute to the exploitation of blacks in the United States and elsewhere. He urged black workers to take over America by sabotaging US factories and ports "while the brothers fight guerrilla warfare in the streets." And Huey Newton and the Black Panther Party denounced the American Dream as defective and called for the destruction of the capitalist system. Nothing of the kind was seen this time around, as OWS was committed to non-violence, even if there were radical voices inside the movement. By and large, OWS was not a mob trying to overthrow capitalism per se. A faulty redistributive system and cronyism were what protesters denounced, but they also highlighted the need to restore basic capitalist principles like accountability, even if no clear strategy as to how to reach such goals emerged.

Conclusion

The positive legacy of OWS is to have initiated a novel conversation about the basic structure of the US economic system. Yet the civilizational focus mentioned in the introductory chapter to this book helps us understand the limits of a protest movement that is profoundly embedded in American society and culture and the hidden resistance force of existing models. We have seen both how the growing interconnectedness of the state–market nexus was underestimated by the protesters and how personal qualities such as self-reliance and individual responsibility were reactivated by those who wish to discredit protest movements that try to define crises in terms of class warfare. This sacrosanct idea of freedom can also be found in the political structure and the indomitable belief in the virtuousness of the electoral-representative model, another feature which OWS failed to recognize. To disconnect it from these fundamentals and present it otherwise would be a misperception.

Predictably, even if an increasing number of Americans believe class conflict has escalated in the United States, most still believe in the fairness of the American capitalist model. A December 2011 Pew survey on public perceptions of capitalism vs. socialism showed how little those perceptions have changed over time, 50 percent saying they still have a positive view of the term "capitalism" (vs. 40 percent who have a negative view). Those figures are largely unchanged from a 52 percent to 37 percent balance of opinion in a similar survey taken in 2010. Likewise for "socialism": in 2011, figures of 60 percent negative/31 percent positive were the same as 2010. Again, these figures show how much riches and power are ascribed to personal qualities of industry or talent in the United States, and that those who have little or nothing only get what they deserve.

More importantly, perhaps, public opinion is clearly ambivalent in its responses about how to change the system. While an increasing majority (77 percent) say they think there is too much power in the hands of a few rich people and large corporations (up from 60 percent in 1941), about as many still think that the rich got rich "mainly because of their own hard work, ambition or education" (43 percent) as "because they know the right people or were born into wealthy families" (46 percent). These findings are largely unchanged from a similar Pew survey in 2008. What this means is that even though half of Americans admit they live in a class society, the other half stills clings to the "land of opportunity" narrative.

While there has been a significant shift in public perceptions of class conflict in American life, this does not necessarily signal an increase in grievances toward the wealthy. Nor do the data suggest growing support for government measures to reduce income inequality. In other words, without going as far as saying that anti-systemic movements are bound to fail in the United States because of these powerful cultural/ideological forces, OWS's dispiriting message had few chances of lasting long in a nation which has always prided itself on being optimistic and forward-looking, and is defined by a liberal capitalist model so deeply anchored in individual responsibility and personal freedom. On the other hand, to look at it from a more positive perspective, we may recall once again the analyses made by social movement theorist Frances Fox Piven (1979, 2012) and say that the legacy of OWS will perhaps reside in the establishment of multiple beachheads, the infiltration of multiple issues and the political linking of multiple sites. The outcome of disruptive movements is often not felt right away, but momentum builds over the long term, underground, once the phase of drama and disturbance subsides.

I will leave the last word to Todd Gitlin (2012, p. 220):

> Theorists have been proclaiming this the age of late capitalism for decades, but if it is indeed late, it keeps getting later. Capital continues to find new ways to grow, creative destruction and all. We are not witnessing the global *Götterdämmerung* of the political elites or their institutions. They persist if for no other reason than that no new world is yet emergent within the shell of the old.

This lack of alternative is what many on the Left such as Leo Panitch *et al.* (2013) have regretfully come to acknowledge. Although capitalism is in economic crisis, as witnessed by the eruption of movements like OWS and other similar protests across the globe, in the United States at least, it remains politically secure for the time being.

Notes

1 The Congressional Budget Office (CBO) reported that from 1979 to 2007, the highest income 1 percent of the population saw after-tax household income grow 277 percent, while for the 60 percent of the population in the middle, incomes grew less than 40 percent (CBO, 2011, p. ix).
2 Which only paid a meager $2,000 apiece in reality.
3 Although the push for the bank transfer movement began with Kristen Christian, a young art gallery owner from Los Angeles who created a Facebook page urging her fellow citizens to move their money out of banks, Occupy Wall Street protesters became some of the most visible supporters of Bank Transfer Day.
4 Research on Lexis/Nexis shows that between October 2010 and September 2011, the number of articles with the term "greed" fluctuates between 452 and 728 a month. But for the single month of October 2011, when Occupy Wall Street was in full swing, 2,285 articles mention the term.
5 www.teamster.org/content/teamsters-occupy-wall-street-protest-sothebys-auction.
6 These actions remind one of former mayor Richard Daley in 1968, who militarized the city and "colluded" with agents provocateurs to help consolidate public opinion against the anti-war movement.

References

Boltanski, L. & Chiapello, E. (1999). *Le nouvel esprit du capitalisme*. Paris: Gallimard.

Congressional Budget Office. (October 2011). Trends in the distribution of household income between 1979 and 2007. Retrieved from www.cbo.gov/ftpdocs/124xx/doc12485/10-25-HouseholdIncome.pdf.

Cyrus, M. (2012, January 23). *Liberty walk* [Video file]. Retrieved from www.youtube.com/watch?v=EcTKcr67uLw.

Dean, J. (2012, January 13). The meaning of Occupy Wall Street for the Left. Talk delivered at the James Connolly Forum, Troy, New York. Retrieved from: http://jdean-icite.typepad.com/i_cite/2012/01/occupy-wall-street-and-the-left.html.

Eckholm, E. (2012, February 11). Occupy Movement regroups, preparing for its next phase. *New York Times*.

Engler, M. (2011, October 21). The future of the Occupy Movement: Solidarity and escalation. *Dissent*. Retrieved from www.dissentmagazine.org/blog/the-future-of-the-occupy-movement-solidarity-and-escalation.

Fastcompany. (2011, November 2). *Infographic: Who is Occupy Wall Street?* Retrieved from www.fastcompany.com/1792056/infographi-who-occupy-wall-street.

Frank, T. (1998). *The conquest of cool: Business culture, counterculture, and the rise of hip consumerism*. Chicago, IL: University of Chicago Press.

Gitlin, T. (2012). *Occupy nation: The roots, the spirit and the promise of Occupy Wall Street*. New York: IT Books.

Hacker, J.S. & Pierson, P. (2010). *Winner-take-all-politics: How Washington made the rich richer and turned its back on the middle class*. New York: Simon & Schuster.

Heath, J. & Potter, A. (2004). *Nation of rebels: Why counterculture became consumer culture*. New York: HarperBusiness.

Interactive Brokers. (2012, March 14). *Join the 1%* [Video file]. Retrieved from www.youtube.com/watch?v=ChKIecFPL8A&feature=player_embedded.

Krugman, P. (2011, November 24). We are the 99.9%. *New York Times*. Retrieved from www.nytimes.com/2011/11/25/opinion/we-are-the-99-9.html.

Luntz, F. (2011, November). Republican governors conference. Retrieved from http://news.yahoo.com/blogs/ticket/republicans-being-taught-talk-occupy-wall-street-133707949.html.

NBC News/Wall Street Journal. (2012, April 13–17). Study #12336. Retrieved from http://pos.org/documents/wsjapril2012.pdf.

NYC General Assembly Declaration. (2011, September 29). Declaration of the occupation of New York City. Retrieved from www.nycga.net/resources/documents/declaration.

Panitch, L., Albo, G. & Chibber, V. (2013). The question of strategy. *The Socialist Register*, *49*.

Patton, S. (2011, November 16) Why African Americans aren't embracing Occupy Wall Street. *Washington Post*. Retrieved from www.washingtonpost.com/opinions/why-blacks-arent-embracing-occupy-wall-street/2011/11/16/gIQAwc3FwN_story_1.html.

Pew Research Center. (2011, December 15). Frustration with Congress could hurt Republican incumbents. Retrieved from www.people-press.org/files/legacy-pdf/12-15-11%20Congress%20and%20Economy%20release.pdf.

Pew Research Center. (2012, January 11). Rising share of Americans see conflict between rich and poor. Retrieved from www.pewsocialtrends.org/2012/01/11/rising-share-of-Americans-see-conflict-between-rich-and-poor.

Piven, F.F. & Cloward, R. (1979). *Poor people's movements: Why they succeed, how they fail*. New York: Vintage Books.

Piven, F.F. (2012, September 17). Occupy's protest is not over: It has barely begun. *Guardian*. Retrieved from www.guardian.co.uk.

Rasmussen Reports (2012, January 5). 51% see Occupy Wall Street protesters as public nuisance. Retrieved from www.rasmussenreports.com/public_content/politics/general_politics/january_2012/51_see_occupy_wall_street_protesters_as_public_nuisance.

Romney, M. (2011, December 28). *Davenport, four years earlier* [Video file]. Retrieved from www.youtube.com/watch?v=yiILEtKsz8o.

Sawhill, I. (2011, October 20). OWS and the demise of the American dream. Brookings Institution. Retrieved from www.brookings.edu/research/opinions/2011/10/21-ows-American-dream-sawhill.

Smith, K. (2011, November 20). With friends like these.... *New York Post*. Retrieved from www.nypost.com/p/news/opinion/opedcolumnists/with_friends_like_these_MpQ1qfIQgX0iOcoRnpJlCL.

Stein, J. (2011, October 12). OWS: A sign of our times. *Dissent*. Retrieved from www.dissentmagazine.org/blog/ows-a-sign-of-our-times.

Time Magazine (2011, November 14). Can you still move up in America?

Weiss, L. (1998). *The myth of the powerless state: Governing the economy of a global era*. Oxford: Polity Press.

12 The Giving Pledge

Philanthropy and the reinvention of American capitalism

Laurence Cossu-Beaumont

As early as October 2008, in the immediate aftermath of the credit crunch, *The Economist* provocatively expressed concerns regarding the health and viability of the Anglo-Saxon model of capitalism when it ran a printed issue about "Saving the system." Repeatedly columnists suggested a "fatigue" of the American brand of capitalism and claimed "the Anglo-Saxon model ha[d] taken a knock" (*The Economist*, 2009). The paper later contended that the grievances of the Occupy Wall Street movement were "legitimate and broader than previous rages against the machine" (*The Economist*, 2011). In the chorus of outcries about the shortcomings of capitalism and denunciations of the inequalities it had failed to breach, also emerged the even less anticipated voices of capitalists themselves. Indeed, Warren Buffett, who was incidentally the wealthiest billionaire on *Forbes*' list for 2008,[1] the crisis peak year, soon argued that, in the wake of the recession and efforts toward recovery, more sacrifices should be demanded from "the super rich," or as he had it, "my super rich friends."

> While the poor and middle class fight for us in Afghanistan, and while most Americans struggle to make ends meet, we mega-rich continue to get our extraordinary tax breaks.... [Last year] what I paid was only 17.4 percent of my taxable income – and that's actually a lower percentage than was paid by any of the other 20 people in our office. Their tax burdens ranged from 33 percent to 41 percent and averaged 36 percent.
>
> (Buffett, 2011)

Interestingly, as protesters marched on Wall Street and Zucotti Park, the wealthy of America remained vocal and "occupied", for their part, the public discourse. While Buffett was instrumental in denouncing the unfair nature of the American capitalist model and its role in the unraveling of the crisis, Bill Gates also contributed to this conversation. His take on the debate was not a call for congressional action and increased taxation, but a suggestion that philanthropy was an appropriate means to counter capitalism's failures (Ben-Ami, 2013). Buffett and Gates may both be viewed as the very embodiments of the financial and entrepreneurial aspects of American capitalism; they are figures easily identifiable for the general public. What's more, they have built corporate empires before stepping down, at least for Gates, to focus on their charitable foundations.[2]

In May 2009, Gates and Buffett discreetly launched *The Giving Pledge*, a philanthropic initiative inviting a dozen American billionaires to commit to donating at least half of their wealth. The givingpledge.org was officially launched in August 2010 with the 40 first participants (Strom, 2010; *The Giving Pledge*, 2010). High-profile figures like New York then-mayor Michael Bloomberg or Hollywood director George Lucas have since joined the group, which grew to about 80 participants within two years (*The Giving Pledge*, 2012) and to almost 130 by May 2014 (*The Giving Pledge*, 2014). Pledgers range from traditional dynasties such as the Rockefellers to new and media-friendly tycoons such as Facebook's Mark Zuckerberg or shareholder activist Carl Icahn. Most pledgers, however, are less high-profile, and their commitment, though not legally binding, is publicly stated in a pledge online. While philanthropy is nothing new in the context of American capitalism and its excesses, as the nineteenth-century Robber Barons and philanthropists exemplified, this chapter offers a discussion of twenty-first-century philanthropy in the aftermath of the Great Recession and questions the opening of a new era (Zunz, 2012, p. 298).

How do the choice of "going public" and the discourse of the wealthy inform us on the health of American capitalism, on the severity of the crisis of the model and on the possibilities for its renewal? As other contributions to this volume, this chapter starts from the hypothesis offered in the introduction: a civilizational approach may be apt to consider if/how the impact of the Great Recession reached beyond the subprime crisis, the local foreclosures and the global downturn to challenge a flawed American model of capitalism. To address the task set in the introduction and speculate on whether the Great Recession fostered significant shifts in the capitalist model – or at least in its ideological underpinnings – this chapter examines a specifically American approach to the excesses of capitalism and the redistribution of wealth through individual initiative: philanthropy. The latter is now understood as the practical "donation of money to good causes" though its etymology goes back to a more religious dimension (namely the "love of God for humanity") that may be of interest in the discussion (OED).

The privileged object under scrutiny, *The Giving Pledge*, may be defined by two tenets: "going public" and "going global." In other words, the philanthropic initiative is rooted in communication and publicity as its main strategy and endeavors to attain levels of charitable investment never reached before. As such, it offers ground for reflection on its contribution to the criticism and renewal of a capitalist model that needs correction, as acknowledged by the most successful financiers, entrepreneurs and capitalists. The billionaires' unprecedented commitment first interrogates the erosion of the American capitalist experience, from gateway to individual success and national economic strength to liability for both American households and entrepreneurs, as well as for the nation's world status, its financial sustainability and its broader ideological legitimacy. The billionaires' public commitment then offers a platform for a reflection on the resilience or failure of the model – in other words a critical discourse stemming from the inside, rather than from outside agents such as government or civil society. The chapter's aim is not to survey the figures and channels of American philanthropy.[3] The discussion will rather be rooted in the "civilizational" approach suggested in the introduction by examining the recent discourse of American capitalist-philanthropists through the editors' proposed *focale* ("a cultural prism that spotlights specific ideological representations while obscuring other ideational elements to make sense of the past, the present and the future of American capitalism" – see the introduction to this volume). This focus on the current discourse of philanthropy with regards to the tradition and culture and in connection with the Great Recession may allow one to both re-embed the American brand of capitalism in its essential historical and cultural *milieu* and favor a dynamic vision of American capitalism.

After a more thorough presentation of *The Giving Pledge* through its online discourse and press releases, this chapter will go on to explore the question of the US economic and ideological paradigm through this new flagship of American philanthropy by first raising the likelihood that the success of *The Giving Pledge* may evidence a watershed brought about by the Great Recession and acknowledged by successful capitalists themselves. Namely, that American capitalism has evidenced a need for redeeming and redressing – and perhaps reforming? This question will be examined through the discourse of individual pledgers who donate and invest but also yearly discuss best practices in charity, public policies ("partnering with government to maximize impact") and social entrepreneurship (*The Giving Pledge*, 2014). The chapter will then turn to the fact that this new age of philanthropy led and endorsed by IT entrepreneurs and social network magnates, as well as its venturing outside American borders, may seem to entail a renewal if not reinvention of the American philanthropic tradition whose embeddedness in the American capitalist model may now have to be redefined.

The Giving Pledge: philanthropists go public

The Giving Pledge is considered to have been launched in May 2009 by Bill and Melinda Gates, along with Warren Buffett, all well-known long-term philanthropists who personally contacted fellow billionaires and set out to convince the wealthiest Americans to "pledge at least 50% of their net worth to charity during their lifetimes or at death" (Loomis, 2010). The initiative first remained strictly confidential, although the first dinner held in New York City in May 2009 and hosted by David Rockefeller was leaked to the press by one of the guests. As a result, the following dinners and meetings were held with even greater discretion and any released information is now strictly controlled. Loomis' 2010 *Fortune* article is one of the few published with authorized quotes from the Gateses and from Buffett, and only so because of Loomis' personal ties with the latter. The secrecy and coopted-only rule contrasts with the transparency advocated through the online pledges. Potential "great givers" – in Buffett's words – at the first dinner counted 14 guests and included New York's historical dynasty – the

Rockefellers – and Wall Street figures such as Pete Peterson, Julian Robertson and George Soros. Rockefeller, Peterson and Robertson joined *The Giving Pledge* within a few weeks. Other notable guests were Mayor Bloomberg and media tycoons Oprah Winfrey and Ted Turner; both Bloomberg and Turner became pledgers. Two prominent philanthropist couples had flown in from California, the Broads – from insurance company SunAmerica – and the Morgridges – John Morgridge was the former chairman of CISCO. Both couples joined the Pledge soon after.

Since 2009, *The Giving Pledge* has grown into a group of 127 signatories (May 2014 press release) whose make-up offers an interesting panel of the pillars of the American economy. More Wall Street financiers and hedge fund founders followed Buffett's lead. More traditional business sectors are present, such as retail (Home Depot's Arthur Blank, or Chuck Feeney who founded Duty Free Shoppers) or real estate (Tad Taub). America's innovative entrepreneurs are also well represented: Microsoft's co-founder Paul G. Allen, Oracle founder and CEO Larry Ellison, AOL's Steve Case; the next generation of high-tech prodigies is also represented with Mark Zuckerberg and his Facebook co-founder Dustin Moskovitz, and most recently Paypal's Elon Musk.

Interestingly, most of the guests of this first dinner and early pledgers were known philanthropists already, with foundations of their own. The task set, then, was not to recruit new givers or to raise money for a specific cause but seemingly to gather forces for increased visibility and efficiency. The only actual deed of *The Giving Pledge* takes the form of a sober website where each pledge is published and of discreet annual encounters where ideas and methods are shared and debated. The early pledgers of 2009 – Rockefeller, Peterson, Robertson, Bloomberg, Turner, the Broads and Morgridges – joined by merely publishing their individual pledges on the *Giving Pledge* website. The actual giving of their wealth was already well under way through their own personal initiatives and foundations. Still, the network, the powers added of the members, and the media and social capital are behind-the-scene assets of undeniable importance.

In that respect, philanthropists accepted to go public about their commitment to charity in the same way companies that open to public investment to gain in capital and scope also become accountable and commit to transparency and communication.[4] The endeavor thus borrowed from corporate common sense and practices, as well as the ancient Greek tradition,[5] but also departed from the traditional form of American philanthropy, supposedly fostered by individual choice and conducted privately. In August 2010, Larry Ellison, founder of Oracle, specialized in business software, and one of the world's richest men (*Forbes*, 2015) joined *The Giving Pledge*. The full content of his online pledge is reproduced here:

> To whom it may concern,
> Many years ago, I put virtually all of my assets into a trust with the intent of giving away at least 95% of my wealth to charitable causes. I have already given hundreds of millions of dollars to medical research and education, and

> I will give billions more over time. Until now, I have done this giving quietly – because I have long believed that charitable giving is a personal and private matter. So why am I going public now? Warren Buffett personally asked me to write this letter because he said I would be "setting an example" and "influencing others" to give. I hope he's right.
>
> (Larry Ellison)

Ellison summarizes here the specificity of the Gates/Buffett philanthropic initiative as one of communication and visibility insofar as he, Ellison, like many early pledgers, was already a committed philanthropist. The fact that Ellison's pledge is brief and only about "going public" reflects the novelty of *The Giving Pledge* that thus appears to be about discourse as much as charity. Other participants confirm this definition by reminding that their commitment to give away most of the wealth had been decided and implemented before *The Giving Pledge* even existed and that their joining the group is meant to stimulate other wealthy donors. Paul G. Allen from Microsoft mostly insists on the "worthy challenge to make our giving plans public" (Allen, 2010); others state their decision, not to donate but to join, was triggered by the will "to inspire others to give" (Dubin, 2012) or "encourage others to do the same" (Forstmann, n.d.). Ted Forstmann, who made his fortune in private equity and passed away in 2011, further provides evidence that philanthropy may have taken a new turn for the very reason that it is going public as never before. While Carl Icahn admits that he "never considered going public about [his] intentions" (Icahn, n.d.), Forstmann's claim exemplifies the traditional approach to charity: "I've always believed that you don't really talk about giving" (Forstmann, n.d.). This novelty, a break from a heretofore individual and private practice, is where a civilizational focus may enrich our understanding of American capitalism, by focusing on discourse and on this "rare insight into the workings of and motivations behind American philanthropy" (Acs, 2013, p. 126). Indeed, though single figures such as Carnegie or Rockefeller were known for their realizations and legacies, rarely did philanthropists formally voice their motives and intentions and form a united community of dozens conversing about those motives.[6] This is what the online pledges provide in the form of "stories."

When it comes to the defining moment of *The Giving Pledge*, Loomis' privileged access to Buffett and thus unique account of the "first supper" offers an interesting insight. Indeed the 2009 symbolical launching of *The Giving Pledge* at the Rockefeller-hosted dinner actually consisted of the guests sharing "stories" (Loomis, 2010). These "riveting" stories are those ultimately presented by the participants in their online pledges. In congruence with the editors' endeavor to understand the cultural substrate and dynamics of American capitalism in the aftermath of the Great Recession, the pledges offer a reading of capitalism's flaws and merits by an array of engaged, powerful and influential agents. The present methodology that consists of screening the state of capitalism through a culturally defined lens (an American discourse) borrows from Braudel's early injunction that the economy is aptly grasped through, not just ideology, but the wider *milieu* in which it is implanted, from which it stems and which he called *civilization* (Braudel, 1982, 1995). *The Giving Pledge*, because it publishes story after story of capitalists who ponder on their road to success, makes up an interesting *history* of American capitalists. But as French historians have shown, discourse plays an important role in the writing and making of history (Ricoeur, 1985; Veyne, 1971). Likewise, *The Giving Pledge* plays a performative function in the American capitalist ecosystem insofar as they portray a positive vision of America's capitalism and realize a re-writing, in the crisis, of America's past values and themes of success. French historian Jacques Le Goff pointed to the interest of the "mentalities" or collective and shared mindset represented in such objects as customs, rites and images, also calling for an "embedded" approach of individual discourse or production, not to be detached from their cultural framework. An epoch's (artistic or discursive) representations are more than the reflection of the time's concerns and ideals, they are as many active productions of what culture is. While Le Goff's (2006) object was medieval society, his success in accounting for how both the elite's and the laymen's viewpoints shaped society serves this chapter's purpose well. The pledges may indeed be considered as representative of a certain American "mentality," both in their contemporary writing and in the way they publicly address, pursue or renew the past tradition of capitalists and philanthropists, to actively create a legacy of their own.[7]

At first glance, the "going public" appears as the defining character of the new philanthropic initiative, a "concept … intriguing" for some (Cooperman & Cooperman, 2010). Ellison felt he had to react to the Gateses' insistence at making "an explicit commitment" (Gates & Gates, 2009): "I have long believed that charitable giving is a personal and private matter" (Ellison, 2010). Such "marketing" strategy may seem to open a new era in modern America's philanthropy; in the past rich donors remained discreet about their "intentions and the thinking that lies behind them" (Buffett, 2009). This new need for publicity could appear as a response to the rising discontent about American capitalism in the aftermath of the Great Recession. However, the collection of online pledges, available on *The Giving Pledge.org*'s front page,[8] make up a highly visible American narrative whose pieces are remarkably consistent and timeless. In this sense, they seem to rejoin the most deeply rooted beliefs of the American "mentality." Quite a few pledges refer to the American Dream and just as many to the "opportunities" made available to all in the United States. Glenn Dubin, for instance, reflects upon his "personal attempt to perpetuate the American dream." The investment fund manager goes on to write that he "started [his] career with nothing but opportunity" (Dubin, 2012). The occurrences of "American Dream" and America's "opportunities" are numerous enough in the hundred or so pledges[9] to create a pattern in the collective discourse offered. Even a British pledger, Lord Ashcroft, businessman and Conservative Party official, marvels at "the most appealing traits of American life" and calls himself a self-made man (Ashcroft, 2013).

Capitalists here re-validate the sense and meaning of American capitalism as the path to success through their individual stories that are stunningly similar. Each individual pledge both addresses the moment and refers to the values and paradigm of the American nation-building – from work ethics to organized benevolence, from rags-to-riches story to social utility. Collectively the pledges forcefully reaffirm that, in spite of the crisis and the need for correction that their very action and public statement point to, they are acting within the frame of American capitalism that offers failures, but successes as well, and fundamentally shapes American society. Interestingly, through the discourse displayed on givingpledge.org, American civilization does not come across as solely capitalist, similarly to what was hinted at in the introduction to this book: "we depart from the claim that 'economic capitalism' defines American civilization as its sole 'driving force'" (Braudel, 1995). The pledges interestingly remind of the historical, societal and cultural forces at play in American capitalism beyond irrational practices and faulty ethics. The "thinking that lies behind" the pledgers' intentions (Buffett, 2009) is mostly a contemporary re-writing of the American Dream narrative, beyond economic considerations. So while the success of *The Giving Pledge* first seems to mostly raise the question of the collective responsibility of "the super rich," it actually does so while celebrating America through individual success stories.

Giving back: the American narrative

The civilizational approach developed in this chapter may borrow here from historian Pierre Nora's (1997) *lieux de mémoire*. Nora's demonstration of how space can help define a nation's identity – through institutions, museums and monuments, but also more abstract locations and symbolic repositories of collective memory – serves here to suggest that *The Giving Pledge*'s materiality, in the form of discourse deposited online, makes it an effective *lieu de mémoire*. Givingpledge.org is about expressing and transmitting a community's vision of its own identity. The donating and actual charity is achieved elsewhere, in the respective foundations of the signatories while on givingpledge.org capitalist entrepreneurs and financiers define themselves as holders of a national experience, as transmitters of values and ethics that have made, not just their individual success, but the exceptional destiny of their nation. They have, in their lifetimes, actualized the national American Dream, and now decide, for posterity, to join a community whose legacy aims at bringing about change while perpetuating the great American narrative. Indeed the self-made man narrative informs many of the pledge letters. It does so in a twofold way: by rooting philanthropy in the middle-class experience of success or in the immigrant's success story. What's more, as a correlate to the individual rise to the top is the "moral" responsibility that comes with it, also a recurring theme of the pledges, which then may be seen as forming a "Gospel of Wealth in the 21st Century" (Acs, 2013, p. 126).

The self-made man narrative

The earlier pledges reflect a consistent will to inscribe the unprecedented philanthropic initiative in perennial tradition rather than in the urgency of the present.

Both Toby and Leo Cooperman – former CEO of Goldman Sachs – on the one hand, and John and Tashia Morgridge, on the other hand, joined in 2010.

> The fact that Toby and I are even candidates to make the pledge is a testimony to the American Dream. Let me explain.
>
> I am the son of a plumber who practiced his trade in the South Bronx. I am the first generation American born in my family as well as the first to get a college degree. My education is largely public school based – public grade school, high school and college all in the Bronx. I had a short stint at the Columbia University Graduate School of Business where I earned an MBA and this opened the door for me to Goldman Sachs. I joined the Firm the day after graduation as I had a National Defense Education Act Student Loan to repay, had no money in the bank, and a six-month-old child to support.
>
> (Leon and Toby Cooperman)

> In 1955 we graduated from the University of Wisconsin-Madison, got married and headed west so John could attend the Stanford Graduate School of Business and Tashia could start her teaching career. All of our possessions fit into our 1950 Ford and all of our wealth fit into a back pants pocket. It was the start of a glorious adventure!
>
> (John and Tashia Morgridge)

These pledges are examples, if not of the rags-to-riches story the philanthropists of the nineteenth century could boast of, at least of the prevalence of the opportunities offered in America to the children of the middle-class. Cooperman and Morgridge, however, are children of the baby-boom generation, whose climbing of the social ladder was real and spectacular but may have come to an end (Stiglitz, 2012).[10] Still, the repetition, pledge after pledge, of the vast possibilities opened by the American educational, entrepreneurial and business environment reinforces the myth of an American Dream tied to the merits of free market, capitalism and democracy that the pledgers have come to embody and often reaffirm in their narratives.

> The free enterprise system and a domestic economy dependent on private investment and economic freedom provided an opportunity for me to live the American Dream. All Americans should have equal opportunity and the freedom … to create jobs and to contribute to the economic growth.
>
> (Joe Craft)

Also recurring in the pledges is the theme of immigration and success. Some of the early American pledgers are indeed immigrants themselves, such as Michele Chan and Patrick Soon-Shiong, a South African-born surgeon, researcher, founder of bio-tech firm and minority owner of the LA Lakers, or second-generation immigrants like John Paul Dejoria, the son of Italian/Greek immigrants who was raised by a single mother and is the co-owner of Paul Mitchell Hair Products. Along with George Mitchell, the son of Greek immigrants who came through Ellis Island, they narrate their individual achievements that also make the Great American Dream come true:

> America has been a land of opportunity for us, as it has for so many immigrants. We are proud to be Americans and we want to see our country strong and healthy. We are blessed to have resources and expertise to contribute.
>
> (Michele Chan and Patrick Soon-Shiong)

> Being a first generation American has many rewards. Among them is having the opportunity to succeed in this free country, and then succeeding enough to have the privilege of knowing that "success unshared is failure."
>
> (John Paul Dejoria)

> I was born in Galveston, Texas, to Greek immigrant parents and was a teenager during the Great Depression. Although I grew up in a very meager, yet loving, environment, I always considered myself fortunate to live in the United States where opportunities were unlimited.... As I've been blessed with good fortune for decades and have lived the American dream, I'm pleased to take the Giving Pledge.
>
> (George Mitchell)

These pledgers all speak in the same voice about the American experience, before turning to what is their main topic: philanthropy. The latter is thus defined here, not in connection with the contemporary situation of crisis, inequality, social mobility stalled or a capitalist model gone wild but with regards to an American identity and tradition. As such they offer a compelling perspective onto a recognizable aspect of American civilization, both in belief and discourse. *The Giving Pledge* unfolds as rooted into the American narrative. In this context, the philanthropic endeavor appears less as a correction of the acknowledged failures of capitalism than as a celebration of the merits of the American environment and an impulse to give back.

The gospel of wealth in the twenty-first century

The impulse to give back is not only connected to the American experience, but also to "moral obligations" in the words of Bill Gates (Loomis, 2010). The consideration of a moral duty cannot but evoke Carnegie's legacy. This has been suggested by Buffett himself, who has referred to the pledges as modern-day "Gospels of Wealth" and been echoed by observers of American philanthropy (*The Economist*, 2012; Acs, 2013). Pledgers formulate their sense of duty or responsibility to give back, some explicitly referring to their illustrious predecessors:

> We are deeply indebted to our community and our country for the many opportunities granted to us, and for a social and economic environment in which we could make the most of those opportunities. We consider it our responsibility to ensure the same opportunities for others.
>
> (Laura and John Arnold)

> I began my career on Wall Street nearly 50 years ago. From a modest upbringing in Queens, New York, I have been fortunate enough to accumulate great wealth. And with that wealth comes responsibility – those who have benefitted the most from our economic system have a responsibility to give back to society in a meaningful way … Rockefeller, Carnegie, Frick, Vanderbilt, Stanford, Duke – we remember them more for the long-term effects of their philanthropy than for the companies they founded, or for their descendants. And by giving, we inspire others to give of themselves, whether their money or their time.
>
> (Carl Icahn)

Carnegie's 1889 claim known as his "Gospel of Wealth" is indeed re-scripted and re-written in several compelling ways. This discursive practice is a process envisioned by the historians of "mentalities," a process whereby communities seize and redefine, in their modern era, the tenets of a national tradition – which thus finds itself both preserved and dynamically continued. First of all, Carnegie's nineteenth-century prescriptions to fellow wealthy Americans entailed a pragmatic obligation to live modestly and "to set an example of modest, unostentatious living"; then to refrain from indulging in the European patrimonial, aristocratic, ostentatious tradition and "provide moderately for the legitimate wants of those dependent upon him; after doing so to consider all surplus revenues which come to him simply as trust funds" to be passed on to the community (Carnegie, 1889). *The Giving Pledge* signatories also address the question of lifestyle and inheritance.

> This pledge will leave my lifestyle untouched and that of my children as well. They have already received significant sums for their personal use and will receive more in the future.
>
> (Warren Buffett)

> I got married three years ago for the first time at the age of 52 and Mei Sze and I have a one-year old son. While I intend to provide him a level of security, I would never consider leaving him the vast amount of wealth that I have been fortunate to accumulate. The bulk of my estate will go to our foundation.
>
> (Jeff Greene)

> Wealth is created. If that wealth is all passed on to another generation its benefits are often greatly underutilized as those who inherit the wealth view

> their mission as one of maintaining it. The better path is one that allows wealth to be activated as a force to make the world a better place through endless avenues.
>
> (Dan and Jennifer Gilbert)

> When you think about it, no other approach seems to make sense. Passing down fortunes from generation to generation can do irreparable harm. In addition, there is no way to spend a fortune. How many residences, automobiles, airplanes and other luxury items can one acquire and use?
>
> (Herb and Marion Sandler)

Here are four examples of what a few other pledgers tackle – that is to say the belief that families and heirs should be provided for but not with the whole wealth accumulated. The latter is indeed to be redistributed outside the family, as Carnegie instructed through his condemnation of the traditional bequest of whole estates to heirs. The initiators of *The Giving Pledge* abided by this theme central to their recruiting pitch to fellow billionaires. Indeed, it is reported Melinda Gates insisted the spouses should be invited to the enrolling dinners and made active pledgers as well because "it affect[ed] their kids" (Loomis, 2010). While the practices of twenty-first-century American philanthropy *The Giving Pledge* may epitomize seem to follow in Carnegie's footsteps, so do the underlying principles. The "moral obligation" to give back repeated through many pledges calls attention to the spiritual and religious origins of an American "gospel" of wealth. Carnegie's conviction was admittedly rooted in the "Protestant work ethics." Weber's writings have established the genealogy of American capitalism whose "spirit," as the title of his study phrased it, is embedded in this "Protestant ethic" (Weber, 2002). It has, in time, come to define a specifically American outlook on work, financial success and even national identity. While hard work, modesty and giving back may have, through the centuries, shed the spiritual and religious motives they originally inherited from Calvinist asceticism, the twenty-first-century pledges delineating the contours of the American capitalist experience at the same time as they do those of philanthropy still echo this traceable source.[11] They evidence, however, the diversity of the modern American experience.

The twenty-first-century Gospel of Wealth is no longer solely Protestant and, as American society, is made of different backgrounds and experiences, whose diversity is reflected in the pledges. Although a rare pledger refers to his Protestant upbringing and inspiration in the "Gospel of Jesus Christ" (Green, 2010), there is also room, in the new Gospel of Wealth, for a secular understanding:

> I am not a particularly religious person, and believe that my limited time on earth is all that I am going to get. And I have lived with that understanding, doing my best to extract as much out of life as I can.
>
> (Ackman and Ackman, 2012)

Other pledgers maintain their religious faith has been determining in their commitment to philanthropy. However, if Carnegie's Scottish roots used to symbolize the Anglo-Saxon origins of the early immigrants who built the nation, twenty-first-century philanthropists claim much more varied influences when it comes to religion. Catholic and Jewish pledgers, representing the history of the later waves of immigrants who successfully joined the American path to success, intend to formulate their own version of the Gospel of Wealth. Henry Samueli, founder of Broadcom, links *The Giving Pledge* to the *Tzedakkah*, the Jewish charitable tradition, which is considered a *Mitzva*, a moral duty. In that sense, the very same principles are maintained, including the religious imprint, but also altered to become open to diversity (Samueli & Samueli, 2011). Leon Cooperman articulates the connection in his pledge:

> Toby and I feel it is our moral imperative to give others the opportunity to pursue the American Dream by sharing our financial success. The case for philanthropy has been stated by others in a most articulate way and in words that have impressed me: In the early 1900s Andrew Carnegie said "He who dies rich, dies disgraced." [...] Well before all these gentlemen expressed their thoughts, it was written in the Talmud that "A man's net worth is measured not by what he earns but rather what he gives away."
>
> (Leon Cooperman)

In a similar way, Tom Monaghan, founder of Domino's Pizza, ties in his Catholic faith to the present impulse to charity:

> I came into the world penniless and as a Catholic Christian, I know that I cannot take any of it with me, so it has long been my desire to use the material resources that I have been blessed with to help others in the most meaningful ways possible. My faith has always been a central part of my life; not that I have always lived it perfectly, but it has been the consistent guiding force as far back as I can remember. My early experience of the Catholic faith, taught to me by the Felician sisters when I was in the orphanage during my formative years, served as a foundation for what I would believe to be the most important things in life. As I built and expanded Domino's Pizza for 38 years, my desire to spread the faith also grew.... Also, as a Catholic, I would not be living out my faith if I did not use the abundant resources God has given me to help others.

Giving back here becomes inspired by more than one faith when it comes to religion. The pledges thus reflect the making up, if not of American society, but of American billionaires, and thus offer diverse but coherent narratives of a collective American experience while re-writing a modern Gospel of Wealth. While pledgers mostly depart from Carnegie's Protestant inspiration, they may still be pointing at its resilience in the American psyche, yet another instance of what Sacvan Bercovitch (2011) called "the Puritan origins of the American self" –

that is to say the unique way New England Puritanism not only shaped a seventeenth-century emerging American identity, in the light shed by Weber for capitalism, but lingered in the rhetoric of modern America; this, Bercovitch argues, is perceptible in the contemporary American imagination, and we may add in the context of this chapter, in the collective memory and discourse about modern America as yet another way to understand *The Giving Pledge* as a *lieu de mémoire* in the making. For, once the Puritan foundation of the philanthropic endeavor has faded, as it is in the pledges under consideration, all that remains is the American myth of the self-made man succeeding and giving back; all the more so as the unprecedented philanthropic initiative is never justified by the severity of the crisis, nor echoes the surrounding criticism.[12] It is justified by a celebrated and renewed American model of capitalist opportunities and tradition of giving back.

Where *The Giving Pledge* departs the most from Carnegie's rationale and legacy is when it comes to the political implications of the philanthropic commitment. Twenty-first-century pledgers, though some of them are well-known for their political statements[13] and sometimes for their political ambitions,[14] mostly stay away from any political agenda. Carnegie defended the sustainability of capitalism in the context of his clear indictment of socialism. *The Giving Pledge* is careful to evidence no such ideological aim. Figures of philanthropy who are more clearly advocating political clout such as the Koch brothers or George Soros are not part of *The Giving Pledge*. Buffett visibly distances himself from the ideological core of Carnegie's vision that linked the wealthy's responsibility to "give back" to the "masses" as a way to keep social unrest at bay (*The Economist*, 2012).[15] And while the launching of *The Giving Pledge* in 2009 and 2010 coincides with the rising criticism that triggered the 2011 Occupy Wall Street Movement, there is no direct response to the charges against capitalism. The signatories' letters, however, indirectly counter the critical atmosphere with their discourse that is a pledge to capitalism, assert that capitalism is the best way and the right way to accumulate wealth and ultimately to redistribute it through philanthropy. They offer no alternative and represent another form of trickle-down process, the wealthy "giving back" to the community, money but also exemplary models of success. Ironically, Buffett's own pledge, in 2010, anticipates the OWS formula that opposed the 99 percent to the rich and powerful 1 percent. Buffett explains that his version of *The Giving Pledge* is to give virtually all of his wealth away, with the full agreement of his family:

> Were we to use more than 1% of my claim checks (Berkshire Hathaway stock certificates) on ourselves, neither our happiness nor our well-being would be enhanced. In contrast, that remaining 99% can have a huge effect on the health and welfare of others.
>
> (Warren Buffett)

Another equation opposing "the upper 1 percent of Americans [...] now taking in nearly a quarter of the nation's income every year" to "the other 99 percent" was the symbol of the OWS protest that was originally coined by Joseph Stiglitz in his 2011 article "Of the 1%, by the 1%, for the 1%," another instance of discursive *lieu de mémoire*, through which Stiglitz subverts Lincoln's celebration of the American (democratic) experience to denounce the flaws of twenty-first-century American political economy (Stiglitz, 2011). In a parallel only made possible retrospectively by the matching of these symbolic figures, Buffett plans to return 99 percent of his wealth to the 99 percent of Americans left out of the riches of capitalism.

The American grand narrative that the stories reproduce almost to a caricature in the various pledges describes philanthropy as an unprecedented social initiative in scope as in motive. Yet one should note how embedded in the American collective psyche this discourse is. Depicting America as a land of opportunity for all, the pledges constantly suggest a historical and moral continuity with the perennial quest of the nation, as they do with the tradition of American philanthropy as a quintessentially moral drive for social improvement. Still, American philanthropy viewed throughout history has been coined as intrinsically innovative (Zunz, 2012, p. 3). This very theme of innovation, that is not only at the heart of entrepreneurship but also of philanthropy, is prolonged, modernized and extended into a new concept and practice: philanthro-capitalism (Bishop & Green, 2010).

Giving with returns: philanthro-capitalism

A survey of the pledgers' profiles reveals that they mostly belong to a generation born before or shortly after World War II (GlassPockets.org). Business sector emergence and profitability also matter when it comes to giving. The high-tech, internet and software sector accounts for one-quarter, just about the same as the banking and investment sector. The other notable sectors are more traditional and include industrial manufacturing, mining and energy, entertainment, retail and finally real-estate (GlassPockets.org). Of course, the numerical discretion of the young innovators of the New Economy and the strong show of bankers, investors and financiers who were prominent in the "glorious financial" years raises the question of the way the philanthropic endeavor presents itself as an innovative response and also a relevant and socially responsible response to the Great Recession. While the health of the nation's economy is at stake, and its very model of prosperity or sustainability jeopardized by the lingering inequality, the irony is that a significant number of *The Giving Pledge* signatories have been or are still involved in the sector deemed responsible for a finance-driven economic crisis. The excesses of financial innovation, in the form of credit derivatives for instance, have fueled and unleashed criticism at the unethical and predatory practices of investment bankers and hedge funds managers. We may ponder on the paradoxical popularity of a philanthropic discourse that pervades the public space and celebrates the merits of a free-market system and its opportunities, while another public but critical discourse develops in the press and academia to denounce that the way many philanthropic icons have made their personal success

– notably financiers – is also a sign of a collective loss of measure and integrity that ultimately contributed to the crisis and threatens the nation's strength and wellbeing.

Generally speaking, free enterprise, market opportunity and the centrality of entrepreneurship are hailed in the pledges: "a domestic economy dependent on private investment and economic freedom provided an opportunity for me to live the American Dream" (Craft, 2012) or "We live in an amazing country – because of our capitalistic society and free enterprise system, I was able to work my way out of poverty" (Hamm & Hamm, n.d.). In that sense, capitalism's underlying principles and practices find themselves not criticized but upheld, as is an optimistic and enthusiastic vision of social mobility. While some pledgers do allude to the failings evidenced by the economic polarization of American society, these views remain marginal on the whole, as well as within the given pledge in which such nuance is expressed. If Arthur Blank, co-founder of The Home Depot, acknowledges that "the gap between rich and poor in America is growing," he goes on explaining that philanthropy "alone cannot repair all of the social injustice in our county or the world. It can, however, inspire good will, spark innovation and provide thought leadership" (Blank, 2012). In other words, philanthropists envision their charity endeavor along the same lines as their professional trajectories. Philanthropy is not meant to correct the failings of capitalism, but rather to borrow from its accomplishments: a constant innovative spirit, an unrelenting drive toward more efficiency, the highest returns on investment possible are the most frequently quoted means and ends that lead to successful philanthropic ventures. In his statement, Carl Icahn's personal perspective blurs the lines between business, on the one hand, and philanthropy, on the other. Philanthropy becomes a social business and a form of social enterprise that borrows its techniques from the for-profit sector:

> The principles that have guided my career in investing are the ones that I use in my approach to philanthropy. As a shareholder activist, I have focused on acquiring control of undervalued companies (which are often poorly managed). I believe I have unlocked substantial shareholder and bondholder value and have improved the competitiveness of American companies. In a similar vein, I want to maintain America's position as the world economic leader by improving the competitiveness of its educational system.
>
> (Carl Icahn)

Icahn suggests that both his competence as shareholder activist and his vision for philanthropy partake of the same passionate drive for competition, efficiency and value creation that explains and serves well American competitiveness. His success as a visionary investor is transferable to his philanthropic initiatives. The consistent discourse held by most pledgers on their capitalist environment and the business culture they thrived in offers ground for further discursive observation of the metaphors and words they use to qualify their quest. The pledges not only encapsulate the billionaires' inspiration to "give back," but also their firm intention to "give with returns." This is the third tenet that appears in the pledges read collectively: first comes the unprecedented move to "go public," then the legitimation of the personal inspiration to charity in connection with a very American celebration of success, and ultimately a firm commitment to efficiency. This may come in the form of detailed descriptions of the actions taken or of the pledger's foundation's guidelines:

> At the Foundation, we focus on areas where (1) philanthropic investments can lead to solutions that are self-sustaining in the long-term, (2) we can leverage a relatively small investment to create a large impact on total societal benefit and (3) the market does not presently yield optimal results, due to inefficiencies, lack of adequate information or other reasons. These guiding principles have led us to invest in a number of areas including education reform, health care, social services and social justice.
>
> (Laura and John Arnold)

The first two mission statements are most interesting since they point to the rational calculus that conditions a strategic, focused and efficient investment supposed to yield larger returns. The capitalists in *The Giving Pledge* thus intend to do more than speak out and give away. Their agency as powerful and efficient individuals is repeated through the letters. They insist through the letters on the importance of self-efficacy and personal success in businesses. Shrewd management may be the innovative spur they bring to philanthropy. The pledge letters provide examples of such a transfer of competence from business to charity, as exemplified by Seagram heir Charles Bronfman, that remind that risk-taking lies at the heart of business – and is probably at the heart of philanthropy too.

> We have never been "risk" averse. In fact, we've continuously experimented with "outside the box" programming. Our family of private operating foundations has played different roles in the lives of our grantees, not only financially but in terms of governance, evaluation, quality assurance and partnership.
>
> We have taken risk capital to initiate programs, then incubate them and, after indicating successful potential, sought partners in each. As that project learned to stand on its own feet, we lowered our financial input, and our guidance until each could be completely independent. There are roughly a dozen examples of this kind of successful initiative.
>
> (Charles R. Bronfman)

The "dozen examples" of innovative, experimental and successful initiatives recalled in one pledge serves as a springboard for creating a tightly knit discursive community, gathered around a common philanthropic and business experience and core values. The spirit of entrepreneurship seeks to accomplish more than a much needed relief in designated fields for charity, it strives to transform the practices of philanthropy – by borrowing the "lessons learned" from the corporate experience and by sharing individual experiences. This is also the advantage of a community in the making and the resulting social capital that is here shared. Some pledges even imitate the tone and methodology of an annual letter to shareholders:

> **We want to make as big an impact as possible**
> We are a spend-down foundation and therefore act with urgency to make significant contributions that have both an immediate and lasting impact.
>
> **We are focused on achieving results**
> One of our core competencies stems from our experience as CEOs of the second largest savings bank in the country. We understand the critical importance of due diligence, an important part of which is evaluating the management of potential grantees. We offer technical assistance, i.e., how to improve strategic and business plans; goals and objectives; budgets; etc.
>
> **We are willing to take risks**
> In essence, in many ways, we are venture capitalists. We are willing to take risks and make bold strategic investments in areas not adequately addressed by government, industry, universities or the non-profit sectors.
>
> (Herb and Marion Sandler 2010)

The Bronfman family (both brothers, Edgar and Charles, heirs to their father's company and philanthropic deeds, signed *The Giving Pledge*) does offer a long-term experience other pledgers, of more recent wealth, are looking for. The Sandlers are clear about their aims and means borrowed from their corporate and banking experience; they remain bankers and "venture capitalists" while acting as philanthropists; they are intent on creating lasting value and delivering the most efficient returns possible. Hence the importance of measuring out impact and developing "result-oriented giving" (Wylie, 2010). The most innovative dimension of *The Giving Pledge* lies in the forging of a community that will make a major quantitative and qualitative difference, the community being more than the sum total of its participants and donations. Sharing innovative management skills, social capital, bonds and ties transform individual philanthropy into a collective force and provide more potent and efficient tools to its members, making philanthropy bolder, more efficient and less isolated in its methods.

> I'm so appreciative to Bill and Melinda Gates and Warren Buffett for creating a forum of philanthropic thought leaders. Many of the pledgers are farther down the road on their journey of giving back, and I look forward to learning from, and collaborating with them.
>
> (Sarah Blakely)

> We also look forward to working with the dozens of others who have made the Giving Pledge commitment to share lessons, perspectives and best practices. We have learned a lot over the years both through our philanthropic successes and our failures, and believe that by working together and exchanging lessons learned, the impact of the backers of the Giving Pledge can be enhanced. Our individual commitments are significant, but the power of our collective commitments can be greater than the sum of the parts. That is why we are joining with Bill, Melinda, Warren, and so many others to make this public commitment.
>
> (Steve Case)

Many pledges echo this idea of an innovating forum or of an emerging leadership. AOL's Steve Case, just like Sarah Blakely (2000 founder of Spanx, a lingerie company), expresses his wish for dialogue and the exchange of "lessons learned" with experienced counterparts. This is the purpose of the only other public deed of *The Giving Pledge* – apart from a website: the annual meetings between signatories. Case reported that the 2012 meeting allowed unearthing the growing relevance of public–private partnership (*The Economist*, 2012). The discussions within the "forum" of innovative and leading thought *The Giving Pledge* seeks to be, though discreet and not made public, do point to a conversation between capitalism and philanthropy. In 2012, one of the most discussed topics that stemmed from the community gathered by Gates and Buffett was "impact investing." Impact investing focuses on "investments made into companies, organizations, and funds with the intention to generate measurable social and environmental impact alongside a financial return"; impact investing represents an interesting case in point where philanthropic endeavors and capitalistic practices are reconciled through the giving away of funds and the drive for business returns. Philanthropy is no longer about giving money away and making a difference by pouring significant funds into areas of choice. The philanthrocapitalists intend to be as successful in their charity endeavor as they are in their business career and they plan to use their collective expertise and the pioneering spirit induced by their yearly exchanges. Richard Branson has also indicated in his pledge that this is the worthy contribution of *The Giving Pledge*:

> We want the value created by the Virgin Group to be used to invest in new collaborative approaches to addressing issues, where business, governments and not-for-profits join forces to create a healthy, equitable and peaceful world for future generations to enjoy. We started by trying to give a voice to the young people of the 1960s and hope our "Giving pledge" will help many generations to come. We look forward to working with Bill Gates and Warren Buffett in expanding the number of people who are part of this pledge outside America. We are honoured to be joining this great group of leaders as part of a movement where all sectors are working together towards radical new approaches to solving issues that will help to truly change the world for the better.
>
> (Richard and Joan Branson)

The "radical new approaches" in the form of innovative partnerships "where business, governments and not-for-profits join forces" are echoed in one of the activities of the Bill and Melinda Gates Foundation: its 2011 report on "Innovation with Impact: Financing 21st Century Development." Innovation and new partnerships are the cornerstones of Gates' vision of aid to development. To him, a new era of development and progress is at hand if donors promote "the basic tools of development by making them cheaper, easier to use, and more efficient – or by inventing wholly new tools" – in other words innovation applied to aid (Gates, 2011). Innovation also adequately describes the "new partnerships" Gates envisages such as " 'triangular partnerships' among rapidly growing countries, traditional donors, and poor countries, because they exploit the comparative advantages of many different countries." Here, with the "comparative advantage," as elsewhere in the report, Gates adopts a capitalist's view he defines as that of a "businessman, [who] believe[s] the free market fuels growth." In other words the working tools of capitalism should benefit aid and development plans as well. The report is particularly important because its findings were presented, by Gates himself, at the G20 Summit in Cannes in November 2011. Here is reached the final step of Gates' assignment, also reflected by *The Giving Pledge*: transforming philanthropy from a personal and privately conducted practice to a global one; global because it attains levels of donations and efficiency never considered before by gathering forces and ideas; global because it leaves the private sphere of family foundations to become public and even speak to international organizations. The great philanthropists' mingling with politics is no longer about pushing through legislation that might be favorable in terms of tax policy and revenue and the governments' interest for philanthropic organizations is no longer its being able to channel philanthropic resources and charities for local action (Zunz, 2012, p. 5, p. 104). There, too, a new form of partnership is being formed, or at least a dialogue engaged. Buffett echoes this when he promises leverage and expertise to "make the subsequent expenditure of public monies more effective" (Wylie, 2010). This runs counter to the original intuition one may have had of American capitalists being discredited by their responsibility in the global economic crisis. Ironically, philanthropy offered capitalists a platform to promote their methods – and perhaps model. Tom Seyer, an investment banker and one of the signatories of *The Giving Pledge*, argues:

> [Philanthropy] transforms the image of private enterprise from an old-fashioned extractive model where people are taking resources out of the system for their benefit and their families to a more regenerative model of capitalism where they are putting resources back into society.
>
> (Wylie, 2010)

On closer inspection, rather than an opportunity to consider the flaws of the American model of capitalism, this "regeneration" of capitalism here suggested looks like an overhaul of capitalism by capitalism – for capitalism? – if one may be allowed to imitate Stiglitz's re-reading of Lincoln's phrase. And while critics have compared *The Giving Pledge* to a cynical publicity stunt aimed at redeeming the Wall Street rogues, it does unfold an interesting discourse of capitalists on the American model for observers interested in American civilization. The success of the pledge is such that it even reaches beyond the borders of the United States, and in this sense too is "going global."

Conclusion: going global

The chapter will conclude on the idea that this new age of philanthropy led and endorsed by a generation of American businessmen and financiers, as well as IT entrepreneurs and social network magnates, along with its reaching out outside American borders, may seem to entail if not a reinvention at least a renewal of the American philanthropic tradition whose embeddedness in the American capitalist model may have to be redefined. Indeed, the "going global" turn taken in 2013 evidenced at the same time the very American identity of *The Giving Pledge* and its leaving the American geographic and civilizational space only. As of 2013, more than a dozen new pledgers have joined who are not American. Of course Anglo-Saxon countries such as Britain (Richard Branson, Lord Ashcroft, Ann Gloag John Caudwell, Chris and Jamie Cooper-Hohn, Mo Ibrahim, David Sainsbury) and Australia (Andrew and Nicola Forrest) were the first represented. More difficult was the transition to countries like China, Russia and Saudi Arabia, where dinners were held, because of "cultural hurdles that ranged from civic modesty to perpetuating family dynasties" (*Forbes*, 2013). Though it addressed successful international businessmen, the philanthropic endeavor was too American to be readily understood and accepted by other world capitalists, thereby confirming the civilizational aspect of American philanthropy. Victor Pinchuk, leader of Ukraine's steel, stated that he originally misunderstood the idea and believed he would become bound by contract to donate (*Forbes*, 2013). He describes in his pledge his own path, as his country's, to the free market economy, interestingly echoing the Americans' rapport with capitalism. In South Africa, Patrice Motsepe, a mining magnate, also feels the need to find a cultural identity closer to home for his joining the Pledge and thus refers to an African tradition of compassion he calls *Ubuntu/ Botho* (Patrice & Precious Motsepe, n.d.).

The Giving Pledge letters first seem to evidence a buoyant American narrative resisting the crisis as well. The twenty-first-century business leaders may have breached economic and technological frontiers, but they offer the same rags-to-riches story the self-made man tradition has passed along for generations. Yet *The Giving Pledge*'s discourse and its development model online signal the emergence of a new era of Philanthropy 2.0. that self-reflects on American capitalism itself. Far from condemning the excesses that led to the Great Recession as much of the contemporary discourse did, the pledgers seem keen on inducing an evolution of philanthropy along the lines of the American business model and its healthy capacity to spur and reward innovation. In that respect, the resilience of the American brand of capitalism after the serious blow of the Great Recession is more an instance of reinvention than permanence and can be read through the pledges. The ongoing process of the philanthropic endeavor gone public and gone global may continue to serve to delineate a model whose definition seems to be dynamic.

Notes

1 "Buffett is currently the world's 3rd richest" according to *Forbes* 2015 list of the world's richest.
2 This falls into the American philanthropic tradition of "managed stewardship" as initiated by John D. Rockefeller (1839–1937), for instance, who, like Gates today, devoted his time to his foundation.
3 For a historical survey of the origins of American philanthropy in the nineteenth century and ensuing twentieth-century endeavors, see McCarthy (2003) and Zunz (2012); for a discussion of the tenets and channels of American philanthropy, see Gaudiani (2003); for a study of philanthropy in the light of American entrepreneurship, see Acs (2013).
4 Or publicity. One cannot but think of Guy Debord's (1967) *Society of the Spectacle* and make the connection between his thesis and the way capitalists here use (new) media to create and control representation of themselves.
5 This is after all the origin of philanthropy, if not in name, in deeds. In both Greek and Roman cultures, euergetism associated the rich's generosity toward the community to the display of their social status and a moral obligation (Veyne, 1976).
6 Ford was convinced of the private nature of charity and even believed in individual gestures more than in institutions (Marquis, 1923).
7 This chapter does not interrogate the "American character" of philanthropy (Curti, 1958) or seek to identify something distinctively "national" in *The Giving Pledge*, but rather to discuss the appropriation and strategy of the initiative and its agents when it comes to American history and culture.
8 Access to the URL the givingpledge.org opens a sober page with the following brief statement: "The Giving Pledge is a commitment by the world's wealthiest individuals and families to dedicate the majority of their wealth to philanthropy." The pledges are listed immediately underneath.
9 Although there are 131 signatories who appear online, not all have proposed a pledge for the public to read.
10 It is difficult to find evidence of another tone, or perhaps less enthusiastic faith in the American opportunities in the younger generation. Indeed, few pledgers are young billionaires and though a few internet moguls born in the late 1960s and early 1970s have joined *The Giving Pledge*, they are too scarce to form a representative sample. True, the half-dozen signatories who are the youngest entrepreneurs do not show any reference to the American Dream, rather their good fortune or luck to have been unexpectedly involved in the internet revolution. However, E-bay's Jeff Skoll and Pierre Omydiar are Canadian. The youngest pledger, Mark Zuckerberg from Facebook (born 1984), did not publish his pledge online. This leaves only very few published pledges to represent the younger generation of American philanthropists. Craig Silverstein, Google's first employee, Groupon's Eric Lefkovsky or Facebook's co-founder, Dustin Moskovitz do not mention any "American" inspiration, but this hardly suffices to conclude that they are collectively more skeptical about the American model.
11 The moral contract that the pledges draw reminds of the original moral and religious covenant of the early settlers with the Mayflower Compact (1620).
12 There may be a few exceptions of pledges that do offer a nuanced acknowledgment of the limits of the market, but these remain marginal (e.g., "the market does not

presently yield optimal results, due to inefficiencies, lack of adequate information or other reasons," Arnold & Arnold, n.d.).

13 The Buffett Rule was meant to be part of the Obama Administration's 2011–2012 tax plan. It followed Buffett's contention that rich Americans were under-taxed and sought to implement a minimum 30 percent tax rate for taxpayers whose revenues exceeded $1 million per year. It did not become a law, however, and failed to pass after a Republican filibuster in the Senate. In the midst of the debates, another pledger took the opposite side. Leon Cooperman was publicly critical of the Obama Administration and accused the president of launching a new class warfare and antagonizing the rich (Freeland, 2012).

14 John Greene ran in the 2010 Democratic primaries for US Senator in Florida.

15 This is a comment on *The Giving Pledge*'s discourse and strategy. Just as philanthropy has been analyzed for the partnerships it has always forged between government and forms of citizens' groups ("philanthropy, governance and the economy were inherently linked" – McCarthy, 2003, p. 6), *The Giving Pledge* does result in a powerful network whose agenda of influence and soft regulation needs to be considered.

References

Ackman, B. & Ackman, K. (2012). Pledge. Retrieved from http://givingpledge.org.

Acs, Z. (2013). *Why philanthropy matters: How the wealthy give and what it means for our economic well-being*. Princeton, NJ: Princeton University Press.

Allen, P.G. (2010). Pledge. Retrieved from http://givingpledge.org.

Arnold, J. & Arnold, L. (n.d.). Pledge. Retrieved from http://givingpledge.org.

Ashcroft, M. (2013). Pledge. Retrieved from http://givingpledge.org.

Ben-Ami, D. (2013, March 15). Bill Gates' attack on capitalism is nothing to cheer. *Guardian*. Retrieved from www.theguardian.com/commentisfree/2013/mar/15/bill-gates-capitalism-attacks.

Bercovitch, S. (2011 [1975]). *The puritan origin of the American self*. New Haven, CT: Yale University Press.

Bishop, M. & Green, M. (2010). *Philanthrocapitalism: How giving can save the world*. New York: Bloomsbury.

Blakely, S. (n.d.). Pledge. Retrieved from http://givingpledge.org.

Blank, A. (2012). Pledge. Retrieved from http://givingpledge.org.

Branson, R. & Branson, J. (n.d). Pledge. Retrieved from http://givingpledge.org.

Braudel, F. (1982). *Civilization and capitalism, 15th–18th century, vol. II: The wheels of commerce*. New York: Harper [Originally published as *Les Jeux de l'échange*, 1979].

Braudel, F. (1995). *A history of civilizations*. New York: Penguin Harper [Originally published as *Grammaire des Civilisations*, Flammarion, 1987].

Bronfman, C.R. (n.d.). Pledge. Retrieved from http://givingpledge.org.

Buffett, W. (2009). Pledge. Retrieved from http://givingpledge.org.

Buffett, W. (2010, June 16). My philanthropic pledge. *Fortune*. Retrieved from http://archive.fortune.com/2010/06/15/news/newsmakers/Warren_Buffettt_Pledge_Letter.fortune/index.htm.

Buffett, W. (2011, August 14). Stop coddling the super-rich. *New York Times*. Retrieved from www.nytimes.com/2011/08/15/opinion/stop-coddling-the-super-rich.html.

Carnegie, A. (2006 [1889]). *The gospel of wealth essays and other writings*. New York: Penguin.

Cooperman, L. & Cooperman, T. (2010). Pledge. Retrieved from http://givingpledge.org.

Craft, J. (2012). Pledge. Retrieved from http://givingpledge.org.

Curti, M. (1958). American philanthropy and the national character. *American Quarterly, 10*(4), 420–437.

Debord, G. (1995 [1967]). *The society of the spectacle*. New York: Zone Books.

Dejoria, J.P. (n.d.). Pledge. Retrieved from http://givingpledge.org.

Dubin, G. & Dubin, E. (2012). Pledge. Retrieved from http://givingpledge.org.

Economist, The. (2008, October 11). Saving the system. Cover.

Economist, The. (2009, October 1). Market fatigue. Retrieved from www.economist.com/node/14530138.

Economist, The. (2011, October 22). Rage against the machine. Retrieved from www.economist.com/node/21533400.

Economist, The. (2012, May 19). Spreading gospels of wealth. Retrieved from www.economist.com/node/21555605.

Ellison, L. (2010). Pledge. Retrieved from http://givingpledge.org.

Forbes. (2013, February 19). The Giving Pledge goes global: Warren Buffett details America's latest "export." Retrieved from www.forbes.com/sites/randalllane/2013/02/19/the-giving-pledge-goes-global-warren-buffett-details-americas-latest-export/.

Forbes (2015). The world's billionaires. Retrieved from www.forbes.com/billionaires/list.

Forstmann, T. (n.d.). Pledge. Retrieved from http://givingpledge.org.

Freeland, C. (2012, October 8). Super-rich irony: Why do billionaires feel victimized by Obama? *The New Yorker*.

Gates, B. (2011, November 3). *Innovation with impact: Financing 21st century development*. Gates Foundation. Retrieved from www.gatesnotes.com/Development/G20-Report-Innovation-with-Impact.

Gates, B. & Gates, M. (2009). Pledge. Retrieved from http://givingpledge.org.

Gaudiani, C. (2003). *The greater good: How philanthropy drives the American economy and can save capitalism*. New York: Henry Hold and Co.

Giving Pledge, The. (2010, August 4). Forty US families take giving pledge. Press Release. Retrieved from http://givingpledge.org/press-releases.aspx

Giving Pledge, The. (2012, April 19). Press release. Retrieved from http://givingpledge.org/press/PressRelease_4_19_2012.pdf.

Giving Pledge, The. (2014, May 9). Press release. Retrieved from http://givingpledge.org/press/PressRelease_5_9_2014.pdf.

Glass Pockets. (n.d). Eye on the Giving Pledge. Retrieved from http://glasspockets.org/philanthropy-in-focus/eye-on-the-giving-pledge.

Green, D. & Green, B. (2010). Pledge. Retrieved from http://givingpledge.org.

Greene, J. & Green, M.S. (n.d.), Pledge. Retrieved from http://givingpledge.org.

Hamm, H. & Hamm, S.A. (n.d.). Pledge. Retrieved from http://givingpledge.org.

Icahn, C. (n.d.). Pledge. Retrieved from http://givingpledge.org.

Le Goff, J. (ed.) (2006). *La nouvelle histoire*. Paris: Editions Complexes.

Loomis, C.J. (2010, June 16). The $600 billion challenge. *Fortune*. Retrieved from http://fortune.com/2010/06/16/the-600-billion-challenge.

McCarthy, K.D. (2003). *American creed philanthropy, and the rise of American civil society: 1700–1865*. Chicago, IL: University of Chicago Press.

Marquis, S.S. (2007 [1923]). *Henry Ford: An interpretation*. Detroit, MI: Wayne State University Press.

Mitchell, G.P. (2010). Pledge. Retrieved from http://givingpledge.org.

Monaghan, T. (n.d.). Pledge. Retrieved from http://givingpledge.org.

Morgridge, J. & Morgridge, T. (2010). Pledge. Retrieved from http://givingpledge.org.
Motsepe, P. & Motsepe, P. (n.d.). Pledge. Retrieved from http://givingpledge.org.
Nora, P. (1997). *Les lieux de mémoire.* Paris: Gallimard.
Oxford English Dictionary (OED). Philanthropy. www.oed.com/view/Entry/142408?redirectedFrom=philanthropy#eid.
Ricoeur, P. (1991 [1985]). *Temps et récit. Tome III: Le temps raconté.* Paris: Gallimard.
Samueli, H. & Samueli, S. (2011). Pledge. Retrieved from http://givingpledge.org.
Sandler, H. & Sandler, M. (2010). Pledge. Retrieved from http://givingpledge.org.
Soon-Shiong, P. & Chan, M. (n.d.). Pledge. Retrieved from http://givingpledge.org.
Stiglitz, J. (2011, May). Of the 1%, by the 1%, for the 1%. *Vanity Fair*. Retrieved from www.vanityfair.com/news/2011/05/top-one-percent-201105.
Stiglitz, J. (2012). *The price of inequality: How today's divided society endangers our future*. New York: W.W. Norton.
Strom, S. (2010, August 4). Pledge to give away half gains billionaire adherents. *New York Times.*
Veyne, P. (1971). *Comment on écrit l'histoire*. Paris: Seuil.
Veyne, P. (1976). *Le pain et le cirque. Sociologie historique d'un pluralisme politique?* Paris: Seuil.
Weber, M. (2002). *The Protestant ethic and the "spirit" of capitalism and other writings.* New York: Penguin.
Wylie, I. (2010, August 9). The great billionaire giveway. *Financial Times.*
Zunz, O. (2012). *Philanthropy in America: A history*. Princeton, NJ. Princeton University Press.

Index

Page numbers in *italics* denote tables, those in **bold** denote figures.

www.ingramcontent.com/pod-product-compliance
Ingram Content Group UK Ltd.
Pitfield, Milton Keynes, MK11 3LW, UK
UKHW020018200926
475702UK00014B/1952
* 9 7 8 1 0 3 2 0 9 8 1 4 2 *